AN
INTRODUCTION
TO MINISTRY

To Cubby & Hyde -
with deep gratitude
and much love

Grant

March 2016

Also available

The Student's Companion to the Theologians
Edited by Ian S. Markham

The Wiley-Blackwell Companion to the Anglican Communion
Edited by Ian S. Markham, J. Barney Hawkins, IV, Justyn Terry, and Leslie Nunez Steffensen

Against Atheism: Why Dawkins, Hitchens, and Harris Are Fundamentally Wrong
Ian S. Markham

A World Religions Reader, 3rd Edition
Edited by Ian S. Markham and Christy Lohr

Understanding Christian Doctrine
Ian S. Markham

Do Morals Matter?: A Guide to Contemporary Religious Ethics
Ian S. Markham

A Theology of Engagement
Ian S. Markham

Encountering Religion: An Introduction to the Religions of the World
Edited by Ian S. Markham and Tinu Ruparell

AN INTRODUCTION TO MINISTRY

A PRIMER FOR RENEWED LIFE AND LEADERSHIP IN MAINLINE PROTESTANT CONGREGATIONS

IAN S. MARKHAM
ORAN E. WARDER

WILEY Blackwell

Library of Congress Cataloging-in-Publication Data

Markham, Ian S.
  An introduction to ministry : a primer for renewed life and leadership in mainline protestant congregations / Ian S. Markham and Oran E. Warder.
    pages cm
  Includes bibliographical references and index.
    ISBN 978-0-470-67330-0 (cloth) – ISBN 978-0-470-67329-4 (pbk.)   1. Pastoral theology–United States. I. Title.
    BV4011.3.M365 2015
    253–dc23

                                                                                                   2015021574

A catalogue record for this book is available from the British Library.

Cover image: © Pearl/Lightstock

Set in 10/13pt MinionPro by Aptara Inc., New Delhi, India

Printed in Singapore by C.O.S. Printers Pte Ltd

1 2016

For Oran:
This book is dedicated to my parents, Joe and Kate, who led me to faith; to Amy, my long-time partner in ministry, who has triumphantly finished the race; to our children and greatest treasure, Zachary, Griffin, and Wesley; and to Barbara, my beloved companion as the journey continues.

I am also grateful for all the communities that have shaped and formed me: St. Matthias Church, Grafton, West Virginia; Trinity Church, Huntington, West Virginia; St. Philip's Church, Laurel, Maryland; the Episcopal Diocese of Delaware; and most especially the congregation of St. Paul's, Alexandria, Virginia, whom I am so privileged to serve and without whose support and encouragement this book could not have been written.

For Ian:
This book is dedicated to my wife Lesley and my son Luke. Few can imagine the impact that ministry has on those close to them, for their participation in the journey I am extraordinarily grateful.

I am also grateful for those who helped to nurture my vocation as a priest. Keith Ward, Leslie Houlden, and Richard Harries at King's College, London; Giles Legood, who embodies so many priest-like qualities; Richard Burridge, Martyn Percy, Gareth Jones, and Lewis Ayres, who were there every step of the way; and finally, Don Hamer and Bill Eakins at Trinity Episcopal Church in Hartford and Heidi Hadsell of Hartford Seminary, who supported me through the process.

Contents

Acknowledgments

This is a book that emerged from our respective contexts – a parish priest and a seminary dean. We are grateful to those in our contexts who supported this venture: the Vestry of St. Paul's Episcopal Church and, in particular, the team of priests – Judith Harris Proctor, Ross Kane, and Sam Mason; and at Virginia Seminary, the leadership team – Melody Knowles, Heather Zdancewicz, Barney Hawkins, Katie Glover, and Justin Lewis-Anthony – who recognize that such work is a legitimate part of a work week.

We were fortunate that the Seminary supported this venture with the appointment of two outstanding research assistants. Ms Shannon Preston was careful, attentive, and gifted, as she tracked down books and articles and carefully read the draft as it emerged; Mr Gregory Millikin was talented, energetic, and thorough, as he made sure that everything was in place; and we are grateful to Ms Samantha Gottlich who did the index.

We are both Episcopal priests who were committed to writing a text that can serve the wider Church, so we were very grateful that the following people helped represent their respective traditions and gave the draft manuscript a very close reading: Ms Katherine Malloy (Methodist), the Rev. Dr Nathaniel Phillips (Presbyterian), Dr Christy Lohr-Sapp (Lutheran), and Dr Heidi Gehman (United Church of Christ, UCC). It is such a relief that our readers are not going to be subject to our earlier drafts; and we are so grateful for the generous gift of their time.

The team at Wiley-Blackwell was impressive. Ms Camille Bramall was efficient and capable at the copyediting and proofing stages. Finally, we are grateful to Ms Rebecca Harkin, the commissioning editor from Wiley-Blackwell. Rebecca has that extraordinary gift of being able to take the seed of an idea and improve it. She has been attentive and helpful. It is an honor to work with a person so committed to innovative excellence.

Ian Markham and Oran Warder

Introduction

We are hopeful. We do not accept the narrative of decline that pervades much of the talk around the mainline. The mainline ethos can have real traction. The so-called Nones (those who profess no religion in surveys) still use words like "spiritual" to describe their world view; young people are attracted to the social affirmations of many mainline congregations; and the reach of the Christ grounded in Scripture continues to impact countless human lives. We believe that leaders of mainline congregations are needed. And we recognize that the challenge is getting the leadership right. So this is where this textbook comes in.

This is the first attempt at a comprehensive ministry textbook for ministers, pastors, and priests who make up the mainline denominations in the United States. We want to provide an ecumenical introduction to the shared craft of ministry that can be read by seminarians everywhere. We want to support those small congregations, where leadership is being raised up with limited training. We want to provide a reference-type textbook for those responsible for training in the various denominations throughout the United States that can provide a foundation for those who are not being trained at a theological college or seminary. We want to provide those who are in discernment and considering the ministry with an insight into what ministry involves.

It is important to be clear about the focus. To make this large project manageable, we needed to place limits on it. So we are concentrating on the United States. Those in other contexts will have a sense of where the United States is in terms of the expectations of the well-rounded congregational leader. Furthermore, we are limiting ourselves to five of the seven in the mainline. Traditionally, the term "mainline" emerged in Philadelphia in 1908 with the emergence of the Federal Council of Churches. It had been applied to the so-called "Seven Sisters" of American Protestantism. These were: the Congregational Church (now the United Church of Christ, UCC), the Episcopal Church, the Evangelical Lutheran

An Introduction to Ministry: A Primer for Renewed Life and Leadership in Mainline Protestant Congregations, First Edition. Ian S. Markham and Oran Warder.
© 2016 John Wiley & Sons, Ltd. Published 2016 by John Wiley & Sons, Ltd.

Church, the Presbyterian Church (USA), the United Methodist Church, the American Baptist Convention, and the Disciples of Christ.[1] The challenge in every chapter was to make sure that we touched on the variety within and across the denominations. To handle seven was difficult; so our focus is on the five largest – the United Methodist Church, the Evangelical Lutheran Church, the Presbyterian Church (USA), the Episcopal Church, and the UCC.[2] However, naturally we hope that readers outside these traditions will find it useful, especially those in the American Baptist Convention and the Disciples of Christ. And it would be lovely if some in the Roman Catholic and Southern Baptist traditions find some of the more "generic" chapters helpful.

The theological approach of the entire book is rooted in generous orthodoxy (to use Brian McLaren's label); it is creedal (incarnational and Trinitarian) and committed to generosity when it comes to other faith traditions and social issues. We are making an argument here. Liberal churches can take extraordinary pride in their lack of doctrinal expectations. By contrast, we believe that a Church grounded in the God revealed in Christ is the reason why that Church should be generous. We want congregations to be innovative and progressive because they believe that God has spoken. We are not interested in a liberal theology that endlessly denies the central claims of the Christian faith. Our sense is that much of the leadership of the mainline shares this ethos. This book is a defense of that approach. The result is a book offering a grounded account of ministry, which is in conversation with the culture and other contemporary trends in the academy. There will be an appropriate recognition of the wisdom derived from feminist and other liberationist theologies.

Given the distinctive nature of this project, it is necessary to be clear about the precise identity of this book. This book is a helpful map; it is not a triple volume comprehensive definitive resource. So we recognize that in many chapters more could be said. It is a bird's eye view of an area. Therefore, this book is a gateway to further study through the annotated bibliography and further questions; it is not the complete description of all the options in any given area. We are making an assumption that there is a growing convergence in the mainline. Our evidence for this is that increasingly we share the Church seasons, lectionary, and an affirmation of certain ethical trends.

In terms of using this book, there are several options. For those who are "reading" for ministry (or perhaps are on an alternative route to ordination), this book might form the basis of the program. Working through one chapter a week would provide a good introduction to the issues in each area. For those who are in discernment and preparing for seminary, this is your preparatory reading. For those in theological education, this is a good reference work. Some readers will want to work through each chapter consecutively; however, it has also been written so each chapter can be read as a standalone. So a teacher or reader can move through the volume in any order they choose.

Ministry in the Church is an extraordinary privilege. It is a calling to service. One is invited by Christ to lead the people of God in worship, to celebrate with a couple as they get married, and to sit by the bedside as a person passes into eternity. One is invited to the most intimate of places in the lives of women and men. It is often holy ground. Yet it is also the hardest of callings. Ministry is often isolating and painful. It requires the capacity to raise money, to run a volunteer organization, to maintain a physical plant, and to handle conflict. All of this is captured in this volume. We invite you to join us on a journey into this world that is both exasperating and magical, both painful and exhilarating, and both deeply serious and yet great fun. And on every page of this book, we hope you realize that ministry is never a journey made alone, but is one in which God promises to walk with you every step of the way.

Notes

1   For a good discussion of the history of the mainline see Jason S. Lantzer, *Mainline Christianity: The Past and Future of America's Majority Faith* (New York: New York University Press, 2012).

2   The American Baptists are larger than the UCC; however, space did not permit sustained discussion of the distinctive Baptist ethos.

Section One

Exploring the World of Ministry

1

Sensing the Call

We begin this chapter, and indeed this entire book, in the place where we will end. We begin and end in the knowledge that we, all of us, are known and loved by God. We begin and end in the knowledge that God summons us into relationship, invites us to share in his divine life, and calls us to ministry in the world. How we hear and respond to that call is the topic of this first chapter and sets the stage for the unfolding of this text.

This famous prayer of *Thomas Merton* (1915–1968) acknowledges the challenge and difficulty, as well as the hope and promise, of all who make this journey:

> God, we have no idea where we are going. We do not see the road ahead of us. We cannot know for certain where it will end. Nor do we really know ourselves, and the fact that we think we are following your will does not mean that we are actually doing so. But we believe that the desire to please you does in fact please you. And we hope we have that desire in all that we are doing. We hope that we will never do anything apart from that desire. And we know that if we do this you will lead us by the right road, though we may know nothing about it. Therefore, we will trust you always though we may seem to be lost and in the shadow of death. We will not fear, for you are ever with us, and you will never leave us to face our perils alone.[1]

Thus we set out to explore what it means to be called by God. How do we hear that call? How do we know it is a call from God? What could following that call mean for our everyday lives? What is the role of the community in discerning a sense of calling? How do we prepare ourselves and open ourselves to perceive and respond? Even to begin to answer these important questions requires some definition of terms as well as a common understanding of the nature of *discernment*, neither of which is simple or easy.

An Introduction to Ministry: A Primer for Renewed Life and Leadership in Mainline Protestant Congregations, First Edition. Ian S. Markham and Oran E. Warder.
© 2016 John Wiley & Sons, Ltd. Published 2016 by John Wiley & Sons, Ltd.

> ### Thomas Merton
>
> Thomas Merton was born in 1915 and perhaps is the most influential American Roman Catholic writer on spirituality. In 1941 he became a Trappist monk and, while a Trappist, he became a strong advocate of civil rights. Later in life, he became interested in other religious traditions, especially Zen Buddhism. Thomas Merton died in Bangkok in 1968. His legacy is a significant range of publications of which his autobiography, *The Seven Storey Mountain* (1948, Harcourt Brace and Company), is one of the best known.

Call and Vocation

Part of the confusion is that words like *call* and *vocation* are often used interchangeably. This is understandable since the word vocation comes from the Latin *vocare*, which literally translated means "to call." The confusion comes in the application of these terms. The word vocation can be rightly understood in a number of different ways. The dictionary offers three standard definitions: one being a summons to perform a certain function or career, especially a religious one; another refers to a function or career to which one believes he or she is called; and a third refers to any career, profession, or occupation.[2] Notice that there are both religious and secular meanings implied in each of these definitions.

For our purposes, writing from a mainline perspective, we will follow the pattern established in what has become a classic text in Christian discernment, *Listening Hearts: Discerning Call in Community*. In this book, the term *vocation* is used in the broadest sense, while the term *call* is reserved for something more specific. For instance, someone might have a vocation as a choral director and yet respond to a call to serve a particular choir at a particular time in a particular place.[3] The title of this book is derived from the Judeo-Christian understanding that the heart is more than flesh; it is the very core of being, the hub of mind, body, and spirit. It is in the heart where we enter into communion with God and one another, and it is the place where we struggle to understand our vocation and God's call.[4] The premise of this text is that God's call involves obedience, God's call involves some form of ministry, and God's call involves community.

Pointing to the origins of the word *obedience*, from the Latin, *audire*, which means, "to listen," the authors of this book contend that every true call is a call to obey.[5] Obedience refers to the deep listening of the heart, which requires a response. For people of faith, that response is ministry. In this sense, ministry is not simply the doing of good deeds, but more specifically refers to "something that Christ does in us and through us and that we do in and through Christ."[6] Christian vocation, therefore, involves our striving to hear and respond to God's call in ways that conform to a living and active partnership with Christ.

According to this understanding, being obedient, or listening for God's call to ministry, requires discernment. This term, which is so crucial to our understanding of vocation and call, comes from the Latin *discernere*, and means "to separate," "to distinguish," or "to sort out." In the realm of classical spirituality, discernment has to do with identifying what spirit is at work in a specific situation. In this sense, discernment helps one to determine the source of a call, helps one to determine to whom a call is directed, and helps one to determine an appropriate response. It also helps one to determine if one is being deaf or blind to a call, rejecting or ignoring a call, or resisting or avoiding a call. Discernment itself is a gift from God and is a matter of both hard work and a generous amount of grace. This is particularly true since we are bombarded by any number of voices. The voices of ego and pride, of culture and career, of success and self-interest, can compete with, and drown out, the voice of God. How, then, are we to differentiate these voices, sort out the spirits, and discriminate between our will and God's will?[7]

Unfortunately there are no rules and no definitive answers, and the rules that do exist, even the most sincere and well intentioned, are imperfect and incomplete. For example, we can look to the experience of a sect of early *Quakers* who were convinced that God's "true" call was always contrary to one's own will. The assumption was that any "cross" to one's personal will provided an opportunity to take up the cross of Christ. This line of thinking produced some rather absurd results when some Quaker Friends were discovered walking naked through the streets of their community simply because it was clearly "contrary to their own will and inclination" and therefore was most certainly an action taken in "obedience to the Lord."[8] Another definitive test or rule regarding the true call of God, far less dramatic than the last, yet often far more problematic, is the reliance on particular passages of *Scripture* to determine God's call and will. "Frequently, however, this meant (and can still mean) merely choosing some biblical passages and ignoring others to confirm a pre-charted course."[9] Therefore, Christian discernment cannot be reduced to a set of rules or formulated answers, but rather develops in a relationship with God; that is, our hearts being rooted and grounded in the heart of God. To that end, discernment is better understood as "apprehension rather than comprehension."[10] Using the analogy of driving a car at night, discernment is like the light that is cast only far enough ahead to see the next bit of road. Discernment involves taking risks, it involves making mistakes, it involves having faith in God, and it involves trusting that more discernment will come.[11]

This is precisely why the role of the community is so important and why a life lived in community is so central to the Christian faith. Paul aptly uses the metaphor of the Body of Christ to describe the mutuality and interconnectedness of members. "If one member suffers, all suffer together with it; if one member is honored, all rejoice together with it (1 Corinthians 12:26, New Revised Standard Version, NRSV)." Given this reality, something incredibly important happens when we consult one another within the Christian community. "God calls us each individually but as individuals we see only partially."[12] Other members of the community can have the ability to open our eyes to see things that we might not have seen and open our ears to hear what we might not have been able to hear on our own.

> Even a person who feels absolutely certain about a call may be mistaken in how it is applied. Because God often reveals part of the picture to one person and another part to another person, it is prudent to consult one another to discern God's counsel, guidance, and direction, even if there is no apparent reason to do so. While circumstances sometime require us to act without consulting others, the danger of arrogance and error in proceeding on our own can be great.[13]

So vocation and call require obedient listening, a response that takes the form of ministry, and community discernment. Vocation and call require risk and the possibility of making mistakes. Vocation and call require trust that even when we act in error, more discernment will follow. Central to this understanding of call and vocation is the basic idea that God has called each one of us to do something with our lives, and in the doing of that something our lives will have meaning and purpose.

The pages of Holy Scripture abound with stories of call, and in practically every instance there is a corresponding story of how the call from God is at least initially resisted. In almost every case there is an immediate sense of inadequacy on the part of those being summoned. This is typically followed by a litany of reasons why this particular call is bad idea, which is then typically followed by the suggestion that God would do far better to choose someone else. The classic call stories of the great prophets Moses, Jeremiah, and Isaiah all fit this pattern. Moses, for instance, refuses God's call no less than five times (Exodus 3:11, 13; 4:1, 10 and 13); he also complains that he does not know God's name, is not a person of consequence, has no credibility, and is not a public speaker. Jeremiah famously complains that he is just a boy and does not even know how to speak (Jeremiah 1:6), and Isaiah opines that he is a person of unclean lips who dwells among a people of unclean lips (Isaiah 6:5).[14] And yet, in spite of an overwhelming and sometimes crippling sense of unworthiness, in each story, by the grace and power of God, the call is ultimately heard and heeded. These stories offer both consolation and inspiration as we grapple with similar issues in our own lives.

Practically every book, article, or lecture on the topic of Christian vocation in recent times includes quotes from one or all of the three Bs: Frederick Buechner, Walter Brueggemann, and *Dietrich Bonhoeffer*. Buechner, clearly the most quoted on the subject, sees call and vocation as the intersection of personal passion and the needs of the larger community, or in his words, vocation is "the place where your deep gladness meets the world's deep need." Notice how his thinking begins with self-understanding and moves outward to the world.[15] Similarly, Brueggemann places vocation at the intersection of personal will and divine will, or in his words, vocation is "finding a purpose for your life that is part of the purposes of God."[16] And lastly, Bonhoeffer emphasizes that the very process of obedient listening and responding faithfully to our vocation as disciples requires change and transformation. It means that we are drawn toward something different to our current situation. Echoing the call of the disciples, who immediately left their nets to follow Jesus, he points out that when Christ is done with us, we will not be the same people we were when we started. On the contrary, we may well be at odds with former beliefs, former understandings, and former lifestyles.[17] For Bonhoeffer, to be called as a disciple of Christ is to be changed fundamentally. So for the three Bs vocation has to do with passion, purpose, and the possibility of transformation. Notice that all three interpretations have a public dimension (a movement beyond self) and a future orientation (a movement beyond the present).

Parker Palmer

Parker Palmer's *Let Your Life Speak* is a key manual to those persons entering into a discernment process. It is personal, reflective, and ultimately instructive as to how one may listen to where God may be leading. Our deepest calling is to grow into our own authentic self-hood, whether or not it conforms to some image of who we *ought* to be. As we do so, we will not only find the joy that every human being seeks – we will also find our path of authentic service in the world.[18]

Martin Luther on Vocation and the Ministry of the Baptized

It is a vast understatement to say that the reformed traditions of mainline Christianity owe a great debt to the brilliant theological mind of *Martin Luther* (1483–1546). We are particularly indebted for his recovery of the idea of the "priesthood of all believers," which provides the theological groundwork for our modern understanding of vocation. When he nailed his *Ninety-Five Theses* to the door of All Saints' Church in Wittenberg in 1517 he was protesting Church abuses that he knew firsthand. Living a privileged monastic life he grew increasingly uncomfortable with the growing wealth of the Church and the growing poverty of the general populace.[19]

Philipp Melanchthon, a contemporary of Luther and fellow reformer, described the monastic life in this way:

> Everyone knows how much hypocrisy, ambition, and greed there is in monasteries; how ignorant and cruel those illiterate men are; how vain they are in their sermons and in thinking up new ways of making money. There are other vices, too, which we would rather not talk about. Though once upon a time they were schools of Christian instruction, they have degenerated as from a golden age to an iron age, or as the Platonic cube degenerates into bad harmonies which, Plato says, cause destruction. Some of the richest monasteries just feed a lazy crowd that gorges itself on the public alms of the church.[20]

It is against this backdrop that Luther sets out to be an agent of change. He railed against monastic life and promoted a Christian life returned to the fundamental principles of the love of God and the love of neighbor. He believed that a true Christian should have no other thought than the needs and concerns of his neighbor. This basic notion is the driving force behind his developing theology and the foundation for his emerging understanding of vocation.[21]

As previously discussed, today we appreciate both the secular and religious understandings of the word vocation, yet in Luther's day there was no such distinction. On the contrary, it was understood that only those in religious orders received the gift of vocation. Luther thought differently. He believed and championed the radical notion that all Christians had a calling in life. In particular, he felt that every Christian was called to live a life that consisted of faith in God and love of neighbor. Vocation for Luther was simply a function of Christian love. This, he believed, was true regardless of station, status, class, or office. For Luther, vocation was not simply understood as an occupation, but as relationship. Even more far-reaching and controversial, Luther would come to believe that even the most common and lowly work of society was equal to, if not greater than, the work of the religious orders of the day.[22]

It is little wonder that Luther found himself in such trouble with the established Church when he wrote words such as these:

> However numerous, sacred and arduous they (vows of monkery and priesthood) may be, these works in God's sight are in no way whatever superior to a farmer laboring in a field, or a woman looking after a home. Rather all are measured by him by faith alone. … Indeed it occurs quite frequently that the common work of serving man or maid is more acceptable than all fastings and other works of monks and priests where faith is lacking.[23]

For Luther, it is through *baptism* that we receive our religious vocation, our ordination for ministry, and our welcome into the priesthood of believers. The calling of all the baptized is then to spread the love of God through Christ in all that they do, whether in religious order in the Church or in daily work in the world.

> Therefore, both vocations – the Ministry, and the vocations of secular life which serve love to one's neighbour, spring from the same source and arise out of the same Gospel. Since the ministries which serve faith and those which serve love take their origin in the same source, they possess the same dignity and are different aspects of the same priesthood.[24]

Again, Luther in his own words, "As many of us as have been baptized are all priests without distinction. … For thus it is written in I Peter 2, 'Ye are a chosen generation, a royal priesthood, and a priestly kingdom.' Therefore we are all priests, as many of us as are Christians."[25]

It is this legacy that lives on today in the denominations of the mainline; all in one way or another have been shaped and formed by the premise that all are called to ministry through baptism. The question for mainline Christians therefore, is not "Have I been called to ministry?" but instead, "To what ministry am I being called?"[26] It is critical to note at this point that Luther did not advocate for an end to ordination, nor did he wish to abolish the role of clergy, but rather wanted to make certain that a call to serve in this capacity stood in the shadow of baptism and not apart from it.

Denominational Perspectives

It is this fundamental shift in the understanding of vocation that has been inherited by mainline Christianity. At this point we will now explore the manner in which various denominations have dealt with the distinction between the ministry of all the people of God and the representative ministry of the clergy.

We will begin with *The Book of Order of the Presbyterian Church USA* that states:

> All ministry in the church is a gift from Jesus Christ. Members and officers alike serve mutually under the mandate of Christ who is chief minister of all. … One responsibility of membership in the church is the election of officers who are ordained to fulfill particular functions. The existence of these offices in no way diminishes the importance of all members to the total ministry of the church. These ordained officers differ from other members in function only … when women and men, by God's providence and gracious gifts, are called by the church to undertake particular forms of ministry, the church shall help them to interpret their call and to be sensitive to the judgments and needs of others.[27,28]

The Book of Discipline of the United Methodist Church, the book of law for this denomination, offers a similar statement:

> Ministry in the Christian Church is derived from the ministry of Christ, who calls all persons to receive God's gift of salvation and follow in the way of love and service. The whole church receives and accepts this call, and all Christians participate in this continuing ministry. Within the church community, there are persons whose gifts, evidence of God's grace, and promise of future usefulness are affirmed by the community, and who respond to God's call by offering themselves in leadership as ordained ministers.[29]

The candidacy manual for the Evangelical Lutheran Church in America offers the following:

> It is by Christ's gift that all baptized persons are called to ministry. Every baptized believer is given gifts and abilities for ministry. Every baptized believer is called to ministry in daily life. Some are given gifts and abilities which equip them to provide leadership in one of the rostered ministries of this church.[30]

Quite similarly, the canons of the Episcopal Church state that every *diocese* of that denomination shall:

> make provision for the affirmation and development of the ministry of all baptized persons, including: (a) Assistance in understanding that all baptized persons are called to minister in Christ's name, to identify their gifts with the help of the Church and to serve Christ's mission at all times and in all places. (b) Assistance in understanding that all baptized persons are called to sustain their ministries through commitment to life-long Christian formation.[31]

The Episcopal Church's "Outline of the Faith" also affirms that, "the ministers of the Church are lay persons, bishops, priests and deacons."[32]

A closer look at denominational literature reveals that each denomination has its own unique review process for helping the Church to determine which ministry best suits those who present themselves seeking such discernment. For those seeking ordination there are a few general assumptions that seem to permeate all of the literature: (i) there is an assumption within each denomination that the gifts necessary for ordination will be readily apparent to the Church; (ii) there is an assumption that candidates for ordination will be supported by their home congregations in pursuing the call to ordination; (iii) there is an assumption that this support is operative for at least 6 months before moving forward; (iv) there is an assumption that a local congregational process occurs prior to judiciary level process; (v) there is an assumption that this discernment and these series of interviews happen over an extended period of time; and lastly (vi) there is an assumption that it is the work of the church to decide who is suitable for ordained ministry and who is not. The corollary to the last item is the assumption by all mainline denominations that not everyone who senses a call to ordination should, in fact, be ordained. Generally speaking, the candidate's desire to be ordained is not a deciding factor. Therefore, in mainline denominations it is either explicit or implicit that community discernment (at the local and judiciary levels) is integral to the vocational process, with each church reserving the right to discriminate.[33]

In the United Methodist tradition, the historic questions asked of all candidates for ordained ministry are found in *The Book of Discipline*. These questions contain John Wesley's own standards for pastoral leadership and have been in use since he first asked them in 1746:

1. Do they know God as a pardoning God? Have they the love of God abiding in them? Do they desire nothing but God? Are they holy in all manner of conversation?
2. Have they the gifts, as well as evidence of God's grace, for the work? Have they a clear, sound understanding; a right judgment in the things of God; a just conception of salvation by faith? Do they speak justly, readily, clearly?

3. Have they fruit? Have any been truly convinced of sin and converted to God, and are believers edified by their service?

> As long as these marks concur in them, we believe they are called of God to service. These we receive as sufficient proof that they are moved by the Holy Spirit.[34]

Aside from the implicit assumption that not all persons seeking ordination would be found suitable, these questions do expect that candidates would have a high level of commitment and would also exhibit a certain degree of spiritual maturity. These questions also strongly suggest that those candidates who do possess these particular gifts will be readily apparent to the Church.

> Those whom the Church ordains shall be conscious of God's call to ordained ministry, and their call shall be acknowledged and authenticated by the Church. God's call has many manifestations, and the Church cannot structure a single test of authenticity. Nevertheless, the experience of the Church and the needs of its ministry require certain qualities of faith, life, and practice from those who seek ordination.[35]

One final example is found in *The Evangelical Lutheran Candidacy Manual*:

> Candidacy Committees have the responsibility to determine which form of ministry is most appropriate for the individual's gifts and abilities. When an individual's gifts are not suited for rostered ministry it is the responsibility of the committee to clearly indicate that and direct the individual to the important ministry of the baptized. When an individual does possess those characteristics which enable a person to serve in rostered ministry the committee will need to affirm and support the candidate in the process of preparation and formation.[36]

All of these examples point to the reality that a call to ordination in the mainline is not solely a matter of a personal sense of call, or simply the affirmation of the local congregation, but also requires the official approval of the larger denominational body.[37] In the mainline, a call to ordination is a multi-layered, multi-faceted, and deeply interconnected process that requires prayerful discernment at all of those levels.

A Compelling Alternative View

Returning now to the broader topic of call and vocation as it relates to the ministry of all of the baptized, and not just those seeking ordination, we conclude this first chapter by offering a slightly different perspective. This alternative view, while not diametrically opposed to the traditional overview that we have provided, is a reaction against the large and popular strand of contemporary evangelical theology that emphasizes that one finds one's call and vocation by searching for and finding God's will. In his article, "No secret plan: Why you don't have to find God's will for your life," Philip Cary criticizes this thinking not only as anxiety producing and unhelpful, but also as profoundly unbiblical.

Rather than embracing the idea that God's will is elusive – something out there waiting to be found – he contends that God's will is unambiguous, revealed in Scripture, and is right in front of us. Rather than praying that we find God's will in every moment and every decision (from whom we will marry, to what career we will choose, to what we will have for dinner) he suggests that we pray for wisdom and understanding to make these, and all decisions, as responsible and faithful moral agents. Citing the prophet Micah's admonition that we are to do justice, love kindness, and walk humbly with God (Micah 6:8), Cary also echoes the 10 commandments and Jesus' summary of those commandments, which compel us toward love of God and love of neighbor. Cary suggests that this is the will of God, this is what God asks us to do, and that nothing more is required of us. All we have to do is apply it. "Anyone who tells you that you need to do more in order to be 'in the will of God' is teaching falsehood."[38] This understanding of vocation and call fits well with Brueggemann's idea of locating our purpose within the purposes of God.

Understanding God's will, revealed in the whole *Word of God*, does not tell us what to do in every situation we encounter, and Cary believes this leaves the door wide open for mischief on the part of those who would look for formulas, simple answers, or foolproof methods for making these decisions. Rather, Cary contends that there are no recipes; there is only wisdom. He defines wisdom as the heart's ability to discern: the ability to discern what is good and what is evil, the ability to discern between a positive choice and a negative choice, the ability to discern constructive decisions from destructive ones. The heart's intelligence is "not a method or formula you can apply to a particular situation simply by applying the rules, but a habit of the heart developed through personal experience that includes making mistakes."[39] Any attempt to follow a prescribed method in search of a short cut, or as a guarantee against failure, disrupts the arduous task of acquiring wisdom.

Referring to the "Parable of Talents" (Matthew 25:14–30), Cary says that the work of the steward begins as soon as the master leaves town. In the parable, the steward has been entrusted with talents, has been commanded to do business with them, and is expected to make good investments. What have not been given to the steward are specific, step-by-step instructions about which investments to make and which to avoid. Those decisions are left to the steward. While it is conceivable that the steward could invest using a formula or method, it is more likely that the master expects the steward to employ the virtues of wisdom. It is clear that when it comes to proficiency in this work, there is no substitute for practice. The task is to learn in our own hearts how to carry on God's work in the world, thus acquiring the virtue of wisdom and becoming a co-worker with God. In the parable, the steward, who refuses to decide, refuses to invest, refuses to risk failure, and buries the talents, is deemed not only disobedient and slothful, but even wicked.[40]

In summary, Cary believes that the frenzied search for God's will in every moment of our lives is misguided. He suggests that our time, energy, and resources, as stewards of the master, as God's co-workers, as individual moral agents, would be better spent praying for the ability to discern. "For we already know God's will for our lives, he wants us to discern good from bad which includes making good investments for His kingdom."[41] In this process of taking risks, making mistakes, and learning from them, our hearts are remade into hearts of wisdom. It takes time and much effort for this to happen, and "the Lord does not short-circuit the process by making our decisions for us."[42] We believe Cary's view, while alternative to a popular strand of contemporary evangelism, is in fact consistent with the traditions of the mainline.

And so we end where we began, setting out on a journey not fully knowing where the road will lead, or what might happen along the way. We walk by faith and trust, knowing that we are loved and known by God, invited into relationship and community, and called to serve. We strive to locate our passion within the needs of the world, we strive to find our purpose within the purposes of God, and we strive to discover our truest selves within the transforming love of Jesus. Our vocation and call, with all their challenges and difficulties, with all their hope and promise, are rooted in the heart of the One who summons us and promises to be with us to the close of the age.

Notes

1   Thomas Merton, *Thoughts in Solitude* (New York: Image Books, 1958), 81.

2   Virginia Samuel Cetuk, *What to Expect in Seminary: Theological Education and Spiritual Formation* (Nashville, TN: Abingdon Press, 1998), 57.

3   Suzanne G. Farnham, Joseph Gill, R. Taylor McLean, Susan M. Ward, *Listening Hearts: Discerning Call in Community (20th Anniversary Edition)* (New York and Harrisonburg, PA: Morehouse Publishing, 2011), 103.

4   Ibid., 2.

5   Ibid., 13–14.

6   Ibid., 17.

7   Ibid., 23.

8   Ibid., 24.

9   Ibid., 25.

10 Ibid., 26.

11 Ibid., 27.

12 Ibid., 55.

13 Ibid.

14 Ibid., 14–15.

15 Parker Palmer, *Let Your Life Speak: Listening for the Voice of Vocation* (San Francisco, CA: Jossey-Bass, 2000), 16.

16 Joyce Ann Mercer, "Call forwarding: Putting vocation in the present tense with youth," *Compass Points: Navigating Vocation* (Princeton, NJ: Institute for Youth Ministry, Princeton Theological Seminary, 2002), 29.

17 Cetuk, *What to Expect in Seminary*, 49.

18 Palmer, *Let Your Life Speak*, 16.

19 Cetuk, *What to Expect in Seminary*, 56.

20 Ibid.

21 Ibid., 57.

22 Ibid.

23 Ibid., 58.

24 Ibid.

25 Ibid., 60.

26 Ibid.

27 Ibid., 59.

28 The Presbyterian Church, USA (PCUSA) now uses the title "teaching elders" for what were previously called "ministers of the word and sacrament." There are therefore both "teaching elders" and "ruling elders."

29 Ibid., 59–60.

30 Ibid., 60.

31 Canon III.1.a, b, in *Constitution and Canons for the Government of the Protestant Episcopal Church in the United States of America: Otherwise Known as the Episcopal Church* (adopted in General Conventions 1789–2012 together with the rules of order revised by the Convention) (New York: Church Publishing, 2013), 67.

32 "Outline of the faith: Commonly called the Catechism," in *The Book of Common Prayer* (New York: Seabury Press, 1979), 855.

33 Cetuk, *What to Expect in Seminary*, 60–61.

34 Ibid., 61–62.

35 Ibid., 62.

36 Ibid.

37 Ibid., 63.

38 Philip Cary, "No secret plan: Why you don't have to find God's will for your life," *Christian Century* 127, No. 20 (October 5, 2010), 21.

39 Ibid.

40 Ibid.

41 Ibid., 23.

42 Ibid.

Annotated Bibliography

Badcock, Gary D., *The Way of Life: A Theology of Christian Vocation* (Grand Rapids, MI: Eerdmans Publishing Co., 1998).
Moving away from the idea of vocation as occupation, the author analyzes the Hebrew, Greek, and Latin origins and meanings of the word and provides a survey of various histories and theologies of vocation.

Cary, Philip, "No secret plan: Why you don't have to find God's will for your life," *Christian Century* 127, No. 20 (October 5, 2010), 20–23.
This article counters the popular notion that we are to seek God's will in our lives, or in a particular situation, by arguing that we are to focus more on the task of acquiring wisdom (the ability to discern what is good and what is bad). Using the Parable of the Talents, the author emphasizes that we are given talents with the expectation of the master that they be invested in the kingdom, but without specific details about how to do the investing. Therefore, the wise steward is a co-worker with the master.

Cetuk, Virginia Samuel, *What to Expect in Seminary: Theological Education and Spiritual Formation* (Nashville, TN: Abingdon Press, 1998).
While this primer to entering seminary is focused primarily on the academic, spiritual, and communal expectations with respect to leadership training, Cetuk (a professor at Drew Theological Seminary) sets the context for discussions on discernment and calling. In one chapter, she also includes a brief survey of the discernment processes in various mainline denominations.

Countryman, L. William, *Living on the Border of the Holy* (Harrisburg, PA: Morehouse Publishing, 1999).
This work is viewed as a classic in the exploration of faith, calling, community, and the priesthood of all believers. He defines "priest" from the beginning as one who inhabits the "borderlands" of our experiences and encounters with God.

Farnham, Suzanne G., Gill, Joseph P., McLean, R. Taylor and Ward, Susan M., *Listening Hearts: Discerning Call in Community* (20th Anniversary Edition) (New York and Harrisonburg, PA: Morehouse Publishing, 2011).
For over 20 years this book has served as one of the key manuals for those who are sensing a call to ministry. The primary author, a Quaker, helps frame the questions about major life choices as they relate to the will of God, and suggests how one can listen to the community's affirmation in this process.

Gallagher, Nora, *Practicing Resurrection: A Memoir of Work, Doubt, Discernment, and Moments of Grace* (New York: A.A. Knopf, 2003).
This moving story narrates the personal discernment of the author through recognizing a calling, discerning God's will as a member of her Episcopal congregation, and then navigating the inevitable polity and mechanics of discernment committees and Commissions on Ministry. Throughout the process she returns to prayer and soul-searching as her compass.

Grinenko Baker, Dori and Mercer, Joyce Ann, *Lives to Offer: Accompanying Youth on their*

Vocational Quests (Cleveland, OH: The Pilgrim Press, 2007).

This entry in the Youth Ministry Alternatives Series focuses on the calling of youth to ministry. Chapter 8 is a key to this text, entitled "Whose Calling? Who's calling?", which is a distinction that is entirely appropriate in those sensing God's call at any age.

Mercer, Joyce Ann, "Call forwarding: Putting vocation in the present tense with youth" (lecture given as part of the 2002 Princeton Forum on Youth Ministry).

This lecture explores the various changes in the understanding of vocation within Christian theology, with particular emphasis on the implications of these shifts with regard to youth and young adults.

Palmer, Parker, *Let Your Life Speak: Listening for the Voice of Vocation* (San Francisco, CA: Jossey-Bass, 2000).

Essential reading for a person preparing for a discernment process in ministry of any kind, Palmer's book has been referenced and reflected upon by many others when writing on the topic of call and discernment.

Placher, William C., ed., *Callings: Twenty Centuries of Christian Wisdom on Vocation* (Grand Rapids, MI: W.B. Eerdmans Publishing Co., 2005).

Placher edits together a compendium of writings, passages, and resources from myriad theologians and writers about vocation, calling, and the inspirations of the Spirit. This book provides an excellent resource for looking at the Christian tradition on the subject of call and discernment.

Roscher, Ellie, ed., *Keeping the Faith in Seminary* (Minneapolis, MN: Avenida Books, 2012).

This anthology about particular seminary experiences from various mainline writers contains some valuable testimonials about calling and vocation in Protestant Churches.

Schuurman, Douglas, J., *Vocation: Discerning our Callings in Life* (Grand Rapids, MI: William B. Eerdmans Publishing Co., 2004).

A discussion of calling may be best understood as an exploration of vocation. This book is a look at the Protestant understanding of vocation from a contemporary perspective.

Soughers, Tara, *Fleeing God: Fear, Call and the Book of Jonah* (Lanham, MD: Cowley Publications, 2007).

Soughers, an Episcopal priest, presents the Book of Jonah through the prism of her own discernment process, and offers some powerful thoughts and reflections on calling.

2

The Imperative of Training

Any important role in society needs training. If you want to be a doctor, then you need a 4-year undergraduate degree, a further 4 years of medical education, and then 3–7 years in a residency program. To be responsible for the lives of men and women and make sure that they survive and thrive under your supervision requires an extensive and long training.

There are many forms of ministry in the Church. Some feel called to chaplaincy; some to a form of lay ministry; some are simply called to live out their baptismal vows in the context of regular secular employment. However, the focus of this chapter will be on the leadership of congregations (both lay and ordained). Leadership of congregations is a major responsibility. You are going to be responsible for inviting the loving God who created the cosmos to intersect with the lives of those in the congregation. You will be the person who stands by the bedside of someone as she dies and has to handle the loss and pain of the grieving family. You will be responsible for taking a person and helping him to commit to a volunteer outreach ministry. You are the person who will have to explain the complexities of the doctrine of the *Trinity* (in as far as one is able). You are the person who will have to manage this volunteer organization and deal with budget and staffing issues. This is not easy work. And mistakes, as serious as the ones doctors may commit, can happen and when they do, the damage is significant.

The best ecumenical statement about the nature of ministry was the highly regarded statement produced by the World Council of Churches in the early 1980s. It was called *Baptism, Eucharist, and Ministry*. The text explains that ministry is grounded in the "whole people of God," to whom the Spirit of God has given a range of different gifts. The text recognizes the threefold pattern of ministry – *bishop*, *presbyter*, and *deacon*. And at the same time it notes that modified versions of that pattern are emerging as the Church adapts to the

An Introduction to Ministry: A Primer for Renewed Life and Leadership in Mainline Protestant Congregations, First Edition. Ian S. Markham and Oran E. Warder.
© 2016 John Wiley & Sons, Ltd. Published 2016 by John Wiley & Sons, Ltd.

changing nature of society. For our purpose, the text describes the conditions for ordination and writes:

> Candidates for the ordained ministry need appropriate preparation through study of scripture and theology, prayer and spirituality, and through acquaintance with the social and human realities of the contemporary world. In some situations, this preparation may take a form other than that of prolonged academic study. The period of training will be one in which the candidate's call is tested, fostered and confirmed, or its understanding modified.[1]

The World Council of Churches

In the early part of the twentieth century, it was clear that various denominations of Christendom had splintered over theological issues. A movement to reconcile these denominations began, and dialogue between churches was initiated in what is now called the "ecumenical movement." In 1948, the first World Council of Churches (WCC) convened in Amsterdam featuring representatives of Catholic and Protestant denominations. Today, the WCC boasts the participation of 349 global churches, falling under the guidance of this mission statement:

> The World Council of Churches is a fellowship of churches which confess the Lord Jesus Christ as God and Savior according to the scriptures, and therefore seek to fulfill together their common calling to the glory of the one God: Father, Son and Holy Spirit.[2]

Training for ministry is important and difficult. It needs to include both spirituality and the social sciences. In addition, there is a tension between the skills necessary to understand the tradition we are in and the skills necessary for managing and caring for the congregation. There is also an expectation that the person trained is an appropriate grace-filled vessel. If one's doctor is greedy, one can still trust the doctor's judgment in matters of health; if the priest is greedy, then he or she is not reflecting the values of the Gospel.

So it is not surprising that every mainline denomination in the United States sets out a necessary process for training.

Processes in the Mainline

Getting accepted into the ordination process and getting trained are difficult. All the mainline denominations are very concerned with attracting the most able and training them as effectively as possible. Many start the process and a significant number are finally told that "no call is recognized." This can be painful and difficult. It is hard to offer yourself to the Church only to find that the Church does not think this is your vocation. However, this selection process is important. The Church needs to be confident that the gifts and skill sets of an individual are suitable for ministry. Most Christians are called to serve God in a vast variety of professions. The task of leading a congregation is neither better nor worse than these other callings. It is different. And the Church has a responsibility (however painful it sometimes is) to recognize (and encourage) the call in some and to explain that God's call lies elsewhere for others.

Acceptance into the process is not necessarily a promise of *ordination*. Training takes time. And the Church has a responsibility to make sure that the person in the process is still suitable for ordination. So there are a variety of stages in the process. Ordination is never sure until the hands are laid on a person's head. This means that the process is both time-consuming and unsettling. Time-consuming because the training is extensive, and unsettling because one is never sure that ordination will happen (despite all this training).

Although this uncertainty is necessary, we do take the view that it would be good if all the mainline denominations could ensure that after a rigorous examination of the candidate, once he or she is in the process, then the outcome is likely to be successful. It is not right that as membership of a committee changes or a new bishop arrives there is suddenly a reexamination of applicants who are already in the process. Churches need to be thorough, but they don't need to be cruel.

In addition, there is some evidence that two types of applicants for ministry can be seriously disadvantaged by the process. The first is applicants from ethnic minorities. When progress through society is made difficult because of racism, it is hard to cope with a system of interrogation and suspicion. The second type is the most able applicants. For example, if a person graduates from an elite school and has the choice of a high-paying position in finance (where she is being offered a signing bonus) or struggling through the process towards ordination. When the initial enquiry is met with a lack of encouragement, it is not surprising that some of the most able opt out of the ordination process.

There are some applicants who might find it difficult to enter the process. For the lesbian, gay, bisexual, and transgender (LGBT) community, some in the mainline will welcome and others will discourage. The United Methodist Church, for example, continues to affirm the historic Christian line that confines sexual intimacy to heterosexual marriage. This means that an openly gay applicant will not be received into the process. Even in a denomination that officially welcomes gay applicants, there are localities that are more conservative and might hesitate to take the applicant forward. In addition, there are some parts of the Church that are nervous about ordaining women. Although all the mainline affirm the ordination of women, there are localities within the different denominations that are more hesitant.

The processes are different in each denomination. These are brief descriptions of the five traditions we are focusing on in this book.

The United Methodist Church

There are a number of different options in the United Methodist Church. The first is the *elder*. Elders are called to preach and teach the Word of God, administer the sacraments, organize the Church for its mission and service, and administer the discipline of the Church.[3] The second is a *deacon*, "called to lead in service, word, compassion, and justice and equip others for this ministry through teaching, proclamation, and worship and who assist elders in the administration of the sacraments."[4] Both elders and deacons complete 2–3 years of provisional membership to clergy orders, depending on the location and annual conference expectations. *The Book of Discipline* says those who are "not ordained as elders who are appointed to preach and conduct divine worship and perform the duties of a pastor shall have a license for pastoral ministry." This may include provisional elders who have been commissioned by the annual conference, local pastors, associate members, deacons in full connection who are seeking to qualify for ordination as an elder, and licensed or ordained clergy from other denominations who have a training equivalent to the studies for license as a local pastor but do not meet the requirements for provisional membership. Those licensed for pastoral ministry may perform the duties of pastors but only while appointed to a particular charge or extension ministry. And the third is the locally ordained pastor (who may be part-time). The locally ordained pastor may be elected to associate membership in the Conference after serving for at least 4 years and meeting additional requirements of training. However, in all three cases, there is an expectation of significant initial training.

The process starts with the pastor in a congregation. It is important the pastor is supportive of the candidate starting the process. There is an assigned text called *The Christian as Minister: An Exploration Into the Meaning of God's Call*, which potential candidates for ministry are encouraged to read, in addition to *Understanding God's Call: A Ministry Inquiry Process*. The precise nature of this training is prescribed by *The United Methodist Book of Discipline* and the General Board of Higher Education and Ministry. Certain seminaries are approved by the United Methodist Church to be a place for training – this includes the United Methodist seminaries (such as the Candler School of Theology at Emory University and Duke Divinity School), as well as other ecumenical institutions such as Harvard Divinity School and Yale Divinity School.

For those who are feeling called to local ministry or a licensed pastoral ministry, there is a Five-Year Basic Course of Study. This covers all the basics and can be delivered in a variety of ways. As with all mainline denominations, one does need to have the call recognized by the Church. The district superintendent is a key person: he or she will invite the candidate into, and help oversee, the process. The Clergy Session of the Annual Conferences needs to elect the candidate into provisional membership; and a bishop needs to commission and finally ordain you. This process can be demanding and difficult. Like all the mainline denominations the Methodists strive to discern whether there is an authentic call and whether the training has been adequate.

The Presbyterian Church (USA)

A key theme for Presbyterians is the idea of a "covenant relationship." So the relationship to God is important, along with the relationship with each other. There are three partners in the covenant relationship. These are the "individual under care," the session of the congregation (this is the leadership team of the congregation), and the presbytery to which the congregation belongs (presbytery is the group of local elders and ministers in that area). Normally, the presbytery will delegate its responsibility to a committee or ministry team, which is called the Committee on Preparation for Ministry. The ultimate decision-making responsibility resides with the presbytery. *The Handbook on Ministry* explains:

> The session will make recommendations about whether the person should be enrolled as an inquirer, and may be asked to share what it is discerning about the individual's sense of call and developing ministry gifts during the process. It will continue to provide pastoral care and support to the person as it does to all its congregational members. But it is the presbytery that has the responsibilities for oversight of the person's preparation, to make a decision about suitability for ministry, and finally to assess readiness to seek a call to ministry that would require ordination as a teaching elder.[5]

The focus of the training is on five key areas. These are: first, education for ministry, which normally takes place at a seminary and results in a Masters of Divinity degree; second, spiritual development, which is aided by a required unit of clinical pastoral education; third, interpersonal relationships; fourth, personal growth; and fifth, professional development. The language of covenant continues to shape the process. So there are covenant agreements that set out the progress that is needed in any particular area.

At the end of the training process, the candidate is then "certified." This means that subject to a call to a congregation, the process recognizes that the candidate is ready for ordination.

The United Church of Christ

The United Church of Christ (UCC) has a strong congregational polity. This means that local congregations are self-governing, so the process must start within a local UCC congregation. This congregation will be part of an association. The candidate should be received as "a Student in Care of Association."[6] The two committees that are formed for the student focus on examining the "applicant with respect to fitness, aptitudes, Christian experience, and commitment."[7] Along with the other mainline denominations, the expectation for the full-time minister is a bachelor's degree and a Masters of Divinity degree from a theological seminary.

As with the Presbyterians, the association is responsible for organizing the ordination service, which representatives of the different Churches should attend.

The Episcopal Church

The Episcopal Church process starts in a congregation. A discernment committee is formed to determine whether there is sufficient evidence of a call. If approved, the aspirant then moves to the diocese (the regional organization of various congregations under the control of a bishop). Normally the bishop delegates authority to a commission, which will oversee both the discernment and the training.

Typically training in the Episcopal Church involves seminary training. The type of seminary is at the discretion of the bishop. There are some local ordained options for those who cannot relocate. Increasingly, dioceses and groups of dioceses are organizing regional (and unaccredited) training.

The standing committee of the diocese is responsible for finally recommending a candidate to the bishop for ordination. This is normally done after all the training and just before the ordination to the diaconate. All priests in the Episcopal Church are first required to be "transitional" deacons (of course some people are called just to be deacons and their training is less onerous and normally the work is unpaid), before being ordained as priests by the bishop.

The Lutheran Church

There are four steps to the process in the Evangelical Lutheran Church of America (ELCA). The Church talks of four rostered ministries, which are: (i) a commissioned associate in ministry of Word and service; (ii) a consecrated diaconal minister of Word, witness, and service; (iii) a consecrated deaconess of Word and service; and (iv) an ordained minister of Word and sacrament (this is a pastor).

Focusing on the "candidacy process" for a pastor, there are four steps. These are: first, entrance/candidacy. The person interested in ordination works with the local congregation and a synodically based candidacy committee to explore his or her call to ministry. There is an application and all the normal checks (background check and psychological evaluation). The second step is endorsement. This often happens while in seminary. The idea here is for the synod and seminary to check in on the progress to date. The third step is approval. Once again this involves the seminary and the synod. This is the crucial step where a person will be approved for ordination. Finally, the last step is assignment. This is the moment when one can be assigned to one of the nine regions of the ELCA and then ultimately to a synod. The norm for a pastor is a 4-year Masters of Divinity – 3 years of academic study and a 4th year of internship, although like much of the mainline second career applicants receive a more abridged training. In addition, clinical and pastoral education is also required.

Residential vs. Non-residential Seminaries

Increasingly, persons who are seeking ministerial leadership positions in mainline churches need to consider how to undergo their training. For centuries, the pattern meant a student enrolled in a graduate program (such as a Masters of Divinity) at a "residential" seminary – a fully enclosed academic campus in which seminarians live, worship, and study as they complete their degree. In the past couple of decades, prospective ministers have looked toward "bi-vocational" ministries, and similarly, non-residential education. Today, many seminarians across many denominations may partake in part-time studies while maintaining their existing careers or jobs. But this is not to say that residential seminaries have gone the way of the dinosaur – many denominations have seminaries that provide the resources for a full intensive education that encompasses residency on or adjacent to a full-time academic campus.

Figure 2.1   Virginia Theological Seminary
Source: Courtesy of Virginia Theological Seminary, www.vts.edu

Key Features of Training

For all mainline traditions, it is important that the clergy person be well formed in the Christian tradition. So the key features are: a good grounding in Scripture (one needs to know the Bible and be able to interpret the Bible intelligently), theologically literate (know the key theologians of the Church), historically sensitive (understand the journey of faith over the years), ethically aware (understand how the tradition calls us to live lives of love rather than egotism), congregationally effective (understand the world of worship and know how to preach), and pastorally sensitive (able to be there when there is a need).

In this book, we have chapters on these areas. They form the basis of a good academic foundation. Naturally, there are many other areas that are considered important. So, for example, it is helpful to have an understanding of the arts, or of other religions, or of the challenge of distinctively missional context (a diverse urban setting for ministry is quite different from a more homogeneous rural setting). One important discovery that one makes as one starts the training is that there is always more to know. No program of training can cover everything. As a clergy person in the making, one needs to anticipate that the training will last a lifetime.

One entirely distinctive part of the training is the need for personal integrity and spiritual depth. The word normally used in theological education is "formation." One needs to be formed to be ready to serve. It is grounded in that beautiful biblical image of the potter and the clay (Isaiah 64:8): God needs to shape us into beautiful pots appropriate for the work of ministry.

Now this is where training gets tricky. In the end, one can trust the medical judgment of a doctor or the legal judgment of lawyer, even if they do not pray. The graduate training of a doctor or a lawyer need not include expectations around prayer. However, with a clergy person it is vitally important that the person be authentic. One needs to be a person of prayer; one needs a disciplined internal life; one needs to have integrity in one's relationships; and one must have a sense of God and a joy in living the Christian life. Naturally, clergy are not immune from the struggles, temptations, and brokenness of all human life. So there are moments when it can be so hard. And we need to bring our brokenness as part of our authenticity to our ministry, but one should always be a work in progress. We need to give God the space to transform us so we are ever more effective as ministers of the Gospel.

Formation

The place to start with formation is discipline. The work of giving God the space for our lives to be transformed is a work of discipline. One must clear time every day for prayer and study. This must be a priority; the busier you are the more important it is to keep the time for devotions intact. Different traditions have different forms of devotions. For the Lutherans and Episcopalians, it is an expectation that one observes the "daily office" (short liturgies that involve certain prayers, canticles, and readings); for the Methodists, UCC, and Presbyterians, there is more flexibility. Naturally there are a whole of host of aids for Bible study and prayer, some of which are listed at the end of this chapter.

Another important part of formation is spiritual direction. Accountability is important in formation. It is very easy for patterns to emerge in a life that betray the Gospel. So finding a "prayer partner" or a "spiritual director" (the terminology depends on which tradition you are in) is vitally important. Ideally a clergy person should aim to meet up with them every 4–6 weeks or so (any more often and there is nothing to say, and any less the accountability is less effective). It should be a time where the challenges of ministry and of one's own personal journey are shared. The conversation should range widely, discussing worries around relationships and children, as well as those moments when doubts and fears are real. Naturally, the conversations should be kept in the strictest confidence. Such sharing is serious and holy work.

These two features – dedicated daily time with God coupled with spiritual direction – form the pillars of formation. Other aspects include searching out opportunities for collegiality and retreats. Collegiality in a clergy group is important because it ensures we remain sensitive to the spectrum of God's work in the world. Part of formation is learning to live with people who hold different opinions from you. So finding a good clergy group with whom you can discuss differences of polity and faith is healthy. Increasingly, there are clergy groups who are forming co-ed soccer teams, which then combine exercise and collegiality with a witness. Wellness is an important part of formation. We are called by God to love our neighbors as ourselves. This means that the commandments include "love of self." To give, give, give to others with no self-care is very unwise. Studies show that lack of self-care is a key factor in clergy misconduct.[8] In addition, the Episcopal Church discovered that clergy who exercise and take care of themselves are much more likely to lead a growing church. So a good diet, regular exercise, and taking a vacation are all-important ingredients in a well-formed clergy person.

New Models of Training

Earlier in the chapter we looked at the mainline emphasis on a graduate degree from a seminary. This expectation has its roots in the ideal of a "learned clergy." Gregory Jones and Kevin R. Armstrong muse on the roots of this concept when they write:

> This ideal has been built partly on the image of the pastor as a professional, but it is rooted also in an emphasis on the pastor as preacher and teacher. Many of the earliest colleges and universities were founded in order to cultivate a learned clergy. The founders of Harvard College, for example, sought to avoid leaving "an illiterate Ministry to the Churches, when our present ministers shall lie in the dust." … When the time came that the colleges felt a need for a more focused studies for future clergy, they endowed professorships of divinity, formed departments around them, and eventually established the divinity schools whose work it was, and is, to create a learned clergy for the church.[9]

Jones and Armstrong go on to reflect on the challenge that the concept of the learned clergy has posed for American Christianity. They want excellence grounded in a wider set of skills. However, an additional challenge to the learned clergy has come from a more practical and logistical place.

A graduate degree is difficult for many people to obtain. It is not so much the raw intellectual ability, but the challenge of finding the time for such sustained training. Many mainline congregations are very small. Often the size of the congregation reflects the small town. If the town has a population of 5000 people, then it is not surprising that the congregation in the local mainline church is small. Raising up leadership for these congregations is difficult. The congregation cannot afford a full-time clergy person. So the position will have to be part time or even voluntary. To require a 3-year graduate degree (with all the inevitable debt) is unreasonable.

As a result many mainline denominations are developing alternatives. Using books such as this, they are working to design a curriculum that can facilitate appropriate and sufficient training to lead the small congregation effectively. One can now train online or in weekend and week-long intensive programs. These options are opening up theological education in an important and effective way.

The other important trend is around the form the training takes. Even with the 3-year graduate degree, there are many different types. Some are delivered in partnership with congregations (a major feature of the training for the Lutheran Church); others have a focus on chaplaincy as a ministry setting (for the military, prisons, hospitals, and schools); and others strive to be aggressively missional in approach.

Lance R. Barker and B. Edmon Martins have collected some excellent examples of alternative models for theological education. The "mutual ministry" model, which is aimed at small rural congregations, involves "localized, corporate learning … that seeks to engage – over a period of time – a majority of the members of the congregation."[10] The Southern Conference Ordination Preparation Education (SCOPE) is aimed at African Americans in the UCC who need a distinctive program that recognizes the cultural and historical experience of African Americans. The Theology Among the People (TAP) program is another UCC program that focuses on both lay and ordained education in small groups. The United Methodist Church developed the Course of Study Schools, which operates in partnership with the seminaries, but offers a more flexible residence experience in preparation for licensed pastoral ministry. The Presbyterian Church has a program for "Commissioned Ruling Elders" to engage in a modified course of study, which includes online study. The idea here is to provide a training where a person can assist and serve when a teaching elder is not available. All of these programs stress the need for training, but do so in more gentle ways than the traditional 3-year graduate degree.

Conclusion

There is an imperative to the trained. Ministry is difficult and demanding work. As one discerns a call, it is often the case that one imagines that the simple combination of a love for Jesus coupled with energy is all that needed. It is commonplace to resent the demands around training that the process to ordination puts on the future clergy person. However, once in the world of training, almost everyone then understands why it matters so much. There is just so much to learn. It is good to learn Greek or Hebrew or, preferably, both. It is important to understand the different ways in which the Church has understood the Trinity. Learning how to preach well is essential. Relating well to the young as well as the old is hard; yet some of the basics can be taught. Managing a volunteer organization is difficult. Time is needed to learn how to be a personnel manager and a financial specialist. Congregational dynamics are tricky, so conflict management skills are important. And, of course, it is vitally important to learn how to be present with a person in need.

Perhaps the most important part of training is the work of formation. We are called to live the Gospel we preach. This is fundamental. And we need the years to give God the space to make that true of us. Training takes time; it is best not to resent it, but to love every moment of it.

Notes

1   Baptism, Eucharist, and Ministry, Faith and Order Paper No. 111 (Geneva: World Council of Churches, 1982) as found in *William H. Willimon, Pastor: A Reader for Ordained Ministry* (Nashville, TN: Abingdon Press, 2002), 45.

2   "About us," World Council of Churches, http://www.oikoumene.org/en/about-us (accessed May 28, 2015).3 *The United Methodist Book of Discipline*, 2012, 303.2.

3   *The United Methodist Book of Discipline*, 2012, 303.2.

4   Ibid.

5   *Advisory Handbook on the Preparation for Ministry*, 32, as found at http://www.pghpresbytery.org/forms/pdfs/cpm/CPM_Advisory_Handbook.pdf (accessed June 18, 2015).

6   *United Church of Christ Manual on Ministry*, produced by the Parish Life and Leadership Ministry Team. Section 2: Student in Care of Association, 5 as found at http://d3n8a8pro7vhmx.cloudfront.net/unitedchurchofchrist/legacy_url/1300/mom-2002-20student-1.pdf?1418424768 (accessed May 28, 2015).

7   Ibid., 5.

8   see Nils Friberg and Mark R. Laase, *Before the Fall: Preventing Pastoral Sexual Abuse* (Collegeville, MN: Liturgical Press, 1998).

9   Gregory Jones and Kevin R. Armstrong, *Resurrecting Excellence: Shaping Faithful Christian Ministry* (Grand Rapids, MI: Eerdmans, 2006), 111. The quotation from Harvard College comes from a 1643 pamphlet called *New England's First Fruits* by the president, Henry Dunster.

10 Lance R. Barker and B. Edmon Martin,eds, *Multiple Paths to Ministry: New Models for Theological Education* (Cleveland, OH: The Pilgrim Press, 2004), 36.

Annotated Bibliography

Barker, Lance R. and Edmon Martin, B., eds, *Multiple Paths to Ministry: New Models for Theological Education* (Cleveland, OH: The Pilgrim Press, 2004).
Thanks to the Lilly Foundation, this is a useful survey of some of the more innovative programs that have started to emerge for training.

Calian, Carnegie Samuel, *The Ideal Seminary: Pursuing Excellence in Theological Education* (Louisville, KY: Westminster John Knox Press, 2002).
The then-president of Pittsburg Theological Seminary sets out the case for why training at a seminary is so important.

Foster, Charles R, Dahill, Lisa E., Golemon, Lawrence A., and Wang Tolentino, Barbara, *Educating Clergy: Teaching Practices and Pastoral Imagination* (San Francisco, CA: Jossey-Bass, 2006).
Sponsored by the Carnegie Foundation for the Advancement of Teaching, this book has become the classic in respect to theological education. A masterful survey and discussion.

Jenkins, Davod O. and Rogers, P. Alice, eds, *Equipping the Saints* (Cleveland, OH: The Pilgrim Press, 2010).
An important collection of essays that describes the best practices in ministry formation.

Jones, Gregory and Armstrong, Kevin R., *Resurrecting Excellence: Shaping Faithful Christian Ministry* (Grand Rapids, MI: Eerdmans Publishing Co., 2006).

An important text that stresses the centrality of learning the practices of ministry. The theme is the importance of living as faithful disciples of the Gospel.

Willimon, William H., *Pastor: A Reader for Ordained Ministry* (Nashville, TN: Abingdon Press, 2002).
A really helpful reader that sets out the primary ecumenical texts around the nature and purpose of ordained ministry.

Resources for Daily Devotions

- Barnhill, Carla, *The Green Bible Devotional* (New York: Harper Collins, 2009).
  An environment-focused devotional built on daily scripture readings. There are many specific daily devotionals written like this one focused on care for creation.
- Clairborne, Shane, Wilson-Hartgrove, Jonathan and Okoro, Enuma, *Common Prayer* (Grand Rapids, MI: Zondervan, 2010).
  A popular book of daily prayer particularly in US "New Monastic" movements.
- Nouwen, J.M., *Bread for the Journey* (San Francisco, CA: HarperSanFrancisco, 1997).
  Three hundred and sixty-five devotional readings by spiritual writer Henri Nouwen.
- Northumbria Community, *Celtic Daily Prayer* (San Francisco, CA: HarperOne, 2002).

There are many books for daily prayer in the Celtic Tradition. This book of daily prayers follows the morning and evening offices of the Northumbria Community, an ecumenical Christian community in Northumbria, UK.
- Taizé, Prayer for Each Day (Chicago, IL: GIA Publications, 1998).
  A book of ecumenical daily prayer based on the Taizé community following the liturgical seasons.
The One Year Bible: Arranged in 365 Daily Readings (Iowa Falls, IA: World Bible Publishers, 1991).
Read the NRSV in 1 year.
There are many daily devotions available for access online or to be sent to your email. In addition, each denomination provides their own daily devotion online and/or in the form of daily prayer or the daily office.

Alternative Resources for Training

- Asbury Theological Seminary Extended Learning.
  You can complete two thirds of your Masters of Divinity through Asbury's extended learning program.
- The Lutheran Theological Seminary and Lancaster Theological Seminary have teamed up to provide a Distance Learning Collaborative Program.

It allows you to take courses online staying in your location.
- University of Dubuque's Theological Seminary's Christian Leadership Program.
  A distance education technology recommended by the Presbyterian Church and open to those training for leadership in other Christian denominations.

3

Church Dynamics: Exploring Congregational Culture

From bookshelves to blogs, there is no shortage of published material devoted to the renewal of the mainline Church. All seem to agree on the urgent need for change, yet there is no consensus on the form, direction, or shape that change should take, nor is there a consistent understanding of what constitutes a renewed Church. With these issues in mind, we offer an overview of congregational dynamics. These dynamics help to explain the present state of the Church and also offer a glimpse of what the Church can become. While we agree that there is a need to change, we also believe that the elements of renewal are found not from outside the institution, but rather from within the mainline tradition itself. Rather than the wholesale replacement of beliefs, customs, and structures, we contend that the future of the mainline rests in the rediscovery of the best and most fundamental qualities and characteristics of the reformed experience. We believe that our renewal rests on our being more of ourselves and not less so. We believe that our renewal rests on claiming our truest identity rather than becoming something we are not. We believe that our renewal rests on mining the unique gifts and treasures of our tradition rather than discarding them. Thus the change that we are suggesting is not a shift in belief (adapting the theology of the mega-church movement), not a shift in program (acquiring the latest Church growth strategy), and not a shift in structure (organizing our way into a new future). The change that is required is the transformation of congregational culture. The corollary to this change is the leadership required to guide that transformation.

In this chapter we will explore congregational dynamics from a number of perspectives. We begin with a review of the elements of the Church culture and a brief history of the discipline of congregational studies. We will then look at some of the theoretical tools used to help analyze, assess, and understand the complexities of congregational life, and lastly delve into congregational transformation and leadership based on the reclaiming of the theology of mission that is the foundation of mainline Christianity.

An Introduction to Ministry: A Primer for Renewed Life and Leadership in Mainline Protestant Congregations, First Edition. Ian S. Markham and Oran E. Warder.
© 2016 John Wiley & Sons, Ltd. Published 2016 by John Wiley & Sons, Ltd.

> **James Hopewell**
>
> Broadly recognized at the founder of the discipline of congregational studies, James Hopewell (1929–1984) was a missionary in West Africa, trained in the field of comparative religion, and over the course of his ministry became fascinated with the nature, culture, and life of local congregations. He was particularly interested in understanding the resilience of congregations and the application of the rapidly developing world of social sciences to the life of the Church.

Hopewell and the Field of Congregational Studies

Any review of the development of congregational studies as a distinct field of academic pursuit must include the pioneering work of *James Hopewell*. Broadly recognized as the founder of the discipline of congregation studies, Hopewell was, in his early career, a missionary in West Africa. He was trained in the field of comparative religion, focused on Islamic studies, and over the course of his ministry became increasingly fascinated with the nature, culture, and life of local congregations. He was interested in both the challenges facing local congregations and their amazing resilience. He set out to learn more and read widely on the subject, only to find the existing literature incomplete and unsatisfying.

What fascinated Hopewell was the ability of congregations to hold together in the face of seemingly overwhelming pressure, and he found little accounting for this in the congregational literature of the day. He also found that the field of congregational studies, like the literature, was fragmented and failed to account for the subtleties and nuances of congregational life. He would come to believe that any critical understanding of congregational life would require systematic analysis, and that analysis would require tools of theory.[1] Before beginning our examination of congregational analysis, some critical background and context will be helpful.

Congregational studies emerged in the early twentieth century, in the shadow of the rapidly developing world of the social sciences. Often viewed as a weak application of the largely secular principles used to study other social institutions, it would take decades for the field of congregational studies to be acknowledged and recognized as a respected area of study in its own right. Eventually the field was established squarely within the discipline of what is known as "qualitative" research as opposed to the more traditional "quantitative" approach to research. That is, rather than exploring congregational life using strictly statistical surveys, questionnaires, and other rigidly quantifiable analysis, the goal would be to search for deeper meaning, and a richer understanding of congregational life, utilizing more flexible tools of assessment.[2]

Early practitioners also had to define the scope of their work and distinguish between whether or not the goal for their findings were to be of "extrinsic" or "intrinsic" value to the Church. Extrinsic study would be undertaken with the hope that the research could contribute in some meaningful way to the wider Church, that the findings would be applicable on a more global, macro-level. An intrinsic approach has no such goal and would be undertaken simply to foster understanding and for the benefit of the community being studied.[3] It is within this framework that the discipline of congregational studies would emerge. Generally speaking, this field of exploration, within the American mainline Church experience, tended toward qualitative and extrinsic research. The goal was the discovery of deep common understandings and meaning that could be applied more universally to the larger Church.

It is in this context that James Hopewell began his groundbreaking work, which would become known at "ecclesial ethnography." His classic book, *Congregation*, was published in 1987 posthumously, and remains a standard text for those who study congregations. He begins this work with an observation made by the theologian Wade Clark Roof, that in congregations, theological doctrines are always filtered through the social and cultural experiences of the people. The result is what Roof referred to as the "operant religion" of the congregation, which might differ dramatically from the more "formal religion" of the historic creeds. Hopewell believed that it was in understanding the operant religion of a congregation that one could begin to see how belief systems function in people's everyday lives.[4]

Utilizing his experience as a missionary and his skill and training as a social scientist entering an alien culture, Hopewell observed, interviewed, and immersed himself in the life of a congregation with the goal of understanding its unique history and how that history informed its current role and self-understanding. Hopewell began to see congregational life as an unfolding narrative, and found that a storytelling approach was far more effective in exploring people's fundamental beliefs than direct questioning. He found that if he asked directly about a specific theological belief, people would either be embarrassed or uncomfortable in their response, or resort to the language of formal religion and give him the answers that they thought he wanted to hear. He learned that it was more important to learn the language of the operant religion of the congregation, which is the language of story. He found that in a local congregation, members participate in religion far more easily than they can explain it. He believed that it was here, at the intersection of participation and explanation, that the organized and official doctrines of the Church produce a particular slant that becomes the operative religion which forms the basis of personal belief, and shape the unique culture of the congregation.[5]

As time went on Hopewell arrived at the brilliant insight that forms the heart of his thinking and the heart of the seminal book. He would contend that congregations can only be understood and fully appreciated on the basis of narrative; that is, the stories that members tell about themselves and their community is they struggle not only for survival, but also for meaning. Put another way, congregational culture is a unified system based on narrative. His basic theory is that:

> [C]ongregational culture is not an accidental accumulation of symbolic elements but a coherent system whose structural logic is narrative. As congregations first come into being, he argued, they construct a narrative that accounts for their nascent identity. They attract to their fellowship those who want to participate in the unique local drama enacted there. They maintain their integrity against incursions by reiterating their distinct local history. And they encounter the world by identifying similarities between its stories and their own.[6]

The rest of his work is an elaboration on this theory about the power of narrative in shaping and sustaining congregational life and his contention that anyone working within congregations must be aware of this dynamic.

Building upon this foundational work, the field of congregational studies has continued to grow and develop. Yet two of Hopewell's fundamental approaches and practices remain. The first is to draw on the insights of the broader perspectives of the social sciences (anthropology, sociology, psychology, etc.); and the second, to enter every local congregation as one would enter a foreign country or culture. The discipline continues to be shaped and defined as the quest to interpret the unique history, narrative, and culture of a congregation. A more contemporary definition of congregational studies, which echoes these same themes, is from Jackson W. Carroll in his *Handbook for Congregational Studies*. He contends that the goal of congregational studies is to study:

> seriously and appreciatively, through disciplined understanding, their present *being* – the good and precious qualities that are within them – as a means of grace themselves that enable the transformation of congregations into what it is possible for them to *become*.[7]

At this point, it is also important to offer a word of caution. Humility is the hallmark of this work, and yet the dangers of arrogance are an ever-present hazard in the work of congregational studies.

> To speak of "discovering" congregational culture may sound a bit presumptuous. After all, religious leaders have been confronting distinctive congregational cultures for centuries. Think of how immigrant congregations fought over changing the liturgy to English, or of the battles that took place when Irish clergy were sent to serve Polish parishes. And we are familiar at another level with the skirmishes that have taken place over church dinners – do we use fine china or paper plates – and building designs – Gothic or modern? Such clashes are not trivial. Ways of life and basic self-understandings are at stake in such controversies. Clearly, cultural differences have been facts of life in our congregations for as long as we can remember.[8]

One example of how Church ethnographers veered off course occurred in the 1960s when a prominent group of sociologists and theologians became preoccupied with the idea of religion's role as a "tottering sacred canopy over the whole American culture."[9] They fretted about the blandness of American congregations, the suburban captivity of the Church, their increasing homogeneity, and their growing irrelevance to public life. According to this perspective, congregations seemed to have made a deal with the dominant culture: "churches could have Sunday morning, nice buildings and tax exemption, but they had to stay away from corporate boardrooms, executive suites, smoke-filled rooms and other places central to the nine-to-five world."[10]

While not completely unfounded, this perspective "obscured the generative and nurturing role that congregations played at the local or subcultural level."[11] What they failed to see was the amazing resilience and adaptive capabilities of congregations that prompted Hopewell's interests. What they failed to see was that congregations built structures of value and belief that incorporated their own historical narrative as well as larger cultural events. These discoveries helped to "bring into view the distinctive character of the congregation and challenge us to stop taking these institutions for granted."[12]

Reading a Congregation

Learning to appreciate the local congregation, speak its narrative, and become part of its life is essential for those who would also seek to lead that congregation. Yet there are many who believe that congregational leaders are, too often, not adequately prepared for the task.

> At the seminary, students learn distinct styles of worship, varieties of biblical hermeneutics, modes of theologizing, approaches to pastoral care and models of leadership. Some observers of theological education are so disillusioned by the depths of this enculturation and its lack of fit with the cultures of local congregations that they conclude that the only thing the seminary equips students to do is to attend seminary.[13]

While this is an extreme position, it does point to the importance of equipping people with the skills to "read" the local congregation that they seek to serve. Sadly, even when attempts are made to prepare potential leaders, they are taught a variety of methods and practices that are to be applied generically, as if every congregation is the same.[14]

> These explorations of congregational culture also challenge those who lead these institutions, and those who seek to shape their leaders, to learn to read a new kind of text: a congregation. The discovery of congregational culture poses an interpretive challenge as sizable as that presented by the scriptures themselves. Think of how much we invest in preparing people to read the scriptures. We need to make an equal investment in preparing people to interpret congregational life.[15]

And yet, the ability to "read" a congregation is only part of the task. Once the text of the congregation is read as a whole, the next challenge is to navigate the cultural divides that exist within congregations.

> With intermarriage, denominational switching, higher education, career mobility and the complex spiritual pilgrimages taken by so many church members, one cannot assume that members and leaders share a worldview. In addition to learning to identify who and what is in the room with us, we need to learn to work with cultural diversity, to negotiate differences, to bring to the surface hidden values, and to turn congregations into places of healthy cultural exchange. Decisions about hymns, sermon illustrations, church suppers and mission priorities are occasions where church leaders can help or hinder people in passing on, transforming and creating a local culture that can give meaning and value to their lives.[16]

Abundant grace and humility are required to traverse this varied and ever-changing landscape, along with a deep sense of awareness that none of us is culture-free. We each bring our own perspectives, world view, and biases along with us. Yet the complex and complicated web of relationships and connections that constitutes the local congregation is at the same time the very place that helps to provide strength and stability amid external chaos and confusion, is a deep reservoir of belief and value amid societal skepticism, and contains institutions that foster meaning and purpose amid a larger culture of relativism and apathy. It is the local congregation that bears within it the creative imagination and ability to bring people together in such a way that they can embrace a new reality which can bring both life and hope to the world beyond its doors.

Returning briefly to Hopewell, the key to congregational transformation rests in the ability to tap into the local narrative and connect that narrative to the challenges being faced by the congregation. Acquiring such critical understanding, Hopewell believed, requires critical analysis, and critical analysis requires the tools of theory.[17] Our next section is an overview of various tools of theory that can be used for assessment and analysis, but note at the outset, that all are vehicles, in one way or another, of connecting to the congregational narrative.

Tools of Assessment and Analysis

There are a number of ways to observe the dynamics of congregational life, as well as a number of resources available to Church leaders to engage in a process of observation, assessment, and analysis. These are essentially tools that provide various frameworks and perspectives of congregational dynamics. The hope is that they might lead to deeper understanding. We will review four resources: congregation size, congregational life cycle, appreciative inquiry, and contextual assessment.

Congregational size

This theoretical framework, the work of Arlin Rothauge, is one of the earliest, and remains one of the most important frameworks for understanding church dynamics. Based on his extensive research, Dr Rothauge concluded that size was the major determining factor in the culture and behavior of congregations. In his original framework, American congregations were divided into four categories. He was quick to add that his theory intended no judgment about congregations based on their size, there was no optimal size, but rather focused on the defining characteristics of each category, and eventually led to more research about the particular dynamics when a congregation transitioned from one category to another. Each transition was filled with its own unique opportunities and challenges.[18] Dr Rothauge's four categories based on congregational size are:

1. *Family size*. This category has an average Sunday attendance of 50 or less. This size is aptly named, because the dynamics of these congregations are like those of a family. There is usually a matriarch or patriarch and typically one or two actual blood-related families. The clergy tend to function as "chaplain" to the family. More recently different models of sacramental and pastoral leadership have been developed to serve smaller congregations. These include a mix of lay and ordained leaders, bi-vocational clergy, and clergy serving multiple congregations as part of a team.
2. *Pastoral size*. This category has an average Sunday attendance of between 50 and 100. The pastor is truly at the center of the dynamics of this congregation. He or she is responsible for most of the programming, teaching, preaching, and direction. Congregants want to know their pastor and attribute much accountability to that person and role. The pastor is also a primary conduit for welcoming newcomers and for their incorporation into the community.
3. *Program size*. This category has an average Sunday attendance of between 150 and 350. Programs dominate the dynamics of the life of this size congregation. People become part of its life through participation in one of these programs, or small ministry, or

fellowship groups. This size congregation is often served by a staff of multiple lay and ordained professionals. One of the most difficult points of growth in this category is encountered when the average Sunday attendance reaches about 200.

4. *Resource size.* This category has an average Sunday attendance of more than 350 worshippers. These congregations are the most complex in terms of organizational dynamics. There are more programs and groups, and often subsidiary organizations (schools, foundations, community organizations). They will usually have many human and financial resources for mission.[19]

Congregational life cycle

It is the same Arlin Rothauge who also provided this framework for exploring congregational dynamics. Uniting the study of organizational dynamics and the human life cycle and applying them to congregations, Dr Rothauge believed that local churches experienced the breadth of the life cycle from birth, to growth and development, to stability, to decline, and sometimes even to death. His premise is that every congregation like every human institution, and every living organism, is somewhere on the life cycle continuum. He also believed that there were two imperatives for congregational leaders. The first was to know where a congregation currently resides on the continuum, and the second was to address that knowledge in an appropriate, intentional, and strategic way. He used what he called the three "Rs" to describe the appropriate intervention: redefinition (shifting the mission), redevelopment (growing in a new direction), and resurrection (death and rebirth). The focus of any intervention is the essential reengagement with mission and the creation of a strategic plan for health, growth, and renewal.[20]

Appreciative inquiry

A more recent framework for congregation assessment comes directly from the field of organizational development and is called appreciative inquiry. As the name suggests, this framework focuses on helping organizations, in this case congregations, identify their peculiar strengths and the patterns of strength that are reflected in the life of the congregation.[21] One of the great benefits of this approach is that it is, by design, positive and affirming. Starting with assessing strengths and assets helps the community to recognize that these corporate attributes do exist and that alone has the effect of being hopeful and encouraging. Rather than focusing on shortcomings and weakness, this approach seeks to build on strength.[22]

Contextual assessment

Based on the recognition that no congregation exists in a vacuum, this approach focuses on researching and gathering information about the wider context in which the church exists, its neighborhood and community. This can be as simple as intentional neighborhood walks to more formal engagement. One way to gather information is to invite community leaders and neighbors into the church for conversation and discussion of local issues. Another way is to conduct a survey of the neighborhood, local businesses, civic association, or perhaps equip church members to make personal visits. Still another way is to research the many public documents available that provide information about the local community, from census data to tax records. There are also professional services available to congregations. One such resource is MissionInsite,[23] an organization that can provide up-to-date, useful, and relevant information about congregations and local demographics. This group has the capability to produce a snapshot portrait of the local community. This kind of information is invaluable when discussing ways to engage the neighborhood and the world beyond the church.[24]

All of these analytical tools are designed to raise awareness of congregational dynamics, to surface resources within the congregation, and to draw upon the powerful and potentially transforming narrative that exists at the heart of congregations. Such transformation is never easy.

Cultural Change: Demographics

The *USA Today* Diversity Index shows diversity has surged in the last 50 years and is expected to continue rising. The US index rose from 20 in 1960 to 55 in 2010. Driven by changing attitudes and a record wave of immigration, the pace of change varies widely, sometimes even in adjacent counties.

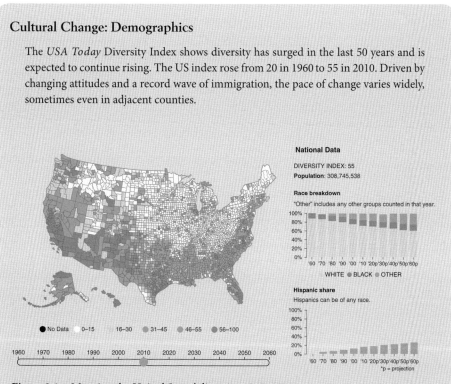

Figure 3.1   Mapping the United States' diversity, 1960–2060
Source: "Mapping the USA's diversity, 1960–2060," from Marisol Bello and Paul Overberg, "Growing pains: Multicultural explosion rattles residents," *USA Today*, November 10, 2014. Available at: http://www.usatoday.com/longform/news/nation/2014/11/10/northern-virginia-diversity-race/18079525 (accessed May 28, 2015). Map: Paul Overberg, *USA Today*, Amanda Astey, Sarah Frostenson, Anthony DeBarros and Gannett Digital. Data: *USA Today*, analysis of data from Census Bureau, NHGIS, and ProximityOne.

Cultural Change

The kind of congregational transformation we are referring to is not a change in Church polity or structure, nor is it a change in programming, nor is it a change in worship style, although all of these might well be affected. Rather, what we are suggesting is much more basic and fundamental, and difficult. We are suggesting the transformation of congregational culture, and we are suggesting that such a transformation takes place within the context of the wider culture.

We live in a nation and exist in a society that is brimming with diversity, and yet our congregations rarely reflect that diversity. This is not a new phenomenon and has been the historical norm in America since the colonial era. This is true in spite of the fact that the United States has become home to a broadly diverse population. This is also true in spite of the fact that "our patterns of ethnic specific religious interaction continued in the US even as people learned to speak English and adapted to the dominant culture."[25]

There are three prevailing theories of American cultural interaction. The first is the idea of "Anglo-conformity," which implies that any new ethnic group becomes completely assimilated into American culture, which itself remains unchanged. The second is the "melting pot" theory, which implies that any new ethnic group becomes completely assimilated as the cultures meld together to form a new dominant culture. The third is the theory of "cultural pluralism," which implies that any new ethnic group coexists alongside the dominant culture with neither being changed in the interaction. While all three of these ideas exist, in theory, none has become the norm. The reality could be more aptly described as "structural pluralism," which acknowledges that there is a large amount of conformity and acculturation on the part of new ethnic groups, while at the same time there is still a large amount of separation. This is particularly true in local congregations.[26] "Without God's initiatives that transform us personally and as groups, our behaviors tend to be limited by cultural and human habits. Encounters with those who were different often led people to withdraw and to protect what was familiar."[27]

For congregational transformation to happen, leaders not only have to be adept at "reading" the congregation they are called to serve, they also have to recognize and appreciate the existing congregational culture, while at the same time developing the ability to reach across multicultural contexts and create an environment whereby God's reconciling action becomes evident in the life of the Church and its missional engagement.[28] In the next section we take up the topic of transformational leadership from the perspective of mission.

Leadership and Mission

Two themes undergird this chapter on Church dynamics and culture: the first is that congregational change cannot happen without leadership; the second is that congregational transformation cannot happen apart from mission.

In his exceptional book, *Transforming Congregations*, James Lemler, outlines the six key practices for faithful and effective transformational leadership.

1. *Clarity of purpose and mission.* Leaders have the primary responsibility for articulating mission. Although mission is discerned collaboratively, it is embodied and proclaimed by the leader.

2. *Intentional leadership of transformation and change.* Leaders cannot be satisfied with the status quo, on the contrary, they must be continuously involved in change, planning for change, and holding before the congregation the possibility of transformation.

3. *Creating and building relationships.* Leadership involves inviting others into partnership. Leadership involves encouraging the development of caring, sustaining, and nurturing relationships throughout the entire congregation.

4. *Learning stance.* Leaders model continuous learning and are responsible for engaging the entire congregation in the ongoing process of development and formation.

5. *Clear, confident, consistent, collaborative.* These certainly apply to all leaders, but especially in faith communities and especially to clergy. Establishing patterns of clarity and communication, coupled with consistency in action, builds trust. Collaboration allows for movement in mission together. Of these, perhaps the most essential is confidence: in God, in the Gospel, in the community, and in one's own skills and abilities. This includes confidence in making decisions, risking failure, and claiming the authority to lead.

6. *Vision and hope.* Congregational leaders set the tone for the entire congregation. It is incumbent upon the leader to create and hold before the people a vision of the future that embodies hope and promise.[29]

Another helpful resource for congregational leadership is Anthony Robinson's book, *Transforming Congregational Culture*. In this text, Robinson argues that the hope for the mainline Church rests within the unique gifts, experience, and even the "genius" of the mainline Church itself, and he draws heavily on the work of Ronald Heifetz in his now classic text, *Leadership Without Easy Answers*. In this book, Heifetz highlights the difference between what he calls "technical work" and "adaptive work." Technical work refers to a situation where there is a clearly defined problem with a corresponding clearly defined solution. Both are clear, and an appropriate response is straightforward. An adaptive work, on the other hand, describes a situation that is not so clear. The problem itself may be unknown, and therefore so is the solution. Addressing the "adaptive challenge" requires ongoing learning and ongoing change, since the exact source of challenge is not necessarily known, or is a complex mix of possible causes.[30]

Robinson makes the case that the mainline Church is now clearly facing an adaptive challenge and offers six strategies for congregational leaders. These are strategies designed to assist in shifting Church dynamics and transforming the Church culture:

1. *Get on the balcony.* Heifetz uses the metaphor of a dance floor. In the midst of the constant movement it is difficult to see what is going on. It is difficult to discern any patterns of activity or relationships. In order to detect such patterns, the leader is required to get above and away from the fray. The idea is to get some distance in order to perceive the whole. From the balcony, leaders can look for gaps between what the congregation

claims as core values and what is actually happening on the dance floor. It is from this vantage point that a leader might also discover which norms or current congregational strategies are no longer relevant or productive.

2. *Identify the adaptive challenge.* With society and culture now officially declared secular and religiously pluralistic, it is difficult to know where the Church fits within this changing context. There is no longer a religious establishment and the Church is now one voice among many. One important skill for leaders to acquire is to ask questions, especially questions about purpose. What are the vital few things that a congregation must do to accomplish that purpose? Another skill in addressing adaptive challenge is to draw out conflicts. Some of the conflict may be destructive, but some conflict may provide valuable opportunities for learning and important adaptive work.

3. *Regulate distress.* When engaging adaptive challenge, resistance, pain and distress are inevitable. Leaders must prepare for and expect trouble. If everyone is happy and content, chances are that nothing is being accomplished. One of Heifetz's favorite images for adaptive work is a pressure cooker. In order to be effective a pressure cooker needs heat, but also needs to maintain a holding environment for things to cook. If there is no heat, nothing happens. If there is too much heat, the top blows off. Leadership involves regulating the distress with an eye toward keeping the stress at a productive level. Three skills are particularly useful in regulating distress: (i) sequence and pace the work, don't overload the agenda. Not everything can or should happen at once. (ii) Plant seeds and take small steps, some seeds will take root and many small steps begin to add up when moving toward a goal. (iii) Engage change by addition and subtraction; people are much more likely to let go of something that is no longer useful with something new to focus on and embrace.

4. *Maintain disciplined attention.* It is critical for leaders to stay focused on the work at hand. Persistence is the key, but sadly too many clergy give up too quickly.

5. *Give responsibility back.* While leadership is essential, success does not rest completely with the leadership team. It takes the entire congregation to shift the culture. It is a partnership. Leaders must learn to give responsibility back.

6. *Protect leadership from below.* Back down on the dance floor, it is important for leaders to recognize, value, and protect the partnership between leaders and followers. Good leaders call forth and enable the leadership gifts of others, even those from outside or those who are new to the congregation.[31]

Transformational leadership is not easy work. There are no foolproof methods, no step-by-step training sessions, and no instruction manuals. There are only those leaders who faithfully engage the work in their particular time, place, and situation.[32]

The other ingredient for transformation is mission. When we speak of mission we are referring to its primary purpose. God's mission, God's primary purpose, is reconciliation, the redeeming and restoring of all creation. The Church's mission, the Church's primary purpose, is the local manifestation of that larger purpose in a particular time, place, and context.[33] In the current age, the Church is faced with a unique opportunity as it seeks to fulfill its mission. Darrell Guder, one of the most articulate North American Mission Theologians, describes the call and the opportunity this way:

> Two things have become quite clear to those who care about the church and its mission. On the one hand, the churches of North America have been dislocated from their prior social role of chaplain to the culture and society and have lost their once privileged positions of influence. Religious life, in general, and the churches in particular, have increasingly been relegated to the private spheres of life. The churches have a great opportunity in these circumstances, however. The same pressures that threaten the continued survival of some churches, disturb the confidence of others, and devalue the meaning of them all can actually be helpful in providing an opening for new possibilities. Emerging into view on the far side of the church's long experience of Christendom is a wide vista of potential for the people of God in the post-modern and post-Christian world of North America. The present is a wildly opportune moment for churches to find themselves and to put on garments of their calling, their vocation.[34]

When commenting on the current period of decline in the mainline Church, some critics place the blame on the ethical and moral changes in the Church. In actuality, "the primary reason for our decline is that we have not envisioned and become engaged in ministries of evangelism, invitation, and hospitality in our congregations in ways that meet the present rapidly changing world around us."[35] It is along these lines that Guder continues:

> This is a time for dramatically new vision. The current predicament of churches in North America requires more than mere tinkering with long-assumed notions about the identity and mission of the church. Instead, as many knowledgeable observers have noted, there is a need for reinventing or rediscovering the church in this new kind of world.[36]

This is an urgent moment for the Church, yet it is also a hopeful one. It is clear that the congregations that will be most effective in the twenty-first century will be those with strong leadership, and those with a clear mission and purpose. They will be of various sizes, they will worship in various styles, and will exist in various locations, and they will draw deeply from the best of their various traditions.

Practicing Congregations

In her book, *Practicing Congregations*, Diana Butler Bass beautifully captures the notion that at the heart of congregational transformation, the result of faithful leadership and attention to mission, is spiritual renewal. Indeed, strong congregations in the twenty-first century are intentional communities where people experience the living God, "they use practices and discipline reflecting the core identity of the congregation's mission" in order to aid in their transformation in faith.[37] Practicing congregations are "communities that choose to rework denominational tradition in light of local experience to create a web of practices that transmit identity, nurture community, cultivate mature spirituality, and advance mission."[38]

All agree on the urgent need for change in the mainline Church. Practicing congregations are leading the way. Mining the riches of the tradition, reclaiming a theology of mission, and raising up transformational leaders are marks of a renewed and renewing Church. The urgency is real, but so is the hope and opportunity of the present moment.

Notes

1   James F. Hopewell, *Congregation: Stories and Structure* (Philadelphia, PA: Fortress Press, 1987), xi.

2   John Williams, "Congregational studies as resource and critique for a mission-shaped church," *ANVIL* 26, no. 3 and 4 (2009), 243–253. Available at: http://www.biblical studies.org.uk/pdf/anvil/26-3_243.pdf (accessed May 28, 2015).

3   Ibid.

4   Ibid.

5   Ibid.

6   Hopewell, *Congregation*, xii.

7   Charles E. Bennison, with Kortright Davis, Adair Lumis and Paula Nesbitt, *In Praise of Congregations: Leadership in the Local Church Today* (Cambridge, MA: Cowley Publications, 1999), 5.

8   James P. Wind, "leading congregations, discovering congregational cultures," *Christian Century* 110, No. 4 (1993), 105–110.

9   Ibid.

10   Ibid.

11   Ibid.

12   Ibid.

13   Ibid.

14   Ibid.

15   Ibid.

16   Ibid.

17   Hopewell, *Congregation*, xi.

18   James Lemler, *Transforming Congregations* (New York: Church Publishing, 2008), 72–74.

19   Ibid., 72.

20   Ibid., 75.

21   Ibid., 64.

22   Ibid., 112.

23   www.missioninsite.com

24   Ibid., 71–72.

25   Mark Lau Branson and Juan F. Martinez, *Churches, Cultures and Leadership* (Downers Grove, IL: IVP Academic, 2011), 15.

26   Ibid.

27   Ibid., 17.

28   Ibid., 13.

29   Lemler, *Transforming Congregations*, 148.

30   Anthony B. Robinson, *Transforming Congregational Culture* (Grand Rapids, MI: Eerdmans Publishing Co., 2003), 12–13.

31   Ibid., 124–136.

32   Ibid., 136.

33   Lemler, *Transforming Congregations*, 2.

34   Darrell Guder, ed., *Missional Church: A Vision for the Sending of the Church in North America* (Grand Rapids, MI: Eerdmans Publishing Co., 1988), 16–17.

35   Ibid., 18.

36   Ibid.

37   Ibid., 52.

38   Ibid.

Annotated Bibliography

Bennison, Charles E., with Davis, Kortright, Lumis, Adair, and Nesbitt, Paula, *In Praise of Congregations: Leadership in the Local Church Today* (Cambridge, MA: Cowley Publications, 1999).

Charles Bennison, with his co-authors Kortright Davis, Adair Lummis, and Paula Nesbitt, offers this comprehensive look at the field of congregational studies in a manner that opens this discipline and its insights to all who care about the local church and its future.

Branson, Mark Lau and Martinez, Juan F., *Churches, Cultures and Leadership* (Downers Grove, IL: IVP Academic, 2011).

The goal of the book is to help congregational leaders "see differently" and to gain the skills and competencies needed for the multicultural contexts of the current age, the focus of this engagement being mission.

Guder, Darrell, *Missional Church: A Vision for the Sending of the Church in North America*

(Grand Rapids, MI: Eerdmans Publishing Co., 1998).

Hopewell, James F., *Congregation: Stories and Structure* (Philadelphia, PA: Fortress Press, 1987).

A seminal voice in the field of congregational studies, Hopewell explores the resilience and coherence of local congregations. The core of his theory of congregations is his contention that congregational culture is not an accidental accumulation of symbolic elements but a coherent system whose structural logic is narrative. For Hopewell, narrative has power and functions as God's work with congregations.

Lemler, James, *Transforming Congregations* (New York: Church Publishing, 2008).

This text, part of the "Transformations" book series of the Episcopal Church, focuses on congregations as the frontline of mission. The goal is to provide ideas and resources to help adjust congregational patterns in order to better serve a changing world.

Robinson, Anthony B., *Transforming Congregational Culture* (Grand Rapids, MI: Eerdmans Publishing Co., 2003).

Drawing upon the work of Ronald Heifetz, the author applies Heifetz's leadership theory to mainline congregation, focusing on the adaptive work required of clergy to lead congregational transformation.

Wind, James P., "Leading congregations, discovering congregational cultures," *Christian Century*, 110, No. 4 (1993), 105–110.

This article stresses the importance of understanding and the ability of leaders to "read" congregational culture in such as a way as to lead effectively and faithfully, respectful of the complex and deep narratives in the community that have the power to transform.

Williams, John, "Congregational studies as resource and critique for a mission-shaped church," *ANVIL* 26, No. 3 and 4 (2009), 243–253. Available at: http://www.biblicalstudies.org.uk/pdf/anvil/26–3_243.pdf (accessed May 28, 2015).

In this article, John Williams argues that the burgeoning discipline of congregational studies should be seen as a constructive and critical partner in the quest for fresh expressions of Church oriented to mission.

Section Two

Cultivating the Skills for Effective Ministry

4

Worship and Mainline Ritual

Much of this book focuses on the work that the leader of the congregation must do outside the congregation. It looks at careful study of Scripture, the need for a coherent theology, the importance of effective pastoral care, and the challenge of church administration. However, it is worth remembering that a key aspect of congregational leadership is creating an outstanding worship experience.

For Christians, the *Holy Spirit* is the primary provider of an "outstanding worship experience." However, the human agent is important. Although it is true that poor preaching and dreadful music can still create an occasion where God is worshipped and the people of God encounter God, it is even better when the people of God work in an imaginative and conscientious way to ensure that the experience offered to God is our best. There is nothing wrong with striving for excellence in worship. It is not incompatible with faithfulness.

The Basics

We live in an age where there are so many competing options for our time away from work – from reading a good newspaper in Starbucks to sports for your children. When you are working 50 or 60 hours a week (an 8am to 8pm day is very common), the leisurely Sunday morning is very precious. The Church of the Holy Comforter (i.e. the comforter you pull up over yourself as you snuggle back to sleep) is a constant temptation on a Sunday morning.

In addition, expectations for "entertainment" (and in a sense this is where worship needs to be compared – church competes with other forms of relaxation on a Sunday morning)

An Introduction to Ministry: A Primer for Renewed Life and Leadership in Mainline Protestant Congregations, First Edition. Ian S. Markham and Oran E. Warder.

are high. Sporting events are exciting; musical events are polished; lectures are informed, snazzy, and use PowerPoint and Prezi effectively; and the movie theater is just a delight. Meanwhile so much of the time church is boring. Music is dull; sermons are too long, boring, and delivered without any technological aids; and the *liturgy* is delivered without any passion.

In the mainline denominations, a good worship leader must make sure that the hour (ideally), perhaps 1 hour 15 minutes, is outstanding.[1] If men and women are going to make church their priority, then it is important that we do everything we can to make sure that they don't regret that decision. The worship experience should always strive for excellence: it should always be outstanding. So what are the important priorities?

Worship is about worshipping God. For some it is hard to worship when leading worship. The worship leader has to think ahead constantly; she (for this chapter she is inclusive of he) must prepare for the next stage of the service. Yet such anticipation should not excuse the presider from also seeking to worship. In the end this occasion is about God. Robert Hovda makes the point well when he writes, if the presider "fails to communicate a sense of prayerful performance, of being (first of all) a worshiper and a member of the worshiping assembly, then he or she is not a leader but an intruder. And the gifts of such a one or such a group damage rather than enhance worship."[2] One comes to the liturgy as a worshipper seeking to be in the presence of God.

There are three basics that always must be covered. First, it is important that one can be heard and seen. When you join a congregation as the new worship leader, do take several weeks just to sit in different parts of the church experiencing the worship experience as a member of the congregation. In this way, you will notice the pillar that obstructs the view, the way that sound moves around the space (meaning that in some places hearing is easy and in others it is much harder), and focus of those around you (some sections of the church will be especially worshipful, others will be texting on their iPhone). This is vitally important information for the worship leader to have. You might feel that you are "hitting the sermon out of the ballpark," but if folks cannot hear then no one else will be sharing your feeling.

The second basic requirement is to cultivate a presence. For the mainline, the presider at the worship experience is given some help. Appropriate attire in the form of vestments and the location of the presider at the front and the center are tools to help give the worship leader a sense of presence. Studies have shown that when it comes to presentations, the visual and hearing impact are more important than the content. Typically, studies have shown that the impact of a presentation is weighted 50% on appearance, 30% on delivery, and just 20% on content.[3] Dressing right and speaking clearly are really important. All of this creates a "presence." The congregation should be aware of the person entrusted with the responsibility of leading the worship.

The third requirement is to be interesting, use humor effectively, and rehearse. Voice training is important; one should cultivate a voice that is interesting. Using humor to relax a congregation is a good way to make a congregation receptive. To laugh one must listen. And once a person has started listening, it is likely that they will stay with you. And rehearsal is essential. Everything should be done well. You do not teach a server how to prepare the table for *communion* during the liturgy itself.

These are the basic requirements for effective worship oversight. The next stage is the organization of the liturgy.

The Basic Mainline Service Structure

Barbara Day Miller helpfully sets out the basic structure of a mainline service. There are four stages: "gathering for praise," "hearing God's Word," "responding in faith," and "sending forth."[4]

Figure 4.1   Source: (a) © Bob Daemmrich/Alamy; (b) © Peter Noyce PLB/Alamy.

Gathering for praise will include music, a call to worship, a hymn of praise, and a prayer. In the more liturgical seasons, there will be a recognition of the moment in the church calendar (normally marked by a special prayer – often called a *Collect*). Hearing God's Word is the moment when Scripture is read and the sermon is preached. The precise number of readings from Scripture can vary considerably. The maximum will be four (normally, an Old Testament lesson, an Epistle, a Gospel, and a Psalm), but it can be as few as just one. The sermon will then seek to apply the insights from the biblical texts to the contemporary situation facing the congregation. Responding in faith can include a whole range of activities. For some traditions, it is the chance for a renewal at the altar (an altar call); for others, it is a creed followed by the prayers of the people. Many traditions will include the confession at this stage and the offering of the tithes. In addition, this is the section where there is communion or the *Eucharist*. The "exchange of the peace" will either happen here or in the gathering section. There are good arguments for both locations: the Lutherans tend to think the gathering is the right place for greeting each other, while the Episcopalians tend to locate the peace after the confession and before the offering. Finally, the people need to be "sent forth." There is always some conclusion to the liturgy (which is normally a hymn, blessing, and some type of dismissal).

This basic structure does vary across the different traditions in the mainline. The Episcopal Church, for example, makes the sacrament of the Eucharist not simply a response to the Word, but the climax of the liturgy in its own right. And many United Church of Christ (UCC) congregations do not include Holy Communion as part of the response to the Word, but instead concentrate on making prayer the primary response. Nevertheless, this basic order (even if the significance of the divisions varies) is found across the mainline.

Significant Rituals

The first and most important ritual is *baptism*. Baptism is the rite of initiation into the Christian tradition. Most of the mainline Churches practice infant baptism, although adults who convert or recommit to Christianity can be baptized. It is theologically the moment when the drama of human sinfulness being transformed by the death of Christ is enacted. As a child emerges from the water, the promise of God made possible in Christ is realized. A baptism can be a joyous occasion. Normally, it is the opportunity for a baby to be brought to God; it expresses the intention of families to support that child in the Christian faith; and many parents take it as an opportunity to give a special role to friends and siblings in the child's life by making them godparents.

The symbolism of baptism is rich. In Paul's letters, baptism is linked both to the Jewish practice of circumcision (see Colossians 2:11–12) and the Exodus (1 Corinthians 10:1–5). In both cases the emphasis is on the new life made possible by Jesus. In Romans, Paul brings these themes together when he writes:

> Do you not know that all of us who have been baptized into Christ Jesus were baptized into his death? Therefore we have been buried with him by baptism into death, so that, just as Christ was raised from the dead by the glory of the Father, so we too might walk in newness of life. (Romans 6:3–4)

The word "baptism" comes from the Greek word, which means "to immerse." The symbolism is clear: as we are immersed in water we are dying with Christ and as we come out of the water, we are symbolically rising with Christ. Baptism is the moment we are transformed by grace to be freed from egotism and selfishness and invited into a new life of love and hope.

Two other rituals are central in a human life. The first is to do with the decision to find a life partner – to get married; and the other is the moment of death – the funeral. With the first, a marriage is a real opportunity for evangelism. Normally, the minister or priest needs to ensure that she is authorized to perform marriages by both the secular and religious authorities. Most churches require some form of marriage preparation. A good program will cover both the more conceptual (the theology and symbolism of marriage) and the more practical (how do you resolve disagreements). Processes around the handling of persons who are divorced getting remarried vary. Some Churches tend to be very informal (with the emphasis being on the pre-marriage counseling to ensure that the next relationship is stronger) compared to other churches wanting some sort of formal process and perhaps external confirmation (e.g. the Episcopal Church requires people to check with the bishop of the diocese). The actual service also varies considerably. In the UCC and the Presbyterian Church, often the couple can design their own service and even write their own vows, while in the Lutheran Church, there is an expectation that the couple will follow the pattern suggested by the Evangelical Lutheran Worship.

The funeral service is where the life of the departed is celebrated in the light of the Gospel promise of resurrection. A good funeral is a precious gift to the grieving family. It is an opportunity to bring some closure to the aching loss of a loved one. Given the pastoral and the theological need to merge, this is important work that needs to be done well. It is important for the minister to know the family and to have a sense of what should be lifted up and recognized and what, given the occasion, might be given less emphasis. Human lives are increasingly complex; so the children from the first marriage might not appreciate an excessive celebration and affirmation of the second marriage. Again the practice around funerals in the mainline varies. For the UCC and the Presbyterian Church, there is much more space where the family can make suggestions; and for the Episcopal Church, there is a particular structure provided by the Book of Common Prayer.

Holy Communion

This section will work through different understandings of the Lord's Supper or Holy Communion or Eucharist or even *Mass* (depending on which part of the mainline to which one belongs). The name is deeply symbolic. Lord's Supper captures the basic idea that we are participating in a remembrance: we are remembering the act of betrayal that led to the death of Jesus. And we are doing so because we believe that through the death and resurrection we are redeemed. The Eucharist means Thanksgiving. It captures the idea that the prayer being said over the elements creates a moment of divine grace where the divine life found in the elements can become part of our lives. For the purposes of this discussion, we shall use the term Eucharist.

The Eucharist is based on the *Last Supper*. Jesus brought his disciples together hours before he was arrested (see Luke 22:7–20; Matthew 26:17–29; Mark 14:12–25; 1 Corinthians

11:23–26). In this meal, Jesus explained to the disciples that the bread was his body and the wine his blood. Paul in 1 Corinthians explains that Jesus took bread:

> and when he had given thanks, he broke it, and said, "This is my body which is for you. Do this in remembrance of me." In the same way also the cup, after supper, saying, "This cup is the new covenant in my blood. Do this, as often as you drink it, in remembrance of me." (1 Corinthians 11:24–25)

At this extremely poignant moment, Jesus asked his disciples to eat bread and drink wine in remembrance of him. From the time of Jesus onwards, the Eucharist or the Lord's Supper became a central Christian ritual.

How this event is understood varies considerably. All the mainline Churches have been in conversation with the Roman Catholic Church. For Roman Catholics, a proper understanding of the Eucharist (or Mass as they prefer) is *transubstantiation*.

Transubstantiation is grounded in Aristotelian terminology and philosophy. *Aristotle* (384–322 BCE) distinguished between the "substance" and the "accidents." The essential nature is the "substance," while the shape, color, and general outward appearance are "accidents." Using this distinction, although the appearance of bread and wine remains the same, it does, nevertheless, become the body and blood of Jesus. The Eucharist then is a miracle of divine grace. In the act of taking the Eucharist, one takes into one's body the divine and redeeming power of God in Christ.

The mainline traditions are nervous about the use of Greek philosophy to understand the mystery of the Eucharist. Martin Luther, who is the major influence on both the Lutherans and the Anglicans, became increasingly suspicious of the use of Aristotelian philosophy in Christian doctrine. Instead of distinguishing between the accidents and the substance, Luther wants Christ present in both. He draws an analogy with the doctrine of the Incarnation: in the same ways the Godhead permeated all of humanity so Christ permeates all the bread. He writes:

> And why could not Christ include his body in the substance of the bread just as well as in the accidents? In red-hot iron, for instance, the two substances, fire and iron, are so mingled that every part is both iron and fire. Why is it not even more possible that the body of Christ be contained in every part of the substance of the bread?[5]

Luther then believes in the "real presence," sometimes known as *consubstantiation*. For Luther, because Jesus in the Bible states that "this is my body," it must be so. The power of the sacraments is made possible by God and received by the faith of the believer.

This means that the Lutherans in their statement "The Use of the Means of Grace" describe their understanding of the Eucharist in the following way (paraphrased here from *Called to Common Mission*, a Lutheran proposal for concordance with the Episcopal Church from 1999): "We believe that the Body and Blood of Christ are truly present, distributed, and received under the forms of bread and wine in the Lord's Supper."[6] The statement goes on to explain that the elements can include red or white wine, unleavened or leavened bread, and gluten-free or non-alcoholic alternatives are encouraged. The expectation is that Lutherans should take the Eucharist weekly and the invitation is only issued to baptized Christians.

The Episcopal Church is very similar to the Lutherans. They describe the Eucharist in the following way: "This is the family meal for Christians and a foretaste of the heavenly banquet. As such, all persons who have been baptized, and are therefore part of the extended family that is the Church, are welcome to receive the bread and wine, and be in communion with God and each other."[7] There is a lively debate within the Episcopal Church about opening up the table to Christians who are not baptized. The canons (i.e. the rules) continue to restrict the Eucharist to those who are baptized; however, many congregations argue that given Jesus took table fellowship with anyone, it follows that congregations should be equally willing to do so.

The Presbyterians tend to follow *John Calvin* (1509–1564). Calvin took the line that the sacraments were signs of a reality that God had already performed. When defining a sacrament, he writes:

> It seems to me that a simple and proper definition would be to say that it is an outward sign by which the Lord seals on our consciences the promises of his good will towards us in order to sustain the weakness of our faith; and we in turn attest our piety towards him in the presence of the Lord and of his angels and before men.[8]

The emphasis here is that sacraments are signs of work that God has already done. In the Eucharist, the bread and wine are witness to a spiritual reality of redemption. There is a lovely humility in Calvin's view. He admits it is difficult to make sense of what exactly God is doing. So he wrote: "Now if anyone should ask me how this takes place, I shall not be ashamed to confess that it is a secret too lofty for either the mind to comprehend or my words to declare. … I rather experience it than understand it."[9] In both cases, for Calvin, the agent at work is the Holy Spirit and that work needs to be trusted.

According to the Presbyterian Missional Society web site:

> The Presbyterian/Reformed understanding of the Lord's Supper is one of thanksgiving and remembrance for the self-offering of Jesus Christ once and for all time on a cross in Jerusalem. Christ's perfect sacrifice of love and service is not re-enacted or reactualized at the Lord's Supper; rather, in the joyful feast of Eucharistic celebration, we offer our praise and thanksgiving to God for this amazing gift. Furthermore, the sacrament that Christ instituted for the remembrance of him takes the form of a simple meal — a sharing of bread and wine. Therefore, it is Presbyterian practice to refer to the Lord's table rather than an altar.[10] To be sure the memorial (or *anamnesis*) of Christ's death and resurrection is an integral part of the sacrament of the Lord's Supper."

Anamnesis

anamnesis (/ænæmˈniːsɪs/; Ancient Greek: ἀνάμνησις

Anamnesis is the critical concept in liturgy and worship in the mainline, as in Catholicism, that embodies the act of remembering the saving acts God has already done, while also pivoting to focus on the saving God will still do. This bears heavily on the Eucharist, where the words of institution, "Do this in remembrance of me," illustrate anamnesis in action – as we remember Christ's institution of the Lord's Supper, we turn to ask God to bless the holy gifts of bread and wine so that they may become the body and blood of Christ in the world present to us.

For Presbyterians, the heart of the liturgy is a fourfold action: take, bless, break, give. The bread is taken; it is blessed and broken; and then it is given to the people of God.

The big debate within the Presbyterian tradition is the frequency of the celebration of the Lord's Supper. The recent Presbyterian publication *Invitation to Christ* explains:

> The Directory for Worship in the Presbyterian Book of Order encourages the "appropriateness" of frequent celebrations of the Lord's Supper. A few congregations have begun celebrations of the sacrament as often as each Lord's Day and on other occasions of special significance in the life of the Christian community. But frequency alone is not the basic issue. Some believe we need to restore the Biblical pattern of the Lord's Supper on each Lord's Day to provide a disciplined reminder of a divine act that will help centralize and "re-focus" the rhythm of our daily lives.[11]

In terms of participation, it is open to all who are baptized. It is the responsibility of the elders to ensure that it is the baptized who receive. In the case of an unbaptized Christian who comes forward, the elders should permit that person to be fed, but then follow up with appropriate ongoing formation.

The United Methodist Church has a distinctive understanding of communion (to use their preferred term). One can sense in their official pronouncements the Anglican influence, from which the Methodists emerged. In *This Holy Mystery*, the Methodists insist that the Communion is not primarily a remembrance or memorial. They write:

> For United Methodists, the Lord's Supper is anchored in the life of the historical Jesus of Nazareth, but is not primarily a remembrance or memorial. We do not embrace the medieval doctrine of transubstantiation, though we do believe that the elements are essential tangible means through which God works. We understand the divine presence in temporal and relational terms. In the Holy Meal of the church, the past, present, and future of the living Christ come together by the power of the Holy Spirit so that we may receive and embody Jesus Christ as God's saving gift for the whole world.[12]

It is almost as if they are in-between Luther and Calvin: it is a transcendent moment of grace that enables us to receive Christ. The bread should look and taste like bread; and the non-baptized are welcome to the table. This latter point is central to Methodism. The open table is really emphasized as a key part of communion.

Many members of the UCC are much more radical. They have sympathies with *Ulrich Zwingli* (1484–1531), who is the most radical of the big three reformers. For him, the sacraments are just "signs or ceremonials."[13] On the Eucharist, he finds it absurd to say that "Christ is literally there." It would mean that Christ is literally "broken, and pressed with the teeth."[14] Instead we should interpret the phrase "this is my body" more metaphorically. It is analogous, explains Zwingli, to a wife who shows someone her husband's ring and says "This is my late husband."[15]

This means that for the UCC communion is properly understood as a sacred memorial, but one that should be understood as a present reality that involves dining with the risen Christ. So the UCC web site explains:

> The United Church of Christ Book of Worship reminds us that "the invitation and the call (to the supper) celebrate not only the memory of a meal that is past, but an actual meal with the risen Christ that is a foretaste of the heavenly banquet at which Christ will preside at the

end of history. … A joyous act of thanksgiving for all God has done, is doing, and will do for the redeeming of creation; a sacred memorial of the crucified and risen Christ, a living and effective sign of Christ's sacrifice in which Christ is truly and rightly present to those who eat and drink; an earnest prayer for the presence of the Holy Spirit to unite those who partake with the Risen Christ and with each other, and to restore creation, making all things new; an intimate experience of fellowship in which the whole church in every time and place is present and divisions are overcome; a hopeful sign of the promised Realm of God marked by justice, love and peace.[16]

It is important to note that although this is a remembrance, it is also an anticipation; it is an anticipation of the Kingdom (or to avoid the associations of monarchy, the terminology used here is Realm of God) to come. So what seems to be a lower view of the sacraments is still an elevated vision of everything that is involved. In terms of invitation, the UCC is clear. The Book of Worship puts it, "open to all Christians who wish to know the presence of Christ and to share in the community of God's people."[17] All are welcome to this anticipation of the "Realm of God."

> ### Transubstantiation vs. Consubstantiation vs. Memorial
>
> Catholicism teaches transubstantiation, or the notion that in the consecration of the elements of bread and wine in the Eucharist, they are transformed literally into the body and blood of Jesus Christ (leaving merely the aura or image of bread and wine to our human eyes). Martin Luther, in the Protestant Reformation, developed a contrasting concept – the bread and wine are infused with the Holy Spirit during the Eucharist, and the "real presence" of Christ is likewise clear in the Eucharistic gifts, but the elements are clearly still bread and wine. Finally, on the farther end of the spectrum, such as in the Geneva branch of Christianity following the Reformation, the Eucharist may be thought of as simply a memorial of the saving acts of Christ – and thus, the bread and wine are merely bread and wine, and the Eucharistic prayer enacts a memorial to the Lord's Supper at most.

Conclusion

Being an effective worship leader is a vitally important part of effective ministry. The gathered people of God need to be fed; and the worship meal needs to be excellent. One cannot underestimate the importance of the basics – make sure readers and musicians rehearse and that the congregation can see and hear.

Any tradition should have a good self-understanding. It is important that a congregation is educated into the shared understanding of baptism and the Eucharist. Such a shared understanding binds a community together. A community that is formed with such a shared understanding also helps with the guest. The guest will appreciate the worship experience so much more when they understand what is going on. So inculcating the shared understanding is important.

The leadership of worship is a privilege. It is an honor and a trust. A well-executed worship service creates the space for the meaning of the liturgy and sacraments to shine through.

Notes

1   It is important to note that some mainline African American congregations, in particular, love the longer service. The dynamic music and rich community can enable men and women to enjoy a full 3-hour morning.

2   Robert W. Hovda, "Liturgy's many roles: Ministers? ... or, intruders?" in John F. Baldovin, ed., *The Amen Corner* (Collegeville, MN: Liturgical Press, 1994), 154.

3   We are grateful to Barbara Brown Taylor for these data. She presented this at the "Tom Bowers Preaching Training Session" at Virginia Theological Seminary, November 2, 2012.

4   Barbara Day Miller, *The New Pastor's Guide to Leading Worship* (Nashville, TN: Abingdon Press, 2006), 31.

5   Martin Luther, *Babylonian Captivity of the Church* (1520), in James F. White, *Documents of Christian Worship: Descriptive and Interpretive Sources* (Louisville, KY: Westminster John Knox Press, 1992), 198.

6   "Agreement #5" in *Called to Common Mission, A Lutheran Proposal for a Revision of the Concordat of Agreement* (ECLA, 1999), retrieved from http://download.elca.org/ELCA%20Resource%20Repository/Called_To_Common_Mission.pdf, (accessed June 1, 2015). See also "Background 33 A" in *The Use of the Means of Grace: A Statement on the Practice of Word and Sacrament*, Evangelical Lutheran Church in America, (ELCA c/o Augsburg Fortress, 1997), 37.

7   http://www.episcopalchurch.org/page/holy-communion (accessed May 29, 2015).

8   John Calvin, *Institutes of the Christian Religion*, IV, 13, 1–26 (1559), in White, *Documents of Christian Worship*, 132.

9   John Calvin, *Institutes of the Christian Religion*, XXI, Library of Christian Classics, John T. McNeill, ed., trans. Ford Lewis Battles (Philadelphia, PA: Westminster Press, 1960), Chap. 4.17.32.

10 Presbyterian Missional Society, "Sacraments: Lord's Supper," http://www.presbyterianmission.org/ministries/worship/faq-lordssupper/ (accessed June 1, 2015).

11 Presbyterian Church USA: "Invitation to Christ," http://www.pcusa.org/media/uploads/sacraments/pdfs/invitationtochrist.pdf (accessed May 29, 2015).

12 The United Methodist Church, *This Holy Mystery*, 13. Available at: http://s3.amazonaws.com/Website_Properties/what-we-believe/documents/this-holy-mystery-communion.PDF (accessed May 29, 2015).

13 Ulrich Zwingli, *Commentary on True and False Religion* (1525), in White, *Documents of Christian Worship*, 132.

14 Ulrich Zwingli, *On the Lord's Supper*, as found in White, *Documents of Christian Worship*, 201.

15 Ibid., 201.

16 United Church of Christ web site. Available at: http://www.ucc.org/worship/communion/ (accessed May 29, 2015).

17 United Church of Christ, *Book of Worship*.

Annotated Bibliography

Baptism, Eucharist and Ministry, Faith and Order Paper No. 11 (Geneva: World Council of Churches, 1982), 10–19.

Blount, Brian K. and Tubbs Tisdale, Leonora, eds, *Making Room at the Table: An Invitation to Multicultural Worship* (Louisville, KY: Westminster John Knox Press, 2001).

An excellent collection of essays that explores diversity in our worshipping communities.

Bradshaw, Paul F., *Eucharistic Origins* (London: SPCK, 2004).

A good overview of Eucharistic origins up to the fourtth century.

Dix, Dom Gregory, *The Shape of the Liturgy: New Edition* (New York, Continuum, 2011).
Explores the relationship of the liturgy to the agape meal.

Hellwig, Monika K., *The Eucharist and the Hunger of the World* (Lanham, MD: Sheed and Ward, 1992).
Explains how the Eucharist is meant to overflow and that those receiving also help feed the world.

Irwin, Kevin W., *Models of the Eucharist* (New York: Paulist Press, 2005).
The focus in this chapter has been on the mainline. This book looks at different Catholic understandings of the Eucharist such as Cosmic Mass, Memorial, Lord's Supper, Sacrifice, Food for the Journey.

Koenig, John, *The Feast and the World's Redemption* (Harrisburg, PA: Trinity Press International, 2000).
The concluding chapter is especially rich as Koenig looks at the implications for the liturgy.

Long, Kimberley Bracken, *The Worshiping Body: The Art of Leading Worship* (Louisville, KY: Westminster John Knox Press, 2009).
The centrality of our body in worship is explored and discussed.

McCall, Richard D., *Do This: Liturgy as Performance*. Notre Dame, IN: University of Notre Dame Press, 2007).
A description of how a minister should approach liturgy.

Macquarrie, John, *A Guide to the Sacraments* (London: SCM Press Ltd, 1997).
Probably the great classic on this topic.

Miller, Barbara Day, *The New Pastor's Guide to Leading Worship* (Nashville, TN: Abingdon Press, 2006).
Tons of practical and helpful advice. It describes in detail what you actually do the first time you are leading worship.

Wainwright, Geoffrey, *Eucharist and Eschatology* (London: Epworth Press, 1971).
Another classic that sets out the significance of the Eucharist and its relationship to eschatology.

White, James F., *The Sacraments in Protestant Practice and Faith* (Nashville, TN: Abingdon Press, 1999).
A good ecumenical discussion of the sacraments.

Willimon, William H., *Word, Water, Wine and Bread: How Worship Has Changed Over the Years* (Valley Forge, PA: Judson Press, 1980).
A very accessible history of worship from the Jewish practices to the present.

Denominational Documents

Episcopal Church: See "An outline of faith commonly called the Catechism," *The Book of Common Prayer* (New York: Seabury Press, 1979), 875.

ELCA: "The use and the means of grace." Available at: http://padrepoint.wordpress.com/2011/10/22/text-the-use-of-the-means-of-grace (accessed May 29, 2015).

PCUSA: "Invitation to Christ." Available at: http://www.pcusa.org/media/uploads/sacraments/pdfs/invitationtochrist.pdf (accessed May 29, 2015).

UMC: "This holy mystery." Available at: http://s3.amazonaws.com/Website_Properties/what-we-believe/documents/this-holy-mystery-communion.PDF (accessed May 29, 2015).

UCC: Available at: http://www.ucc.org/worship/communion (accessed May 29, 2015).

5
Reading Scripture Thoughtfully

The primary vehicle through which we learn about the past is the written text. These words communicate down through the centuries to the present. Christians believe that God has spoken definitively through the Eternal Word made flesh – Jesus of Nazareth. As we we will see in Chapter 6, the second person of the Trinity (the Son), who is the revealing element of God, interpenetrated Jesus of Nazareth to show the world decisively what God is like. Knowledge of what Jesus was like depends on a text. And for Christians, the text that tells us what Jesus is like is the Bible.

For the mainline, the Bible comprises the Old Testament (the Hebrew Scriptures) and the New Testament. There are some 13 books, which are known as the *Apocrypha*, which are considered worthy of study, but not considered as Scripture. The books that make up the Bible are known collectively as the *canon* of Scripture. The word *canon* comes from the Greek and literally means "rod." The idea here is that of a straight rod, which can be used as a rule (like a ruler). In this chapter, we shall start by looking at the history of the canon and then move to the five distinct approaches to the Bible that are found within the mainline.

The Dead Sea Scrolls

The story of the Dead Sea Scrolls is remarkable. A young boy entered into the caves of Qumran in Israel. There he discovered the scrolls that clearly had great archeological import – these were excavated and studied and described as the "Dead Sea Scrolls" in 1946. Among their many revelations were the affirmations of texts of the Bible, particularly the Hebrew Bible books.

An Introduction to Ministry: A Primer for Renewed Life and Leadership in Mainline Protestant Congregations, First Edition. Ian S. Markham and Oran E. Warder.
© 2016 John Wiley & Sons, Ltd. Published 2016 by John Wiley & Sons, Ltd.

The History of the Canon

One of the first discoveries that any student of Scripture must make is that the Bible did not drop fully formed from heaven. If we pause and think about it, then we clearly realize that the text had a distinctive and complex history, but we become so accustomed to the unity implied by the leather cover around these books.

The history of Scripture intersects with the history of *Judaism*. Our Old Testament (sometimes called the "First" Testament or "Hebrew Bible") comprises the sacred corpus of Judaism. Traditionally, the Jewish Bible has 24 books. It consists of the *Torah*: "Law," the first five books of the Bible, "Prophets" (in Hebrew, *Nebiim*), and "Writings" (in Hebrew, *Ketubim*). It is from the Hebrew words that we get the designation for the Hebrew Scriptures of *Tanakh* – *Ta* for Torah, *Na* for Nebiim and *Kh* for Writings. Christians have the same books, but count them differently. For Judaism, instead of 1 and 2 Samuel, 1 and 2 Kings, and 1 and 2 Chronicles being separate books, they are single books and counted as one each.

The canon of the Hebrew Bible was a major discussion well into the early centuries of the Common Era. Josephus, the Jewish historian writing in approximately 95 CE, in his polemic *Against Apion*, explains that the Jews had a settled canon of 22 (instead of the 24 we would expect) books. Lee Martin McDonald suspects that there was much greater fluidity of usage in Judaism, and the Jews outside Israel (the Jews in the diaspora) were even using other books outside the canon.[1] Part of the evidence of this is the Greek translation of the Hebrew Bible called the *Septuagint*.

The Old Testament is written in Hebrew; the New Testament is written in Greek. The reason for the difference is Alexander the Great, who swept through the Middle East bringing Greek learning and language to the region. By the time of Jesus, the Hellenistic influences (i.e. the Greek cultural influence) were very significant. From 331 BCE, there was a significant Jewish population speaking Greek in Alexandria, Egypt. A translation was needed for that generation and subsequent generations to stay in touch with their Jewish faith.

There is a delightful legend involving 70 (or perhaps 72) elders of the Jewish faith who arrived in Alexandria. According to Philo, the Jewish philosopher living in Alexandria, the translators worked in isolation from each other and yet produced identical translations. The truth behind the legend is simply this: as the Greek language became more and more popular, a translation was needed. The initial translation was simply the Torah, but later the rest of the Hebrew Bible was covered. However, the work of translation did not stop with the Hebrew Bible, it extended to those books which we now call the Apocrypha.

It is the Septuagint that is largely responsible for the order of our Old Testament. The Torah is at the beginning of both, but Ruth is moved up in the canon. However, it is the extra books that became the Apocrypha which are interesting. The Septuagint supplements the book of Daniel with two stories that are not in the Hebrew Bible – one at the beginning, *The History of Susanna*, and one at the end, *Bel and the Dragon*.

The Bible of the early Church is the Septuagint. This is the one that is quoted in the New Testament. There is some argument among scholars as to the impact of those additional books that, ultimately, were not recognized as Scripture by the Jewish community. There is clear allusion to the Apocrypha in the New Testament, but nothing that would count as direct quotation.

The story of the New Testament canon is complex. To start with, a congregation might just have access to this or that letter or Gospel. However, usage seems to determine which books became part of the canon. An important criterion in determining legitimate texts was "closeness" to the apostles (those who witnessed the resurrection of Jesus). So the Church, quite rightly, excluded the later second century, many of which were Gnostic (a form of Hellenistic heresy) "Gospels." Instead, the books chosen were letters written by Paul to particular congregations (these books are probably the earliest texts written in the New Testament) and then the Gospels, which were believed to have a connection with an apostle (so Mark was linked with Peter, Luke was linked with Paul, and Matthew and John were apostles). Modern scholars are probably right that these links with the apostles are tenuous. However, the fact that this criterion mattered so much did mean that those texts, which are manifestly written decades later, were excluded.

Marcion

Sometimes doctrine comes about with thanks to those who vehemently disagree with the mainline. Marcion (circa 85–160 CE) is one such example. In the second century, Marcion attempted to construct an early "New Testament," a canon to complement the Hebrew Scriptures, but which spoke to the salvific work of Christ in our world. Marcion's arrangement of Scripture had a different order, and missed some epistles and books that entered into the final canon – and ultimately, he was deemed a heretic for the sake of the Church's greater goal of arranging a proper arrangement of books that would form the official New Testament.

It was the heretic *Marcion* (circa 85–160 CE), who suggested the first canon. Marcion took the view that the Old Testament God was clearly incompatible with the New Testament God, and therefore the canon of the New Testament should be limited to those texts that kept their distance from the Old Testament. He went for the Gospel of Luke and the epistles written by Paul. This position was rejected by the Church, but the fact that Marcion proposed a certain set of authoritative books did encourage the Church to think through this issue with some care.

The canon of the New Testament was not formalized until the early third century. A key person was Athanasius of Alexandria (circa 296–373 CE). In this 39th festal letter, we have the first list of 27 books that we know today. Athanasius did recognize that there were other books in circulation. The *Didaché* (the Lord's teaching through the 12 apostles to the nations) and *The Shepherd of Hermas* (a book of visions that reflects on the nature of desire and forgiveness) were included in many lists of approved and popular texts by certain congregations. However, Athanasius insists that these texts should not be included in the canon, but can be read and studied as edifying. Athanasius is a good summary person. He is the one who accurately captures the books that had, through usage in various congregations, become authoritative.

The mainline recognizes as Scripture the 66 books (39 in the Old Testament and 27 in the New Testament). The Episcopal Church and the Lutherans give a special status to the books that comprise the Apocrypha, while the Presbyterians, United Church of Christ (UCC), and Methodists do not.

Approaches to Scripture

The primary approaches to Scripture among the mainline are as follows.[2] The first is the conservative evangelical approach, which stresses the immediate engagement of the reader with the text. The second is the liberal–experiential approach, which stresses the importance of the experience of God behind the text. The third is the Christological approach, where the Barthian distinction between the two Words is important. (Karl Barth is the distinguished Swiss theologian who stressed the centrality of Christ in the interpretation of Scripture.) The fourth is the ecclesial approach (ecclesial is a technical word for "church"), where the community of interpretation is central. This is the approach taken by Stephen Fowl's influential book *Engaging Scripture*. The fifth approach is the liberationist approach, where the prophetic stand of Scripture tends to challenge the other parts of the text.

Starting then with the conservative evangelical approach, this is found as a significant minority in all the mainline. For the Anglicans, James Packer, the author of *Knowing God* would be representative. For the Lutherans, John Warwick Montgomery has defended the inerrancy of Scripture.

Both Packer and Montgomery link Christology with their view of Scripture. In Christ, the human and the divine are perfectly woven together; likewise, in Scripture, the human and divine are perfectly woven together. When the modern world started to treat the Bible "just like any other book," the agency of the Holy Spirit was denied. The result was "higher criticism" that undermined the unity and integrity of Scripture.

Kern Robert Trembath describes this evangelical approach to Scripture as "deductivist." He defines such an approach as "one that reflects the understanding that knowledge is grounded upon beliefs which are not subject to empirical verification but nevertheless guide or influence empirical observations."[3] Such approaches tend to start with the doctrine of God and then, given such a doctrine of God, attempt to determine what sort of Bible would be expected. This approach does not start with the text and then try and work out what God is doing, but operates the other way round. Now, as Trembath admits, John Warwick Montgomery would contest the claim that his approach is deductive (starting with God and then coming to Scripture). In fact, Montgomery would claim that he is advocating an "inductive inerrancy" (i.e. that a careful reading of Scripture demonstrates that it is a text without errors). However, Trembath is right: Montgomery does not demonstrate that a natural reading of the text suggests a text with no errors at all.

It is not surprising that the majority of scholars in the mainline are moving away from this approach to Scripture. Christian Smith calls this approach "Biblicism" and insists that in the end it cannot be used consistently. Smith writes:

> Biblicism is impossible. It literally does not work as it claims that it does and should. Biblicism does not live up to its own promises to produce an authoritative biblical teaching by which Christians can believe and live. Instead, Biblicism produces *myriad* "biblical" teachings on a host of peripheral and crucial theological issues. Together those teachings lack coherence and are not infrequently contradictory. Biblicism does not add up.[4]

This is more than the traditional objections to inerrancy. Christian Smith takes for granted that Genesis one does not read like a historical, scientific narrative (it is much more like a poem); the books of Chronicles and Kings do disagree; it is not clear exactly how Judas died; and it is difficult to believe that the sun stopped moving in Joshua – especially given the sun is not moving in relationship with the earth. Instead for Christian Smith, an evangelical himself, the problem is that the reality of the pluralism of interpretations is not taken seriously. Smith illustrates this very well in one very long sentence:

> Divergent views based on different readings of the Bible also involve many other significant topics – including the role of "good works" in salvation, proper worship protocols, the value of reason and rationality in faith, *supersessionism* (whether God's "old covenant" promises to the Jews have been replaced by the "new covenant"), martial submission and equality, the legitimacy of creeds and confessions, the nature of life after death, the possible legitimacy and nature of ordained ministry, the morality of slavery, the theological significance of Mary, the ethics of wealth, views of private property, creation and evolution, the nature of depravity and original sin, salvation of the Jews, use of statues and images in devotion and worship, the status of Old Testament laws, the importance of a "conversion experience," the perseverance of the saints, church discipline, birth control, tithing, dealing with the "weaker brother," the meaning of material prosperity, abortion, corporal punishment, capital punishment, asceticism, economic ethics, the wearing of jewelry and makeup, celibacy, drinking alcohol, homosexuality, the "anti-Christ," believers' relations to culture, church-state relations, and – last but not least – the nature and purpose of the Bible itself.[5]

Conservative evangelical scholars would argue that if we cannot be confident about the Bible then how can we be confident about our theology? The response to this is that it looks like God has not given us such confidence. At the very least, conservative evangelicals must concede the appearance of error in the text. And this would then provoke the obvious question: why does God undermine our confidence in the text by allowing the appearance of error? Christian Smith is right: "Biblicism forces a gap between what the Bible actually is and what its theory demand that the Bible be."[6] We need to treat the Bible as the book that God has actually given us, rather than wish for a book that is different.

A further related difficulty is worth noting. This approach to Scripture tends to have a deep suspicion of hermeneutics. Hermeneutics is the task of interpreting Scripture. We all know that the Bible is interpreted by different people in different ways: some people think Genesis is more like a poem, others sees it as scientific history. These are differences of interpretation.

In an important book called *The Fall of Interpretation*, James Smith (sorry, yet another scholar called Smith) argues that evangelicals are too often inclined to see interpretation of the text as a consequence of *the Fall*. So in Eden, we enjoyed an intimacy with God, where interpretation was not necessary. However, as sin entered the world, so a distance arises between humanity and God that requires interpretation. Those committed to the inerrancy of the Bible want the text to be free from the challenge of the Fall. They want a reliable communications system. So James Smith writes:

> Metaphysics and fundamentalism have an extremely reliable – I should say "infallible" – postal system. It is a telecommunications network equipped with unbreakable lines, virus-proof computers and the latest technological advances. Acquiring this inerrant technology means always receiving God's Word unmediated and unaffected by the postal and telecommunications system.[7]

For James Smith, there are two difficulties with this. The first is that in truth the setting and location of the reader does affect the interpretation of the text. Who we are and how we look at the world have a significant influence on our reading of the Bible. The second is that we should not see interpretation as a result of the Fall. Instead it is part of the divinely intended structure of creation. God made us so we would have to struggle with the challenge of interpretation. Direct uncomplicated access was never the idea.

We turn then to the second approach within the mainline. This we are calling the "liberal–experiential" approach. The classic account was provided in 1929 by C.H. Dodd (1884–1973). For Dodd, revelation is less contained in the actual sentences that make up the Bible, but instead in the experiences that humanity has of God that lies behind the sentences. So we are less interested in the struggle to harmonize the actual words of Jesus across the Gospels, and more interested in the experiences of the disciples that gave rise to the Gospels. It is the experience behind the text that matters, not the actual words of the text.

C.H. Dodd also saw the revelation as "progressive." Dodd writes:

> We observe a process that as a whole must be called progressive. At each stage of the process we observe individuals who gathered up in themselves the tendencies of the process, criticized them by some spontaneous power of insight, and redirected the process in its succeeding stages. That which these individuals contributed was a vision of God, determined by what they themselves were.[8]

For Dodd, the climax of this process was Jesus. It is in Jesus we have the fullest disclosure of the nature of God. For Dodd, the prophets of the Old Testament – the Hebrew Bible – were definitely inspired, but their insight was always partial. However, while the fullest disclosure is in Jesus, the process of disclosure continues into the present day. Scripture is the poetic and artistic masterpiece that captures a process into which we are all invited.

This approach is called liberal–experiential because it is liberal, in that a particular text is not binding on the Church and it allows a pluralism of interpretations, and is experiential because it is the experience behind the text that matters. The text itself is less important.

Critics of this approach have a number of concerns. The first surrounds the actual authority of Scripture. Is a closed canon a good idea? Could we in principle add texts to Scripture – insert sections of Shakespeare and take out the book of Revelation? It seems to some critics that this approach does not justify exactly why these books matter. The second is that the image of "progressive" revelation is seen by some as anti-Jewish and as assuming an almost evolutionary (things are just improving slowly over time) world view.

However, there are strengths. It takes us away from a fixation on the actual text; it places revelation in a larger context. It does not impose on the Bible something it is not. This entire approach has had a very significant impact on the mainline. However, although Dodd believes that Jesus is the climax of the biblical revelation, it was the work of Karl Barth (1886–1968) and others that made Christ the lens through which we interpret Scripture.[9] It is this that is our third approach.

The third method we are calling the Christological approach. In Christian Smith's study of Biblicism, he concludes with an appeal for evangelicals to make Christ the interpretative lens of Scripture. Read the text through what we have learned of God in Christ. This is the key to this position. Smith correctly gives much of the credit for this approach to Karl Barth – the brilliant theologian who dominated much of the early twentieth-century European theology.

The central insight of this approach is to distinguish between the two Words. For Christians, the primary Word of God is the Word Made Flesh. So the author of John's Gospel explains in that remarkable beginning:

> In the beginning was the Word and the Word was with God and was God. ... And the Word became flesh and dwelt among us. (John 1:1, 12)

Christians believe that the definitive disclosure of God is the Eternal Word. It is the life, death, and resurrection of Jesus, which primarily tells us who God is. We learn about God from the person of Jesus.

Once the Eternal Word Made Flesh (i.e. Jesus of Nazareth) is considered the primary Word of God, then we can turn our attention to the written word (i.e. the Bible). For Karl Barth the purpose of the Bible is to witness to the Eternal Word. It is in the text of Scripture that we learn everything we need to know about Jesus; and what we know about God in Christ can and should inform our interpretation of Scripture.

The advantages of this position are easy to see. It means that we have a vitally important interpretative lens through which Scripture is interpreted. It is the encounter with Christ that is central; and the purpose of Scripture is to facilitate that encounter. Karl Barth had an interesting line on higher criticism. Basically, he was uninterested. The fact that Moses did not write the Pentateuch was incidental to the effectiveness of the Pentateuch to point us to the God revealed in Christ who is calling all humanity to live as God required.

The fourth approach makes the community of the Church central. In the United States, the group of theologians who stress this approach are loosely gathered around the "post-liberal" school. It was George Lindbeck, the remarkable theologian who spent most of his career at Yale, who suggested that the significance of the community of interpretation has been so often overlooked in theology. For Lindbeck, all knowledge comes through communities. If you are in science, then an interpretative community of scientists becomes your conversation partners and the lens through which you make sense of data in your discipline. What is true in science is also true in theology. Now for Lindbeck, this does not result in relativism (the view that there is no way of deciding between different community interpretations), but it is a recognition that discovery of truth depends on joining a community because there is no other way in which knowledge in any discipline can be transmitted.

Lindbeck has had a major influence on contemporary mainline theology. The best defense and development of a post-liberal view of Scripture is the remarkable *Engaging Scripture* by Stephen Fowl. Fowl describes his argument thus:

> [T]he central argument of this book is that, given the ends towards which Christians interpret their scripture, Christian interpretation of scripture needs to involve a complex interaction in which Christian convictions, practices, and concerns are brought to bear on scriptural interpretation in ways that both shape that interpretation and are shaped by it.[10]

Fowl distinguishes between three accounts of interpretation. Determinate interpretation seeks clarity; this is the approach that wants to uncover the meaning of the biblical text. Anti-determinate interpretation wants to exercise a "hermeneutics of suspicion" (i.e. it wants to look for the ulterior motives that underpin many traditional interpretations). Fowl takes the work of Derrida as his way into this approach. Against these two approaches, Fowl wants to argue for an underdetermined interpretation. This approach "recognizes a plurality of interpretative practices and results."[11] Crucial to this approach is an emphasis on the ways in which Christians attend "to the question of how they can order their lives, practices, *and* their biblical interpretation with a sufficient vigilance to read scripture in such a way that they avoid sinful practices."[12] The idea here is that the Christian community is central; it needs to be a community that makes forgiveness, repentance, and reconciliation central. In addition, the agency of the Holy Spirit is central in this process. In the same way as the Holy Spirit is vital in the process of interpretation around the inclusions of Gentiles in the early Church, so the work of the Holy Spirit will be central when it comes to contemporary discussions around inclusion.

The fifth approach is a liberationist approach. The term "liberationist" captures a movement that wants to read Scripture with the ethical priority of liberating the reading so the text supports an agenda of freedom and justice. For advocates of this approach, the text is too often a vehicle of oppression. This movement has its roots in the liberation theologians of South America who argued that the individualist gospel of the west is serving the interests of the rich and powerful, while in actual fact the text of Scripture supports a political community-orientated reading. In other words, the focus of so much preaching is on personal salvation that leads to life after death. Yet the story of the Exodus (where an oppressed people are in slavery and then liberated by God's intervention) and the preaching of Jesus (which talks a great deal about the evils of excessive wealth with virtually nothing about sex) are all about freeing the people from the challenge of oppression.

From this vantage point, the text needs to be read in a liberating way. So although there are texts that support slavery, the doctrine that every person is created in the image of God should enable us to see that slavery is incompatible with the biblical insight. Although there are texts that support patriarchy, Paul's insight that "there is no longer Jew or Greek, there is no longer slave or free, there is no longer male and female; for all of you are one in Christ Jesus" (Galatians 3:28) implies a fundamental equality between the sexes. Although there are texts that appear to denounce homosexuals, a liberationist reading stresses that the gospel values of justice should lead us to recognize that such texts emerged from a culture unaware of the reality of sexual orientation.

Critics of this approach worry about whether this is too reductionist. Scripture is no longer a text about God's relationship with humanity, but a political agenda. However, many in the mainline combine this approach to the text with one of the earlier approaches.

Pew Study – Biblical Illiteracy

Given the ever-increasing challenge of biblical illiteracy, in their book *Move*, authors Greg L. Hawkins and Cally Parkinson, citing their extensive research, claim that regular Bible reading is the single greatest factor in spiritual growth.

> The power of being immersed in the Bible is undeniable. We know that reading and reflecting on the Scriptures is critical to spiritual growth ... there may be nothing more important we can do with our time and effort than encouraging and equipping our people in this practice.[13]

Conclusion

All Christians are in conversation with Scripture. It remains the central authority for our life and witness. Compared to the Roman Catholic and Evangelical tradition, the mainline tends to be more liberal. The text of Scripture is carefully read in context. Almost all the leadership in the mainline recognizes the legitimacy of what is called "higher criticism" (approaches to the biblical text that recognize the way in which different sources have been compiled). The majority of Christians in the mainline do not think there is a conflict between the truth of science (namely, the processes of natural selection) and the message of Genesis 1 (namely, that God creates the world). So although there are significant representatives of the first interpretative approach – the conservative evangelical approach, the majority of the main line would identify with one of the other approaches.

It is the approach to Scripture that lies behind the more generous theology that shapes much of the mainline. Any of the strategies that shape approaches two to five frees the Christian to be more generous to other faith traditions, more committed to social justice, and less obligated to defend passages that seem to authorize genocide.

For critics of the mainline, this is a problem. The text of Scripture is not being treated as authoritative. For defenders of the mainline, this is the strength. Scripture is being treated seriously and not forced to be something it is not.

Notes

1 See Lee Martin McDonald, *The Origin of the Bible: A Guide for the Perplexed* (London and New York: T&T Clark International, 2011), 67f.

2 There are several different ways in which this debate can be handled. The five positions identified here are our own.

3 Kern Robert Trembath, *Evangelical Theories of Biblical Inspiration: A Review and Proposal* (New York and Oxford: Oxford University Press, 1987), 8.

4 Christian Smith, *The Bible Made Impossible: Why Biblicism is not a truly Evangelical Reading of Scripture* (Grand Rapids, IL: Brazos Press, 2011), 173.

5 Ibid., 27–28.

6 Ibid., 128.

7 James K.A. Smith, *The Fall of Interpretation: Philosophical Foundations for a Creational Hermeneutic* (Downers Grove, IL: InterVarsity Press, 2000), 47.

8 C.H. Dodd, *The Authority of the Bible, Revised Edition* (Glasgow: Collins Fount, 1960), 255.

9 For the purposes of clarity, Barth was not directly in conversation with C.H. Dodd; he was working on a much larger canvas, mainly involving Schleiermacher.

10 Stephen Fowl, *Engaging Scripture: A Model for Theological Interpretation* (Oxford: Blackwell, 1998), 8.

11 Ibid., 10.

12 Ibid., 61.

13 Greg L. Hawkins and Cally Parkinson, *Move* (Zondervan, 2011), 119.

Annotated Bibliography

F.F. Bruce, *The Canon of the Scripture* (Glasgow: Chapter House, 1988).

This text remains a classic. He takes a careful, informed line, which both explains the selection of books and defends the selection.

Stephen E. Fowl, *Engaging Scripture: A Model for Theological Interpretation* (Oxford: Blackwell, 1998).

One of the most imaginative books looking at Scripture to be published in the past 30 years. Fowl makes the role of the Church central in the interpretation of Scripture.

Lee Martin McDonald, *The Origin of the Bible: A Guide for the Perplexed* (New York: T&T Clark International, 2011).

Worth reading alongside Bruce. For McDonald, the evolution of the canon is more complicated and more open. A good model of contemporary scholarship.

Kern Robert Trembath, *Evangelical Theories of Biblical Inspiration: A Review and Proposal* (New York and Oxford: Oxford University Press, 1987).

A solid survey of historical and contemporary approaches to biblical inspiration among evangelicals.

Christian Smith, *The Bible Made Impossible: Why Biblicism is Not a Truly Evangelical Reading of Scripture* (Grand Rapids, IL: Brazos Press, 2011).

The problem with an approach that claims inerrancy and certainty for Scripture is that it ignores the actual way the Bible is. Even evangelicals are forced to admit a range of plausible readings of the text, this pluralism is evidence that such an approach to Scripture does not work. Instead, the key is to read the text through the lens of Christ. In so doing, one arrives at a much more authentic evangelical approach to Scripture.

James K.A. Smith, *The Fall of Interpretation: Philosophical Foundations for a Creational Hermeneutic* (Downers Grove, IL: Intervarsity Press, 2000).

Smith makes the interesting argument that we need to move away from seeing the challenge of interpretation as a result of the Fall and instead see it as built into the very structures of creation. An interesting argument that puts Derrida and evangelical scholars in the same camp.

6

Connecting the Theological Dots

Theology literally means "talk" (from the Greek word *logos*) about God (from the Greek word *Theos*). For many Christians, the very word "theology" provokes some apprehension. Doctrines of the *Trinity* or *Incarnation* or *Atonement* are rightly perceived as difficult and complicated. As a result, many leaders of congregations are tempted to avoid explicit theology.

Yet theology is important. Christianity is a tradition that invites a person into a particular world view – a particular understanding of how the world is. Articulating this worldview is the work of "theology." The doctrinal claim that "there is a God" means that we live in a world intended by divine agency, rather than a cosmic fluke or accident. It means that the universe is here for a purpose. We are not simply complex bundles of atoms that emerged from nowhere and ultimately face extinction when we die. It is an entirely different way of seeing the world. And it is the work of *doctrine* to express that different way of looking at the world. In addition, Christians believe that God has spoken: in other words, we know what God is like because God has told us. Along with prophets and the disclosure of God in history, for Christians, the primary disclosure of God is a life – the life of Jesus of Nazareth; this life is our ultimate authority as to what God is like. Given we believe in the Incarnation, we find ourselves forced to talk about one God who relates to us in three contrasting ways. This entire narrative – this world view – has embedded within it a set of beliefs. Learning to understand and explain these beliefs is important. A good congregational leader needs to be able to connect the theological dots.

This chapter will start with a brief description of the heart of the Christian world view, namely the claim that God was in Christ and therefore God is triune. This description captures the work that the Church did in the initial centuries when the major creeds were written. It is a description that is shared across the entire ecumenical Christian family. Then in the second section, we will look at certain differences in theological outlook, which emerged

An Introduction to Ministry: A Primer for Renewed Life and Leadership in Mainline Protestant Congregations, First Edition. Ian S. Markham and Oran E. Warder.
© 2016 John Wiley & Sons, Ltd. Published 2016 by John Wiley & Sons, Ltd.

during the *Reformation* and continue to shape the differences between the denominations that make up the mainline. Finally, in the third section we introduce a tension that is found within each denomination and across the mainline, namely the "liberal" and "conservative" divide.

Mainline Shared Beliefs

Christianity has Jewish roots. The Hebrew Bible is an important part of the Christian scriptures. Abraham is credited as the "father" of the *Abrahamic faiths* (Judaism, Christianity, and *Islam*). He is the one who made *monotheism* central and stressed the demands that God wants to make on all lives. Jesus is a Jew. He grew up believing that the one true God had a covenant relationship with the Jewish people. However, as he attracted disciples, so those close to him saw more in the life, much more.

Elsewhere in this book, we have looked at the nature of the Bible. We saw that interpreting Scripture is not easy; and there are plenty of disagreements about the historicity of this or that. So what follows is the picture of Jesus emerging from Scripture that proved important for subsequent doctrine.

The *Gospels* are carefully woven together stories about Jesus. Stories about blind people regaining sight and the lame walking were central. The teaching of Jesus included a call for transformed values, where the poor were affirmed and the rich were challenged. In addition, Jesus had a message about himself. He was not simply a *Rabbi* (teacher), but also an agent who anticipated and in some sense embodied the coming reign of God. He claimed to have the authority to forgive sins; people marveled at the authority underpinning his teaching. The writers of the Gospels struggled with this side of Jesus. Mark (the earliest of the four gospels) sees Jesus as an agent of the *eschaton* (the end of the world); Matthew sees Jesus as the new Moses bringing the new law; Luke sees Jesus as the agent who realigns the world in accordance with God's values; and John brings all these images together with the resolute declaration that Jesus is the pre-existent Word Made Flesh.

These stories about and reflections on Jesus found in the Gospels run parallel with another significant trajectory. It is worth remembering that when we look at the New Testament, the order of the books is misleading. The order might lead us to suppose that the Gospels were written before the Epistles (letters). However, the truth is the opposite. Most of the Epistles were written before the Gospels. Many of the Epistles are written by the apostle Paul. And here you see the development of worship of Jesus.

Larry Hurtado's major study on "devotion to Jesus in earliest Christianity" is enormously important. As one reads the New Testament, the affirmation "Jesus is Lord" pulsates throughout the text. So many passages are a celebration of Jesus (e.g. Colossians 1:15–20, Acts 2:36, and Philippians 2:1–11). Hurtado shows that this devotion to Jesus did not emerge gradually but exploded onto the scene. Hurtado writes:

> Christians were proclaiming and worshipping Jesus, indeed, living and dying for his sake, well before the doctrinal/creedal developments of the second century. … Moreover, devotion to Jesus as divine erupted suddenly and quickly, not gradually and late, among first-century circles of followers. More specifically, the origins lie in Jewish Christian circles of the earliest years.[1]

The sudden eruption, coupled with its home amongst Jewish monotheism, is clear evidence of the remarkable impact that the totality of Jesus' life, death, and resurrection had on the first Christians. Here we have Jews, who at considerable personal cost, believe in one God yet want to pray to and worship Jesus.

Monotheistic Jews know that one can only worship God. So if these Jews looked at Jesus and wanted to worship Jesus, then their practice meant that they were worshipping God made flesh. This provokes two questions: can we trust the closest witnesses to Jesus that this life is indeed God made flesh? And second, how is it possible that God can be one, yet be manifest in bodily form as a human?

On the first, there are many reasons why we can trust the closest witnesses. The Gospels have, to use J.B. Phillips' lovely phrase, the "ring of truth."[2] The selection of Gospels was very considered. By the time the early Church was making decisions about the canon of the New Testament, there were plenty of books purporting to be Gospels. They had lots of choice. Many of them were much more interesting and spectacular. *The Infancy Gospel of Thomas*, for example, had some great stories about Jesus as a child, which includes the story of Jesus creating clay birds into which he breathed life.

However, the early Church rejected such Gospels. They wanted texts as close as possible to the apostles. They wanted the texts that were restrained and considered; the texts that accurately reflected the life of Jesus. The four Gospels reveal a man who was constantly reaching out to others, understood that he had a significant role, issued a challenge to all he met, and was willing to die for these values. The way death is handled and the stories of his triumph over death in the resurrection are powerful and compelling. In addition, almost all of these early witnesses were martyred for their convictions. They paid the ultimate price for their beliefs. So today, as we read the New Testament, we can understand why the disciples believed Jesus worthy of worship.

The second question about the Christian belief about the nature of God in the light of the Incarnation is answered by way of the *Creeds*. Thanks to Dan Brown's *The Da Vinci Code* the Creeds are viewed with some suspicion. Dan Brown suggests that a Roman Emperor, fearful of divisions in the Empire, deliberately forced through an orthodoxy, which crushed many counter traditions. The truth is much more complicated than Brown suggests.

Although it is true that the Creeds were a result of considerable argument and that the Roman Emperor *Constantine* (272–337 CE) was interested in doctrinal unity, the Creeds were ultimately driven by sound theological considerations. The two most important texts were the Creed emerging out of the *Council of Nicaea* in 325 CE and the declaration emerging out of the *Council of Constantinople* in 452 CE. In the first the issue was monotheism; in the second the issue was the Incarnation.

The solutions of the Church to the conundrum of how monotheists can believe that God can be present as a human and simultaneously the Creator of everything are very imaginative. The starting point is a biblical image. Scripture talks about God as "Father" and Jesus as the "Son." Now this metaphor is understood by the *Church Fathers* to capture the difference between the source – the Father, the Creator – and the revealer – the Son. In the same way as we often see a parent in the looks or behavior of a child, so we are invited to see the nature of God, the Father, in the revealer, the Son. Starting with this metaphor, an argument developed that led to the doctrine of the Trinity, which had the following steps:

1. The Son has perfectly interpenetrated the life of Jesus of Nazareth so that we can see God in that life. In the same way that words are expressions of thoughts, so Jesus is the Word of God (the expression of God's thoughts in human form). If you want to know what God is like, then you need to look at the life, death, and resurrection of Jesus.
2. Now God's "speech" in Jesus cannot simply start in Jesus' life. This would undermine the nature of God as unchanging. The speech of God must always be part of God. In addition, given we believe in one God, the two aspects of God must be connected.
3. Therefore the Father and the Son must be in some perfect eternal relationship.

These three steps were formulated at the Council of Nicaea in 325 CE. Prior to that Council, *Arius* (ca. 256–336 CE) was arguing that monotheism means that everything must be created by the source (by the Father). However, *Athanasius* (296–373 CE) (his great rival and the man who did more than anyone to shape the debates at Nicaea) insisted that monotheism needs the Son to be in an eternal relationship with Father. This is because of step 2 – the Word of God – the eternal Wisdom of God – is part of God. God's speech doesn't just begin. In addition, Athanasius argued that God's appearance to humanity in Jesus is how God is in every respect. Michael Higton, in a rather nice summary of former Anglican Archbishop of Canterbury Rowan Williams, writes:

> [T]here is nowhere we can go in God, no extra we can think about or point to, no reservation, no sanctuary, in which God is not engaged, involved, loving, and relational. God is love, all the way down.[4]

Athanasius

Athanasius was the great hero of the orthodox. But he was extremely pugnacious. When he first started taking issue with the heretic Arius, he was in his early 20s. According to William Placher, "He had according to tradition, unusually dark skin, a hooked nose, and a red beard, and he was so small that his opponents called him a dwarf."[3] There was a time apparently when he once grabbed Emperor Constantine's horse and hung on to the bridle until the Emperor had conceded a theological point. As a result he occasionally made himself unpopular; so much so, he was exiled five times to different parts of the Empire. He did however, live a good long life. He died when he was about 80.

Now thus far, the focus has been on the Father and Son. There is another important biblical metaphor – the Spirit – that needs to be developed. In the original draft of the Creed, the Spirit gets a mention (just one line "We believe in the Holy Spirit"), and over the next 30 years or so the concept of the Holy Spirit is clarified.

The primary function of the Holy Spirit is to find a way of talking about the aspect of God that makes God present to us. Primarily the work of the Father is "Creator" (which is mainly a past event); and primarily the work of the Son is "Revealer" and "Redeemer" (which is also a past event). As Jesus, the physical embodiment of the Word is removed from the presence of the disciples at the *Ascension*, so the Spirit is sent. The Spirit is the aspect of God that constantly makes the Father and the Son real to the Church. In fact all of God's agency is mediated through the agency of the Spirit.

As the Church found itself talking about God in these three ways, so the Church determined that the language of the Trinity was essential. As John Macquarrie puts it, "the doctrine of the Trinity safeguards a dynamic as opposed to a static understanding of God."[5] It is actually intended to protect monotheism. The doctrine of the Trinity links these three elements together to create a unity. So Christians have their sense of God as source, revealer, and agent in the present, but all three are part of the one.

Now as the Church sorted out the concept of God implied by the reality of worshipping God in Jesus, it then turned its attention to the dynamics embedded in the life of Jesus himself. Clearly Jesus was human; he walked, talked, ate, and slept. However, given the Church is worshipping Jesus, Jesus must also be God. Exactly how these two relate is obviously tricky.

Chalcedon attempted to resolve this problem. Now interestingly, although both Nicaea and Chalcedon were controversial, Chalcedon was more so. However, the majority of Christians found it compelling. Against two extremes, Chalcedon opted for the middle way. One extreme was *adoptionism* (the view that Jesus was a human who was especially commissioned by God to be an agent of God); this view stresses the humanity of Jesus. The other extreme was *docetism* (the view that Jesus was completely God and his bodily flesh was simply a cloak that covered his divinity). Chalcedon rejected both by affirming both. Jesus is completely God and completely human. It set rules for our language – for our talk about God. Never say anything about Jesus that implies that he is less than fully human; and never say anything about Jesus that implies that he is less than fully God. Chalcedon does not seek to answer the question as to precisely what Jesus is. Instead it seeks to preclude inappropriate talk.

There were many reasons why this position made sense to the Church. *Soteriology* (the theory of how Jesus saves us) and *liturgy* (the various rituals of the Church) were important. However, the primary purpose of the language is to safeguard the amazing idea that in a life you can see the Eternal Wisdom of God. The language makes sure that we really have a life and, simultaneously, a God in all God's greatness visible in that life.

The purpose of this summary is to sketch out a way in which we can understand the achievement of these councils. In all its brevity, it attempts to show that these Creeds matter. They are real attempts to struggle to make sense of the grammar of the Christian faith – to make our talk about God and God's relations to Jesus and to the present intelligible. Although there are plenty of theologians who are continuing the conversation, the account offered above is one that captures the intent and achievement of the Fathers.

When it comes to doctrine, the "official" position of the mainline continues to affirm these councils and the achievement of these Creeds. Recognition as a "Christian denomination" depends on this. Later in this chapter, we shall look at the "progressive" and "conservative" divide.

The Four Ecumenical Councils Concerning the Nature of God and Christ

Council of Nicaea (325 CE). Establishment of a creed of beliefs.

Council of Constantinople (381 CE). Approval of the Nicene Creed, and a condemnation of Apollinarianism.

Council of Ephesus (431 CE). Repudiated Nestorianism, affirmed Mary as the "theotokos" (God-bearer).

Council of Chalcedon (451 CE). Affirmed Jesus Christ as both fully divine and fully human.

Theological Outlooks Arising from the Reformation

It is Martin Luther who gets the credit for the Reformation. Luther was born in Saxony. He became a priest in 1507 and a professor of biblical studies at the University of Wittenberg in 1512. It was his knowledge of Scripture that made him uncomfortable with the approach taken by the Roman Catholic Church. As we will note in Chapter 7, he revisited certain biblical themes and made them central to his theology. Instead of a theology that depended on "works" (paying the *penance*, buying *indulgences*), Martin Luther argued that faith and grace were what mattered. He rediscovered the major themes of Paul's Epistle to the Church in Rome. It isn't what we do that matters, but what God has already done. It is not that we work hard to become righteous, but that God through Christ has already made us righteous. As he developed these arguments, so a new tradition slowly emerged. He inspired the tradition that we know today as the Lutheran denomination.

Carl Braaten, a contemporary Lutheran theologian, has identified eight principles that capture the essence of Lutheran theology. The first is the *canonical principle*. For Luther, Scripture matters because it conveys the Gospel (the good news). The second is the *confessional principle*. The Church confesses (shares) its insights with others and often these take the form of statements of faith. The third is the *ecumenical principle*, a recognition of deep connections with other Christians. The fourth is the *Trinitarian principle*. The doctrine of salvation depends on all three persons of the Trinity being in operation. The fifth is the *Christocentric principle*. For Luther, the work of Christ on the cross is central. The sixth is the *sacramental principle*; Christ really is present in the bread and the wine. The seventh is the *law/Gospel principle*; we are ultimately saved through faith not works. The eighth is the *two kingdoms principle*; there is a complex link between salvation and the kingdom of God.

Meanwhile in Geneva, John Calvin was starting to articulate his distinctive theology. Calvin was trained in theology in Paris. In 1533 or so, Calvin read Martin Luther's writings and this was a factor in his break from the Roman Catholic Church. He was given an opportunity to create a "proper Christian society" when he moved to Geneva. Here, he not only had the space to write and reflect and create his distinctive reformed theology, but he also implemented a particular political vision of society.

A distinguished Bible scholar, Calvin immersed himself in the biblical world view. He was not striving to create a new religion, but to "reform" the current Christian tradition. The control on his theology was the Bible. If an idea was not in Scripture, then it should be discarded. A polity emerged that stressed the importance of the lay voice. He argued that the biblical witness does not simply affirm God's central role in the drama of salvation, but God's central role in the drama of creation. For Calvin, God is sovereign. God is in control of everything that happens: and humans are deeply mired in sin. His theology stressed the doctrine of *predestination*. From eternity past, God chose those who were redeemed. All of this can be found in his *Institutes of the Christian Religion*. He inspired the traditions that are known in the United States as the Presbyterians and the Congregationalists (the United Church of Christ, UCC).

Back in England, *King Henry VIII* (1491–1547) needed a male heir. His current wife was Catherine of Aragon, and he wanted to marry Anne Boleyn. Having opposed Martin Luther and written a book defending the seven sacraments, for which he was honored by the Pope, he did not want to make a radical theological move away from the Roman Catholic Church. However, for a whole host of complex reasons, an annulment was not granted by the Pope. So King Henry VIII took a dramatic step. He declared himself "head" of the English Church. The Pope no longer had authority over the English Church. It took his daughter – *Queen Elizabeth I* (1533–1603) – to create the distinctive outlook of Anglicanism. Theologically, this was a tradition that walked in-between Rome and Geneva. It shared the sacramental emphasis of Rome and the emphasis on the Bible of Geneva. The Anglican tradition had emerged; the Episcopal Church was to become an offspring of this tradition.

English Anglicanism had its own problems in the eighteenth century. So much so, that a society emerged in Oxford known as the "Holiness Society." A group of young men, wanted to recover the piety of the early Church, and felt that this needed a revival. Two brothers proved important – *John and Charles Wesley*. John Wesley (1703–1791) was an inspired preacher and organizer; Charles Wesley (1707–1788) was a gifted preacher and hymn writer. Although neither saw themselves as leaving the Church of England, they finally felt impelled to allow the "ordination" of other ministers to be permitted. As a result a new denomination had emerged; the Methodist Church had been born.

At this point distinctive theological approaches had emerged across the mainline. The Lutherans and the Anglicans were closest to the Roman Catholic Church. The Presbyterians, UCC, and the Methodists were further away.

Liberal and Conservative

The Reformation provoked a certain theological spectrum to emerge. *The Enlightenment* provoked a different theological spectrum to emerge. Where the Reformation provoked questions that interpreted theological language in different ways, the Enlightenment provoked questions that challenged theological language.

The Enlightenment describes a European movement of the seventeenth and eighteenth centuries, which stressed the importance of reason. *Immanuel Kant* (1724–1804), the great Prussian philosopher, was the person who used the expression "Enlightenment." For Kant, we were moving from an age that made arguments from authority central, to an age that made reason central. Kant credits *David Hume* (1711–1776), the Scottish philosopher, for waking Kant from "his slumbers." Hume's theme that pervades all this philosophy is "how do you know?" Hume wondered about miracles (and provided strong arguments for skepticism); he didn't think the arguments for God's existence were that convincing (although he was mischievous in the *Dialogues Concerning Natural Religion*, where he appeared to suggest that the modern day deist design advocate was convincing); and even science he found puzzling.

The Enlightenment created a new theological divide. This time it was between those who wanted to change the faith in the light of modernity and those who did not. This was the liberal–conservative divide. Unlike the denominational divides, this one crosses denominations. So we find that liberal Lutherans, Episcopalians, and Methodists have more in common with each other than they do with their own conservative counterparts within their own denomination. The world has slowly changed. Conservatives across denominations work together (on such things as abortion) and liberals across denominations work together (on such things as gay rights).

For the liberals, the faith must adapt or die. The Episcopal bishop John Shelby Spong is representative. In a series of books, he has sketched out a powerful manifesto for a modern faith. His primary theme is that "we must change or die."[6] In the end, he argues, a faith that clings to outmoded ethics or cosmology cannot survive. So he wants a faith that takes seriously biblical criticism. We know that the Bible is not without error; we know that the values of the Bible in various passages are pre-modern (it affirms slavery, patriarchy, and homophobia); and we know that the Gospel authors were not journalists (they had a pre-modern understanding of the past, which meant that they were more than happy to "invent" stories about the past that applied to their present). Spong wanted a faith that made sense of science. There is no question that evolution enabled humanity to emerge on this planet. Science makes the traditional miracle unlikely (the Bible treats epilepsy as if it were demon possession). Indeed he went so far to say that we need to move beyond *theism* (belief in a personal God) into a more spiritual realm. Spong also wanted a faith that sets forth a progressive ethical agenda. The Church, he argued, is constantly playing catch-up. Over the equality of women, the Church was one of the last organizations to allow women to have leadership roles in Church (and still the extremes hold out); over racial equality, the Church did not take a lead; and over gay rights, the Church continues to be resistant. Spong argued that we need to get ahead of this curve.

There is no doubt that Spong has kept many people in the Church. He writes for those in exile – those who have a spiritual sense but cannot cope with the hypocrisy and implausible of the Church. These women and men love his books and enjoy listening to him speak.

The conservatives have their own representatives. The list is long: John Scott (Anglican), James Packer (Anglican), Tim Keller (Presbyterian), George Lindbeck (Lutheran), and Stanley Hauerwas (Methodist). The themes pervading all their work is the impoverished conceit of liberalism. It is impoverished because the faith that remains is abstract, limited, and unsatisfying. It was C.S. Lewis who observed that a "skeptic is much more likely to travel further in to Christianity then the liberal assumes."

If you are going to believe in the Christian drama, then you want to believe God who discloses the reality of God in Scripture and in Christ. You want to believe in divine agency, which might from time to time take a miraculous form. You are unlikely to lay down your life for the sake of a Gospel of skepticism.

For the conservatives, the key issue is authority. This chapter started with the recognition that Christian theology assumes that somewhere, somehow God has spoken. God has revealed God to the world. It was Karl Barth, the great Swiss reformed theologian, who made this point central to his theology. He insisted that any coherent theology depends on *revelation*. We need God to tell us. For Barth, if God has not spoken, then we are all *agnostics* because we are all guessing what God is like.

Contentious Theological Issues

Since the beginning, theological issues rarely go away. The original questions that divided the Church (how can God be human, and the nature of the Trinity) continue to be a matter of conversation today. Significant issues emerging from the Reformation (nature of the sacraments, ecclesiology, and baptism) are still present, but perhaps less pronounced in the Christian consciousness. These differences between denominations have dissipated. Evangelicals from each tradition are willing to come together and stress rather more their agreements than doctrinal disagreements; liberals (who have a looser connection with doctrinal formulations) are willing to do the same. It is for these reasons that interest in ecumenical agreements is limited: for example, many lay people in the Anglican and Lutheran Churches do not realize that we have a concordat that permits extensive cooperation and mutual recognition.

The energy in contemporary theology is primarily around *methodology* (how exactly do we "talk about God," i.e. our system). The primary conversation in the mainline at the start of the twenty-first century is around three groups: the first is the revisionist group; the second is the postliberals; and the third is the liberationist group. We will conclude this chapter by looking at these three in some detail.

Methodology in Theology

The roots of *revisionism* are two distinguished twentieth-century theologians. *Paul Tillich* (1886–1965) was responsible for stressing the imperative of linking the Christian tradition with the ever-changing nature of modern society; he used the phrase "correlation" to describe this approach. One should seek to correlate the questions of modernity with the rich resources (and in a sense "answers") of the tradition. *A.N. Whitehead* (1861–1947) provided much of the content of a revisionist theology. Where traditional theology worked with a set of assumptions that God was timeless and disconnected from the world, Whitehead inspired *process theology*, which saw God within time and intimately connected with the world.

It was 1973 when the Chicago theologian David Tracy coined the expression "revisionism." For Tracy, the work of the theologian is to "revise" the tradition so it works in the present. For Tracy, "the revisionist will … try to rectify earlier theological limitations both in the light of the new resources made available by further historical, philosophical, and social scientific research and reflection and in the light of the legitimate concerns and accomplishments of the later neo-orthodox and radical theological alternatives."[7]

For Tracy, the revisionist theologian isn't afraid to recognize that mistakes have been made in the past and to recognize that theology must change to accommodate insights generated by science and historical studies, but also should learn from the liberation theologians (more about liberation theologians in a moment). The goal is to produce a theology that is intelligible to those outside the Church. We revise our theology to ensure it is a "public theology."

Tracy's work birthed a school – an entire approach taken by other theologians. Some are more conservative (they take the tradition more seriously) and others are much more radical (they are willing to question tradition in a variety of ways). Robert Neville in Boston has stressed the importance of other religions in revising the faith. Edward Farley wants to stress the importance of experience and with starting with humanity and this world, rather than God and heaven. Peter Hodgson used the phrase "constructive theology" – theology is a construct that needs to be built. And the Mennonite theologian Gordon Kaufman is the most radical of the group. He admits that much of his theology is "agnostic"; and God is reinterpreted to be a symbol that is less oppressive to the poor and yet still places a demand on humanity.[8]

Revisionism should be linked with the liberal theology described earlier in the chapter. The second school is the more conservative reaction to this theology. Writing back in 1989, William Placher compares the revisionist theologians and the *postliberals* when he writes:

> To oversimplify, the concern of the *revisionist* theology which dominates most academic circles in the United States is to preserve the *public* character of theology, that is, to find ways in which Christians can explain what they believe and argue for its truth in ways that non-Christians can understand. For the recently emerged *postliberal* theology, the theologian's task is more nearly simply to describe the Christian view of things.[9]

Placher goes on to clarify:

> Postliberal theologians note ad hoc conjunctions and analogies with the questions and beliefs of non-Christians, but their primary concern is to preserve the Christian vision free of distortion, and they mistrust systematic efforts to correlate Christian beliefs with more general claims about human experience, which seem to them always to risk constraining and distorting the Christian "answers" to fit the "questions" posed by some aspect of contemporary culture.[10]

The postliberal school has its roots in the theology of the famous Lutheran theologian George Lindbeck. It was in his book, *The Nature of Doctrine* (1984), that Lindbeck argued for a "cultural-linguistic" approach to religion.[11] A religion is a language – a discourse of beliefs and practices – that emerges from a community that seeks to make sense of the world. The task of theology is to understand the grammar of faith – to see how all the parts connect together and provide a compelling set of beliefs and practices. Once Christians are clear about their own self-understanding, it is possible for them to converse with others.

For the postliberal theologian the opening section of this chapter is crucial. It is the historic Creeds that capture of the essence of the Christian discourse. To be a Christian is to live within this Incarnational and Trinitarian narrative and appreciate its power and vision. The first two methodologies have dominated the North American theological academy. The third has its roots in South America. And this is the approach of *liberation theology*. There are two sources that have influenced this theology: the first is the Second Vatican Council of the Roman Catholic Church, also known as "*Vatican II*" (1962–1965); here a theology emerged that stressed the importance of Roman Catholic social teaching. The second source of liberation theology is the reality of income inequality in some parts of South America. When Scripture is read from the vantage point of the poor, then the Exodus is not simply a spiritualized journey from captivity to sin into hope, but also speaks to the deepest yearnings of the poor who recognize the political need to escape from the slavery they find themselves in and find ways to live in dignity.

The classic text for liberation theology is Gustavo Gutiérrez's *A Theology of Liberation*. It is a *contextual theology* – one that stresses that the shape of a theology looks different depending on the vantage point of those doing the theology. It is a theology that stresses the political. The God of Scripture actually did hear the cries of those in slavery and set them free in the Exodus; the Jesus of the New Testament did actually stress the imperative of selling everything you have and giving it to the poor. For liberation theologians, God has a *preferential option for the poor*.

With its close connection with the Roman Catholic Church, it was inevitable that the approach would be carefully examined by the Roman Catholic authorities. In 1984, the Sacred Congregation for the Doctrine of the Faith expressed concern about the elements of the theology that owed an explicit debt to Marxism. It is true that the Marxist insight that the superstructure of a culture (the law, theology, and philosophy) often reflects the economic base (which in a capitalist economy includes unjust economic relations) is developed by many liberation theologians. According to these theologians, it was the need of the rich to protect their wealth that led to the emergence in the west of a theology that stressed the afterlife and turned people into "souls on legs." However, beyond this, the debt to Marxism was less than many claimed.

Liberation theology is important because it birthed many other contextual theologies. Where liberation theology starts with the experience of the poor, feminist theologies focus on the experience of women. *Black theology* concentrates on the history of oppression of persons of African descendent. *Gay theology* stresses the primarily heterosexual emphasis of the Christian tradition. There is a shared emphasis. Scripture looks different depending on the context of the reader.

This debate about methodology is important. A key issue is the attitude to "tradition." Is the tradition the problem or the resource? For those at the more liberal end of the spectrum, the tradition can be a problem. In the case of liberation theology, a tradition of interpretation has emerged that stresses the voices of the privileged. For contextual theologies, the tradition has supported and underpinned certain forms of oppression. Many "revisionist theologians" affirm the insights of contextual theology. The tradition needs to be revised so it can speak effectively to the voices of the marginalized in society. The postliberals are at the more conservative end of the spectrum. It might sound odd to talk about "postliberal" being conservative, but this is the right way to think about this movement. Lindbeck's work has inspired a whole movement of what John Webster has called the "theologies of retrieval."[12]

Webster's designation is helpful: these are theologies that take the tradition seriously and see the tradition as a resource rather than a problem.

For the clergy person it is important that we become familiar with these key theological debates. Once one understands these different approaches, one can start to understand the different theologies that are found in different congregations and different denominations.

Conclusion

It is important that the Church has a wide theological spectrum. We need the conservatives who stress the importance of authority: how do we know that this or that idea really comes from God? And we need the liberals who stress the importance of engagement with contemporary culture: what exactly could we learn from this or that idea? It is also good that there is a spectrum of different theological stories underpinning the different mainline denominations. The Lutherans stress the cross; the Anglicans the Incarnation; the Presbyterians stress election; the Methodists personal devotions; and the UCC stress social justice. The plurality of approaches can and should be seen as a good thing.

Yet it is important that there is a shared story around which the Church coalesces. This story is that in the life, death, and resurrection of Jesus, we see God; it is a story of how God encountered humanity to overcome our propensities to egotism and invite us into new life in Christ; it is a story that promises all of us who struggle the hope of divine agency that can make a difference.

Notes

1   Larry W. Hurtado, *Lord Jesus Christ: Devotion to Jesus in Earliest Christianity* (Grand Rapids, MI: Eerdmans, 2003), 650.

2   This phrase comes from the title of his book. See J.B. Phillips, *Ring of Truth: A Translator's Testimony*, (Wheaton, IL: Shaw Books, 2000).

3   William Placher, *A History of Christian Doctrine* (Philadelphia, PA: Westminster Press, 1983), 73.

4   Mike Higton, *Difficult Gospel: The Theology of Rowan Williams* (New York: Church Publishing, 2004) 42.

5   John Macquarrie, *Principles of Christian Theology*, revised edition (London: SCM Press, 1977), 197.

6   see John Shelby Spong, *Why Christianity Must Change or Die: A Bishop speaks to Believers in Exile* (San Francisco, CA: Harper Collins, 1998).

7   David Tracy, *Blessed Rage for Order: The New Pluralism in Theology* (Chicago, IL: University of Chicago Press, 1996), 32.

8   Gordon Kaufman, In the Face of Mystery: A Constructive Theology (Cambridge, MA: Harvard University Press, 1993), xiii.

9   William Placher, *Unapologetic Theology: A Christian voice in a pluralistic conversation* (Louisville, KY: Westminster John Knox Press, 1989), 154 (his italics).

10 Ibid., 154.

11 George A. Lindbeck, *The Nature of Doctrine* (Louisville, KY: Westminster John Knox Press, 1984).

12 John Webster, 'Theologies of retrieval' in John Webster, Kathryn Tanner, and Iain Torrance, eds, *The Oxford Handbook of Systematic Theology* (Oxford: Oxford University Press, 2007), 584.

Annotated Bibliography

Braaten, Carl E., *Principles of Lutheran Theology*, Second edition (Minneapolis, MN: Fortress Press, 2007).
The classic statement of how exactly Lutherans differ from other traditions. Working through eight principles, Braaten not only explains key Lutheran ideas, but also restates the ideas in conversation with contemporary scholarship.

Brian Hebblethwaite, *The Essence of Christianity* (London: SPCK, 1996).
Solid, clear and accessible. A good introduction.

Higton, Mike, *Difficult Gospel: The Theology of Rowan Williams* (New York: Church Publishing, 2004).
This is not simply an excellent introduction to the theology of Rowan Williams, it is also a masterful exercise in systematic theology and apologetics. Higton has organized Williams and provided a compelling introduction to the Christian faith through Williams' writings.

Markham, Ian S., *Understanding Christian Doctrine* (Oxford: Blackwell, 2008).
An attempt to offer an Anglican approach to theology, which makes the issue of theodicy central.

Migliore, Daniel L., *Faith Seeking Understanding: An Introduction to Christian Theology*, second edition (Grand Rapids, MI: Eerdmans Publications Co., 2004).
A reformed approach to Christian doctrine.

Placher, William, *Unapologetic Theology: A Christian voice in a Pluralistic Conversation* (Louisville, KY: Westminster John Knox Press, 1989).
This is a great book. It is a both a solid introduction to philosophy and an exploration of the postliberal approach.

Polkinghorne, John, *Science and Christian Belief: Theological Reflections of a Bottom-Up Thinker* (London: SPCK, 1994).
A distinguished physicist reflects on how best faith and science can be reconciled.

Radford Ruether, Rosemary, *Sexism and God-talk: Towards a Feminist Theology*, (Boston, MA: Beacon Press, 1993).
Rightly acclaimed as a classic. A pioneering text that worked hard to think through the relationship of theology to patriarchy.

Ward, Keith, *Religion and Community* (Oxford: Oxford University Press, 2000).
One in a series of four volumes that reflects on the challenge of formulating an account of the Christian faith, which takes seriously both the insights of other faith traditions and of science.

Webster, John, Tanner, Kathryn, and Torrance, Iain, eds, *The Oxford Handbook of Systematic Theology* (Oxford: Oxford University Press, 2007).
Written by an international team of theologians, this has become a classic introduction to systematic theology. It is especially helpful on the nature of revisionism and liberation theology.

7

Church History

No one just falls out of the sky; no church just starts from nothing. We all have a past; and understanding the past is crucial to our identity. So much of the practice is justified in the past. The basic approach of the tradition is grounded in the thought of certain key people who shaped the tradition. Services can just look strange unless one has a sense of a tradition; and the assumptions made by members are often grounded in the views of those who shaped the tradition.

Church history is an important part of any training. In this short chapter, we shall look at the reasons for studying Christian history; the different approaches to that study; and a brief overview of the mainline denominational histories.

Why Study Christian History?

It was in *Jesus Christ Superstar* that Judas berated Jesus and asked a simple question:

> You'd have managed better if you'd had it planned. Why'd you choose such a backward time and such a strange land? If you'd come today you would have reached a whole nation. Israel in 4 BC had no mass communication.[1]

The question is a good one. Why did God choose the Jewish people? Why did God choose the first century? And, of course, the questions can be extended. Why did Christianity catch on in Europe? Why did Rome become so significant? Why did it grow from being a Jewish movement to the largest religion in the entire world?

Many of these questions at a very practical level are answered by Church history. Church history is in a real sense the study of the movement of ideas and practices among humans.

An Introduction to Ministry: A Primer for Renewed Life and Leadership in Mainline Protestant Congregations, First Edition. Ian S. Markham and Oran E. Warder.
© 2016 John Wiley & Sons, Ltd. Published 2016 by John Wiley & Sons, Ltd.

Every idea has to have a home. Why was it Isaac Newton who had the idea of gravity, thereby giving European culture a head start on the scientific revolution? Why was it the culture of India that probably birthed the oldest game in the world – chess? When you ask historical questions you are asking questions about how the past shapes the present to create new possibilities for the future.

And when you are studying Church history, you are studying the *providence* of God – God's movement in human history. Andrew F. Walls makes the point well when he writes:

> A similar process of reflection on Christian history as a whole might consider how that history is one of successive linguistic and cultural translation. The Incarnation itself is a great act of translation, God translated into humanity, the whole meaning of God expressed in human categories. But the incarnate Christ is not humanity generalized, but God expressed in the culture-specific terms of first-century Jewish Palestine. The only humanity we know and recognize as human is culture-specific. So the process of Christian expansion is the story of various re-translations of the original into other cultural media as Christ is received among people of different languages and cultures.[2]

Walls is right – God did not take the form of a generalized humanity in Christ, but a particular form of humanity (male and Jewish). From that moment of translation, the Gospel has been translated countless times since. Church history is an attempt to understand that journey – a journey that has touched every part of the globe.

There are two skills that one learns through Church history. The first is the significance of interpretation. When it comes to the past, we have to work hard to select the appropriate sources, give them appropriate weight (take into account any bias), and then offer a narrative that makes sense of what has happened. It is important to recognize that no-one comes to the study of the past without a lens. Justo L. González points out how often the lenses about the past have focused on the dominant cultures. Therefore he calls for a recognition of the "*postmodern*, polycentric map of Christianity [our emphasis]."[3] For González, it is vitally important that significant numbers of women and persons of color join the ranks of professional Church historians. He gives four reasons: the first is that women and persons of color "have a closer acquaintance with poverty and powerlessness in our own communities."[4] This is important because there is a greater emphasis on the context of the past, especially those situations where a minority is coping with an oppressive majority. The second reason is that the emergence of women in the historical guild has forced "all historians to look again at the historical record to see what it said about women."[5] For a long time, a guild dominated by men only focused on men in the past: given women make up half of the human race, it is good to see this being corrected. The third reason is there is now a greater interest in the "daily life of Christians."[6] The past isn't just ideas; the past is lived lives, where people are sick, taking out the garbage, and coping with the rigors of daily living. The final reason is that there is a greater interest in "the practices of popular religion that a generation ago were easily dismissed as '*syncretistic* [our emphasis].'"[7] Again this is linked with the lived religion rather than the theoretical religion. As we revisit the past, we discover, for example, that many Japanese Christians absorbed aspects of Shintoism or Confucianism.

For González, this is a much-needed shift for interpretation. We have shifted from a male, theoretical, intellectual reading of the past to a much greater sensitivity to the communities of women and those groups outside the elites. For this shift to occur, it has been necessary for people to join the academy and read the past with a different set of lenses.

The second skill is the appreciation of the sheer variety of practice and belief embedded in the past. Church history is the best cure for the sin of assuming that all Christians are alike. Different Christians have formed different communities with very contrasting understandings and views. Coptic Christians are different from Baptists from Alabama; the Church of Pentecost in Ghana (the largest Christian Church) is different from the Messianic Jewish Alliance of America (Jews who believe in *Yeshua*). And even Roman Catholics of today are quite different from the nineteenth-century Roman Catholics (before Vatican II). As one moves into the world of Church history, one becomes aware of just how varied Christianity is. It becomes a challenge to make sense of this variety.

Different Approaches to Study

Dyron B. Daughrity identifies five contrasting approaches to Church history. The first is the chronological approach. This is where one tells the story of Christianity from its origins to the present day. Starting with the apostolic age, Daughrity moves through "post-apostolic, illegal age," "Constantine and Byzantine age," "pivotal age," "fractured age," "global expansion age," and "recession and indigenization age."[8] This is a way of dividing and organizing the past – others would do it in a different way. The point is that it is taking the past and breaking it into segments.

The second is the denominational approach. This will be the focus of the approach taken later in this chapter. The idea here is to tell the story of the past through a particular trajectory. One difficulty with this approach is fairness. Ideally one needs to be a member of the denomination because that ensures that one has an insider's knowledge of the tradition; however, one drawback of being an insider is the challenge of being fair.

The third is the sociological approach. Daughrity explains, "Sociology is a massive field of inquiry. At its most fundamental level, it is the study of society. There are numerous methodologies that are properly considered sociological. Common to all of them, however, is the attempt to count, measure, and interpret."[9] For Daughrity, the best sociological history is the work of Rodney Stark. Stark's work is fascinating. He shows how a small number of Christians in 40 CE (probably not much more than 1000 in total), grew steadily to almost 32 million in 350 CE.[10] And the sociological factors working in favor of the growth of Christianity included attracting Jews from the diaspora, women, and slaves.

The fourth approach is the geographical approach. This is another way of telling the story of Christianity. The story is different in different places. The Middle East (where Christianity started and now is a small group) is quite different from South America (where Christianity is the largest group). The immediate challenges in each area are different. When it comes to the strength of Christianity, Islam is a major issue in the Middle East, while European colonization is central to South America.

The fifth approach is the biographical approach. The first four approaches focus on corporate narratives (narratives of groups), but individuals have a dramatic impact as well. So, to take Daughrity's example, the story of *St. Augustine of Hippo* (354–430 CE), who was a Manichee who converted to Christianity and became, perhaps, the most influential bishop of the early Church, is the story of a life that had a dramatic impact on the Church. The biographical approach to Church history concentrates on these individuals and their biographies and the impact they had on the development of the Church.

Augustine of Hippo

An incredibly influential "patristic" father of the Christian faith and Christian theology, Augustine was a bishop in the Church's early Northern African strand. Augustine developed theological insight and, thus, doctrine, relating to baptism and initiation, piety, ethics, original sin and the Fall, and theology related to the sacraments. He is the benchmark to which Christian theologians in the west must measure.

In all these cases, the careful reading of texts is central to the enterprise. The past comes to us through texts (primarily, it is only recently that you get pictures and images), so the understanding of the text is central. In Jean Comby's useful introduction to the study of Church history, she explains that there are eight elements to the careful reading of a text.

Denominational Tree

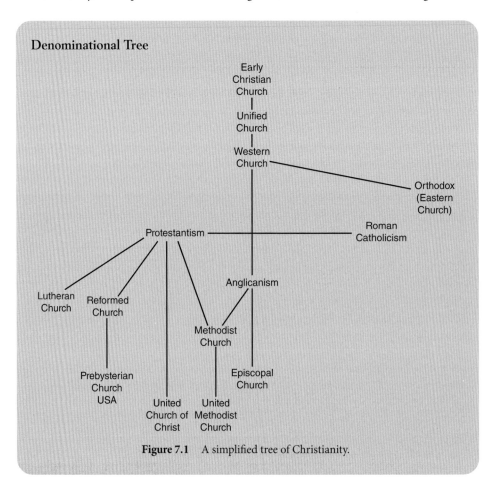

Figure 7.1   A simplified tree of Christianity.

These are: "a part of the whole" – so locating the text in the wider corpus; "understanding" – working hard to understand what is written (and with some texts from the past this can be very difficult); "translation" – recognizing that a translator has already made some decisions about meaning; "literary genre" – treat poetry like poetry and so on; "incidental information" – notice the incidental detail that can tell us more about the time than the direct message of the text; "where does the truth lie?" – ask about accuracy; "confronting the evidence" – make an effort to look at how different historians are reading a text; and "letting our surroundings be changed" – allow yourself to be transported back to the past and do not judge the past by the standards of the present.[11]

The great joy of all this hard work is that slowly one has a sense of the Christian tradition. Countless men and women in the past make up the Christian story. It eliminates any sense of being alone; one is part of a vast and rich tapestry of human life.

Denominational History: An Overview

Using the second of Daughrity's approaches, let us now look briefly at the history of the mainline that exists in the United States.

All five of the traditions that we are considering under the heading "mainline" are products of the Reformation. In one sense they are all traditions that broke away from the one unified European Church. It is worth noting that we should not identify the unified European Church with the Roman Catholic Church. The modern Roman Catholic Church is as much a result of the Reformation as the Protestant denominations. Although there appears to be continuity because the authority of the Bishop of Rome is affirmed by the Roman Catholic Church, there are many other elements (not least the attitude to political power) that the modern Roman Church shares with the other movements emerging from the Reformation. Naturally, even the unified European Church is itself a result of division because there was an earlier split from the Eastern Orthodox Churches.

The Reformation takes different forms in different places. Perhaps the best known Reformer is Martin Luther. Martin Luther was an Augustinian monk in Saxony, Germany. It was when he discovered that the Pope was authorizing the sale of indulgences to cover the cost of funding St. Peter's in Rome that he erupted. He took action, nailed 95 theses on his door, and was finally excommunicated by the Pope. This is the moment when the Lutheran tradition was born. Certain themes emerged in Luther's writing. He stressed the centrality of the grace in the work of salvation; our charity and payments for indulgences (i.e. works) were not the way. Instead it was the simple response to the work of God in Christ. "Justification by faith" was a key slogan. He translated the Bible into the vernacular. And as the printing presses were invented, a Bible translated into the German language suddenly had a major readership. A different way of being a European Christian had arrived.

In 1638, Lutherans from Sweden were looking for a place to practice their religious tradition and made their way to Wilmington, Delaware (it was then known as Fort Christina). These settlements attracted Finnish and German Lutherans, although the congregations formed were under the jurisdiction of the Church of Sweden. Austrian Lutherans made their way to Georgia in the early 1700s. The Salzburger Lutherans founded a community called Ebenezer, which by 1741 had 1200 people.

It is interesting that just across the English Channel from Europe was the English Tudor Crown. To start with, *King Henry VIII* was an opponent of Lutheran theology. He wrote a treatise defending seven sacraments against the views of Martin Luther. However, relations with the Pope changed as the issue of producing a male heir became apparent. Henry needed his marriage to Catherine of Aragon annulled. Rome refused to accede to the request. The result was the break with Rome and the English monarch becoming the Supreme Governor of the *Church of England* under the Act of Supremacy of 1534. From this political start, a distinctive Anglican ethos started to emerge. *Thomas Cranmer* (1489–1556) was a key person liturgically and wrote the *Book of Common Prayer*. The compromises that shaped the Elizabethan Religious Settlement created the sense of *Anglicanism* as the tradition located in-between Rome and Geneva.

As the English settled in the United States, so the Anglican tradition came with them. The first permanent colony in North America was Jamestown in 1607. Naturally, a tradition grounded in the English Church had problems after the Revolutionary War. It was in 1789, the American Prayer Book explains, "when in the course of Divine Providence, these American States became independent with respect to civil government, their ecclesiastical independence was necessarily included."[12] So the Protestant Episcopal Church was born. It had links with the Church of England, but there were significant differences. Decision-making resided with the General Convention, instead of a king or parliament. The first General Convention was held at Christ Church, Philadelphia, on September 27, 1785. So an Anglican Church developed in the United States, independent and yet linked through the ties of history and liturgy; this was the Episcopal Church.

It was not just the Roman Catholics who were unhappy with the emergence of distinctive Anglican tradition in England at the Reformation. At the other end of the spectrum were the Puritans; their goal was to "purify" the Church of Catholicism. They were influenced by John Calvin of Geneva. The Puritans triggered their own English civil war. They executed King Charles in 1649 and Oliver Cromwell governed as Lord Protector. Hope for a Puritan England died with the restoration of the monarchy in 1658.

Due to earlier persecution of Puritans, many made their way to America. It was in Plymouth, Massachusetts (1620) that the first Puritan colony was formed. Between 1630 and 1640, some 20 000 English Puritans settled in New England. This is the genesis of the Congregational Church, which later merged with other denominations (namely, the Reformed Church, the Christian Churches, and the Evangelical Synod) to form the United Church of Christ (UCC).

Back on the continent of Europe, John Calvin had been following the emergence of a Protestant theology very closely. He broke with the Roman Catholic Church in 1533. After a short period of imprisonment, he fled to Basel and started writing his famous *Institutes of the Christian Religion*; the first edition was published in 1536, which was the same time he moved to Geneva. It was *John Knox* (1514–1572) who took Calvin's ideas to Scotland; and it is from Scotland and Ireland that Presbyterians made their way to the United States.

The first Presbytery was founded in Philadelphia in 1706; 83 years later, Philadelphia hosted the first General Assembly of the Presbyterian Church in the United States of America (PCUSA). The "First Great Awakening" of *George Whitfield* (1714–1770) had a positive impact on the Presbyterian Church of America, especially for those groups settled in the north. Slowly, the distinctive emphasis on governance and recognition of the centrality of developing a biblical theology turned the Presbyterian Church into a significant part of the mainline.

Finally, John Wesley, a brilliant preacher, founded a movement in Oxford that slowly swept America. Wesley was an Anglican who was interested in encouraging renewal within the Church of England. Along with his brother Charles (an extraordinary and gifted poet and hymn writer), the Holy Club emerged in Oxford, which sought to deepen the prayer lives of those who belonged to and initially sought reform within the Church of England. John Wesley became a popular preacher reaching groups that were often neglected, for example tin miners in Cornwall. John Wesley made a trip to Georgia in 1735, which introduced him to the piety of the Moravians. Methodist congregations started developing in the 1760s. American Methodists left the Church of England, formally, in 1784 at the so-called Christmas Conference, which was held in Baltimore. This was partly a response to the position of the Church of England over the Revolutionary War, but it was also because, unlike the Anglicans, Methodists wanted traveling preachers, or circuit riders, who could reach out to the frontiers of America.

A key person in American Methodism was *Francis Asbury* (1745–1816). He was the first Methodist bishop who advocated for itinerate preachers who ideally were young and single. He did not want clergy who settled down, but clergy who were willing to travel. By the 1850s, the Methodist movement was the largest Protestant group in the United States; it founded many schools and universities. And it became the largest of the groups within the mainline.

This brief history of our five denominations that make up the subject of this book illustrates the different historical trajectories. Although the roots are all European, they took different strands of the European Reformation and created a distinctive set of traditions in the United States.

One issue they all had to reckon with was slavery, which was a crucial part of the distinctive ethos of these traditions in the United States. America needed cheap labor. Starting in 1619, significant numbers of Africans and Creoles (those of mixed descent) were captured and brought to the United States. It was a cruel and wicked trade. It was based on race; it made men and women legal chattel until they died; their children were bound to the white master for their lives; and brutal force could be used to maintain order. All of the mainline denominations were, at best, complicit in, at worse, supportive of the institution of slavery. And even after slavery was made illegal, legal segregation continued to shape America right up until the civil rights era of Martin Luther King Jr. As with the emancipation of slaves, the churches' role in civil rights was very mixed – some were supporters of civil rights, others hostile.

Listening to the past is important. Sometimes the present emerges out of the past: the genesis of a tradition can help us to understand the distinctive DNA of that tradition. The stress in the UCC on the autonomy of the local congregation, and the simplicity of the worship is grounded in its distinctive founding. The interest of the *Anglican Communion* (the worldwide membership of Anglicans who recognize the importance of the *Archbishop of Canterbury*) in the election of bishops in New Hampshire (where Bishop Gene Robinson – the first openly gay bishop in the Communion) is intelligible when you understand the history. The story of the past helps us to understand the present.

Sometimes the present is a reaction to the past. A good illustration of this is the affirmation across much of the mainline in support of gay and lesbian rights. The first decade of the twenty-first century in the United States has been a season where lesbian, gay, bisexual, transgender (LGBT) rights have been at the forefront of the culture wars. At the start of the twenty-first century, polls showed the majority of Americans did not feel that marriage could be extended to persons with a same-sex orientation. The evangelicals and the Roman Catholics were especially opposed. Although many in the mainline were conservative, among religious groups the mainline took the lead. One reason for this was that the mainline had been haunted by the way it came slowly to support the rights of African Americans. So in response the UCC, the Episcopal Church, the Lutherans, and the PCUSA have sought to be at the vanguard of gay and lesbian rights. The United Methodist Church has been slower, partly because of its strength in more conservative parts of the country, and the General Conferences of the United Methodist Church include international delegations from outside the United States, which tend to oppose the ordination of gay and lesbian clergy.

Different Narratives About the Past

Telling the story of the past has power. One important advantage that the secularist has is that our language of the past tends to denigrate the Christian tradition. So, for example, the term Enlightenment is used to describe the rise of science and affirmation of reason that emerged in the seventeenth century in Europe. So the "light is being turned on," it comes just after the *Renaissance* (a rebirth of ancient Greek architecture, practices, and literature – in the fourteenth to the sixteenth centuries), which comes just after the Middle Ages or even the Dark Ages. This is the language that favors modernity. A light is turned on as Europe escapes the clutches of the medieval Church.

The secular bias in terms of reading the past is embedded in our language and widely used by all historians. A self-congratulatory narrative of modernity triumphs in our labels for the different periods. When feminists suggest that the term "history" should be replaced by "herstory," they are making an important point. Our language makes certain assumptions, which includes a certain vantage point. Challenging this is important.

Applying History to the Congregation

History helps to illuminate the present in vitally important ways. The focus of this chapter has been on the macro-story of the Church. A congregational leader needs to know the story of Jesus, the emergence of the Jesus movement in the Church, the development of the Creeds, the conversion of Constantine, and the slow spread of Christianity around the globe. In addition, congregational leaders need to know the story of their own particular traditions. This will help illuminate the reasons why things are done in a particular way.

However, the need for a historical sensitivity is also a local need. A good congregational leader needs to learn the story of the particular congregation. It is amazing how congregations repeat certain patterns. So a congregation that has had clergy leadership that is abusive often ends up repeating the same mistake with a subsequent call. The identity of a congregation is embedded in the story that is told. Learning that story is an imperative.

Once one has the story of the past, one is able to start shaping that story. A good congregational leader needs to combine the macro-stories of Christianity and the denomination with the micro-story of the congregation. Leadership involves telling the strongest possible narrative of a congregation so that the identity of the congregation is clear. A congregation with a clear identity is more likely to endure and succeed. So, for example, a UCC congregation that has a strong history of inclusion, perhaps located in an urban setting, can combine the following: first, the stories of a Christ who ate with everyone; and second, the persecution of the initial settlers. The result is a congregation that is willing to be friendly to everyone. This grounds the congregation's own context and story in the context and story of Christian history, thereby making the identity of the congregation stronger. Every opportunity should be taken to link these themes together.

Differing Views of Church History

Church history is the record of God's gracious, wonderful and mighty deeds, showing how by his Spirit and Word he rules his Church and conquers the world.
Nils Forsander, *Life Pictures from Swedish Church History*[13]

Violent, irrational, intolerant, allied to racism and tribalism and bigotry, invested in ignorance and hostile to free inquiry, contemptuous of women and coercive toward children: organized religion ought to have a great deal on its conscience.
Christopher Hitchens, *God is Not Great: How Religion Poisons Everything*[14]

Forsander and Hitchens provide two different views of Church history. Who do you think is closer to the truth?

Conclusion

History is not optional. An understanding of the past is essential. A good training will not simply include content (the dates when this or that happened), but also the capacity to read and interpret history with some sensitivity.

It is important to be self-aware in the analysis and telling of the past. One needs to be sensitive to one's assumptions of what is normal. It is so tempting to judge the past by the standards of the present. But we need to be as kind to the past as we trust the future will be to us. So, for example, perhaps we are blind to animal rights; and perhaps the future will judge harshly those of us who are not committed vegetarians; but we hope this will not be the only criterion used to judge our lives. So we should be equally respectful to the past. *Thomas Aquinas* (1224–1274), the great Dominican Friar of the thirteenth century, made wicked assumptions about women and Islam, but he also formulated a remarkable, generous, and innovative theology for his time. It should not stop us recognizing his cultural blindness, but, at the same time, we must allow the past to be understood on its own terms.

History is fun. Over and over again, the past surprises us. There is no linear line from confused to enlightened. Innovation, brilliance, and quirky insights are all found in different places and at different times. Finally, we conclude this chapter where we started. Studying history is a theological task. One is detecting the work of God in history. The story of our collective human past is the remarkable story of God's relationship to us all. This is the most exciting part of being a historian.

Notes

1 Andrew Lloyd Webber, 'Superstar,' taken from *Jesus Christ Superstar*.

2 Andrew F. Walls, "Eusebius tries again", in Wilbert R. Shenk, ed., *Enlarging the Story: Perspectives on Writing World Christian History* (Maryknoll, NY: Orbis Books, 2002), 19.

3 Justo L. González, *The Changing Shape of Church History* (St. Louis, MO: The Chalice Press, 2002), 19.

4 Ibid., 23.

5 Ibid., 24.

6 Ibid., 25.

7 Ibid., 26

8 Dyron B. Daughrity, *Church History: Five Approaches to a Global Discipline* (New York: Peter Lang, 2012), 5.

9 Ibid., 84.

10 Rodney Stark, *The Triumph of Christianity* (New York: HarperCollins, 2011), 156–157.

11 Jean Comby, *How to Read Church History* (London: SCM Press, 1985), 7.

12 *Book of Common Prayer*, 1662, 7.

13 Nils Forsander, *Life Pictures from Swedish Church History* (Rock Island, IL: Augustana Book Concern, 1913).

14 Christopher Hitchens, *God is Not Great: How Religion Poisons Everything* (New York: Twelve, Hatchett Book Group, 2009).

Annotated Bibliography

Cameron, Euan, *Interpreting Christian History: The Challenge of the Churches' Past* (Malden, MA: Blackwell Publishing, 2005).

Cameron makes the important point that "the knowledge of Christian history is essential to anyone who wishes to understand the present-day Christian Churches, or to assume any position of leadership within them." He stresses the importance of interpretation and vantage points.

Coakley, John W. and Sterk, Andrea, eds, *Readings in World Christian History* (Maryknoll, NY: Orbis Books, 2004).

This is the best collection of primary sources – a very helpful resource.

Comby, Jean, *How to Read Church History* (London: SCM Press, Ltd, 1985).

A helpful introduction to some of the central challenges in studying Church history.

Daughrity, Dyron B., *Church History: Five Approaches to a Global Discipline* (New York: Peter Lang, 2012).

An excellent survey of five major approaches to the study of Church history. Daughrity illustrates how the same subject matter can be looked at in completely contrasting ways.

Gonzalez, Justo L., *Church History: An Essential Guide* (Nashville, TN: Abingdon Press, 1996).

This shorter introduction gives overviews of major periods of Church history with suggested reading for each.

Gonzalez, Justo L., *The Changing Shape of Church History* (St. Louis, MO: Chalice Press, 2002).
One of the most prolific writers; in this book Gonzalez makes the case that the new voices (women and scholars of color) are so important for a proper understanding of our past.

Gunneman, Louis H., *The Shaping of the United Church of Christ* (Cleveland, OH: United Church Press, 1999).
A solid survey of the history of the UCC.

Herring, George, *An Introduction to the History of Christianity* (New York: Continuum, 2006).
An interesting journey through the various periods of Christian history.

Littell, Franklin H., *Illustrated History of Christianity* (New York: Continuum, 2001).
Rightly acclaimed as both helpful and interesting. A good text to begin with.

MacCulloch, Diarmaid, *Christian History: An Introduction to the Western Tradition* (Werrington, Epworth Press, 1987).
Probably one of the greatest historians of our time. He writes in a clear and compelling way.

MacCulloch, Diarmaid, *Groundwork of Christian History* (London: Epworth Press, 1987).
Almost anything written by MacCulloch is worth reading.

MacCulloch, Diarmaid, *A History of Christianity* (London: Allen Lane, 2009).
Probably the best one-volume history.

Marty, Martin E, *Lutheran Questions, Lutheran Answers* (Minneapolis, MN: Augsburg Books, 2007).
A popular and gentle survey of the history of the Lutheran tradition.

Mullins, Robert Bruce, *A Short World History of Christianity* (Louisville, KY: WJK Press, 2008).
Makes the case that a story approach is better than an encyclopedic approach.

Prichard, Robert, *A History of the Episcopal Church*, third revised edition (New York: Morehouse Publishing, 2014).
Locates the emergence of the Episcopal Church in the wider trends of the United States.

Shenk, Wilbert R., ed., *Enlarging the Story: Perspectives on Writing World Christian History* (Maryknoll, NY: Orbis Books, 2002).
A good discussion of the changing nature of the Christian story.

8

Preaching the Word

> And Jesus said to them,
> "Go into all the world and preach the gospel
> to the whole creation."
> Mark 16:15 Revised Standard Version

The Purpose

From the very beginning, the proclamation of the Word has been a fundamental task of the Church and central to the life of the Christian community. Karl Barth famously reminds us that in proclaiming the Word of God, we are proclaiming Jesus Christ, the Word Made Flesh; we are proclaiming the Bible, the written words of Scripture; and we are proclaiming the preached word, giving words to the Word. It is the preached word and the sacraments that constitute the Church's proclamation.[1] It is through this proclamation that the fundamentals of the Christian faith are taught and that the truth of Scripture is held up to contemporary interpretation, experience, and understanding.

The goal and purpose of this proclamation is reconciliation, healing the breach that exists between God and us and healing the breach that exists among God's people. It is in the proclaimed Word that our narratives are intertwined with the biblical narrative and thus our story becomes grounded in God's story.

The Churches of the mainline hold that it is through both the Word and sacrament that God is present in the midst of the gathered community. The mainline also holds that the proclaimed Word exists not only for the gathered community but for the sake of the whole world; thus the task of preaching remains of vital importance.

An Introduction to Ministry: A Primer for Renewed Life and Leadership in Mainline Protestant Congregations, First Edition. Ian S. Markham and Oran E. Warder.
© 2016 John Wiley & Sons, Ltd. Published 2016 by John Wiley & Sons, Ltd.

The Problem

It was Lutheran Walter Burghhart who once said, "It is indeed true that, as in the story of Balaam (in Numbers 22), the Lord can speak through the mouth of an ass, through the dullest and most plodding of preachers. But this is not an ideal, just a fact."[2] Robert Farrar Capon, perhaps rather more charitably, makes the same point when he writes:

> Great *sermons* will always be in short supply. Even in the case of the first-rate preachers, the church occasionally has to settle for third-rate performances. And in the case of second-rate preachers … well, let's just say that there are more of them than any kind. That's not a criticism. It's one of the facts of church life. I'd only make matters worse if I tried to change the situation by making preachers feel guilty about it. It's that way in every occupation. The world's supply of top-notch saxophonists is miniscule compared with the armies of honkers who live down the street from you – and the same thing goes for you … as a preacher.[3]

Every generation in the Church has produced exemplary preachers and yet there has never been a golden age of preaching. On the contrary, every generation seems to bemoan the demise of preaching. Our current age is no exception. Most modern critics point to two main areas of concern. The first is an eroding sense of theological sophistication and the second is the overwhelming (and detrimental) influence of larger cultural movements.

In terms of the decline of theological understanding, it is no longer assumed that members of mainline congregations know the traditions of their respective denominations. Nor is it assumed that members possess an even rudimentary understanding of the fundamentals of the Christian faith.[4] The blame for this is often leveled directly at preachers.

Additionally, in this fast paced, multi-media, information age, the cultural ground is shifting beneath our feet. Consumerism (the notion of church shopping), radical individualism (viewing belief as an entirely personal matter), the move toward simplicity in all things (easy solutions, easy answers, the simpler the faith the better), the tendency to be suspicious of concepts and abstractions (the increasing inability to create an image in one's mind), and the death of tradition (the triumph of the new over the old), all contribute to the challenge of preaching in the current age. Add to this the radical secularization of culture (the absence of transcendence), the emergence of a new spirituality (a revolt against secularism yet often thin on theological substance), and the idea of *postmodernism* (a new age response that challenges the modern concepts of reason and science as overarching narratives) and the task is even more difficult still.[5]

The result of these forces, along with the competing pressures for preachers to manage, pastor, fund, and grow congregations, is preaching that can be more geared toward shortened attention spans and with less theological depth. The heart of the problem, as defined by Michael Pasquarello is that the study of preaching has become the study of the mastery of skills and techniques for effective communication rather than the practice of being "mastered" by the Word of God.[6]

This chapter seeks to take seriously the current realities that define and shape the Church and challenge the mainline preacher of today. What follows starts by touching on the history of the craft, which is located in the fundamental connection between sound and word. We then move to the preaching event, before examining a fundamental divide in preaching between those who see it as a task from above and those who see it coming from below. The rest of the chapter deals with practicalities: length, narrative, humor, and preaching to children. The purpose of this broad overview of the preaching task is to link Scripture with the challenge of reinterpretation and communication in the modern generation. The goal is not to create virtuoso performances but to promote the faithful, week-to-week, Sunday-to-Sunday, proclamation of the Word that will feed, nourish, and strengthen the people of God.

Reuniting the Word and Sound: The History of a Craft

The Gospels emerged in an oral culture. In the midst of the assembly, God's Word was spoken and God's voice was heard speaking in the present. Stories of Jesus were told, and the telling of these stories and sayings constitute preaching. Yet almost from the start there began the shift away from sound to the page. Collections of the sayings and stories of Jesus were gathered into a new literary genre, the Gospel. The apostle Paul wrote sermons in the form of letters, or epistles, which are radically different from the Gospels of the Jerusalem Church in that they are not narratives of Jesus but rather centered on conceptual arguments (influenced by classical rhetoric). If Paul knew the stories of the life and ministry of Jesus, with the exception of the crucifixion and resurrection, he did not incorporate them into his proclamation. In the succeeding generations, the shift from oral proclamation to the written word continued. With the invention of the printing press, the sound all but died away.[7]

In the ancient world, reading and sound went together. Augustine was said to have been astounded and utterly disappointed when he first visited *Ambrose* (ca. 337–397 CE) in his study. Augustine expected to overhear the great scholar reading from a sacred text. What he found was Ambrose reading, but doing so without making a sound. For ancient people a word was not a marking on a page, but a sound uttered (literally *outtered*).[8] This has relevance to our discussion as a reminder that the ancient Scriptures existed primarily as sound.

One of the tasks of the preacher is to rediscover the connection between word and sound, to differentiate between the spoken word and the written word, and to remember that the sermon is prepared for the ear and not for the eye. Thomas Long writes that "a 'written sermon' is a contradiction in terms," a sermon occurs not in the writing but in the preaching.[9] The work of the preacher is to lift the words off the page, to give oral testimony to an ongoing and lively conversation happening between the preacher, the Scripture and tradition of the Church, and the gathered community. Episcopalian Robert Farrar Capon suggests that in preparing a sermon the preacher must learn to trust his or her *talking mind* and *listening ear*. His advice is to learn the sound of one's ordinary talking voice and then ruthlessly remove anything in the sermon that does not match that same sound.[10] This, of course, takes practice and persistence, yet, at the very least, rehearsing a sermon out loud allows the preacher to hear how the sermon sounds and not simply how it reads.

Barbara Brown Taylor on Preaching (from *The Preaching Life*)

Watching a preacher climb into the pulpit is a lot like watching a tightrope walker climb onto the platform as the drum roll begins. The first clears her throat and spreads out her notes: the second loosens his shoulders and stretches out one rosin-soled foot to test the taut rope. They both step out into the air, trusting everything they have done to prepare for this moment as they surrender themselves to it, counting now on something beyond themselves to help them do what they love and fear and most want to do. If they reach the other side without falling, it is skill but it is also grace – a benevolent God's decision to let these daredevils treat the high places where ordinary mortals have the good sense not to go.[11]

The Preaching Event

If sermons are the proclamation of the spoken Word of God in the midst of the congregation and not simply words on a page, then the preaching event takes on a sacramental function. Somehow, in the process of proclamation, God is present.

Thomas Long, a Methodist, describes this phenomenon as a coming together of the congregation (the worshipping assembly), the preacher (who is intimately part of the congregation he stands before), the sermon (the action of preaching), and the presence of Christ (God's promise when we gather in his name). He is careful to note that Christ is present in this sacramental moment not because we preach, rather we preach because Christ is present.[12]

In examining the preaching event and its sacramental nature it is crucial to acknowledge the Bible as the primary source for proclamation, and secondly, it is crucial to note the context as the primary source for the interpretation of Scripture.

The Bible and Proclamation

Augustine wrote what is arguably the first textbook on *homiletics*. His book, *On Christian Doctrine*, was conceived as a resource for proclamation. It is worth noting that this work is essentially a manual for biblical interpretation.[13] For mainline Churches, the Bible remains the primary source and the norm for proclamation. This may seem obvious, but it is an assumption that warrants further exploration in the next section. For now, we make the point that part of the preaching event includes the proclamation of the Word of God received in Holy Scripture.

Context and Interpretation

Sermons are written in specific places, for a specific people, at a specific time. Like the original authors of Scripture, the preacher must engage in the task of *hermeneutics*, that is, the process of interpreting the received tradition and applying it to a contemporary situation and setting.[14] Thus knowing and understanding the context, the place and people, in which the preaching event happens is vital. There is a direct correlation between good preaching and preachers who pay attention to, listen to, know, and understand the community in which they are called to preach. Rowan Williams, the previous Archbishop of Canterbury in the Anglican Church, believes that good sermons arise when the preacher engages in twofold listening: listening to the tradition, and listening to the present. In this action, the preacher is thus listening "to and for God so that something emerges almost begging to be put into words."[15] Thus another part of the preaching event includes taking seriously the context in which the sermon is preached.

In spite of the fact that these two elements are inextricably connected, there is some conflict that exists over which is more important. It is a kind of "chicken and egg" discussion that boils down to a question of priority. Where does a preacher begin? Put rather crudely, does the preacher start with the Bible and find ways to apply the text to the community (preach from above)? Or does the preacher start with the community and find a text that addresses community needs (preach from below)?

Preaching from Above

An extreme understanding of this perspective is that it is the preacher's task to *exegete* Scripture, understand the Church's *doctrine*, and embody the Church's traditions in such a way as to find a transcendent, global message. The task is simply to get the message straight and then speak it plainly.[16] The context in this instance is irrelevant. The sermon could be preached anytime, anywhere, to any group of people.

A more nuanced approach might be the example of Karl Barth, who definitely believed that the sermon emerged from Scripture with the expressed purpose to teach Christian doctrine, but in a manner that sought application in contemporary human experience.[17] To clarify, when we speak of doctrine, we refer to the discrete and distinct theological themes that find their source in Scripture and not to the Church's absolute formulations of faith.

Addressing the decline in the theological sophistication of Church members, there is a call for the renewal of doctrinal preaching, teaching sermons that cover the core curriculum of basic Christianity. The goal is essentially the translation of the tradition into a framework that is accessible and understandable. Starting *from above*, the hope is to connect hearers to the biblical narrative, the traditions of the Church, and Christian doctrine in such a way that helps make sense of ordinary experience and offers meaning and purpose to daily life.[18] This perspective seeks to offer a biblical and doctrinal framework to human experience.

Preaching from Below

An extreme understanding of this perspective holds that the sermon is not determined by any text but rather is determined solely by the needs of those in the pew. The sermon exists only to serve the religious needs of the people. The lives of the people are the sacred text at the heart of the proclamation.[19] Therefore the preacher is free to draw on many sources of inspiration insofar as they address the needs of the worshipping community.

A more nuanced approach might be the example of Harry Emerson Fosdick, a Baptist pastor who saw preaching as pastoral counseling. The preacher's job is to be aware of the personal concerns of those in the congregation and seek to respond to those concerns. He describes a good sermon as an "engineering operation" whereby a chasm is bridged. On one side of the chasm are the lives of the hearers, and on the other side are the spiritual gifts that come from the "unsearchable riches of Christ". The goal is to transport those riches from one side to the other.[20]

Another noteworthy example of this perspective is the late televangelist Robert H. Schuller, a minister in the Reformed tradition, who believed that the most important question facing the Church is, "What are the deepest needs felt by human beings?"[21] This is the starting point for the preacher and is precisely where he believed the Church needed to be reformed. He argued that *preaching from above*, that is, imposing a theocentric model, is doomed to fail, particularly when addressing the unchurched. Rather, he believed that the goal is to strive to communicate spiritual reality to those not yet ready to believe, in a way that is respectful and based on a human needs approach and not a theological attack. For Schuller, Church decline is a direct result of the failure to address the emotional and spiritual needs of people. He writes rather emphatically that, "We have been a church first and a mission second. ... So the church must be willing to die as a church and be born as a mission."[22] This perspective seeks to take seriously the deepest needs of the people and address them in a manner that connects, in varying degrees, to the biblical and doctrinal witness and the traditions of the Church.

The conflict that exists between these perspectives is not a contemporary phenomenon. Martin Luther, a clear proponent of biblical and doctrinal preaching, was concerned about the quality and content of the sermons heard in churches of his day. To remedy the situation he produced several books of sermons that could be read to congregations. Otherwise, Luther reasoned that many clergy were not talented public speakers or properly trained, and left to their own devices "the final result would be that everyone preaches his [her] own whims and instead of the gospel and its exposition, we shall again have sermons on blue ducks."[23] Critics, of course, would likely agree that sermons should not be based on the personal whim of the preacher, but on matters that address the deepest desires and real needs of the people, they might well advocate for a sermon on blue ducks.

Form, Structure, and Style

Practically every human enterprise is embedded with structure or form in some variety. This is particularly true of preaching. Often unnoticed, yet critically important, structure and form allow listeners to organize what they are hearing, select where they might focus attention, as well as engage in their own reflection and personal interpretation.

Old preaching manuals provided prescribed structures and forms for sermon preparation. The emphasis was on a certain type of preaching style as being most effective. It appears that it was not until medieval times that sermon form and structure became self-conscious. Thus for the first time a disciplined approach to preaching emerged. The style followed a predictable pattern and outline:

1. the sermon began with a quotation from Scripture;
2. the theme for the sermon was stated;

3. a prayer was offered, and this was followed by;
4. an introduction that included a restatement of the sermon theme;
5. the division (argument) that often included word play and rhyming words;
6. and then a three-point "subdivision."

This perhaps is the precursor to the classic three-point sermon that has been passed on to the modern day. Along with providing structure and form to sermons, it also offered a means for evaluation. Sermons were judged rather objectively against the standard pattern: unity of focus and theme, manner of division, and proof of argument.[24]

Sermon forms and structures, though often transparent, have their own implicit power. Thomas Long even more emphatically states that the sermon's power is in its "structure not its decoration."[25] The current thinking is that there is not an ideal form to be mastered and imitated, but rather the emphasis is on cultivating a variety of forms in order to hold interest and attention, and perhaps even surprise and delight.

There are many sermon models that have been developed, each with many variations. The traditional linear approach in many ways follows the form of the medieval style discussed above. The sermon's structure is basically an outline, complete with headings, points and sub-points, each supporting a stated proposition. Other styles are usually either deductive or inductive in approach. A deductive sermon moves from the presentation of a general truth to the application or illustration of that truth. With this approach there is no ambiguity or discovery. Listeners are given a map and know the destination before setting out. Critics would describe this approach as static and rigid. By way of contrast, an inductive approach moves from the particulars of experience to a general truth. So rather than being told in the introduction what the sermon is about, the listeners are invited on a step-by-step journey that leads to a place of discovery.[26]

One particular sermon form that bridges both approaches is United Church of Canada professor of homiletics Paul Scott Wilson's "Four-Page" system of sermon preparation. His basic idea is that the sermon consists of four pages: the first page highlights trouble in the biblical text, the second page highlights trouble in the world, the third page highlights grace in the biblical text, and the fourth page highlights grace in the world.[27] Worth noting is the flexibility inherent in this system. The pages can be arranged in a linear and deductive manner with the framework quite clear, or the pages can be rearranged in a more organic and random fashion with the framework emerging as the sermon is developed.

Whether experimenting with a variety of styles or developing one's own, attention to structure and form is key. The underlying rule is that sermon structures need to reflect the process of thought, follow an ordered process, embody movement from one point to the next, and have a clear beginning, middle, and end.

Embodying the Word

Thomas Troeger, a Yale professor who is a member of both the Presbyterian and Episcopalian denominations, once described homiletics as "theology processed through the body."[28] There is a growing body of homiletical literature devoted to the subject of embodied preaching. Seen often as simply a cerebral and intellectual exercise, this area of study seeks to enliven the preaching task by integrating movement and sensory experience to the preparation and delivery of sermons. Words and concepts appeal to the mind but sometimes we need more than words to convey meaning and understanding. Our lives are filled with rhythms and movement, the biblical narrative is filled with rhythms and movement, and yet if our worship experience is not grounded with rhythm and movement, our words can be empty and our ability to embody the Gospel in the world is diminished.[29]

The art of homiletics therefore needs to comprehend the notion that preaching is a whole body endeavor. In theological terms, embodied preaching is nothing less than a demonstration of the Holy Spirit. It is the Spirit, that cannot be contained or restrained, that animates the preacher.[30] More broadly speaking, by the Spirit's power, the Gospel is not only embodied in the preacher but also in the whole people of God.

In her book *Transforming Preaching*, Episcopal priest and professor of homiletics at Virginia Theological Seminary, Ruthanna Hooke, offers a useful resource for those looking for practical ways to engage with this topic. Utilizing methods to free the voice for proclamation, incorporating yoga to free the breath and body for fuller expression, the goal is to work toward the integration of the mind, body, and spirit.[31]

A related topic, in terms of a multi-sensory approach to homiletics, is the increased use of audiovisuals in preaching. Many mainline congregations are experimenting with, or have gone completely to, paperless worship services that incorporate PowerPoint slides, music, and movie clips into the sermon itself. Modern humans are becoming increasingly visual, so images and stories have great impact on the imagination and have power to shape consciousness.[32] Some argue that in the postmodern era, indirect forms of communication will become the primary grounds for theological discourse. Imagery, including story, facilitates theological insight.[33] At the very least knowing that people engage and respond to different learning modes, and striving to offer such variety can be quite powerful and effective in the life of a congregation. Yet, care must be taken that the presentation does not overpower the message and that the focus remains on proclamation.

How Long, O Lord, How Long?

Martin Luther once advised, "When you see your hearers most attentive, there conclude."[34] Perhaps his thinking was that a good sermon really does not end but rather continues on in the hearts and minds of the hearer. Perhaps the sermon evokes an emotional response or elicits some call to action, or ignites some combination of both. At the very least, the sermon may offer a challenge, a new perspective, or an invitation that warrants further reflection. As a general rule, it is best to conclude even while listeners are fully engaged, rather than waning with diminishing attention. If a sermon does follow some basic structure, form, and flow, then it will be readily apparent to hearers when a sermon has reached its conclusion. One only hopes that the preacher realizes this as well.

There is much debate about the ideal length of a sermon. In the mainline there remains a wide spectrum of opinion and practice. Some subscribe to the phrase attributed to either Mark Twain or John Wesley, "no souls are saved after the first ten minutes" of the sermon; for others, the first 10 minutes are simply the warm up. While rarely is there heard a complaint that a sermon was too short, there is often comment that perhaps the preacher went on too long. Consistently finding the right balance is a challenge.

In reality there are several issues at play. The first is the expectations of the congregation. Even within denominational norms there are local norms, with every congregation exhibiting its own culture around preaching. This culture is molded by past experience and the role of preaching within that particular liturgical context. The sermon might well be viewed as the "main event" of the service whose emphasis might be on the proclaimed Word, or the sermon could be seen as one liturgical component among others that constitute the worship experience. Nevertheless, it is critical that the preacher know the norms, culture, and expectations of the congregation. To ignore them is unwise. This is not to say that the culture cannot be changed, but must be altered with a good measure of care and caution.

Illustrations, Narrative, and the Use of Humor

The use of illustrations, narrative, and humor is not a modern homiletical invention. Jesus expertly employed all three devices in his own preaching and teaching. The popularity of these rhetorical tools has waxed and waned throughout the history of preaching, yet it is clear that medieval monks clearly accepted that part of the preaching task was to utilize illustrations and stories and also seemed to readily accept that entertainment was also part of their role and responsibility.[35]

The use of illustrations in preaching is literally intended to shed light on, that is, to bring, deeper understanding. For many, the illustrations are the lifeblood of sermons. The most important note about the use of illustrations is that they are congruent with the overall content of the sermon, and not a disconnected addition. The illustration should not merely help make the point of the sermon but actually be the point of the sermon. The continual issue for preachers is first, where to find good sermon illustrations, and second, how to file them so that they are readily available when needed.

The best source of sermon illustrations is the preacher's life itself and the development of an eye and ear for potential illustrations that will either connect to the biblical narrative or speak directly to the life of a congregation. Reading and listening widely and paying attention to what is happening in the world will provide a constant stream of sermon resources. Consulting the ecclesiastical calendar (the liturgical seasons and special days), the secular calendar (engagement with the wider culture), and the congregational calendar (major anniversaries, special recognitions, and days that highlight a particular emphasis or program) all are potential sources for sermon illustration. Ministry experience is also a rich source for illustration, particularly in addressing common pastoral issues. It is imperative however that the preacher exercise great care and caution with regard to confidentiality and appropriateness. While it may be true that a preacher's life and faith experience is rife with sermon possibilities, and it is important to notice such possibilities, it is also good advice not to view every life event and experience as a potential sermon illustration.

Organizing, storing, and retrieving sermon illustrations present their own set of issues. Some illustrations might be of the nature to have a very short shelf life, while others are more timeless. The temptation with the former is simply to make the sermon fit the illustration rather than the other way around, which is, of course, a temptation that is best to be avoided.

The systems that many preachers have devised to catalogue sermon illustrations range from the less scientific "shoebox" method, to the more elaborate filing systems arranged by Bible verses or major biblical themes. Modern computer systems have made the task a bit easier in that a digital search can screen for different criteria, including key words or phrases, as well as a particular passage or theme. And yet, at the same time, internet research capabilities have also complicated the task in the sense that it is easy to be overwhelmed by too many possibilities. The best advice perhaps is for the preacher to trust his or her own experience in the process of identifying and applying illustration from a variety of sources.

A particular form of illustration that deserves specific attention is the use of narrative. Without question, Jesus sets the standard in exhibiting both the use and power of story in teaching and preaching. Jesus clearly understood that we are a people of story, that our lives are structured through story, and that the various threads and fragments of our human experience are most often stitched together through story. In preaching, the power of narrative rests on the artistic expression and storytelling abilities of the preacher, and also on the story's ability to become a shared story with those who are hearing it. The use of narrative emphasizes the experiential nature of faith and is effective only if the content somehow connects with the experience of the listeners. The same cautions apply to narrative as they do generally to the use of illustrations. If a story is told simply for the story's sake and remains disconnected to the biblical narrative, the power is lost. Critics of narrative preaching complain that, taken to the extreme, preachers risk giving up solid exposition and rational argument for pulpit drama and storytelling.[36]

An ongoing debate within the field of homiletics that is directly related to the use of narrative is whether or not personal narrative has a place in pulpit. Some argue that the preacher should never appear in the sermon, and others argue that the preacher must always appear, given that the preached word is an embodied word and therefore must be proclaimed through the personality and life experience of the preacher. As in previous discussions of such homiletical conflicts, the issue is really a matter of degree. The consensus appears to be moving toward the acceptance of self-disclosure and self-revelation, but not without caution and clarification. While personal stories can provide a point of connection with listeners and add a sense of liveliness to the sermon, there is also the risk of the preacher becoming the focus of the sermon and the message getting lost. This is self-indulgence and not self-disclosure. Yet the sharing of personal story can be powerful if used discreetly and selectively. To do so, be clear about the purpose of the story – why should it be told? And also be clear about appropriate personal boundaries: don't embarrass family members, don't break confidences, don't be portrayed as a hero, and don't use the pulpit as a confessional. But having said this, listeners will, no doubt, connect to a preacher who is not a model of perfection, who shares similar struggles, and who is a fellow companion on the journey of faith.

If narrative is a form of illustration that warrants attention, and if personal narrative deserves particular examination, then the same special consideration must also be given to the use of humor in preaching. Like other considerations there are opposing views, those who see preaching as weighty and serious with no room for humor, and those who make room for a lighter and less serious approach. The use of humor is a complex issue and raises again the importance of understanding the norms, customs, and culture of the preaching context. Yet, even in congregations where the use of humor is normative, it is important to know where the limits are and abide by them. The same rules apply regarding illustrations in general, if a joke is not connected to the message in a direct and meaningful way, it is best not to use it. If a joke appears to be near the edge of acceptability and appropriateness, it is likely unacceptable and inappropriate. Do remember that the standard of good taste is higher for the preacher than for the general public. And lastly, remember that the only person who it is acceptable to make fun of in a preaching context is the preacher.

The Conversation Sermon

There are some mainline congregations that are starting to want sermons in a very different form. One of the most popular is the conversation sermon. This is where two people will stage a thoughtful discussion about the biblical texts. One might ask questions and the other reply; one might take a particular interpretation which the other will challenge; one might articulate the hidden thoughts of those listening ("did this really happen") and the other will engage with those thoughts. Historically, the traditional sermon was important because of the low literacy rates. But in our modern society, where almost everyone has at least a high school diploma, a more conversational sermon might be the way to go.

The Children's Sermon

Generally speaking, the churches of the mainline understand and acknowledge that participation in worship is our primary resource for education and formation. Being present in the midst of the worshipping community on a regular basis has the potential to shape and form participants in innumerable ways. If this is true for adults, it is especially true for children. Children do learn by participation, and finding the right and appropriate level of participation is something that requires careful deliberation. The end result is that some congregations have completely separate worship services for children with an age appropriate sermon, while others insist that all of the congregation worships together with a family sermon designed to reach a broad spectrum of ages. Others offer some variation between these two extremes with the children being invited to either come forward for a children's sermon or being invited to another location for a sermon of their own. In reaction to the latter, a cartoon once showed a child standing in the pulpit making an announcement: "At this time I would like for the children to remain seated in the nave and I invite all of the adults to go now to the basement for the sermon." Our purpose is not to advocate a best practice, but to acknowledge the variation of practices and address the unique issues related to preaching to children.

As mentioned, there are those who believe that both adults and children can be reached in the *real* sermon. The challenging preaching genre of the family sermon seeks to be child-friendly and also to offer sound adult proclamation. The characteristics of this method of preaching include the explicit recognition that children are present and offering them something of their own within the context of the sermon. The use of illustrations and stories provides the ability to catch a child's attention even if they do not understand the whole. Stories in particular allow listeners to engage at various levels of depth and understanding.[37]

There is also the sermon that is explicitly for children, recognizing the fact that children have their own concerns that need be addressed. It is important to also be aware that children do not come to the preaching event as blank slates but have thoughts and ideas about God and religion and have already come to some conclusions. The children's sermon must, therefore, strive not only to approach children at their level of understanding, but also to respect that they have already embarked on a spiritual journey of their own. The sermon is more than simply a lesson to be taught, but also seeks to invoke active engagement and personal involvement.[38]

Given that a children's sermon requires the same kind of thought and preparation that goes into any other sermon, there are also some specific things to keep in mind. Children's sermons are not theological essays and, rather than having multiple elements, would do well to have one clearly articulated point. For the same reasons as stated above, fully embodied, well-told (not read) stories are highly effective. This certainly includes the telling of Bible stories bearing in mind that not all stories from the Bible are meant for children. Conventional wisdom is not to add a moral to the story, but that stories should contain something important and also be entertaining.[39] Stories told in children's sermons should also be *true* in some sense of the word. This is an issue of credibility and trust. "Children have every right to expect that the church is a place where they will not be deceived."[40]

Without talking down to children, the language of the sermon should be kept simple. This does not mean, however, that children cannot grasp deep meaning. Use of analogy (using something that is easily understood to explain something that is not so easily understood) is one of the best ways that children learn. Object sermons and the use of props enjoy a long history in this homiletical realm. Tangible objects help children think concretely, but can also be confusing if connections are not explicit.[41]

In terms of delivery, a conversational style, as opposed to a monologue, seems best. Engaging in eye contact and conveying warmth, openness, and positive energy is key. In addition, it is also crucial to pay attention to non-verbal cues. Children are particularly adept at recognizing inconsistencies between the spoken word that says one thing, and body language that conveys another.

The Socratic method of asking carefully worded questions is also a popular model. Careful wording is key, given the ample opportunity for surprises and digressions, and the inevitable barrage of answers that might come from a question that is perhaps too open-ended (What costume are you wearing for Halloween?). Even then, however, it is imperative for the preacher to continue to model respect by taking the children seriously and by accepting, and not immediately dismissing, the responses that are offered. There are also the unavoidable interruptions that will occur, that may or may not be relevant to the message of the sermon. Accept them with grace, coach the congregation to respond appropriately, acknowledge the interruption before moving on, and if possible, try to ignore the waving hand at least until after the point of the sermon is made. If the congregation laughs at an innocent comment, the preacher may need to interpret the laughter to the child so that the reaction is understood and the child is not embarrassed.[42]

Hard Texts and Controversial Subjects

In much of the mainline, the Sunday scriptures are provided by a common *lectionary*. While most mainline preachers are not required to follow these prescribed texts, particularly if responding to a specific issue or need of the congregation, most see this intentional 3-year cycle of readings as a gift. Not only does the lectionary provide a broad ecumenical connection between mainline churches, but it also challenges preachers to engage difficult texts that might otherwise never be selected for consideration. The use of the lectionary also offers the opportunity to gain a wider theological perspective by being in conversation with Scripture that spans the breadth of the biblical record: the Hebrew Scriptures, the Psalms, the New Testament Epistles, and the Gospels. There are times when common themes are apparent, there are times when serial readings build from week to week, and there are times when the readings speak directly to a specific feast day or Church season. While broadly embraced and appreciated, the lectionary also has its detractors. Critics usually complain that the system is too confining, or that the editing of certain passages reflects a bias of one sort or another. Still most all agree that even with its imperfections, a common lectionary is a great blessing.

When in conversation with the weekly cycle of readings, the preacher is free to discern whether or not to engage a difficult text that arises. If the preacher finds a particular passage uncomfortable or particularly interesting, chances are that the congregation may as well. In that case, further exploration might well be in order.

In addition to difficult texts, there are also difficult topics that confront the mainline preacher. While most mainline congregations would resist a constant diet of sermons focused on current social, economic, or political issues, they might well also resist the complete absence of them. Again, finding balance and proportion is key. Preaching too often on controversial subjects risks deafening the ears of the congregation, while avoiding controversial subjects altogether risks suggesting that the Christian faith is irrelevant and has nothing to offer to the conversation.

When engaging a controversial subject in a sermon, it is important to try to ground the concern theologically, do your best to provide accurate information, be respectful and acknowledge that there are other opinions, find ways to engage the congregation in dialogue apart from the sermon, and keep things in the proper perspective.[43] It is important that the message is sound or really seeks to be the Word of God at that time. Speak with truth as best you know it, speak with love born out of a common relationship, and always speak of hope. Despair is never an appropriate response for the people of God.

But what if there is no good news to be found in a difficult passage or when addressing a controversial subject? Augustine again comes to our aid. He advises that it is important for the preacher to keep studying the Scripture until we have found something that contributes to the law of love and the primacy of God's grace. Yet, if all else fails, and nothing is found, then we are free to invoke the *resurrection hermeneutic*.[44] That is, we can be assured of the fact that the narrative of salvation is at the center of Scripture and is embedded in every text. The cross and resurrection have changed everything. All of creation, and all of the Bible, can be interpreted through the lens of new and unending life.

Common Threads

Feeling a bit under the weather one Sunday morning, a wife once insisted that her husband go on to church without her. Feeling much better when he returned at midday, she was anxious to hear about the service. "What was the preacher's sermon about this morning?" She asked. After pausing to think for a moment he replied, "I don't know, he never really said."

In this chapter we have looked at the preaching task from various perspectives. We do not presume to advance one style or method of preaching over another, nor do we wish to offer techniques for imitation. What we do advocate and what we do encourage is the development of one's own style and method that emphasizes the skills that come naturally, that offers the challenge of continued growth, and that is exercised in a manner that fosters flexibility and variety (which can be the *spice of life* for the congregation as well as the preacher). Whether preaching is done from the pulpit or the center aisle, with a full manuscript, simply an outline, or with no notes at all, each style of preaching can be completely effective, each has its own strengths and weaknesses, and there is a great preacher somewhere who utilizes that very method. The purpose of this section is to look for common threads amid the wide range of homiletic expression.

Regardless of sermon type, unity of theme is of great importance. The ability to articulate the very heart and essence of a sermon in one sentence is a useful discipline. This carefully crafted theme, stated several ways in the body of the text, will leave no doubt as to the content and aim of the sermon. While every preacher will develop his or her own strategy and habits of preparation, and each will develop his or her own weekly rhythms and routines, we strongly advise that one of those habits be the building of the sermon around one, unified, clearly stated theme.

We believe that the difference between a good sermon and a great sermon is not necessarily what was included in the delivery, but what was excluded in the preparation. Revise. Revise. Revise. Edit. Edit. Edit. Delete. Delete. Delete. "God does not do for preachers what they can do for themselves."[45] Continue to refine the sermon with an ear toward how the sermon sounds. The sermon is not the presentation of a written essay but a spoken encounter with the living Word of God. Practice. Practice. Practice. Say it out loud. Listen to the words. Visualize the sermon. Imagine yourself preaching it and imagine the congregation hearing it. Look for rough places, be mindful of transitions, and pay attention to grammar and word choice. Keep refining. The sermon is not over until it is preached.

It is a gift to know which method of preaching works best for you and best serves the hearers within the congregation. Part of determining that method requires the discernment of the preacher's most authentic self, so that the person inside the pulpit matches the person outside the pulpit. This involves being conscious of one's conversational voice quality and tone and then matching that tone with natural gestures and expressions. It involves a sense of humility as well as a sense of humor. It involves taking preaching more seriously and ourselves less seriously. It involves self-awareness as well as self-forgetfulness. Many in the field of homiletics speak of the preacher's need to be transparent, that is, to remove oneself and get out of God's way. Ruthanna Hooke reminds us that this is not helpful advice for preachers. In the first place it is impossible, and second, it is not sufficiently incarnational.

The preacher is not alone in the pulpit: his or her presence offers a quality of presence that is beyond words.[46] We are best as preachers when we are our best and most authentic selves. Tom Long puts it simply and well, "no words have more credibility that those of a truthful preacher."[47]

Another common thread is passion. Preachers are to say what they believe and believe what they say. Embodying the Word, indeed incarnating the Word, requires not simply empathy toward the text, but the engagement of personal feeling and emotion. What genuinely comes from the heart and mind of the preacher will genuinely go to the heart and mind of the listener. Preaching with passion communicates more than words on a page; it communicates the living Word of the living God, who is present in the midst of a living people.

It is also good advice that once the sermon is preached, let it go. Remember that in the mainline the sermon is part of the whole of the service of worship and not its entirety. Remember that everything does not rest on one sermon. Remember that listeners wander in and out of even the best of sermons and connect in different places and at different levels and are moved in any number of ways. So much of what happens in the preaching event is a glorious mystery and, in the end, is best entrusted to God.

In closing, perhaps the common threads of good preaching are most beautifully and best described by Episcopalian author and priest Barbara Brown Taylor: "Genuineness in presentation, clarity of thought, appropriate humor, faithfulness to the biblical text, attention to the sacred dimensions of everyday life and imaginative language."[48]

The preaching life ultimately involves the offering of one's personal faith for the sake of the faith of others. The sermon is ultimately God communicating not only in words, but also in and through preachers created in God's own image.

Notes

1   Richard Lischer, *Theories of Preaching: Selected Readings in the Homiletical Tradition* (Durham, NC: The Labyrinth Press, 1987), 338.

2   John S. McClure, ed., *Best Advice for Preaching* (Minneapolis, MN: Augsburg Fortress Press, 1998), 14.

3   Robert Farrar Capon, *The Foolishness of Preaching: Proclaiming the Gospel Against the Wisdom of the World* (Grand Rapids, MI and Cambridge: Eerdmans Publishing Co., 1998), 55.

4   Robert G. Hughes and Robert Kysar, *Preaching Doctrine: For the Twenty-First Century* (Minneapolis, MN: Augsburg Fortress, 1997), 1.

5   Ibid., 3–10.

6   Michael Pasquarello, III, *Sacred Rhetoric: Preaching as a Theological and Pastoral Practice of the Church* (Grand Rapids, MI and Cambridge: Eerdmans Publishing Co., 2005), 135.

7   Paul Scott Wilson, *A Concise History of Preaching* (Nashville, TN: Abington Press, 1992), 9–25.

8   Ibid., 18.

9   Thomas G. Long, *The Witness of Preaching, Second edition* (Louisville, KY: Westminster John Knox Press, 2005), 225.

10   Capon, *Foolishness of Preaching*, 129.

11   Barbara Brown Taylor, *The Preaching Life* (Lanham, MD: Rowman and Littlefield, 1993), 76.

12   Long, *Witness of Preaching*, 15–18.

13   Lischer, *Theories of Preaching*, 137.

14   Ibid., 187.

15   Rowan Williams, *A Ray of Darkness* (Cambridge and Boston, MA: Cowley Publications, 1995), vii.

16   Long, *Witness of Preaching*, 18.

17   Lischer, *Theories of Preaching*, 338.

18   Hughes and Kysar, *Preaching Doctrine*, 10–14.

19   Jane Rzepka and Ken Sawyer, *Thematic Preaching: An Introduction* (St. Louis, MO: Chalice Press, 2001), 3–5.

20   Lischer, *Theories of Preaching*, 291.

21   Robert H. Schuller, *Self Esteem: The New Reformation* (Waco, TX: Word Books, 1982), 13.

22   Ibid., 12.

23   Rzepka and Sawyer, *Thematic Preaching*, 4.

24   Wilson, *Concise History of Preaching*, 71.

25   Long, *Witness of Preaching*, 117.

26   Rzepka and Sawyer, *Thematic Preaching*, 71.

27   Long, *Witness of Preaching*, 128.

28   Pamela Ann Moeller, *A Kinesthetic Homiletic: Embodying Gospel in Preaching* (Minneapolis, MN: Augsburg Fortress Press, 1998), 7.

29   Ibid., 2–8.

30   James Henry Harris, *The Word Made Plain: The Power and Promise of Preaching* (Minneapolis, MN: Augsburg Fortress Press, 2004), 83.

31   Ruthanna B. Hooke, *Transforming Preaching* (New York: Church Publishing, 2010), 6.

32   Hughes and Kysar, *Preaching Doctrine*, 56.

33   Ibid., 73.

34   Long, *Witness of Preaching*, 192.

35   Rzepka and Sawyer, *Thematic Preaching*, 68.

36   James Henry Harris, *The Word Made Plain: The Power and Promise of Preaching* (Minneapolis, MN: Augsburg Fortress Press, 2004), 113.

37   William H. Armstrong, *Thinking Through the Children's Sermon* (Cleveland, OH: The Pilgrims Press, 2006), 13.

38   Ibid., 12–33.

39   Ibid., 11–62.

40   Rzepka and Sawyer, *Thematic Preaching*, 93.

41   Armstrong, *Thinking through Children's Sermon*, 11–62.

42   Ibid., 87–94.

43   Rzepka and Sawyer, *Thematic Preaching*, 127.

44   Wilson, *Concise History of Preaching*, 66.

45   McClure, *Best Advice for Preaching*, 85.

46   Hooke, *Transforming Preaching*, 22.

47   Long, *Witness of Preaching*, 29.

48   McClure, *Best Advice for Preaching*, 8.

Annotated Bibliography

Allen, Ronald J., *The Teaching Sermon* (Nashville, TN: Abington Press, 1995).
The Bible and the tradition of the Church can bring continuity and identity in an age marked by chaos and confusion. The author contends that the teaching of the Christian faith is the primary way to connect congregations to the power and purpose of the living God.

Armstrong, William H., *Thinking Through the Children's Sermon* (Cleveland, OH: The Pilgrims Press, 2006).
Making children's sermons more meaningful and edifying is the one goal of this book. Too often done poorly and hastily, Armstrong advocates taking the children's sermon seriously and offering children something that specifically addresses their needs, is something of their own, and acknowledges and respects their presence.

Bond, L. Susan, *Contemporary African American Preaching: Diversity in Theory and Style* (St. Louis, MO: Chalice Press, 2003).
Bond shows that, contrary to popular opinion, a monolithic black preaching style does not exist. Rather, there are a variety of preaching theories and styles that actually characterize

African American preaching at the close of the twentieth century.

Clark, Neville, *Preaching in Context: Word, Worship, and the People of God* (Stowmarket, UK: Kevin Mayhew Ltd, 1991).
Writing from the Free Church tradition, Clark decries the development of a separate discipline called "homiletics." This development, he contends, has "obscured the synoptic vision and unified understanding of both the Church and Ministry (p. 7)." This book is an attempt to restore the balance.

Farrar Capon, Robert, *The Foolishness of Preaching: Proclaiming the Gospel Against the Wisdom of the World* (Grand Rapids, MI and Cambridge: Eerdmans Publishing Co., 1998).
The book incorporates the lectures given by the author, at the Seabury-Western Theological Seminary in 1996. There is one consistent point made in these lectures: nothing counts but the cross. The author contends that the problem with modern day preachers is that they tell us nothing of the dark center of the gospel – that we are saved in our deaths and not by our efforts to lead a good life.

Harris, James Henry, *The Word Made Plain: The Power and Promise of Preaching* (Minneapolis, MN: Augsburg Fortress Press, 2004).
Citing that the Black Church is the only institution in American institutional life that is owned, operated, and controlled by blacks, Harris writes of the unique preaching culture that developed in this context.

Hooke, Ruthanna B., *Transforming Preaching* (New York: Church Publishing, 2010).
In this work, the author, a professor of homiletics at the Virginia Theological Seminary, does two things. First, she explores the nature of preaching. Second, she offers interviews with some of the most effective and engaging preachers of the Episcopal Church today.

Hughes, Robert G. and Kysar, Robert, *Preaching Doctrine: For the Twenty-First Century* (Minneapolis, MN: Augsburg Fortress, 1997).
This useful resource documents the major cultural changes affecting twenty-first century preachers. No longer able to assume even basic knowledge about the Christian faith or traditions, the task of the preacher is to use the experience of people as a frame of reference for deeper engagement with the biblical narrative and the traditions of the Church.

Lischer, Richard, *Theories of Preaching: Selected Readings in the Homiletical Tradition* (Durham, NC: The Labyrinth Press 1987).
A systematic sampling of preaching throughout the ages utilizing and excerpting the sermons and writings of a wide variety of preachers, the author identifies major themes in preaching and then offers primary sources that exemplify a particular theme.

Long, Thomas G., *The Witness of Preaching, Second edition* (Louisville, KY: Westminster John Knox Press, 2005).
A second edition of this classic text, Long offers a comprehensive and thorough introduction to the practice of preaching and the formation preachers. Moving from text to proclamation he engages the best of contemporary scholarship and also offers a resource of best practices.

McClure, John S., ed., *Best Advice for Preaching* (Minneapolis, MN: Augsburg Fortress Press, 1998).
This book is an experiment in collaborative homiletical wisdom derived from a cross-section of 27 renowned preachers and teachers of preaching. Contributors responded to a questionnaire regarding best advice for preachers covering a wide range of topics related to the preaching task.

Moeller, Pamela Ann, *A Kinesthetic Homiletic: Embodying Gospel in Preaching* (Minneapolis, MN: Augsburg Fortress Press, 1998).

Sometimes we need more than words in order to make the transition from hearing the Gospel to living it to in the rest of the week. Words and concepts appeal only to the intellect. This work merges the Gospel with kinesthesia and seeks to incorporate movement, sensory experience, and memory as a result of movement, into biblical proclamation.

Moseley, Dan, *Healing Relationships: A Preaching Model* (St. Louis, MO: Chalice Press, 2009).
A series of sermons preached at Chautauqua Institute that includes the author's personal reflections of his own life as a preacher following the death of his wife. The overarching theme is the task of preaching to help heal the breach that exists between God and the created order.

Page, Sue, *Away with Words: A Training Book on the Whole Spectrum of Christian Communication* (London: Lynx Communications SPCK, 1998).
The author believes that the essential communication of faith already exists within each one of us. We are the channels for divine communication, not just in words, but also in what we are and do.

Pasquarello Michael, III, *Sacred Rhetoric: Preaching as a Theological and Pastoral Practice of the Church* (Grand Rapids, MI and Cambridge: Eerdmans Publishing Co., 2005).
The aim of this book is to glean wisdom from the past in order to inform the present and shape the future. If the most serious challenge of modern preaching is the separation from the larger narrative of Scripture, then the remedy lies in rejoining the craft of preaching with the study of theology.

Rzepka, Jane and Sawyer, Ken, *Thematic Preaching: An Introduction* (St. Louis, MO: Chalice Press, 2001).

The authors, both Unitarian Universalists, lead the preacher through a broad range of homiletical resources and ideas. They offer a uniquely practical and comprehensive guide to contemporary preaching.

Schuller, Robert H., *Self Esteem: The New Reformation* (Waco, TX: Word Books, 1982).
If the core of most religious thinking is distorted by fear, guilt, and mistrust, the corrective, according to Schuller, is embracing the divine dignity that God intended to be our emotional birthright as children created in his image. This book outlines Schuller's understanding of the importance of self-love and the practice of pastoral psychology using the Lord's Prayer as a framework for his discussion.

Williams, Rowan, *A Ray of Darkness* (Cambridge and Boston, MA: Cowley Publications, 1995).
Former Archbishop of Canterbury, Rowan Williams offers this sermon collection with the cautionary words that sermons are events, moments in time, and not static written texts. These sermons were written in specific places, for a specific people, in a specific time. In addition to emphasizing the importance of context in preaching, the hope is, of course, that these sermons might speak in some way to a broader and more general audience.

Wilson, Paul Scott, *A Concise History of Preaching* (Nashville, TN: Abington Press, 1992).
Wilson offers a brief but rather comprehensive tour of the history of preaching. Dividing this rather large scope of work into four eras (Early Church, Middle Ages, Reformation, and Modern Times), the author identifies the major issues and offers selections from a few major preachers of each era.

9

Ethics in the Mainline

The sense that faith is linked to character formation is widespread. Indeed for many Christians, the whole purpose of being religious is to be ethical. The precise relationship between faith and ethics is complex. It touches on such historic debates as "faith and works" and "holiness, perfection, and sanctification." However, it is important that a leader of a congregation is aware of the dynamics underpinning the ethical and faith formation.

To start thinking about these dynamics, we shall now look at ethical methodology and ethical issues. Ethical methodology refers to the "approach or method of deciding ethical questions"; the ethical issues are "the current ethical questions of the day."

This chapter divides the discussion of ethics in the mainline into three different headings – sources, expressions, and issues. Each of these issues will now be discussed in turn.

Sources

Natural Law

The *Natural Law* approach is the primary ethical methodology of the Roman Catholic Church. However, both the Anglicans and the Methodists have been influenced by this approach.

Natural Law theorists claim that the approach has its roots in the thought and writing of Aristotle. It was Aristotle who provided the biological framework for the discourse. Aristotle believed that everything in nature was striving to realize its appropriate "end" (*telos* in Greek). So a little acorn has the natural end of becoming an oak tree. According to Aristotle the "right" thing for that acorn is to be left unimpeded and allowed to become an oak tree.

It was the great Dominican friar of the thirteenth century, Thomas Aquinas, who baptized this approach and made it central to his approach to Christian ethics. Aquinas argued

An Introduction to Ministry: A Primer for Renewed Life and Leadership in Mainline Protestant Congregations, First Edition. Ian S. Markham and Oran E. Warder.
© 2016 John Wiley & Sons, Ltd. Published 2016 by John Wiley & Sons, Ltd.

that God as creator had built into creation the purposes (the natural end) of each part. Using human reason (so without reference to revelation – e.g. the Bible), all people should be able to work out what is right and good. So, for example, given it takes a mother and a father biologically to produce a child, and that child then needs care from her or his parents, the institution of marriage and family are God-intended goods. For Aquinas, families, community, even the State, are God-intended goods.

This approach is most controversial when applied to the realm of human sexuality. Here Roman Catholic theorists argue that the purposes of sexual intimacy include procreation. Therefore any sexual activity that is not open to the procreative possibility is not "good." This is the root of Roman Catholic opposition to contraception, masturbation, and homosexuality.

Many mainline theorists are sympathetic to the method of Natural Law, while dissenting from the particular application of Natural Law to sexuality. In the Anglican tradition, many *Anglo-Catholics* (Anglicans who stress the Catholic nature of the Anglican tradition) make this approach central. V.A. Demant, for example, became a prime mover behind the 1940s "Christendom" movement in England, which wanted to see "a social order in which the conscious leadership would be guided by an understanding of the essential nature of the human being, the term 'nature' being used here of what man is in the order of creatures."[1]

This approach has been popular with Anglicans and Methodists. The founder of the Lutherans, Martin Luther, viewed with deep suspicion the Natural Law approach to ethics. He felt that the whole approach owed too much to "pagan philosophy" (which is true) and that it ignored the impact of the Fall. For Luther, when Adam and Eve sinned in the Garden of Eden, the human capacity to discern the truth about ethics also became difficult. The impact of the Fall extended to human reason, which is where our capacity to grasp Natural Law resides. For Luther, we need redemption, the Church, and Scripture to help us see the ethical. Luther's critique meant that, for Lutherans, Scripture was more important than Natural Law when it comes to thinking about the moral life.

Scripture

As we have seen elsewhere the study of Scripture is central to the craft of priesthood. Scripture tells the story of the incarnation of God in Jesus of Nazareth. It is inescapably central. All the mainline traditions take Scripture seriously. All ethical reports from the mainline have a section on the Bible.

However, the mainline are agreed that the use of Scripture in ethics is difficult. The Bible is a collection of books, covering over 1800 years of history (from the approximate time of Abraham to Paul). The ethical injunctions range from the bizarre – "you shall not boil a kid in its mother's milk" (Deuteronomy 14:21) – to the profound – "you shall love your neighbor as yourself" (Leviticus 19:18). Deciding how to interpret the witness of Scripture is a challenge.

Most mainline traditions insist that you cannot take a "proof texting approach." So the fact that capital punishment is encouraged in the Old Testament does not make it binding to us now. Instead one takes one of two strategies to handle the witness of Scripture.

The first is a thematic approach. Richard Hays (a Methodist), in his *The Moral Vision of the New Testament* argues that Scripture should be read through a thematic prism of three images: community, cross, and new creation. Hays explains that on *community* he means, "The Church is a countercultural community of discipleship, and this community is the primary addressee of God's imperative."[2] On *cross*, he means, "Jesus' death on a cross is a paradigm for faithfulness to God in this world."[3] And on *new creation*, he means, "The church embodies the power of the resurrection in the midst of a not-yet-redeemed world."[4]

Using these images, he moves from a descriptive task (that takes the distinctive approach of each author in the New Testament seriously), to a more systematic account of New Testament ethics viewed in terms of the three predominant themes. So for example, Hays tends to be sympathetic to divorce and remarriage, but nervous about the affirmation of same-sex intimacy.

The second approach makes the Incarnation central. As we saw in previous chapters, it was Karl Barth (a giant who has influenced much of the mainline, especially in its more reformed forms) who insisted that it is important to recognize the centrality of the Word Made Flesh in our theology and ethics. "In the beginning was the Word and the Word was with God and the Word was God," writes the author of John's Gospel in its opening verse. The primary disclosure of God is the incarnation of Jesus. Thus the incarnation should be our primary guide when thinking about the moral life (or, our natural ends – the ways God calls us to live in the world). For Barth, Scripture becomes the Word of God as it witnesses to the Word Made Flesh. A recent and important study of Christian ethics has made this approach central. Richard Burridge, an Anglican, has argued that the unifying theme of the New Testament is the "imitation of Christ."[5]

The purpose of the Gospels is to encourage us to live as Christ lived. And the interesting challenge of that ethic is that Jesus is constantly calling us to perfection ("be ye perfect as your heavenly Father is perfect"), yet constantly including us when we struggle. For Burridge, these twin themes of an exacting call to holiness runs parallel with an inclusive community, where all voices need to be heard.

Experience

The above sources for mainline ethics are all influenced by patriarchy and other forms of oppression. In recent years, there has been a growing literature suggesting that deep injustices are not going to be exposed or challenged unless "experience" is taken seriously as a source for moral reflection. By "experience," we mean the human story as lived, especially the story of the oppressed.

Two narratives are becoming more important for Christian ethics – the liberationist and the feminist. The first was provoked by the Roman Catholic movement known as Liberation Theology, which has had a major impact on the mainline. *A Theology of Liberation* by Gustavo Gutiérrez is rightly acclaimed as a classic. His point is simple: any faith that does not take seriously oppression here and now is not a true heir to the biblical faith. He draws attention to the major themes of the exodus (release from actual slavery), the eighth-century prophets, and the Jesus of Luke's Gospel. He was accused of importing Marxism into the Gospel. While it is true that Gutiérrez does use the Marxist insight that often religion can serve the interests of the rich and powerful, it is not true that the text is primarily Marxist. Instead it is a clarion call for a faith that takes the here and now seriously and works hard for a just society as a sign of the coming of the kingdom of God. This requires appealing to the experience of the oppressed as a source for insight into how to enact the kingdom.

The feminist influence on the mainline has been significant. Over the past 30 years, all the major mainline denominations in the United States have moved to the full inclusion of women. Along with the successful campaign for the inclusion of women as pastors, ministers, and priests, the feminist influence has extended into the realms of theology, liturgy, and ethics. In theology, there has been a growing emphasis on a God who embraces nature; and in liturgy, the emphasis has been on inclusive language. In ethics, feminist theology has supported the mainline emphasis on justice for the oppressed. Justice requires that women should be treated equally with men; the widespread violence against women should be unequivocally condemned; and they should have choices and be freed from the oppression of patriarchy.

In recent years, the principle that the "experience" of this or that group needs to be heard has been extended. The experience of gays and lesbians has been a major factor in the extension of rights to the homosexual community. Most ethicists in the mainline are sympathetic to the principle that experience is a legitimate source of Christian ethical thinking.

Methodology

So far the chapter has focused on the different sources that are used by the mainline in thinking about moral behavior and society. The mainline has also been in conversation with the more philosophical approaches to the ethical. Traditionally, philosophers have distinguished between deontological approaches and teleological approaches.

The deontological approach is associated with the great Prussian philosopher Immanuel Kant. He argued that the ethical compromises certain fundamental convictions that we are "obligated" to perform regardless of the consequences. For example, "you shall not lie" is a fundamental obligation that should not be violated. He arrives at this assumption through the "categorical imperative." Kant argued that the fundamental question is this: "What could I legislate as a universal principle of action for all human persons?" For Kant, we are searching for universal principles that rational persons can affirm. For Kant, an ethical person is completely consistent: she always does what is right. So with respect to lying, truth telling might need to be done gently, but one never resorts to direct lies. It means that the ethical obligation is always recognized even when it is difficult.

At the other end of the spectrum we have the consequentialists or teleologists. This position is normally associated with the nineteenth-century movement known as the Utilitarians. John Stuart Mill took the view that the ethical is the quest for the "greatest happiness for the greatest number." This movement inspired prison reform. After all, it is clearly more beneficial for society if a prisoner is changed into a good citizen rather than punished with no hope of change or release.

Ethicists in the mainline often draw on both approaches. They concede that there are many situations where an absolute must simply be observed and no argument could countenance the absolute being violated. Violating the tenets "You shall not rape" or "you shall not torture children" cannot be justified under any circumstances. However, there are some ethicists who do want to recognize that at times a "weighing" of different goods is necessary. The best example is a situation where a mother is carrying an embryo that is the result of a rape.

However, much of this debate has been superseded by a shift. Rather than focus on actions, it is better to focus on character. We do not want men and women constantly calculating the best way forward; but rather, thanks to their well-formed character, they know what is the right thing to do. This is the tradition of virtue ethics.

Virtue ethics

While Roman Catholics have been more excited about Natural Law, the mainline has been getting very excited about the recovery of *virtue ethics*. It was Alasdair MacIntyre's remarkable book *After Virtue*, published in the 1980s, which led to a resurgence of interest in virtue ethics. MacIntyre argued that the contemporary confusion around ethics is due to the fact that we lost the system of ethics in which ethical language emerged. So MacIntyre writes:

> [T]he interminable and unsettlable character of so much contemporary debate arises from the variety of heterogeneous and incommensurable concepts which inform the major premises from which the protagonists in such debates argue. ... What is lacking ... is any clear consensus, either as to the place of virtue concepts relative to other moral concepts, or as to which dispositions are to be included within the catalogue of the virtues or the requirements imposed by particular virtues.[6]

MacIntyre's point is that the language of the virtues was all part of a system – a system that interconnected and provided coherence to a life. Sadly, modernity has lost this system. So the task of communities (e.g. the Church) is to recover the system and reeducate the community into how moral discourse all links together.

The roots of virtue ethics are grounded in the thought of Aristotle. For Aristotle, the ethical way was often the mean between two extremes. So when watching a child unable to swim in a torrential river, the ethical action is the mean between "cowardice" (running away) or "foolhardiness" (just leaping in, regardless of the dangers). The mean between these two extremes is the virtue of "bravery."

One attraction for many mainline ethicists is the emphasis in virtue ethics on the work of formation. We are called to become virtuous people by learning the skills of discernment. So we spend less time creating an ethical system that tells us what to do and rather more time on being shaped by a community to become the people we can be. One attraction of this approach is that the Church is central. The purpose of the congregation is to be the place of training in the virtues.

Stanley Hauerwas (a Methodist) is probably the best-known advocate of virtue ethics. Hauerwas argues that we need to move away from moral rules and focus instead on virtue and character. Part of the work of formation, according to Hauerwas, is a commitment to pacifism, which he considers central to the Christian faith, for the Christian community is grounded in a solidarity that expresses itself in non-violence.[7]

Expressions

These sources express themselves in three contrasting ethical expressions that are found across the mainline denominations. The first can be described as *individual ethical piety*; the second is *political realism*; and the third is *prophetic justice*. The first is popular with those who are lay; the second is found among those who are politically conservative; and the third is found among those who are politically progressive.

Individual ethical piety

Pietism is primarily associated with the Baptist and Pentecostal traditions. However, it is worth emphasizing that this remains an important aspect of the mainline, especially as found among the lay people. For this position, it is the individual Christian and his or her morality that matters. Salvation is the call to the individual to live a transformed life. Once saved the obligation on the Christian is to embark on the process of sanctification (where the Holy Spirit works in our lives to make us holy). Slowly our character is transformed as we shift from egoism and selfishness to a focus on others. As the author of the Ephesians exhorts his readers: "Be kind to one another, tenderhearted, forgiving one another, as God in Christ has forgiven you" (Ephesians 4:32). The vision is of a life that is honest, generous, respectful, with a disciplined internal life.

It was the English Anglican Edward Norman in his Reith Lectures of 1978 who argued for a pietist vision of the Christian faith. For Norman, to turn Christianity into politics is a betrayal of the Gospel. Norman writes:

> I … see the politicization of Christianity as a symptom of its decay as an authentic religion. It is losing sight of its own rootedness in a spiritual tradition; its mind is progressively secularized; its expectations are prompted by world changes; and its moral idealism has forfeited transcendence.[8]

For Norman, this identification of Christianity with a set of socialist and Marxist positions is a big mistake. The political realm is inevitably ephemeral; the fashions in politics come and go. Christianity is about the timeless story of God's gift of salvation made possible through the atoning work of God in Christ. It is the universal story of God's love and invitation to be transformed by God's grace. For Norman, it is completely wrong to reduce Christianity down to a set of political positions.

Instead the focus should be on cultivation of an appropriate spirituality. Norman explains:

> True religion points to the condition of the inward soul of man. … In Christianity, as it was delivered by the saints and scholars of the centuries, men are first directed to the imperfections of their own natures, and not to the rationalized imperfections of human society. … In their pilgrimage through the world, Christians who are wise in their time always return from the fading enthusiasms of unfulfilled improvements to a more perceptive understanding of the inward nature of spirituality.[9]

For the advocates of individual piety, one should not link Christianity with a particular set of policy proposals in the present, but focus on the timeless invitation to let Christ transform our lives and in so doing change the world – one redeemed person at a time.

Political realism

Many pietists in the mainline are politically conservative. However, in the past 30 years, a more robust and ecumenical movement has emerged which has argued that the Christian interest in the political needs to be grounded in an appropriate Christian *anthropology*. Such an approach tends to link Christianity with a more conservative political position.

An inspiration to this movement is a contested reading of *Reinhold Niebuhr*. Niebuhr held the mainline spellbound with his impressive critique and discussion of social issues from the 1930s through to the 1970s. Starting out with an almost Marxist understanding of the social order, Niebuhr writes as a pastor in Detroit, where he calls for transformed working conditions for those working in industry. His classic *Moral Man and Immoral Society* draws attention to the tension between individual acts of kindness and group acts of deep insensitivity. He explores in some detail the way in which good people can form cruel societies. However, while he started on the political left, slowly he moved to the right. A key issue for him was pacifism. Although pacifism was a key virtue of the New Testament, he recognized that pacifism was an inappropriate position for a Church coping with the manifest evils of Adolf Hitler in Germany. So a more nuanced ethical approach emerged. The ideals of the Gospel provide an exacting standard, from which we are periodically forced to compromise as we live this side of the eschaton (the end of the age). He became a resolute defender of democracy, an opponent of Stalin's Russia, and an advocate of the selective use of force by America.

Niebuhr's methodology was grounded in a biblical theology. For Niebuhr the great themes of Scripture provide the interpretative context that makes sense of our experience in the world. The themes were *creation, fall, atonement,* and *parousia*. This biblical religion, as Niebuhr calls it, explains the deepest human needs and wants. They provide an analysis and solution to the situation of the human creature. So Niebuhr writes:

> Man does not know himself truly except as he knows himself confronted by God. Only in that confrontation does he become aware of his full stature and freedom and of the evil in him. It is for this reason that Biblical faith is of such importance for the proper understanding of man, and why it is necessary to correct the interpretations of human nature which underestimate his stature, depreciate his physical existence and fail to deal realistically with the evil in human nature, in terms of Biblical faith.[10]

For Niebuhr one learns from Scripture the true nature of humanity and then formulates appropriate policies for society.

Niebuhr's approach is primarily advocated by those on the political right. They like his methodology, which takes Scripture seriously. They like, even more, his political positions, which tend to support democracy and the market. Before becoming a Roman Catholic, Richard John Neuhaus was a highly influential Lutheran pastor. He made a similar journey to Niebuhr: he was firmly on the left in his early work (even at one point defending the language of "revolution") before moving to the right. For Neuhaus, the Christian commitment to the poor, which he recognized as pivotal, was best realized in a market economy. The poor need to be given a way into an entrepreneurial society; this is a much better way of affirming human dignity and raising living standards than state socialism. Neuhaus had an enormous influence: Max Stackhouse, for example (United Church of Christ), shared many of his key positions.[11] For Stackhouse, democracy was wiser than socialism and the challenges of the market were worth overcoming for the sake of the market.

Unlike pietism, the political realists recognize that there is a legitimate and important Christian interest in the political. For this position, Scripture requires that we grapple with this obligation and interest. However, the result is a politics right of center rather than left.

Prophetic justice

The leadership of the mainline and many of the resolutions voted at the denominational meetings take an approach of prophetic justice, rather than a pietist or realist approach, and tend to be politically left of center. They tend to support welfare programs and government intervention. The major influence on this outlook is the work of liberationist theologians and writers who draw on the biblical theme of prophetic justice.

Although liberation theology is explicitly derived from Gutiérrez, there are mainline precursors who anticipate certain themes. The social gospel movement has its roots in the Christian socialists of the nineteenth century who were working in England. F.D. Maurice believed that the Gospel obligation was to work for the kingdom to be realized in society; his thought was influential on an early American twentieth-century version, led by such men as Walter Rauschenbusch (1861–1918). Rauschenbusch was for much of his ministry a pastor of a German Baptist Church, but his reach extended across the denominational divide toward the mainline.

Rauschenbusch denounced capitalism, which he saw as deeply destructive. He writes, "This triumphant sway of profit as the end of work and existence puts the stamp of mammonism on our modern life."[12]

Rauschenbusch wants repentance: "Social religion," he writes, "demands repentance and faith: repentance for our social sins; faith in the possibility of a new social order."[13] For Rauschenbusch, biblical Christians should be supporters of a socialist and anti-capitalist program.

This approach increasingly influenced the mainline. The biblical imperative that the Church stands with the poor was considered central. The pietist approach was considered a betrayal of the biblical tradition. Scripture deals with community; in the Old Testament it is the Jewish people and the subsequent nations of Israel and Judah; and in the New Testament, it is the community of the Church. Instead of stressing individual conversion, we need to recover the prophet tradition of Scripture, which calls for the realization of the kingdom of God on earth. We need a new social order that works for those most disadvantaged and struggling.

All three of these expressions of Christian ethics can be found across the mainline. Certainly the leadership of the major mainline denominations in recent years has tended to be more sympathetic to the prophetic justice position.

Issues

Culture wars

When you think of Christian ethics, the primary issues that come to the fore are linked to the culture wars, in particular, abortion and gay rights. So in this section, we shall briefly consider these two issues.

Although there are plenty of individuals within the mainline who are sympathetic to the predominantly Roman Catholic and Baptist positions on abortion, the leadership has been more nuanced. The *pro-life* position makes one question central: what is the status of the fetus? Is it a human being? If so, then it must be fully protected under the law. For advocates of the pro-life position, the argument is simple. If a baby is a human, then so must be the 9-month-old fetus inside the womb. The 9-month-old fetus is remarkably similar to the 8-month-old fetus. And whatever point in the process chosen (e.g. viability at about 23 weeks), there is nothing ethically different about the fetus the day before. The only legitimate moment in the entire process when there is a difference is conception (when the sperm meets an egg and implants). On this view all abortion is murder.

The *pro-choice* position wants to contest the initial assumption. They would argue that there is no way that the sperm and the egg should be given full human rights. The vast majority of fertilized eggs do not implant; those that do implant can grow into a variety of different things ranging from twins to the umbilical cord. In fact, historically, the Roman Catholic Church did not take the position that human life starts at conception until the nineteenth century; the older Christian position was that human life started when the soul entered the embryo (traditionally at quickening). In addition, this position made much of the dependence of the fetus on the mother. If, for example, the pregnancy is due to rape, then it is wicked for society to inflict harm on the mother by forcing her to carry the child to birth.

The mainline has struggled over this issue. The Methodist Church tends to be more pro-life. They take the following position: "Our belief in the sanctity of unborn human life makes us reluctant to approve abortion. But we are equally bound to respect the sacredness of the life and well-being of the mother, for whom devastating damage may result from an unacceptable pregnancy."[14]

The Presbyterian Church USA tends to be much more clearly pro-choice. The General Assembly Mission Council explains that the Church believes all abortion decisions should be left with women: "Even as it calls for abortion to be 'an option of last resort,' it places the responsibility for making a decision about a problem pregnancy in the minds, hearts and spirits of women who face 'many complicated and insolvable circumstances.'"[15]

The Episcopal Church in 1994, at its 71st General Convention,

> reaffirmed that all human life is sacred from its inception until death and that all abortion is regarded as having a tragic dimension. "While we acknowledge that in this country it is the legal right of every woman to have a medically safe abortion," the resolution stated, "as Christians we believe strongly that if this right is exercised, it should be used only in extreme situations. We emphatically oppose abortion as a means of birth control, family planning, sex selection, or any reason of mere convenience."[16]

The Methodists, Presbyterians, and Episcopalians are typical. With some reluctance, the drift is in favor of allowing abortion to be a legal option for women.

The other key issue shaping the culture wars is the attitude to marriage. All the mainline Churches have significant internal movements that are arguing for marriage to extend to gays and lesbians. This is an issue that has led some to leave the mainline Churches. For the traditionalist, marriage has been culturally defined for centuries as a relationship between a man and a woman (or on some occasions multiple wives), but no culture has seen a same-sex relationship as needing social and public recognition. So this, for the traditionalist, is not a minor issue. Although one might concede that the references to homosexual acts in Scripture are few, all references to such acts are universally critical. It is very difficult to construct a biblical case for same-sex affirmation. Therefore if Christians are turning to the resources of the Christian tradition (e.g. Scripture and the teaching of the Church) for guidance, then there are good reasons for opposing same-sex marriage.

For those in the gay and lesbian communities, these arguments are analogous to the arguments that traditionalists offered against the emancipation of the slaves or the rights of women. They concede that there are problematic passages in Scripture, but these passages must be set against the overwhelming witness of Scripture that stresses justice and the intrinsic dignity of all people. Given the authors of the Bible did not know about the possibility of a settled same-sex attraction (namely orientation), it is important to be very nuanced in the interpretation of Scripture. Marriage should be extended to people whose orientation is gay as an expression of the Christian commitment to justice and inclusion.

The United Church of Christ has led the way on this issue. It has made inclusion of homosexual people as central to their witness since 1985, when it invited congregations to be "open and affirming." The Episcopal Church made headlines when Gene Robinson was elected Bishop of the Diocese of New Hampshire in 2003, the first openly gay and partnered bishop in the Anglican Communion. Presbyterians have slowly followed and even the Methodist Church is slowly joining this movement.

The Christian Saints

For Roman Catholics, the saints of the Church are models of ethical insight and commitment. And for some in the mainline, the saints are helpful and worthy of reflection. So, for example, St. Francis of Assisi (ca. 1181–1226 CE) was a man who turned away from a life of luxury to become an advocate for the poor. He was raised in an environment of exceptional luxury. While a teenager, he went to war and was captured. While waiting for a ransom from his father, he started to receive visions from God in prison. Inspired by these visions, he started a new ministry that involved rebuilding a church and reaching out to the lepers. He has a complete reorientation of life away from affluence to the poor.

Conclusion

There is a growing consensus within the mainline Churches on issues in Christian ethics. This consensus has two main components. First, a commitment to justice and an emphasis on the poor. The mainline are very conscious of their slow and gradual commitment to supporting the rights of minorities. The Presbyterians, for example, were typical; they found the issues around segregation very difficult to handle. Now the mainline uniformly supports programs that reach out and help the poor to cope. Under former Presiding Bishop Katherine Jefferts Schori of the Episcopal Church, the millennium development goals have been central. The United Methodist Church ran an advertising campaign called "Rethink Church," which made "outreach" ministries central. Striving for a just society has been a central theme of the mainline ethical approach in the past 20 years. Second, there has been a recognition of the complexity of many issues within the culture wars. On abortion, for example, most of the mainline want abortion to be rare and legal. Part of distinguishing the mainline from the Roman Catholics and the more conservative denominations has been a more nuanced position on social issues. In contrast to the Roman Catholic and Evangelical denominations, all the mainline denominations are striving to accommodate and affirm the inclusion of gay and lesbian people. They do this while seeking to keep in the denomination many conservatives who find this issue difficult.

In conclusion it is worth remembering that the ethical for most members of a congregation is very simple. It is trying to be a good parent, child, and partner; it is at the level of the very basic – letting a car out into a queue of traffic or returning the shopping cart to the store or helping a friend who needs some support. It is important for the congregational leader to know about their denominational efforts to think through certain key question; it is also important to remember that where the ethical touches regular living is what really matters for most Christians.

Notes

1 V.A. Demant, *Theology of Society* (London: Faber and Faber, 1947), 70.

2 Richard B. Hays, *The Moral Vision of the New Testament* (San Francisco, CA: Harper-Collins, 1996), 196.

3 Ibid., 197.

4 Ibid., 198.

5 See Richard Burridge, *Imitating Jesus* (Grand Rapids, MI: Eerdmans Publishing Co., 2007).

6 Alasdair MacIntyre, *After Virtue, second edition* (London: Gerald Duckworth and Co., 1985), 226.

7 See, for example, Stanley Hauerwas, *The Peaceable Kingdom: A Primer in*

Christian Ethics (Notre Dame, IN: University of Notre Dame Press, 1981).

8 Edward Norman, *Christianity and the World Order* (Oxford: Oxford University Press, 1979), 15.

9 Ibid., 76–77.

10 Reinhold Niebuhr, *The Nature and Destiny of Man, volume one* (London: Nisbet, 1941), 140f.

11 See Max Stackhouse, "How my mind has changed," *Christian Century*, April 2011.

12 Walter Rauschenbusch, *Christianizing the Social Order* (New York: the Macmillian Company, 1926), 165.

13 Walter Rauschenbusch, *Christianty and the Social Crisis* (Louisville, KY: Westminster John Knox Press, 1992), 349.

14 See the Methodist Church web site: http://archives.umc.org/interior.asp?mid=1732 (accessed June 3, 2015).

15 See http://gamc.pcusa.org/ministries/phewa/womens-reproductive-health-under-attack-and-so-are/ (accessed June 3, 2015).

16 See the Episcopal Church web site http://www.episcopalchurch.org/library/article/episcopalians-show-support-reproductive-freedom-march (accessed June 8, 2015).

Annotated Bibliography

Burridge, Richard, *Imitating Jesus* (Grand Rapids, MI: Eerdmans Publishing Co., 2009).
A superb book outlining the theme that the heart of New Testament ethics is the obligation to imitate the words and deeds of Jesus.

Fletcher, Joseph, *Situation Ethics* (Philadelphia, PA: Westminster Press, 1966).
A very compelling account of situation ethics – a Christian version of utilitarianism. Widely discussed across the mainline.

Lewis, C.S., *Mere Christianity* (New York: Macmillan, 1960).
Lewis is much admired across the mainline. In this book he sketches out his famous ethical argument for the existence of God.

MacIntyre, Alasdair, *After Virtue* (London: Duckworth, 1985).
The classic that has stood the test of time. In a highly innovative argument, MacIntyre outlines the reasons why moral discourse is so difficult in the modern period.

Mackie, J. L., *Ethics: Inventing Right and Wrong* (Harmondsworth: Penguin, 1977).
An atheist gives an account of ethical language.

Markham, Ian, *Do Morals Matter?* (Oxford: Blackwell Publishing, 2007).
An introduction to ethics that explores the main approaches to ethics and some of the main issues that are widely debated in society.

10

Pastoral Presence

When it comes to Christian ministry, pastoral presence is central. Indeed many denominations use the term "pastor" or "minister" to describe their leaders; in both cases, the label clearly identifies the role – this person should be a pastor or should minister (or serve) the congregation. The act of "being there and available" when life gets difficult goes right to the heart of the Christian ministry.

In this chapter, we shall look at the task of being a pastoral presence. The chapter will start by locating the task of pastoral care in a historical setting. Then we shall look at the five main facets of pastoral care. These are:

1. In Christian theology a pastoral presence can be a vehicle of bringing Christ's presence to a person.
2. When we deal with others, we bring out our own complexity; it is important for us to be aware of this.
3. Dealing with people at moments of acute distress and in a crisis is a particular challenge.
4. All mainline traditions have to handle the "confession of sin"; however, the Lutherans and Episcopalians have a more developed view of the role of the pastor/priest in those situations.
5. Pastoral care is different for people in different cultural settings.

The Historical Setting

Pastoral presence has always been recognized as a major part of Christian ministry. *Gregory of Nazianzus* (329–390 CE) writes movingly about fleeing the demands of priesthood partly because of the demands of pastoral ministry. *John Chrysostom* (349–407 CE) wrote *Six Books on the Priesthood*, which deals in some detail with the nature of the pastoral office.

An Introduction to Ministry: A Primer for Renewed Life and Leadership in Mainline Protestant Congregations, First Edition. Ian S. Markham and Oran E. Warder.
© 2016 John Wiley & Sons, Ltd. Published 2016 by John Wiley & Sons, Ltd.

Gregory the Great (590–604 CE) in his *Pastoral Care*, makes the character of the priest central. Andrew Purves summarizes the advice in two syllogisms:

> First: Every art must be learned; the government of souls is the art of arts; thus, the government of souls must be learned. Second: Dangerous diseases must be treated by qualified physicians; diseases of the soul are the most dangerous of all diseases; thus, sin-sickness must be treated by qualified physicians of the soul. Pastors, in other words, must be especially fit through education and maturity for office.[1]

Here we find a dominant characteristic of subsequent pastoral theology – we need people who can see to lead the blind. Whole people, who are redeemed and sanctified, can be effective pastors. According to Purves, there are eight features of a classical approach to pastoral theology. First, "pastoral theology and pastoral care are explicitly confessional in content."[2] This means that one should not think of pastoral care in terms of the social science, but in terms of core Christian doctrine. Pastoral care is grounded in the incarnation and atonement. Second, "pastoral theology is a discipline, and pastoral care is a practice, deeply rooted at all points in the study of the Bible."[3] For the classic theologians, pastoral theology is never secular. They read Scripture as the way to understand people. They did not draw on the secular study of psychology, but on the biblical world view. Third, "ministry is a high calling to a holy office, the faithful exercise of which is necessary for the salvation of Christ's people."[4] This ministry is a calling for the classical tradition. It comes with certain intrinsic authority made possible by the status as pastor or priest. Fourth, "pastoral work demands taking heed to oneself to the end that he or she is theologically, spiritually and ethically a mature person."[5] The ancients knew the importance of the pastor being able to handle the demands of being a pastor to others. One's own life must focus on God; if one is not focused on God, then how can one help others to be focused on God. Fifth, "God will hold pastors accountable for the exercise of the pastoral office and the care of God's people."[6] For the classical tradition, pastoral care is deadly serious. If one sets oneself up to care for the souls of others, then it is essential to get it right. One does not do this work lightly. Sixth, "pastoral care is the art of arts."[7] This is difficult work. It is work best learned from a mentor, who just intuitively knows how to do things with sensitivity and skill. Seventh, "pastoral ministry is contextual and situational."[8] The tradition recognizes the complexity of this work. It recognizes that suggestions or approaches that work for one person will not necessarily work for another. And finally, "pastors deeply committed to the church wrote the classical texts." The Fathers who wrote about pastoral care and pastoral theology were pastors. This was not a dry and academic exercise; it emerged from a ministry of pastoral care. This is one of the reasons why so many themes continue to resonate today.

Now let us turn to contemporary approaches to pastoral care. And we start with the basic conception of pastoral care as the exercise of bringing Christ to those who are hurting.

The Christological Basis of Pastoral Care

The remarkable claim of Christians is that at the heart of the universe is goodness and love enabling everything that is and sustaining everything that is. The disclosure of this truth is

Jesus of Nazareth – the *Messiah* (in Greek, "the Christ") who ushers in the reign of God. As Jesus, the historical person, dies, rises from the dead, and ascends into heaven, so God enables the presence of Christ to take different forms. So Jesus says in Matthew, "For where two or three are gathered in my name, I am there among them" (Matthew 18:20). Paul develops the concept of the presence of Christ in his first letter to the Corinthians, where he explains that the Church is the Body of Christ: "Now you are the body of Christ and individually members of it" (1 Corinthians 12:27). The idea is simple. For these New Testament writers, now that Jesus is no longer physically present, we, as members of the Church – redeemed and restored in God, are the physical presence of Christ in the world. The mystic *St. Teresa of Avila* (1515–1582 CE) makes the point in a delightful way in her poem "Christ Has no Body":

> Christ has no body but yours,
> No hands, no feet on earth but yours,
> Yours are the eyes with which he looks
> Compassion on this world,
> Yours are the feet with which he walks to do good,
> Yours are the hands, with which he blesses all the world.
> Yours are the hands, yours are the feet,
> Yours are the eyes, you are his body.
> Christ has no body now but yours,
> No hands, no feet on earth but yours,
> Yours are the eyes with which he looks
> compassion on this world.
> Christ has no body now on earth but yours.[9]

St. Teresa of Avila (1515–1582 CE)

Carmelite nun and Roman Catholic saint, Teresa of Avila, largely through her autobiographical works, *The Life of Teresa of Jesus* and *The Interior Castle*, forever shaped our subsequent understanding of Christian mysticism, meditation, and spiritual practice.

Pastoral care then is noble work. The Church is the presence of Christ in the world. And when we meet a person who is hurting, we are called to bring the reality of Christ in the form of friendship and hospitality to that person. This means that we can draw on the divine touch as we work with this person in pain. We can pray for God's healing action in that life.

There is a vast difference between secular pastoral care and Christian pastoral care. The secular approach works within a psychological and biological framework. The Christian approach is happy to absorb insights from psychology and biology, but recognizes that we live in a spiritually infused reality, where God can touch and transform situations. It is an additional dimension that transforms the perspective.

So pastoral care is a divine activity: the purpose of pastoral care is to bring Christ to the person who is hurting. For Barbara Blodgett (coming out of the United Church of Christ tradition), a pastor needs to be both a prophet and priest. The prophet involves "speaking out," while "priestliness might best be characterized by standing with."[10] So she is not thinking of the term priest in the sense used by Episcopalians, instead she sees it as a role that any pastor or minister can inhabit. Her primary theme is that a priest is a person who is in "solidarity, especially with those who are suffering."[11]

However, although this is divine work, we remain who we are – men and women mired in sin and complexity. It is to this dimension that we turn next.

The Complex Agents of Care

Naturally the obligation of discipleship is to draw on the resources that God has made available to become more and more Christ-like in our interactions with others. However, we are still in a fallen world. Perfection in our thoughts, discourse, and actions is very difficult, if not impossible. So in the pastoral encounter, we bring our fragility and complexity to the conversation. Each of us is, in the famous phrase of Henri Nouwen (1932–1996), a "wounded healer."

For Henri Nouwen, the modern context of pastoral care is highly distinctive. We live in a highly technological age, which can keep a person on a machine long after any quality of life has gone. We live in a highly impersonal age. Unlike the small town, where there is a small population, but everyone knows everyone else, the city is a place where there are millions of people but no one knows anyone. The city is a highly impersonal and for many a deeply unfriendly place. For those who are working, the sense of job satisfaction can be limited and much of the work is routine. So Nouwen talks about "nuclear man" for whom "life easily becomes a bow whose string is broken and from which no arrow can fly. In his dislocated state he becomes paralyzed. His reactions are not anxiety and joy, which were so much a part of existential man, but apathy and boredom."[12]

For Nouwen, both the persons needing pastoral care and the persons bringing the pastoral care are infected by the predicaments facing "nuclear man" (and he does acknowledge in his acknowledgments that he is sensitive to the "male-dominated language" and hopes women readers "will have patience"[13] with such language). And the distinctive contribution of Nouwen is that the sensitivity of the person bringing pastoral care to his or her own wounds opens up a resource for effective pastoral care.

He illustrates this with a delightful legend from the *Talmud*, which is worth quoting in full:

> Rabbi Yoshua ben Levi came upon Elijah the prophet while he was standing at the entrance of Rabbi Simeron ben Yohai's cave. … He asked Elijah, "When will the Messiah come?" Elijah replied, "Go and ask him yourself."
>
>   "Where is he?"
>
>   "Sitting at the gates of the city."

"How shall I know him?"

"He is sitting among the poor covered with wounds. The others unbind all their wounds at the same time and then bind them up again. But he unbinds one at a time and binds it up again, saying to himself, 'Perhaps I shall be needed: if so I must already be taken so as not to delay the moment.'"[14]

Nouwen explains that this is a good model for the minister. He explains:

Since it is his task to make visible the first vestiges of liberation for others, he must bind his own wounds carefully in anticipation of the moment when he will be needed. He is called to be the wounded healer, the one who must look after his own wounds but at the same time be prepared to heal the wounds of others.[15]

For Nouwen, the primary wound that everyone has is "loneliness." We are born into a deeply competitive world; the result is an increasing separation from others and a pervasive sense of loneliness. However, instead of hating this wound that afflicts both the person needing pastoral care and the pastoral caregiver, we need to learn to appreciate it. So Nouwen writes:

But the more I think about loneliness, the more I think that the wound of loneliness is like the Grand Canyon – a deep incision in the surface of our existence which has become an inexhaustible source of beauty and self-understanding. ... The Christian way of life does not take away our loneliness; it protects and cherishes it as a precious gift.[16]

For Nouwen, we need to recognize that at the heart of the human condition, there is an isolation, which can only be fully known by God. The denial of the truth leads to promiscuity or inappropriate and damaging expectations in a marriage. The caregiver needs to know this truth and live aware of this truth.

In addition to the loneliness shared by all humans, Nouwen adds a second complicating loneliness that is distinctively true of the caregiver. When one serves, for example as a chaplain, one often finds oneself on the periphery. In hospitals, the doctors and nurses are the center of the attention, the person who wants to speak to the fundamental concerns of the patient is on the edge; in the prison, the wardens make the decisions, the chaplain will be lucky to be in the room for the conversation.

Nouwen's thesis could be developed further. The truth about effective pastoral care is that one cannot be present for another without being deeply aware of one's inner dynamics. We are all bundles of insecurities and fears. Often these insecurities express themselves in complex patterns of behavior. Self-knowledge is essential for a caregiver. In understanding ourselves, it may be possible to help others understand themselves.

Good pastoral care is, ultimately, a conversation. It is a three-way conversation, with God, with the caregiver, and with the person needing care. God's grace is needed for both the caregiver and the person needing care.

Acute Distress and the Crisis

Living can be very tricky. Life is fragile. It is very easy for our sense of "normal" to come crashing down. From the traffic accident to a breakdown of a relationship, we are all on the cusp of a crisis. Those things that we fear most do happen. When this happens, we have a crisis; we have people in acute distress.

H. Norman Wright in his book *Crisis Counseling* documents with care the pattern of a crisis.[17] The first phase is "the impact." This is when the spouse has left or the death of a loved one has occurred. It is the moment of shock and numbness. The second phase is "withdrawal and confusion." Sometimes this phase takes the form of anger and resentment. Confusion is commonplace. The woman who has lost her job might decide to just give up and never try and find another job again; or the husband wants to sue the hospital where his wife died. The third phase is a gradual one; this is the phase of "adjustment." This varies considerably from person to person. But this is the season when hope slowly replaces the depression. One never gets over an acute crisis, the presenting issue will haunt a life in some way, but one can find new and other reasons to be constructive. And slowly one starts to rebuild one's life. This is the fourth phase, which is called "reconstruction–reconciliation." It is this phase that leads to growth, hope, and a new and different life. It is the time when perspective has arrived and the tragedy can be located in a bigger picture of hopefulness.

Every situation and every tragedy has a different pattern. It is important not to try and simply take a template and impose it on every situation. However, Bruce Petersen suggests certain guidelines that can be helpful.[18]

1. Respond immediately. In an age when self-care of clergy is considered a priority, it is worth remembering that some things trump the evening in or the good night's sleep. A pastor who is there in those initial moments will be a much-loved pastor. People never forget who was there for them when the crisis initially arises. This is a fundamental of your vocation. It is the moment when a pastor must be the pastoral presence.

2. Assess the situation. There are countless situations where this assessment role is key. There are moments when you need to bring in greater expertise. If, for example, the person is a danger to himself or to others, then you might need a trip to the Emergency Room or to contact the authorities.

3. Bring calm to the situation. Often the most important contribution is a simple touch or a reassuring word. Calm is a great gift. Where others are being hysterical, the pastor can ease the situation with the gentle touch and the prayer.

4. Establish rapport. Often there are many parties to a crisis. So do reach out to all the people in the room – the doctor, the friend who made the journey, and the sibling who is visiting. Let them know who you are and why you are present.

5. Be a good listener. Don't rush to give advice. Instead, pause and listen very attentively. Do not interrupt. Often a crisis can be dissipated by a good listener who clearly demonstrates an understanding spirit.

6. Determine what immediate action must be taken. As time passes, the immediate priority is the safety of all those in the moment. If it is an argument between spouses,

then finding out exactly where people are staying that night is important. If it is a person who has driven to the hospital to find out her child is dead, then the immediate question is how that person gets home safely that night.

7. Help the person set goals for the future. This is almost always in a subsequent meeting or meetings. But as people come to terms with the crisis, they need advice about the future. Inviting them to set a goal is an important part of helping them cope with the crisis.

8. Develop a plan of action to move toward the goal. To move towards a goal requires that initial step. One step at a time and one day at a time are good mantras for this season of slow adjustment beyond the crisis.

9. Evaluate the person's support system. In the immediate aftermath of the crisis, the support networks can be exceptionally strong. The rule for the pastor is to reach out in the weeks and months afterwards. It is as the initial support network dissipates (because people assume that their friend is coping) that a deeper crisis can then set in. The pastor needs to track constantly the support system.

10. Help with acceptance. This is the hard work of helping a person through the phases of the crisis. Acceptance is a vital step to coping constructively with the crisis.

11. Foster a sense of hope. A crisis can generate despair. And despair can be deeply damaging. The pastor is always a symbol of hope in a difficult situation.

12. Commit to follow up. Being there in the moment of crisis becomes a commitment to support the person through the crisis. So always finish a meeting with a commitment to come and visit again.

The primary theological narrative that needs to be in the mind of the person seeking to be the pastoral presence in a crisis is the Gospel narrative of crucifixion and resurrection. At the heart of the Christian drama is the claim that God has been there. God faced the pain and humiliation of suffering and death. God also promises that Good Friday is followed by Easter Sunday. We go through Good Friday to get to Easter Monday. We are the ones that take people through their pain and help them find the resurrection hope and promise from God.

Confession of Sin

So far, all the sections in this chapter apply to all ministers in the mainline. This section is different. This is the where the United Church of Christ (UCC), the United Methodists, and the Presbyterians differ from the Lutherans and the Episcopalians.

However, before we get to the differences, the mainline does share a conviction that the confession of sin is a central act of discipleship. We are all broken; we all struggle; and we all fail. As we strive to be vehicles of love and life in this world, we need to bring our brokenness to God. God promises to forgive the past and provide the resources to transform us into a Christ-like presence. These convictions are shared by all Christians.

And for those members of the UCC, the United Methodists, and the Presbyterians, they participate in a public confession every Sunday in the service and, in addition, are invited to discuss their struggles with their minister and bring them to God. They may pray about areas of difficulties together with their minister; but the confession is made directly to God.

The Lutherans and the Episcopalians share with the Roman Catholic Church a sense that God has invited the priest to play a distinctive role in the *rite of reconciliation*. At one level this is the simple idea that, although we can all know theoretically that we are forgiven, the voice of another person declaring that God has indeed forgiven us can make the theory a reality. The conversation with another truly holds us accountable. Now, of course, this could be a lay person. And all the mainline traditions concur that this can be helpful. So there is another level, in Lutheran and Episcopal polity, which prefers this task to be entrusted to a priest. So Julia Gatta and Martin L. Smith write:

> [T]he rite of reconciliation is most appropriately administered by bishops and priests because they are ordained to act on behalf of the whole church. The ministry of absolution is reserved to them because it is an authoritative action of the church, exercising the power to forgive sin entrusted to it by the Risen Christ. Hearing confessions and pronouncing absolution belongs emphatically to the cure of souls.[19]

In the act of ordination of a priest, it is clear that one of the duties entrusted to this woman or man is the task of hearing confession and pronouncing absolution. It is because of the recognition grounded in the ordination that the polity prefers a priest to play this role.

Interestingly many members of the Episcopal Church and the Evangelical Lutheran Church in America do not realize that confession is available. So only a small number come forward and ask a priest to take them formally through the rite of reconciliation. However, the process can be important and life-changing.

For Episcopalians and Lutherans, this is a liturgical rite. So it is important that there is an understanding that this is now moving from pastoral counseling to confession. During pastoral counseling, one must be discreet; during the rite, the seal of the confessional is an absolute. Even after the person has died, the details of the confession cannot be shared; in fact, the priest should not even discuss the confession with the penitent, although the penitent is free to do so as he or she wishes.

There are several ways in which confession can be undertaken. However, best practice tends to highlight the following. First, there should be a time of appropriate preparation. If this is the first confession, then the penitent should divide his or her life into sections and reflect on the challenges embedded in each section. One should deal with one section at a time: spending three full days looking at every act of unworthiness in a lifetime could be mentally damaging. Second, the room should be appropriately arranged. Two comfortable chairs facing each other and space for kneeling are helpful. Third, the priest must listen with care as the rite is unfolding without interrupting. Allow the memories to come; allow the inevitable pauses to be part of the process. Finally, the priest should reflect on the confession, promise the forgiveness of God, and suggest certain actions (which can be both actions of amelioration, but also actions of thanksgiving) that help the penitent to be freed from the destructive power of sin.

The past is a challenge for all of us. Confession is a good way of coming to terms with the power of the past. One cannot change the past: it sits there unable to be altered. But the impact of the past can be changed. We don't have to live with the crushing guilt or regret. The promise of the Gospel is that we can be freed up from that impact.

> ### Case Study
>
> Some of the hardest cases in pastoral care have to do with the keeping of confidences. So consider the following case study and decide what you would do.
>
> You are sitting in your office and a member of the congregation knocks on your door. It is Harry; he has been finding life difficult ever since his wife Melanie left him. He wants to speak with you, and you invite him to sit down. He starts by reflecting on the breakdown of his marriage. He then pauses and says, "Please can you keep this in confidence." You reply: "Of course." He then starts to explain that he suspects Melanie was having a relationship with his best friend. He thinks that she has had an affair. As he speaks, he becomes more and more agitated. He explains: "This makes me mad. I am going to go around to see Melanie and just have it out with her." He bangs the table. You try and calm him down, but it is clear that he is now very angry and blaming Melanie. He storms out of the room.
>
> You have promised to keep a confidence. Yet you are also aware that Melanie might be at risk. What do you do?

Care for the Sick

One difficult area in pastoral care is the issue of sickness. Pastoral care often involves meeting and supporting those who are sick. So it is important for the caregiver to be clear about the theology of sickness.

First, it is important to undermine any connection between sin and sickness. The question "why me?" is often a Job question. The implicit assumption is that "after all, I am a person of relative virtue, so why do I have cancer?" There are passages in Scripture that tend to imply a connection, but Jesus is clear in John 9 when confronted with the question explicitly:

> As he walked along, he saw a man blind from birth. His disciples asked him, "Rabbi, who sinned, this man or his parents, that he was born blind?" Jesus answered, "Neither this man nor his parents sinned; he was born blind so that God's works might be revealed in him." (John 9:1–3)

The problem here, says Jesus, is not sin, but blindness. And the solution is healing. It is very important for the pastor in any situation to eliminate a sense of guilt that might be part of the situation.

Second, prayer is a gift in a situation of sickness. The pastor should strive to connect the person struggling with the pain with the hope promised in the Gospel. A good prayer should remind the person who is suffering that God is there right alongside them. This is the God of Good Friday who knows exactly what pain involves. In addition, it is important to invite the power of God into the situation; however, this need not (and often will not) take the form of dramatic healing or to be more accurate the form of healing may not be physical. The pattern of life followed by death is set for all of us – something will take us to glory. So inviting the power of God to be made manifest in "coping" or in "enjoying family" or "enjoying the next holiday" or in "being free from pain" (which thanks to advances in palliative care is increasingly possible) might be the prayer that person needs.

Third, think through healing. The Christian tradition is clear: God seeks to put pressure on a tragic and difficult situation and bring wholeness and healing. For some, this will take the form of the Christian hope in the life to come; for others, it will take the form of a dramatic or steady recovery from a situation that looks medically very difficult. Naturally, God alone determines what is best; but as the pastor you can believe God can physically heal. Any robust account of providence should include the possibility of physical healing as an option in this situation.

Different Cultures and Different Pastoral Care Approaches

One size does not fit all. Skilled pastoral care requires a recognition that different situations require different dynamics. So for example "touch" is often used as a way of reaching out. However, touch must be used carefully. Some cultures forbid cross-gender contact (e.g. many Islamic and Jewish groups); others limit touch to certain areas (primarily hands) and would not welcome the hand on a shoulder. So a sensitivity of approach is important to learn.

It takes time to learn about a particular sub-culture. The culture of the United Kingdom is quite different from the culture of New England, which is quite different from the culture of Alabama. In the American South, a bereavement committee is likely to bake for the reception after a funeral service; elsewhere, an Irish family in New England might still observe the traditions of the "wake" (which is normally held in the home of the deceased). Along with regional differences, we have racial and ethnic differences. For many African American and Hispanic families, tragedy is a matter for the entire extended family. Therefore any pastoral care will often involve handing significant numbers of people (all with their own often distinctive pastoral care needs).

Pastoral care in these situations needs to be learned. You must spend time learning to "read" the sub-culture. Modes of address, contact between people, meeting etiquette, departure etiquette, and the symbols and associations that can help to support will all vary. Effective pastoral care depends on living with the people one is seeking to serve. It is very difficult to "drop in from the sky" and to suddenly provide such support.

One needs to understand the people for whom one is seeking to care. One needs to understand the distinctive patterns, narratives, and dispositions that make up a community. This is where the social sciences can be helpful. Carrie Doehring, a Presbyterian, points out the importance of cultural studies:

> Cultural studies have helped pastoral caregivers understand how the social identity of careseekers is shaped by their gender, race, sexual orientation, social class, and religious identities. A variety of theoretical perspectives – feminist and gender studies; gay, lesbian, and transgender studies; African American, Hispanic, Asian American, and other ethnically and racially orientated studies – offers norms for interpreting the careseeker's experience of his or her social identity.[20]

One major theme of Doehring's work is that ineffective pastoral care can be damaging. One needs to operate within a contract of care for "such contracts ensure that careseekers will not be harmed."[21]

The idea that a pastor can make situations worse is important to recognize. Situations are often made worse because of the pastor's failure to understand different cultural settings. Cultural gaps are a major part of pastoral ineffectiveness. To avoid such damaging moments, a good pastor is part of the community he or she seeks to serve.

Conclusion

For those called to ministry, the pastoral role is an important aspect. If a minister is present at these crucial moments of change and upheaval, the congregation will forgive the minister's many weaknesses. If the minister is absent, then a congregation will slowly turn on the minister. Learning the craft of care is vitally important. The pastor needs to be the one who is willing to go to places that others fear. No one wants to undergo the journey of death alone. The pastor is the one who represents the Christian narrative and drama and brings that presence to the hardest of situations and moments.

Pastoral care for Christians is grounded in the cross and resurrection. We do not deny the reality of suffering and pain. Good Friday is all too real. However, we do not think it is the complete story. Good Friday needs Resurrection Sunday. We trust that in the hardest of moments God will take our pain and transform it into hope.

Notes

1   Andrew Purves, *Pastoral Theology in the Classical Tradition* (Louisville, KY: Westminster John Knox Press, 2001), 64.
2   Ibid., 115.
3   Ibid., 116.
4   Ibid., 117.
5   Ibid.
6   Ibid., 118.
7   Ibid., 119.
8   Ibid.
9   See http://www.journeywithjesus.net/PoemsAndPrayers/Teresa_Of_Avila_Christ_Has_No_Body.shtml (accessed June 3, 2015)
10   Barbara Blodgett, *Becoming the Pastor You Hope to Be: Four Practices for Improving Ministry* (Herndon, VA: Alban, 2011), 146.
11   Ibid., 146.
12   Henri J.M. Nouwen, *The Wounded Healer: Ministry in Contemporary Society* (New York: Doubleday, 1972), 8.
13   Ibid., viii.
14   Ibid., 83–84. Nouwen notes that this is taken from the tractate Sanhedrin.
15   Ibid., 84.
16   Ibid., 85–86.
17   See H. Norman Wright, *Crisis Counseling: What to Do and Say During the First 72 Hours* (Ventura, CA: Regal, 1993), 31–40.
18   Bruce L. Petersen, *Foundations of Pastoral Care* (Kansas City: Beacon Hill, 2007), 178–182. Petersen provides the initial list. The descriptions under each point are our own.
19   Julia Gatta and Martin L. Smith, *Go in Peace: The Art of Hearing Confessions* (New York: Morehouse Publishing, 2012), 35.
20   Carrie Doehring, *The Practice of Pastoral Care: A Postmodern Approach* (Louisville, KY: Westminster John Knox Press, 2006), 8.
21   Ibid., 11.

Annotated Bibliography

Blodgett, Barbara J., *Becoming the Pastor You Hope to Be: Four Practices for Improving Ministry* (Herndon, VA: Alban, 2011).
Barbara Blodgett was the director of supervised ministry at Yale Divinity School and is now Minister for Vocation and Formation for the United Church of Christ in Cleveland. The focus of this book is how to become a better pastor. However, her section on "priestliness" addresses the idea of pastoral presence. The title of this chapter comes from her work.

Bloede, Louis W., *The Effective Pastor: A Guide to Successful Ministry* (Minneapolis, MN: Fortress Press, 1996).
A Presbyterian with lots of practical advice. His celebration and affirmation of the "pastoral call" to a home is especially commendable.

Carr, Wesley, *The Pastor as Theologian* (London: SPCK, 2008).
One of the leading UK Anglican voices on the nature of pastoral presence. He makes the Incarnation central to his account.

Doehring, Carrie, *The Practice of Pastoral Care: A Postmodern Approach* (Louisville, KY: Westminster John Knox Press, 2006).
Doehring is a Presbyterian minister and assistant professor of pastoral care and counseling at Iliff School of Theology. This text invites us into a rich and diverse understanding of the challenge of handling the diversity of pastoral care situations.

Elford, R. John, *The Pastoral Nature of Theology: An Uphold Presence* (London: Mowbray, 2001).
Makes the argument that pastoral theology is not a branch of theology but the heart of theology.

Gatta, Julia, *The Nearness of God: Parish Ministry as Spiritual Practice* (New York: Morehouse Publishing, 2010).
A classic text. She examines the way in which a priest is a pastoral figure and the necessity for self-awareness, respect, reverence, and space.

Gatta, Julia and Smith, Martin L., *Go in peace: The Art of Hearing Confessions* (New York: Morehouse Publishing, 2012).
Powerful, thoughtful, and helpful. This is the finest introduction to the task of confession for the mainline. The focus is the Episcopal Church, but it would work well for Lutherans.

Gerkin, Charles V., *An Introduction to Pastoral Care* (Nashville, TN: Abingdon Press, 1997).
Gerkin provides a biblical history and an account of pastoral care that takes psychology, the social gospel movement, and academic pastoral theology seriously. He sees the pastor as "Shepherd of the Flock, Mediator and Reconciler, and Ritualistic Leader."

Howe, Leroy T., *Image of God: A Theology for Pastoral Care and Counseling* (Nashville, TN: Abingdon Press, 1995). Having taught for many years at Southern Methodist University, Howe sets out a theology of pastoral care which is grounded in the conviction that people are made in the Image of God. A solid, although often theoretical discussion of the theological underpinning of pastoral care.

Lartey, Emmanuel Y., *Pastoral Theology in an Intercultural World* (Cleveland, OH: Pilgrim Press, 2006).
Lartey looks at pastoral counseling in an international and global world. He addresses the importance of the pastor meeting people in their own context, which takes into account culture, experience, need, and background.

Nouwen, Henri, *Wounded Healer: Ministry in Contemporary Society* (New York: Doubleday and Co., 1972).

The master of pastoral care analysis. This book provides a wise critique of our situation in modernity and how important it is for the healer to recognize that he or she is part of the modern situation.

Peterson, Bruce L., *Foundations of Pastoral Care* (Kansas City, KN: Beacon Hill Press, 2007).
A textbook for pastoral care that includes considerable practical advice.

Purves, Andrew, *Pastoral Theology in the Classical Tradition* (Louisville, KY: Westminster John Knox Press, 2001).
This book reminds us that pastoral care is deeply entrenched in the Christian tradition.

Wright, Frank, *The Pastoral Nature of the Ministry* (London: SCM Press, 1980).
Often considered as the "father" of pastoral care. This is a classic and important text.

11

Christian Education and Formation

How does one embrace a life of faith? This fundamental question is at the heart of our exploration of Christian education and formation. In this chapter we will explore this question from a variety of perspectives. For instance, does faith grow mostly in an open heart, does it flourish primarily in an enlightened mind, or does it thrive chiefly in hands that serve? Is a lively faith achieved by more and better programming, by intentional small groups, or by the worship life of the gathered community? Is faith acquired instantaneously or gradually, is it obtained individually or communally, is it innate (bubbling up from within us) or is it extrinsic (coming from outside of us)? Is faith static and fixed or is it dynamic and evolving? Is the Christian life more about knowledge to be mastered or is it more a lifestyle to imitate? Is the development of faith predictable or spontaneous?

We confess at the start that the answer to all of these questions, to some degree, is a resounding, yes! Yet we also confess that there are many variables at play in the planting of the seeds, the nurturing, and the flowering of faith. Faith development is not an exact science, with observable and controllable results, nor is it completely illusive, beyond our ability to guide and influence. Faith development is essentially the work of the Holy Spirit, and this chapter seeks to find meaningful ways to partner with the Spirit in this vital work. To that end, we highlight three central themes that we believe are critical to initiating, encouraging, and sustaining a life of faith. The first is the significance of the "domestic church," that is, the important role of households in the promotion of faith. Second, and closely connected to the first, is the development of daily practices, which strengthen and reinforce a life of faith. Last, we emphasize corporate worship as an essential means of integration and a fundamental resource for the shaping of a Christian life. We believe that this combination (individual habits nurtured in households, in partnership with a larger faith community) provides a lively framework in which the Spirit can flourish in the lives of God's people.

An Introduction to Ministry: A Primer for Renewed Life and Leadership in Mainline Protestant Congregations, First Edition. Ian S. Markham and Oran E. Warder.
© 2016 John Wiley & Sons, Ltd. Published 2016 by John Wiley & Sons, Ltd.

Education or Formation?

The naming of this chapter was challenging. Is a life of faith essentially the result of a process of Christian education or is it the result of a process of Christian formation? There is an inherent tension between the two. When we think of the process of education, we usually think of a formal classroom, led by a knowledgeable teacher, teaching cognitive/intellectual lessons, designed to illicit some sort of action, or changed behavior on the part of the student. The knowledgeable teacher imparts wisdom to the student, who in turn does something with this new information. When we think of the process of formation, we usually think of more informal settings led by mentors instead of teachers. The overarching metaphor for Christian formation is that of a journey or a pilgrimage, with the mentor being both a guide and a fellow pilgrim. Formation appears to be more holistic. Rather than simply an intellectual exercise leading to a particular action or behavior, formation has to do with the shaping of character and the nurturing of relationships.[1] The focus is on *being* rather than doing.

The conclusion of this simplistic assessment is inevitably that the work of formation is far superior to the work of education and therefore must be the gold standard for faith development. We believe, however, that congregations are best served by holding the two together, and working to synthesize the best attributes of both.[2] The reality is, of course, that each of us acquires knowledge and wisdom differently, and a more comprehensive approach is certainly more effective. We will say more about this later in the chapter.

Before leaving this topic, it is helpful to underscore the overarching goals of Christian education and formation. For congregations, the aim is to be lively communities that teach and shape faithful and faith-filled disciples, but for what purpose? In his textbook, *Introduction to Christian Education and Formation*, Ronald Habermas, building on the work of others, speaks of the five global tasks of Christian education and formation based on the experience and witness of the early Church. He contends that the first task, based on the Greek idea of *kerygma*, has to do with proclamation, the sharing of the *Good News*. The second task, based on the Greek idea of *koinonia*, has to do with fellowship, the building up of the Christian community, the Body of Christ. The third, based on the Greek idea of *diakonia*, has to do with service, both inside and outside the community of the Church. The fourth, based on the Greek idea of *basileia*, has to do with the embracing of the values of the reign of God (principles of justice, compassion, righteousness, and peace). The fifth task, which is an integration of all of the previous four, based on the Greek idea of *leitourgia*, has to do with the liturgy, the work of the people, in offering of praise, thanksgiving, and worship to God.[3] All of these constitute not only the global tasks of education and formation, but are also, each in themselves, a means by which faith is celebrated and shared.

Internal Crisis or External Threat

The question of faith development in the mainline Church is embedded in a call for the renewal of Christian education and formation in congregations. For many, the future of the mainline rests on this revitalization. In the introduction of her book *Basics of Christian Education*, Karen Tye states the problem by pointing to a recent national study of Protestant congregations. The findings of the study are disturbing and sadly familiar: adults are largely disinterested in Christian education; it is increasingly difficult to keep children involved past the eighth grade; there is great difficulty in recruiting and keeping volunteers; and clergy and parents seem generally disinterested. To make matters worse, many congregations are seduced by pre-packaged, high tech, and quick-fix remedies, rather than engaging in serious and intentional conversation about core issues.[4] Addressing the dire consequences of inaction, Tye quotes Walter Brueggemann, who reminds us that "every community that wants to last beyond a single generation must concern itself with education."[5] He goes on to state the dual purpose of education, to provide both continuity and change. For the Church, this means carrying forth the traditions and teachings that have been central to the life of Christian people throughout the ages, while at the same time acknowledging that God is always breaking forth in new ways, in new contexts and new situations. Brueggemann again, focusing on the dual nature of education, warns that "education must attend both the process of continuity and discontinuity in order to avoid fossilizing into irrelevance on the one hand, and relativizing into disappearance on the other hand."[6]

For Tye, this situation calls for a radical response. From the congregational perspective this requires acknowledgement that the transmitting of faith includes both knowledge and practice, it involves enculturation into a community of faith, as well as personal development. Put another way, and incorporating the work of Daniel Aleshire, she contends that the four tasks of Christian education are first, to learn the Christian story; second, to develop the skills to act out faith; third, to reflect on the story and live a life of faith congruent with that truth; and last to nurture these sensibilities within a covenant community.[7] She also warns that the enemy of Christian education, and a hindrance to revitalization, is the fear of change, the presumption that we know what is right, and the "tyranny of the urgent," which seeks the elusive silver bullet to provide an immediate fix. On the contrary, Tye calls for radical patience and faithful persistence. She also advocates for congregational programs that are experiential in nature, reflective of that experience, and relational in the sense that they are connected to the whole community.[8]

Kenda Creasy Dean

A United Methodist pastor, Kenda Creasy Dean proposes an approach to Christian education that has mission at its core and at the same time offers concrete suggestions about how to live authentic Christian lives. Based on her extensive study and work with American teenagers, she argues that this approach combats the often less demanding, watered down theology that characterizes much of contemporary mainline Christianity.

Along similar lines, Kenda Creasy Dean, who teaches at Princeton Theological Seminary, also argues that our concern about faith development, particularly among teenagers, is primarily the result of an internal crisis. In her important book *Almost Christian: What the*

Faith of Our Teenagers is Telling the American Church, she argues that the combination of a "lightweight hands-off deistic approach to God" on the part of parenting adults, and the proclamation of an "imposter faith posing as Christianity" on the part of congregations has led to the development of what scholars are now calling Moralistic Therapeutic Deism (MTD). This term, coined by sociologists Christian Smith and Melinda Denton, describes a combination of beliefs, not exclusive to any major world religion, currently held by many young people. In response, Dean implores the Church to focus energy on mission with respect to youth and engaging and educating parents in matters of faith.[9]

Others have responded to the current crisis in a different way. Rather than seeing the problem as mostly an internal predicament unique to the mainline, some see a much more aggressive external threat to the wider Church as a whole. "Multiculturalism, naturalism, and relativism have eroded our once moral and ethical system of laws and public education. The challenges facing Christian education in the 21st century are to withstand the onslaught of these humanistic philosophies and to educate believers with the absolute truth found only in the Bible."[10] One could question whether or not a more perfect age of morality and ethics ever existed, and one could argue about the extent to which these external forces have shaped our current reality, and one could argue that indeed the Bible is our primary source and guide, but perhaps a more nuanced and more comprehensive interpretation might be helpful. Arguing from this perspective, Robert Pazmino, building on the work of Columbia University professor Laurence Cremin, defines Christian education as the

> deliberate, systematic, and sustained divine and human effort to share or appropriate the knowledge, values, attitudes, skills, sensitivities, and behaviors that comprise or are consistent with the Christian faith. It fosters the change, renewal, and reformation of persons, groups, and structures by the power of the Holy Spirit to conform to the revealed will of God as expressed in the Old and New Testaments and preeminently in the person of Jesus Christ, as well as any outcomes of that effort.[11]

This approach takes into account the possibility that all truth is God's truth wherever it may be found and cautions that in the postmodern world, "Christian education must avoid teaching Bible and theology as ends in themselves, reducing them to purely cognitive constructs."[12] Rather the ideal is to help "students learn to think in biblical ways, using theology as a guide to categories of thinking."[13] This understanding helps us to see the pluralism of the postmodern world as less of the threat to our existence and more of an opportunity to fulfill our mission.

Given that very soon the United States will consist of a "majority of minorities," the question is not whether congregations will need to explore the obstacles and barriers to welcoming people of different cultures and world views, the question is whether or not it will be morally acceptable for a congregation to represent only one culture in a society of such great diversity. The varied denominations of the mainline, and the congregations within them, are not in agreement regarding the boundaries of inclusion and openness to diversity. There are those who insist that, realistically speaking, the local congregation, given its own unique culture, will in fact exclude people in spite of its intention to reach everyone. They argue that "attempts to reach everyone in general will reach no one in particular."[14]

Yet it is also true that the idea of homogeneity must also be rejected. More and more, little by little, denominations and congregations are realizing that it is a misconception to believe that unity comes from uniformity of belief and practice, but rather from the strength of diversity. There still exists a danger in the mainline for congregations to develop exclusive memberships based on race, class, cultural and economic lines rather than seeing ourselves as a common humanity. Any postmodern Christian education program must start here, with changed attitudes, found in the acceptance and appreciation of diversity coupled with the genuine desire to reflect the whole family of God.[15] In her thorough text *The Church as Learning Community*, Norma Cook Everest begins her work by summoning the words of John Wesley, who reminded his followers, "not to make the parish your world, but make the world your parish." She later reinforces that point by reiterating that the Church's very purpose is to encourage and equip its people for mission. That means being sent out from the congregation into an increasingly pluralistic world. For Everest, the key to engagement is clarity of identity, understanding that we are sent out as Christian people. She rightly advises that "no one is served by our being less of who we are, but rather more of who we are."[16]

A Broader Vision

This inclusive vision of Christian education and formation is captured in Mark Bozzuti-Jones' important book, *Informed by Faith*. In this book he not only assumes a widely diverse and multicultural future for the Church, but he also offers a diverse and multicultural approach to teaching, or more specifically, a diverse and multicultural approach to offering faith. Emphasizing the strengths and distinct contributions of African and Asian cultures, as well as the western tradition that grew out of classical Greek society, Bozzuti-Jones helps to make the connections with the biblical narrative. He also emphasizes the deep Jewish roots of Christianity and this rich tradition that is an integral part of our heritage. In all of these cultures and traditions he highlights the power of word and story to shape lives as well as the critical importance of using word and story, in all its many forms, as a means of passing on our tradition. Scripture – word and story – is meant to engage the individual and the whole community in a life-long conversation, a conversation that is enriched by all of the cultures and traditions that have preceded us.[17]

In addition to framing an argument for a more broadly inclusive approach to faith formation, he also seeks to redefine the task of Christian education in a way that is consistent with this vision. Acknowledging that we usually characterize education as the process or act of educating, he looks more closely at the root meaning of the word. The verb "educate," comes from the Latin *educare*, meaning, to educe, to extract, or to draw out a latent or potential existence. Thus education, in this context, means the calling forth of wisdom that already exists. He proposes that "wisdom is experience and knowledge combined with the power of applying our experiences and knowledge critically or actively in our daily activities."[18] Education is then the process of leading out or calling forth wisdom. The implications of this definition for a broader vision of faith development are quite profound. If wisdom is one of the primary gifts of the Spirit, and all of God's people, young and old, near and far, receive the gift of the Spirit, then the starting point for religious education and formation is to "know and believe that all are gifted in and with the wisdom of God. Educators have the unending task of drawing out of themselves and their students the wisdom that abides in them."[19] Christian education thus requires a reflective life that allows teacher and student to pay attention to the inner movement of the Spirit, paying attention to the questions and answers in our hearts, paying attention to what is happening in our lives, and paying attention to God educating us in our experiences with one another.[20] This perspective recognizes that teachers are not perfect and do not have all the answers, and also that all students, even the very young, have wisdom and experience to share.

Human Development

As mentioned previously in this chapter, all of us acquire wisdom and knowledge in different ways. It is true that all of us learn using a variety of modalities, all of us mature at different rates, and all of us gain maturity yet not in every part of our lives. Given this certainty, the work of Christian education and formation may seem overwhelming, if not impossible. Yet with the help of four major theorists in the field of human development, the task is a bit less daunting. Speaking specifically of Jean Piaget (in the field of cognitive development), Lawrence Kohlberg (in the field of moral development), James Fowler (in the field of faith development), and Eric Erikson (in the field of psychosocial development), we have much to learn about the stages, patterns, and processes of human development. No one theory is adequate, in and of itself, in terms of expressing the breadth of human development, and none offers a complete or comprehensive understanding. However, each one does offer valuable perspectives, unique insights, and bits of wisdom that better enable us to understand the cognitive and emotional needs and the developmental issues of those we are called to serve.

Educational scholar, John Dettoni, after studying the works and insights of these important thinkers, offers a synthesis of their ideas and developed what he calls "Practical Insights for Christian Education and Formation."[21] Briefly stated, he concludes that people are more alike than dissimilar and we would be more effective in our work if we possessed a basic understanding of life stages and development. He also summarizes that maturity is an anticipated process for everyone, and this is an inner process that parents, teachers, and mentors seek to engage. Thus the question is not if a person matures and grows, but how and in what direction. He confirms that our environments can either hinder or enable growth, and that patterns (or outcomes) of development cannot be altered significantly or accelerated. He clarifies that the processes (the procedures that lead to outcomes) can be hindered, but the basic idea is to work with these processes and not against them. He also helpfully reminds us that development is not linear for any of us, and rarely, if ever moves in a straight line. Rather, personal growth is most often random and uneven. Another insight, which is vital knowledge for educators of any stripe, is to remember that human development is essentially an internal reorganization and construction of how we process our experiences. While developing, we constantly reorder our categories of personal experiences and constantly create new categories. The role of parents, teachers, and mentors is to provide stimuli and guidance for these times of internal readjustment, which prompts even more growth and deeper maturity. Last, he offers the sober reminder that when growth and development stagnate, dysfunction occurs. Theologically speaking, anytime there is stagnation and dysfunction, the will of God is frustrated.[22]

Given that James Fowler founded the study of faith development theory, his particular work warrants further exploration. His basic assertion is that faith is generic, that all human beings possess some form of faith, and that faith proceeds through some predictable process of development. Even atheists, Fowler argues, have something that provides meaning to their experiences and draws them toward something that moves them deeper toward understanding and commitment. In terms of definitions, Fowler's contention was that beliefs constitute a significant way that faith is expressed, but that the concept of faith has more to do with loyalty and trust. With regard to the life of the Church, and of particular note for this chapter, Fowler insisted that faith is relational (community being central), is expressed in mutual trust, and leads to both being and doing. Faith is both held and acted upon. His research led him to believe that faith developed through six identifiable stages, congruent with chronological age and maturation, with each stage advancement progressing into a deeper and more comprehensive trust and greater flexibility. He found that the stages were invariant, that is, everyone passed through the same stages. He found that the stages were sequential, that is, they occur in the same order for every person. He also found that the stages were hierarchical, that is, each stage builds upon the previous stages. Having said this, he was also clear that not everyone progressed through all six stages. In fact, his research determined that most adults in the United States remain at stages three or four. His theory is extremely helpful in this discussion because it suggests that faith has the potential to grow throughout the human life span, and that congregations can create intentional programming to encourage that growth.[23]

Learning Styles

There is a rapidly growing body of research, and much written in recent years about learning styles and the methods used in teaching to various learning modalities. The traditional view of teaching was that everyone learned essentially the same way and the students took in information following a similar linear pattern: the teacher taught by presenting information; students took notes; teachers interacted with students by asking teacher-directed questions about the information that was presented; students were tested by repeating the information as a way of showing that they had learned the content of the instruction. Educators now have deeper appreciation for the fact that students receive and process information quite differently. Some naturally prefer visual cues, some verbal or auditory cues, some are kinesthetic learners and prefer to touch, feel, and experience. While all of us in fact prefer some blend of these modalities, in general, visual learners constitute approximately 40%, auditory learners constitute 20%, and tactile–kinesthetic learners constitute the other 40% of students. It is also interesting to note that, while 70% of all students have strong modality preferences, the other 30% can stay focused, without regard to modality, as long as they remain interested.[24]

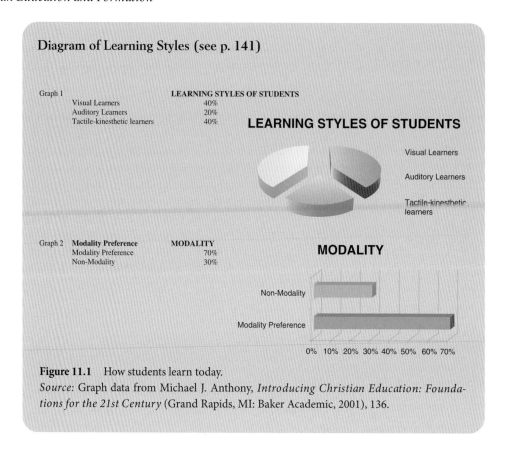

Diagram of Learning Styles (see p. 141)

Graph 1
Visual Learners   40%
Auditory Learners   20%
Tactile-kinesthetic learners   40%

LEARNING STYLES OF STUDENTS

Visual Learners
Auditory Learners
Tactile-kinesthetic learners

Graph 2 **Modality Preference**   **MODALITY**
Modality Preference   70%
Non-Modality   30%

MODALITY

Non-Modality
Modality Preference

0% 10% 20% 30% 40% 50% 60% 70%

Figure 11.1   How students learn today.
Source: Graph data from Michael J. Anthony, *Introducing Christian Education: Foundations for the 21st Century* (Grand Rapids, MI: Baker Academic, 2001), 136.

The challenge for educators, both inside and outside the Church, is to honor preferred learning styles by offering congruent teaching methods. When these efforts are made, amazing things can happen. When efforts are not made, some students will likely be left behind. The sad fact is that students can quickly convince themselves that they are either smart or not smart and it is nearly impossible to overcome that initial impression. "One public elementary school teacher once quipped, 'It takes no time at all for a child to understand the difference between being assigned to the Robin Reading Group or the Buzzard Reading Group.'"[25]

The challenge for church educators is to find a way to teach all those different learning styles in one classroom. In addition to always finding ways to speak, show, and actively engage and experience particular content, Michael Anthony, in his book *Introducing Christian Education*, offers a four-step natural learning process that moves beyond basic modalities to address different types of learners. He suggests that all four steps be considered in every lesson that is prepared. The first group and step one is addressed to *collaborative learners*. The key question in this step is *Why do I need to know this?* It is important for collaborative learners to start with something they already know, and then seek to connect any new information to that past knowledge or experience. The second group and step two is addressed to *analytic learners*. The key question in this step is *What new things do I need to know?* This group needs to learn something new in every lesson or gain some new perspective on something they already know. The third group and step three is addressed to *common sense learners*. The key question in this step is *How does this work?* This group seeks application of the content they are receiving. The fourth group and final step is addressed to *dynamic learners*. The key question in this step is *What can this become?* This future oriented group has the potential to lead the entire class in finding creative ways to use what they have learned.[26] Realizing that almost every classroom, at any given time, consists of students who possess a variety of preferred learning styles, the goal is to consistently and intentionally offer a blend of approaches and teaching methods with the hope of making a substantive and meaningful connection.

Generational Studies

Another area with an extensive and growing body of writing that provides some basic clues about the people we are called to serve comes from the field of generational studies. This approach provides yet another way of seeking to understand and effectively teach God's multigenerational people. While the developmental approach looks at life span, and sociologists look at social grouping, and psychologists study personality and attitudinal categories, the generational perspective seeks to identify the values, beliefs, and actions of certain segments of society. It seeks to ask why certain generational groups believe and act in identifiable ways and in identifiable patterns. Although somewhat vague and imprecise, a "generation can best be defined as a group of people born within a span of about twenty-two years (about the length of time from a mother's birth until she gives birth)."[27] Thus people categorized within a certain generational group are placed there permanently and arbitrarily. Proponents of generational studies contend that this approach provides the strongest basis for generalizing about large groups of people, much stronger than other categories such as race, gender, or geographical region. The common thread, and major determining factor, is their shared experience and memories of that experience, which tend to shape their generational world view. The concept is that a common age combined with a distinct location in history provides a unique shared biography. There have been many attempts over the years to categorize definitively the generations of the twentieth century. In spite of many differences, most keep the number at four, and all mark the beginnings and endings of generations by different historical events or different social circumstances (war, economic crisis, cultural turbulence). By way of example, we will follow the categories popularized by Thomas Rainer. His "Four Bs" generational categories are:

Builders   Born between 1910 and 1945 Account for 76 million births
Boomers   Born between 1946 and 1964 Account for 77 million births
Busters   Born between 1965 and 1976 Account for 44 million births
Bridgers   Born between 1977 and 1994 Account for 72 million births

Those of the *builder* era, sometimes also called the *G.I. Generation*, are thus named because they were alive for both world wars. This group also experienced the Great Depression. As a result of this common history they have developed several common characteristics: strong community spirit, strong sense of family (the family unit is important), tend to be well organized, highly structured, left-brained, friendly, and optimistic. They tend to be in stable marriages and exhibit a can-do pragmatic spirit. They generally rely on intellectual reason to acquire information and less so on emotional or kinetic resources.

The *boomer* era, named for the largest number of births in the last century, were mostly raised by stay-at-home mothers and lived through the Vietnam War and Woodstock, and the anti-authoritarian and countercultural era that followed. More self-centered than their builder parents, this generation has a strong independent spirit which has contributed to the rise of *New Age Spirituality* and the *Self-Help Movement*. They tend to be idealists, champions of causes such as world peace, ending poverty, and creating utopian communities where all of this can be accomplished. Wanting to give more to their children than they felt they received, this generation values a strong work ethic, and a willingness to sacrifice for the welfare and safety of their children. Rejecting many of the values of their parents, boomers have the highest divorce rate ever experienced in the United States. The subsequent fragmentation and blending has led to a new and much broader definition of what constitutes a family. Boomers value excellence in education and expect a high level of personal choice in practically every aspect of their lives.

The *busters*, named for the sharp decline in births, have also been called Generation X (or simply Gen X) because they do not fit easily into any particular category. Trending away from the idealism of boomers, they nevertheless cherish individualism, share a declining view and increased suspicion of institutions, and have a practical approach to life. Busters are ravenous consumers, particularly of technical gadgets. Raised in technology-rich environments, they tend to have shorter attention spans and prefer fast-paced, eye-catching forms of information and entertainment. This group would rather go to the movies than read a book. They are generally pleasure seekers and passive learners, preferring a multi-media presentation of information that includes all three learning modalities (auditory, visual, and kinesthetic). Less biblically literate than the generations before, this group is however open to biblical truth if it can be immediately and practically applied to everyday life. Unlike their forbears who were comfortable with traditional forms of authority found in the Church and in Scripture, and who were moved by well-reasoned intellectual arguments, this generation respond more easily to stories, based in experience, easily applicable, and deeply rooted in the context of everyday life.

The *bridgers*, or *millennials*, are the transition generation linking the twentieth and twenty-first centuries. This is a huge group and a work in progress in terms of identifiable categories and definitive traits. However, some things are clear. This is a multiracial and multicultural cohort. The pulse of this generation runs fast. With little connection to the twentieth century, this group is bombarded by images and technology, is fragmented in terms of focus, and is accustomed to constant change. One major concern about this generation is that this group has been shaped into consumers from birth, well before having the ability to make ethical decisions based on the formation of beliefs and values. One result of this phenomenon is that nothing seems to shock them. As movies, television, and social media continue to push the boundaries of what is acceptable, there is little push back, complaint, or protest. When such disturbing material and content becomes normalized, it is increasingly difficult to discern the difference between what is right and what is wrong.

While there is much to appreciate about generational studies in terms of the challenges and opportunities facing the mainline Church, it is also important to maintain perspective.

This approach is based largely on subjective and anecdotal evidence, is not based on empirical research, and does not take into consideration important societal descriptors (such as race, ethnicity, economic status). Nor does it include in its theoretical framework the important role of family influence. Yet in spite of all this, generational studies provide an invaluable reminder that the Church must be a student of culture, especially when thinking about our approach to Christian education and formation in an ever-changing world. It is wise to gather insights from these theories, while at the same time being aware of their limitations.[28]

Education and Formation in the Small Church

Highlighted in our chapter on church growth and evangelism is the fact that small churches (those averaging fewer than 100 at worship) make up the majority of mainline congregations. Given the predominance of small congregations, their longevity, their stability, and their potential for growth, it makes sense to focus part of our discussion on the unique opportunities for faith development in small churches. The one great misconception is that the small church is merely a scaled down version of a larger one. This false impression has led many pastors to try to adopt the practices of larger churches, which usually leads only to frustration and dissatisfaction. In reality, the small church is governed by a completely different set of congregational dynamics. Small congregations are both quantitatively and qualitatively different.

In her helpful book, *Christian Education in the Small Membership Church*, Karen Tye describes six qualities that exemplify the small church: (i) there is a strong sense of community; (ii) they function like a family; (iii) traditions run deep; (iv) there is a high percentage of participation; (v) there is a simplified organizational structure; and (vi) worship is the primary activity.[29] Of these, we believe that the key dynamic and the primary operating principle is that the small church functions like a family. The old adage about small churches says that they are "hard to get into and even harder to get out of" and this is due mostly to strong family bonds that hold them together.[30] Attendance in the small congregation is not only a Christian duty, but a family obligation. The strength of this familial bond makes the small church extremely effective in transmitting faith as part of its cultural norms.

The success and longevity of a small church pastor is determined by how well they become a part of the family, and not because of any particular pastoral or professional skill. The key to any approach to education and formation in the small church is to build on the existing tradition, to start with what already exists. Change must be evolutionary and not revolutionary and begins with the building of trust and relationships, as well as learning, honoring, and respecting the tradition and culture that are already in place.[31] A pastor will be effective in leading a small congregation by understanding and valuing their preferences, by working within existing traditions to generate new ideas, and by being patient to allow new ideas to take root and new traditions to emerge. It is important to know that even the slightest change is invariably viewed as threatening and that faithfulness and perseverance are essential.[32]

A Life of Faith

Now we have come full circle and return to the fundamental question that began this chapter, *how does one embrace a life of faith?* And we now add the corollary *how do we assist others in this process?* To help answer these questions we also return to our three central themes: the domestic Church (the role of parents, family, and households), the *practice* of Christianity (developing daily patterns), and the congregation (being part of a worshipping community of faith). Reminded that this is ultimately the Spirit's work, we believe that these three, taken together, offer an effective guide to shaping and sharing a Christian life.

An important voice in this particular conversation in mainline Christianity is that of Craig Dykstra, an ordained Presbyterian minister and scholar in the field of practical theology and pastoral ministry. In his book *Growing in the Life of Faith*, Dykstra observes that people learn to play baseball by playing baseball, and he contends that the same is true for learning a life of faith. People come to faith by practice and it is the goal of education and formation to teach these practices which include: corporate worship; telling the Christian story together; interpreting Scripture and the history of the Church; praying; reconciliation; acts of service; giving generously; suffering with and for others; showing hospitality; working for justice and peace; to name only a few. He believes that people come to faith, grow in faith, and are sustained in faith by participating in these practices. He reminds us that whether practiced individually, as a household, or as a congregation these are the practices of the whole Church of God. He also cautions that faith does not simply spring up, that these practices are learned over time and there is no one single practice that is central to obtaining faith. In the end, he concludes, faith is not a task to be accomplished but rather a life to be lived.[33]

Dykstra's work is also helpful in understanding the household or family dimension of this framework of faith. He defines a family as "people who make promises to each other," and goes further to say, "when we see what the promises are we see what the family is."[34] Families are linked by birth, adoption (in the broadest sense of that word), or by marriage. Meant to be an inclusive term, his definition includes both the married and unmarried, those with or without children, and even those living alone (just because we are linked to others does not mean that we live under the same roof). Promises are important to families because they connect us as part of a human matrix. He goes further to add that it is the *promise making* and not necessarily the *promise keeping* that constitutes family, and believes that families are held together by commitments and not necessarily by success. Families fail for all sorts of reasons, sometimes our own doing and sometimes due to circumstances beyond our control, but Dykstra contends that it is not the failure to keep promises that destroys families but the failure to keep making promises.[35] And it is precisely here, in the context of a promise making family, where the Christian practices, which belong to the whole worshipping community, are shared within the family and nurtured in individual members.

We offer Dykstra the last word:

> In my view, an essential task of education in faith is to teach all the basic practices of the Christian faith. The fundamental aim of Christian education in all its forms, varieties, and settings should be that individuals – and indeed whole communities – learn these practices, be

drawn into participating in them, learn to do them with increasingly deepened understanding and skill, learn to extend them more broadly and fully in their own lives and into their world, and learn to correct them, strengthen them, and improve them.[36]

Notes

1   Ronald T. Habermas, *Introduction to Christian Education and Formation: A Lifelong Plan for Christ-Centered Restoration* (Grand Rapids, MI: Zondervan, 2008), 17.

2   Ibid., 17.

3   Ibid., 13–14.

4   Karen Tye, *Basics of Christian Education* (St. Louis, MO: Chalice Press, 2000), 1–3.

5   Ibid., 23.

6   Ibid.

7   Ibid., 10–13.

8   Ibid., 93–117.

9   Kenda Creasy Dean, "Faith, nice and easy: The almost Christian formation of teens," *Christian Century*, August 10, 2010, vol. 127, no. 16, 22–27.

10 Michael J. Anthony, *Introducing Christian Education: Foundations for the 21st Century* (Grand Rapids, MI: Baker Academic, 2001), 14.

11 Ibid., 27.

12 Ibid.

13 Ibid., 33.

14 Ibid., 46.

15 Ibid., 46–51.

16 Norma Cook Everist, *The Church as Learning Community: A Comprehensive Guide to Christian Education* (Nashville, TN: Abingdon Press, 2002), 9.

17 Mark F. Bozzuti-Jones, *Informed by Faith* (Cambridge, MA: Cowley Publications, 2004), 8–24.

18 Ibid., 30.

19 Ibid., 31.

20 Ibid., 36.

21 See John M. Dettoni, and James C. Wilhoit, *Nurture that is Christian: Developmental Perspectives on Christian Education* (Ada, MI: Bridgepoint Books, 1995).

22 Habermas, *Introduction to Christian Education*, 81.

23 Anthony, *Introducing Christian Education*, 83–88.

24 Ibid., 136.

25 Ibid., 130.

26 Ibid., 130–131.

27 Ibid., 237.

28 Ibid., 237–244.

29 Karen Tye, *Christian Education in the Small Membership Church* (Nashville, TN: Abingdon Press, 2008), 1.

30 Anthony, *Introducing Christian Education*, 159.

31 Ibid., 160.

32 Ibid., 161.

33 Craig Dykstra, *Growing in the Life of Faith, second edition* (Louisville, KY: Geneva Press, 1999), 42–44.

34 Ibid., 97.

35 Ibid., 110.

36 Ibid., 71.

Annotated Bibliography

Anthony, Michael J. and Benson, Warren S., *Exploring the History and Philosophy of Christian Education* (Grand Rapids, MI: Kregel Publications, 2003).

This broad study of the history of Christian education stretches back to the Old Testament to the turn of the twenty-first century and reaches into the future. The goal is to apply historical wisdom to the current issues and practice of the ministry of Christian education.

Anthony, Michael J., *Introducing Christian Education: Foundations for the 21st Century* (Grand Rapids, MI: Baker Academic, 2001).
A thorough compendium of many sources and contributors on key facets of Christian education, this text includes both a history of general Christian education plus basic mechanics. Later portions of the book apply theology and theory to practical education.

Astley, Jeff, *The Philosophy of Christian Religious Education* (Birmingham, AL: Religious Education Press, Inc., 1994).
Based on the assumption that philosophy is the basic foundation to the practice and theory of religious education, this volume interprets and offers helpful insights into current major issues facing religious education form a philosophical perspective.

Bozzuti-Jones, Mark F., *Informed by Faith* (Cambridge, MA: Cowley Publications, 2004).
Designed as a catalyst for conversation between religious educators and parents, and for the spiritual refreshment of both, this book examines the history of education in faith communities (African, Asian, and Jewish traditions) and offers a helpful perspective of the role of children in education (as both student and teacher).

Cram, Ronald H., ed., *Understanding Trends in Protestant Education in the Twentieth Century* (Lanham, MD: University Press of America, 1998).
This clinical text is an introduction to the central ideas of twentieth-century Protestant religious education theory and the major theorists, and is also a reflection on the current purpose and understanding of religious education.

Dykstra, Craig, *Growing in the Life of Faith, second edition* (Louisville, KY: Geneva Press, 1999).
Written from the Presbyterian and Reformed traditions, this second edition explores the traditions and practices that help people grow in faith and then helps apply them to the Church in the diverse, modern world.

Everest, Norma Cook, ed., *Christian Education as Evangelism* (Minneapolis, MN: Fortress Press, 2007).
This text, written from a Lutheran perspective, connects solid Christian education to evangelical outreach, and takes a practical approach that incorporates stories, reflections in the development of parish programs, and strategies.

Everest, Norma Cook, *The Church as Learning Community: A Comprehensive Guide to Christian Education* (Nashville, TN: Abingdon Press, 2002).
At its best, every congregation is a community of teachers and learners. This comprehensive book explores this notion in depth and puts forth a vision of the entire congregation as a learning community.

Habermas, Ronald T., *Introduction to Christian Education and Formation: A Lifelong Plan for Christ-Centered Restoration* (Grand Rapids, MI: Zondervan, 2008).
This Christocentric approach to Christian education focuses on the application of Christ's earthly example. Building on the work of others he outlines the text with five global tasks of Christian education and formation: education for evangelism; education for fellowship; education for service; education for kingdom consciousness; and education for worship.

Osmer, Richard R., *The Teaching Ministry of Congregations* (Louisville, KY: Westminster John Knox Press, 2005).

In this dense and data-filled text, the author applies practical theology to the ministry of teaching. This book also takes a more global perspective to the study of Christian education.

Osmer, Richard R. and Schweitzer, Friedrich, *Religious Education between Modernization and Globalization: New Perspectives on the United States and Germany* (Grand Rapids, MI: Eerdmans Publishing Co., 2003).
Looking at issues of modernization, globalization, and postmodernism through a unique comparative and global perspective, this impressive book studies religious education in various contexts, and charts a path to identifying and addressing issues facing the Church in the modern world.

Parrett, Gary A. and Kang, S. Steve, *Teaching the Faith, Forming the Faithful: A Biblical Vision for Education in the Church* (Downers Grove, IL: Intervarsity Press, 2009).
Written as a faithful response to the decline of Christian education and spiritual formation, the authors seek to address both the content and process of religious education by developing a "core curriculum" and addressing the "method" or "process" of faith formation that is not simply catechesis.

Powers, Bruce P., ed., *Christian Education Handbook: A Revised and Completely Updated Edition* (Nashville, TN: B&H Academic, 1995).
This book, written by and for Christian educators, provides a comprehensive resource for the principles and the practice of Christian education in congregational settings.

Tye, Karen, *Basics of Christian Education* (St. Louis, MO: Chalice Press, 2000).
Addressing the vital areas of how to build and maintain a quality Christian education program, this practical book is a concise, practical, and easy-to-use guide. Questions and exercises conclude each chapter to help with application to a particular context for ministry.

Tye, Karen, *Christian Education in the Small Membership Church* (Nashville, TN: Abingdon Press, 2008).
This book is part of series on ministry in small congregations and challenges the notion that small churches are at a disadvantage to larger, program churches in terms of the task of Christian formation. It is written for those serving in the context of small membership churches.

12

Music and Hymnody

While it is true that Christian worship can and does exist in the absence of music, it is also true that every vibrant and growing Christian community has music at the core of its common life. This chapter explores the nature and importance of music in Christian worship, the history and development of music in the life of the church, the form and shape of hymns and religious songs, the tension between traditional and contemporary forms of music in worship, the role of the church musician, as well as the emergence and influence of the music of global Christianity in mainline worship. At the outset, it is important to state the obvious. Any conversation about music, and even our language in describing music, is tainted with judgment and personal bias.

Yet more than simply a matter of taste or personal preference, the music of the Church has the sole task of offering praise and worship to God. The goal of this chapter is not to define "good" or "bad" church music, nor is it to definitively decide between old and new forms of musical expression, nor is it an attempt to create a set of universal standards to discern the suitability of music for use in the church. Rather, our hope is to present an overview of historical and current issues that will encourage faithful conversations about church music within congregations. While some congregations are able to produce the highest quality of musical expression, we believe that every church has within it the God-given resources to offer music that encourages worship and is pleasing to God.

As is often the case, we sometimes do not grasp the value of something until we are deprived of it. This could certainly be said of music in the church. While some traditions forbid the use of music altogether, or at least avoid some forms of musical expression, the churches of the mainline are filled with music. This raises the question of why music is so essential to Christian worship and points to the underlying question regarding the purpose of music in a liturgical setting.

An Introduction to Ministry: A Primer for Renewed Life and Leadership in Mainline Protestant Congregations, First Edition. Ian S. Markham and Oran E. Warder.

Why We Sing

James White, a leading liturgical historian, observes that practically "every choir room has a sign quoting Augustine to the effect that whoever sings prays twice."[1] Affirming the truth of that statement, he expounds on the idea that music offers an additional dimension to worship. Singing requires a deeper level of listening and also requires a deeper awareness and consciousness of what one is doing while singing. Music is a more expressive medium than ordinary speech and can convey greater intensity of feeling. The use of pitch, melody, harmony, tempo, and volume can express a broad range of depth and emotion and adds value to worship. He cautions that although the creation of beauty can be a byproduct of musical offerings, this is not the goal of worship. The primary criterion, he contends, is not the creation of beauty, but rather the dignity of expression.[2]

We sing and make music in the church for the expressed purpose of praising and giving thanks to God. Singing for oneself involves more active participation on the part of the worshiper than listening to someone else sing, no matter how talented they may be. Congregational singing gives everyone the opportunity to offer to God the best sounds that they can create and this offering cannot be adequately replaced by the efforts of another. Fortunately in the church there does not have to be a choice between the two since we often have both.[3]

The function of choral music in worship is a fundamental question. The answer to the question determines the best use and placement of a congregational choir. For instance, if the purpose of choral music is to share the Ministry of the Word, perhaps the best placement of the choir is in the front, facing and singing *to* the congregation. If the purpose of the choir is to create beauty, they will be singing *for* the congregation and their placement is irrelevant as long as the choir can be heard. In most mainline congregations, the role of the choir is to support and encourage congregational singing and this is best accomplished by being placed *behind* or *within* the congregation. White suggests that perhaps the best solution, where reasonably applicable, is the old basilica model that places the choir in the front of the nave with the congregation on three sides. This positioning has the advantage of being able to accommodate all three choral functions.[4]

A Brief History of Liturgical Music

To further explore the role and function of music in Christian worship, a broad and brief overview of the history and development of music in the life of the Church will shed some light on current practice and also highlight issues that continue to challenge us today. We begin with the early Church, whose sounds have "vanished irretrievably beyond the range of our ears."[5] In fact, since musical notation was not invented until the eleventh century, we are unable to recreate the music of the entire first half of the Christian era. Before that time the music was passed on by oral tradition and memory. There are certainly New Testament citations that reference singing, among them Paul's famous admonition that rather than getting drunk with wine, Ephesian Christians should be filled with the Spirit, "as you sing psalms and hymns and spiritual songs among yourselves, singing and making melody to the Lord in your hearts, giving thanks to God the Father at all times and for everything in the name of our Lord Jesus Christ" (Ephesians 5:18–20). We can make reasonable guesses about the content of those psalms, hymns, and spiritual songs that were shared in the early Church, but have no idea how they sounded. We can, however, learn a great deal about early Christian musical thought by exploring the writings of that time.

What is most striking about this exploration is the realization that conflict over music goes back to the earliest Christians. In his insightful and thoughtful book, *A New Song for an Old World: Musical Thought in the Early Church*, Calvin R. Stapert suggests that retrieving the voices of the early Church has particular relevance to us today and makes the point that the circumstances of their times and ours are remarkably similar. For instance, in researching the main developments in musical thought in the second and third centuries, he compares the writings of *Clement of Alexandria* (ca. 150–215 CE), a Greek who was kindly disposed to the assimilation of Greek thought in the evolution of the Church, with *Tertullian* (155–240 CE), who was Latin speaking and absolutely opposed to the Church's acceptance and appropriation of anything pagan, including Greek philosophy. While the contrast between these two positions is quite stark, and that of other early Church figures less pronounced, there nevertheless developed remarkable consistency in their views of music in terms of what was acceptable and what was unacceptable.[6] Generally speaking, there was a widely accepted polemic against pagan influence. Even Augustine, who loved music and wrote of its power to delight and inspire, also wrote of its dangers and warned that Christians should not turn to pagan "theatrical frivolities to discover whether anything valuable for spiritual purposes is to be gathered from their harps and other instruments."[7] He is particularly worried about the power of the attraction of music and the problem of sensual pleasures, that for Augustine, included pleasures of the ears. He was also troubled that music, which he considered a form of rhetoric, could be used to dazzle people with elegance rather than truth.[8] Thus there was always the potential for sinning while enjoying seemingly innocent pleasures. Augustine, by his own experience, knew of our human proclivity to fall in love with the good things in life as if they were ultimate goods. In terms of church music, he points directly to the heart of the problem and warns that delight in music should not be an end in itself but rather a means to inspire love that points beyond itself to the love of God, the source of all good things.[9]

We can be relieved that our early forebears did not reject music completely, but shared a particular enthusiasm for psalmody and hymnody. Their affirmation of these musical forms is proof that they, in spite of their misgivings, had a great appreciation for the use of music in worship. For them, music was a gift and was to be taken seriously and yet they retained their endorsement only for its proper use.

Later in this chapter we will again take up the issue of the inherent conflict that continues to be debated between appropriate forms and expressions of church music, including the persistence of secular influences, yet at this point we return to the history and development of liturgical music. In the first three centuries it is fairly certain that not only was music an integral part of Christian worship, but also it was the possession of the whole worshiping community. It was not until after 313 CE and the conversion of Constantine that worship in general and music specifically would take on more complicated forms. For instance, the use of musical instruments to support congregational singing began to be accepted as long as those instruments were free from any association with pagan rituals. Another related issue that needed to be resolved was whether or not women would be allowed to sing in church. Again, because the association with the popular use of female voices in pagan rites, the practice was slow to gain acceptance.[10]

It was not until later in the fourth century that the role of *cantor* (a soloist who could lead congregational singing) began to emerge, later still for the emergence of a choir. It was the Middle Ages and the monastic development of musical notation that brought significant advances in the realm of church music. The monastic rule of life brought sung daily prayers to the tradition. This included the communal singing of the psalms, liturgical texts, and the use of *canticles* (biblical texts set to music). These daily liturgies took place in a part of the church that would become known as "the choir"; that is, two parallel sections of seats facing each other, divided by an aisle. This configuration leant itself to the creation of a liturgical dialogue that included singing the psalms antiphonally (two semi-independent groups singing alternate musical phrases). In terms of musical style, *Gregorian chant* (simple and ascetic unison singing) was the first to emerge. This was followed in the late Middle Ages by *polyphony* (multiple voices singing simultaneously). The Reformation brought an explosion of expression that ranged from the complete abolition of music in the church, to the use of only the human voice with no instrumentation, to liturgies that were sung entirely. It was Martin Luther, himself a hymn writer, who recognized the enormous potential of music to exemplify the theology of "the priesthood of all believers." The liturgy and music that had become the exclusive property of the learned clergy, in a language unfamiliar to the people, could now once again belong to the whole body of the faithful and invite their full participation in worship.[11]

It took a while, of course, for new liturgical freedoms to be embraced, encouraged, and enjoyed. Initially it was only the psalms that were to be sung by the congregation. In most parts of post-Reformation Europe the state of congregational singing must have been abysmal. In England, very few congregants owned psalm books and it seems that those who did would often neglect to bring them to church. It was the parish clerk who was counted upon to have a copy and to lead the singing using a method that would become known as "lining out." The clerk would read out a line of the psalm that would then be repeated back, sung in unison, and then the clerk would move on to the next and then the next until completed. There was no musical direction or notation, and the singing was undisciplined and painfully slow. "One writer tells of a vicar who, having left his sermon behind, announced a psalm, walked half a mile home and back and returned to find his congregation still singing the same psalm."[12] But things were about to change.

It was *Isaac Watts* (1674–1748) who, appalled at the state of congregational psalm singing, encouraged the Church to move beyond the psalms and toward hymn singing, yet with new words and the use of more familiar and even popular tunes. He set a new standard by introducing the idea that hymns can be evangelical, meaning inclusive of the New Testament, that hymns can be freely composed and not strictly bound to biblical texts or paraphrases of biblical texts, and that hymns can express the thoughts and feelings of the singers themselves. These revolutionary ideas were adopted by John (and especially) Charles Wesley, who transformed congregational singing by making Church hymnody accessible to the people in the pew regardless of their education or background. Their efforts in compiling *A Collection of Hymns for the Use of the People Called Methodists* was intended to serve as a supplemental resource to the established Church, yet fueled a movement that would lead to the establishment of a new denomination. At issue were essentially those who preferred to express their faith on an emotional level and used these hymns as a means of conversion, and those who preferred a more intellectual expression of faith. The publishing of the hymn collection was an attempt by the Wesley brothers to exert some control over the growing movement. Their hope was to keep hymn singing from becoming an "orgy of emotion," to provide authorized tunes and texts, and to keep Christ at the center of the hymns.[13] As a result of their efforts, hymn singing became widely popular and their profound influence continues.

Another important influence on musical expression in the mainline is the experience and contribution of the Black Church. The experience of slaves "who took on the profaned religion of the master and transformed it" articulates the faith of an oppressed people and led to the creation of spiritual hymns that were themselves a means of liberation.[14] In contrast to John and Charles Wesley (whose hymns reflected the need for followers to acknowledge their sinfulness, accept the grace of God as mediated through Jesus Christ, and retreat from the world into the fellowship of Christ's people) the spirituals of the slave tradition acknowledged the slave as a beloved child of God who needed saving, not from themselves and not from the world, but from slavery. The Wesleys longed for freedom from the world, the spirituals hoped for freedom in this world and the next.[15]

John Wesley's Directions for Singing

As found in the preface to his *Select Hymns* from 1761, John Wesley was fond of directing explicitly how to sing and perform these songs of praise:

 I. Learn *these* Tunes before you learn any others; afterwards learn as many as you please.

 II. Sing them exactly as they are printed here, without altering or mending them at all; and if you have learned to sing them otherwise, unlearn it as soon as you can.

 III. Sing *All*. See that you join with the congregation as frequently as you can. Let not a slight degree of weakness or weariness hinder you. If it is a cross to you, take it up and you will find a blessing.

 IV. Sing *lustily* and with good courage. Beware of singing as if you were half dead, or half asleep; but lift up your voice with strength. Be no more afraid of your voice now, nor more ashamed of its being heard, than when you sung the songs of *Satan*.

 V. Sing *modestly*. Do not bawl, so as to be heard above or distinct from the rest of the congregation, that you may not destroy the harmony; but strive to unite your voices together, so as to make one clear melodious sound.

 VI. Sing in *Time*: whatever time is sung, be sure to keep with it. Do not run before nor stay behind it; but attend close to the leading voices, and move therewith as exactly as you can; and take care not to sing too slow. This drawing way naturally steals on all who are lazy; and it is high time to drive it out from us, and sing all our tunes just as quick as we did at first.

Source: John Wesley, "Instructions for Singing," *Select Hymns*, 1761.

Aspects of Congregational Music

In spite of the fact that most mainline Christians know what we like, when it comes to church music, it is also helpful to be reminded that for the most part we like what we know.[16] Our hymnals and songbooks are filled with a vast range of material that includes, no doubt, hymns that represent the breadth of the historical tradition of the Church that we have just reviewed. Most include ancient texts as well as contemporary expressions representing the virtual explosion of new hymns and spiritual songs that have been written and composed in recent decades. Yet whether old or new, it is helpful to remember that there are essentially three different categories of congregational music and essentially three basic hymn structures.

Congregational singing consists of *service music, psalmody*, and *hymnody*.[17] Service music refers to musical settings of the fixed set of words in the liturgy. These are the sections of prayers that are consistently repeated during services and include the *Gloria* ("Glory to God in the highest…") and the *Sanctus* ("Holy, Holy, Holy, Lord God of Power and Might…"). Psalmody refers to the singing of the psalms. The Psalms are the hymnbook of the Hebrew Bible and most congregations follow the Jewish practice of singing these Scriptures as a regular part of worship. The psalms can be sung in a variety of ways (*plainsong, Anglican chant*, metrical versions, paraphrases, etc.). Hymnody, in the broadest sense, and to again borrow from Augustine, is "the praise of God in song."[18] In subsequent generations, and certainly today, more specific and detailed definitions of hymnody have surfaced and continue to be debated. We will enter that conversation in the section of this chapter that examines the tension between traditional and contemporary forms of church music. For now we will embrace the broader definition.

Hymnody

Using this more expansive understanding of hymnody, there are some general rules about the form, structure, and shape of hymns. Again, these categories are generally true whether or not a hymn is old or new, widely loved or barely known, based on a popular singable melody or one that is hopelessly complex. In terms of form, structure, and shape there are essentially three styles of hymns: the western, or linear style; the cyclical, or repeating style; and last, a form that encompasses a combination of both previous styles.[19] Between these three there are innumerable variations, but all start with these basic structures.

Western hymns

The western form is at one end of the hymnody spectrum. The defining characteristic of this style is that it is sequential in form. There are several stanzas that proceed in linear fashion and progress from one concept to the next. These sequential style hymns have a definite beginning, middle, and end. This type of hymn is useful in telling a story, teaching a doctrine, or describing certain aspects of the Christian faith or the nature of God. An example of this form might be a hymn about the Trinity. Such a hymn would have one verse for each person of the Trinity and a final fourth verse in praise of all three. The classic hymn *Come, Thou Almighty King* written by an unknown author in the mid-1700s fits this style:

Come, thou almighty King,
Help us thy name to sing,
Help us to praise!
Father all-glorious,
O'er all victorious,
Come and reign over us,
Ancient of Days.

Come, thou Incarnate Word,
By heaven and earth adored,
Our prayer attend;
Come and thy people bless
And give thy Word success;
Stablish thy righteousness,
Savior and Friend!

Come, holy Comforter,
Thy sacred witness bear
In this glad hour.
Thou, who almighty art,
Now rule in every heart
And ne'er from us depart,
Spirit of Power!

To the great One in Three
Eternal praises be
Hence evermore!
His sovereign majesty
May we in glory see
And to eternity
Love and adore!

Poems of Grace: the Text of the Hymnal 1982
(New York: Church Publishing, 2000), 293–294.

Cyclical hymns

The cyclical or repeating style is at the opposite end of the hymn structure spectrum. Rather than a linear, sequential pattern that leads from concept to concept through a distinct beginning, middle, and end, this form usually involves textual and melodic repetition. In addition to repeating texts and melodies, this form utilizes fewer words and simpler melodies. If the western style focuses on reaching the rational mind, the cyclical style excels at reaching the heart. Without the need for hymnbooks or projected words, the easily remembered and repeated words can lead to prayerful meditation or can be sung while simultaneously performing other liturgical acts like receiving communion or the laying on of hands for healing.

Since the last example was from the mid-eighteenth century, let us chose the ancient Latin text *Dona Nobis Pacem* as an example of this hymn form:

> Dona nobis pacem, pacem.
> Dona nobis pacem.

Jacques Berthier, Taizé: Songs for Prayer
(Chicago, IL: GIA Publications, 1995)

This simple text, which is translated "Give us peace," is often used as a repetitive, cyclical liturgical hymn. It is also often sung as a *canon* (a simple round with all voices musically identical with a new voice starting when the preceding voice reaches the end of the first line). It could be argued that this type of hymn singing is actually more of a spiral than a circle in that each succeeding round has the potential to draw the congregation into deeper communion with God and one another. The music of *Taizé*, a religious community in France that welcomes visitors from around the globe, has become increasingly popular in mainline congregations. This music, almost entirely of the cyclical structure, uses simple texts, translated into many languages and sung simultaneously. On the surface this form of hymnody may appear monotonous, but the use of slight variation in dynamics and intensity in successive cycles can make the experience alive and powerful.

Modern hymns

The third hymn form incorporates the styles and structures of the previous two, and also blends the advantages of both. For instance, a typical hymn in this category would have stanzas in the western style, with linear and sequential structures, and also have a repeatable refrain that would employ the cyclic function. A relatively new and quite popular mainline hymn *Here I Am Lord* is a good example of this structure and hymn type, and contains both of these elements. This hymn was written and composed by Daniel L. Schutte in 1981:[20]

> I, the Lord of sea and sky,
> I have heard my people cry.
> All who dwell in dark and sin,
> My hand will save.
>
> I, who made the stars of night,
> I will make their darkness bright.
> Who will bear my light to them?
> Whom shall I send?
>
> {*Refrain*}
>
> *Here am I, Lord. Is it I, Lord?*
> *I have heard you calling in the night.*
> *I will go, Lord, if you lead me.*
> *I will hold your people in my heart.*
>
> I, the Lord of snow and rain,
> I have borne my people's pain.

I have wept for love of them.
They turn away.

I will break their hearts of stone,
Give them hearts for love alone.
I will speak my words to them.
Whom shall I send?

{Refrain}

I, the Lord of wind and flame,
I will send the poor and lame.
I will set a feast for them.
My hand will save.

Finest bread I will provide,
'Til their hearts be satisfied.
I will give my life to them.
Whom shall I send?

{Refrain}

In addition to being an example of the third hymn style, this hymn also serves as an interesting study of how hymns become part of the mainstream tradition. While it is true that the reforms of Vatican II brought revolutionary change to the music of the Roman Catholic Church, much of it borrowed from the Protestant experience, it is also true that hymns from newer Catholic hymnals have also made their way into Protestant churches. This particular hymn, born out of the music of the Roman Catholic renewal movement, was introduced and quickly embraced as a classic by many mainline denominations.

Traditional and Contemporary Music

This brings us back to the conversation that began earlier in this chapter, a conversation not about the sharing of sacred music among various Christian communities, but the more fundamental conversation about the influence of secular, contemporary music on the established, traditional music of the Church. Every generation of Christians must determine what constitutes acceptable forms of music for worship, and ours is no exception. At the extremes, some have come to believe that the very future of the Church rests on embracing either contemporary or traditional music forms, one or the other, while most fall somewhere in-between.

Our forebears' concern about pagan influences is very much alive. In some corners there are those who attempt to eradicate all contemporary influences and advocate a return to a purer form of Christian practice, while others press for a complete rejection of traditional musical expressions as quaint and arcane, and out of touch with those outside the Church whom they hope to reach. Most, however, tend to take the long view, and acknowledge that the Church, throughout its history, while holding on to the tradition it has received, has also found ways to "baptize" certain profane practices to the extent that future generations would be blissfully unaware of their completely secular roots. Those once suspect practices gain acceptance to the point of becoming part of the tradition. Perhaps the most dramatic example would be the seemingly universal acceptance and use of the pipe organ. This instrument, which is synonymous with church music, was an entirely secular instrument in classical antiquity. Known most notably for its use in ancient drinking establishments, the "king of instruments" has a bit of a checkered past.[21]

In his book, *Music and Vital Congregations: A Practical Guide for Clergy*, William Bradley Roberts argues that the ongoing debate about musical styles in Christian worship represents a false dichotomy and is essentially a "war over nothing."[22] Yet Roberts also concedes that negotiating the diversity of liturgical music styles is the greatest challenge facing church musicians. The way we talk about this diversity is part of the issue because our language often conveys an immediate judgment about what forms are deemed acceptable or unacceptable, legitimate or illegitimate, depending upon one's perspective. If liturgical music is referred to as contemporary, it may not be taken seriously. If liturgical music is called traditional it may be dismissed as outdated. In an attempt to clarify the terms and be more descriptive, one musical scholar referred to church music as either part of the *vernacular tradition* or the *cultivated tradition*. While this classification is helpful, it is still tinged with bias. In the absence of completely neutral language, Roberts chooses to refer to church music as either *classical* or in the category of *popular religious song*. Even more helpfully, Roberts explains that these are not fixed and stagnant categories, but are fluid and flexible over time. Some popular religious songs quickly enter the more standard repertoire of the church's musical life, some take a while to prove themselves as enduring, and many fail to make the transition and fall out of use.[23]

In terms of common practice, some congregations embrace either classical hymns or popular religious songs exclusively, while others have created a hybrid blend of both categories. Some do this seamlessly, while others utilize classic hymns and then have a distinct "praise time" of popular religious songs.[24] This can be theologically problematic if music is used as a stimulus, a summoning of God's Spirit, rather than a response, an acknowledgement that God's Spirit is already present. The Spirit is not at our beck and call and does not simply "show up because we have said the magic words or cranked up enough volume in our praise."[25]

Before a popular religious song becomes part of the classic repertoire, and perhaps is included in a new hymnal or supplemental musical resource, some standards might well be considered for its use in worship. Being clear that he is not a traditionalist and, on the contrary, is a strong proponent of the use of contemporary music in worship, David J. Montgomery, in his book *Sing a New Song: Choosing and Leading Praise in Today's Church*, argues that the setting of boundaries is important and necessary. He writes with concern that the standards for popular religious songs are low in terms of theological depth and literary and musical quality, and laments the "over-riding sense of shallowness, sentimentality and sameness" that seems to permeate many contemporary texts and compositions."[26] He also observes that many contemporary Christian songs are homocentric (highly individualistic with a focus on personal faith to the exclusion of any sense of corporate identity and responsibility), at times express an intimacy that borders on the erotic, and can suffer from bad theology, overused clichés, and careless writing. He is also concerned about what he calls the "appalling self-indulgence, confused and mixed metaphors and a misuse of scripture" that characterizes much of the current musical landscape.[27] Acknowledging that each individual song need not be doctrinally comprehensive, he does suggest, however, that it "should not be incomplete, misleading, or spend a lot of time saying not very much."[28] Last and perhaps most significantly, he also observes a relative absence of contemporary songs that focus on the doctrines of incarnation and atonement and thus, for the most part, an absence of songs on the topic of pain, suffering, sacrifice, or death, which are so central to the Christian faith.[29]

The History of Christian Rock

Christian rock has its origins in secular rock. Rock music in the United States has its roots in the African emphasis on rhythm. Blues comes next. And then we have in the 1950s, Bill Haley and the Comets. This is the start of a movement that includes Elvis Presley and the Beatles. Larry Norman (1947–2008) is acclaimed as the father of Christian rock, with his first album *Upon this Rock* in 1969. For much of the 1970s and 1980s, Christian rock was a niche, distinct, musical area. In recent years, the divide between Christian music and secular music has become less clear with the success of bands such as U2. It was Larry Norman who famously said "Why should the Devil have all the good music?" For many devotees of Christian rock, this has been an important reason for their commitment to this genre.

Conflict between Clergy and Musicians

The current debate between classical hymns and popular religious songs may well be a war over nothing, but it does pose a significant challenge to church musicians and can also be a source of conflict between musicians and clergy. The stories of such conflicts are widespread. In extreme cases the conflict can take the form of underground warfare, or even worse, can undermine the sanctity of the worship service. There is an old joke that captures the latter. An agitated pastor, following a choral anthem, rose from his chair and announced a reading from Acts 20:1, "Now when the uproar had ceased…" The choir sat silently through the reading and the sermon that followed. At the conclusion of the pastor's remarks the choir leapt to its feet and loudly sang another choral anthem, this one based on Romans 13:11, "Now it is high time to awake out of sleep…"[30] Funny, yes, but tragically close to the experience of too many Church professionals. Even the venerable Johann Sebastian Bach had difficulties with his position in the Church. Not long after accepting the ministry of cantor in Leipzig he complained that his new post was not at all as wonderful as he was led to believe, that he was not paid for his work, the city was an expensive place to live, and the clergy were odd and not at all interested in music. He concluded his list of grievances by saying that since he was forced to "live amid almost continual vexation, envy, and persecution," that he would simply have to "with God's help, seek my fortune elsewhere."[31] Bach stayed in Leipzig for 20 more years until his death.

The modern version of this ongoing struggle seems to be based on disagreements over musical style. Aside from issues of personality, ego, and sometimes struggles for power and control, the root of the problem essentially boils down to the fact that clergy and church musicians ordinarily operate out of radically different, and conflicting models and understandings of ministry. Mainline denominations are largely intentional and focused in the formation and training of clergy leaders. Most clergy are seminary-trained and steeped in the ethos and tradition of their respective denominations. In short, clergy are trained to function in the church. By and large this is not so for church musicians. Generally speaking, church musicians are not trained in denominational seminaries and are not intentionally formed for a vocation in the church. Rather, musicians are educated in university schools of music and conservatories where the emphasis is on the acquisition of musical skill and the quality of performance. In short, musicians are prepared to perform for the world and not necessarily to serve the church. So clergy and musician come to their work with a different set of assumptions and sometimes very different goals. Taken to the extreme, a musician might make a music selection that lacks theological judgment, and a clergy person might make a liturgical decision that lacks sound musical judgment.[32]

In addition there are vocational and economic considerations. Good, well-trained organists who are prepared to serve the church are difficult to find and, in this era of shrinking congregational budgets, full-time positions are dwindling. This fact, coupled with the trend to incorporate other instruments in addition to, or in place of, the organ, with additional paid professional musicians has complicated the overall picture. For mainline congregations who continue to embrace a more traditional model, there are several proactive measures that can be taken to strengthen and deepen the role and ministry of the church musician. On a larger scale, denominations can be pressed to be more intentional and focused on the training and formation of church musicians. Congregations can be committed to maintaining and creating full-time music positions (one of the major reasons for the short supply of qualified candidates). This must be coupled with appropriate compensation, a clear ministry description that is regularly updated, and in addition to being musically talented and spiritually grounded, the full-time musician should also be encouraged and supported as a pastoral leader as well as a worship leader in the congregation.[33] Regardless of where an individual congregation falls on the spectrum, it is important to remember the single best way to improve not only the quality of musical expression but also the quality of the overall worship experience is to improve the relationship between worship leaders.[34] Mutual respect and a sense of common mission is key to this relationship.

Add to all this the concern about dwindling Church membership and efforts to attract new members by broadening the musical repertoire of the congregation, coupled with the concern about preserving the tradition of the Church and maintaining the quality of musical expression, and it would seem that conflict is unavoidable. There is also the unrelenting pressure to conform to the wider culture, which, as our early Church forebears remind us, is never neutral to Christianity. As we make changes in style in order to draw people to the Gospel we need to be aware of this dynamic and know where to draw the line. It is crucial to remember that in our "sensation-hungry, pleasure-mad society" sometimes our witness is boldly and intentionally countercultural.[35]

Global Music

One final area of consideration with regard to current trends in mainline church music is to acknowledge the growth and significance of the music of global Christianity. Early missionaries exported music from their home culture and in doing so either intentionally or unintentionally emphasized that Christianity was an entirely foreign religion brought from the outside. Today these churches have expanded and matured and with the rise of immigration and globalization, the experiences of the global Church are now enriching and enlivening our own.[36]

Sharing the Christian faith in a different culture, whether across the world or across the street, always poses a difficult dilemma. At one extreme is the cultural imperialism of our past that seeks to impose faith from outside without regard for existing values and norms, and at the other extreme is cultural relativism that accepts the values and norms of culture even if it means surrendering fundamental Christian tenets. Neither of these is a faithful or acceptable option. Missiologist Andrew Walls offers an alternative that operates within these extremes and suggests that modern evangelists be guided by two principles, what he calls the *indigenizing principle* and the *pilgrim principle*. The indigenizing principle affirms that the Gospel can be at home in any culture. That being the case, the pilgrim principle acknowledges the reality that there is always tension in the relationship between the Christian Gospel and the culture. The task therefore is to communicate the faith in ways that are comprehended but not subsumed by the culture.[37]

Where this intersects with the music of the mainline church is in the recognition that hymns are a means not only of communicating faith within the culture, but also between cultures. The fundamental notion is that everyone and every culture holds some insight about God and hymns are a means by which that insight can be communicated.[38] The incorporation of the songs of global Christianity has begun officially in newer denominational hymnals and supplemental resources and also within the category of popular religious songs. When the people of a dominant culture sing the music of a minority culture (even if not particularly well) a powerful message of unity is sent not only to those in our midst but also to fellow Christians around the world.[39] The communication of faith within and between cultures can only enhance our own understanding and proclamation of the Gospel.

Conclusion

For many people, the music of the church is their only contact with formal religion. This happens at one extreme as sacred music escapes the church and is performed in concert halls, and it also happens at the other extreme, as religious songs sometimes become part of the music of popular culture. At any rate, this recognition serves as a useful reminder that these hymns, psalms, and spiritual songs are often more widely known than the words of the liturgy or of the Bible itself. Within them is the power to touch those who hear them in deep and often unconscious ways. This can happen at any level of musical sophistication, within any musical style, and within any congregation. At the heart of this experience is an encounter with the living God.

Notes

1 James F. White, *Introduction to Christian Worship* (Nashville, TN: Abingdon Press, 2000), 112.
2 Ibid., 111–115.
3 Ibid., 113.
4 Ibid., 114.
5 Calvin R. Stapert, *A New Song for an Old World: Musical Thought in the Early Church* (Grand Rapids, MI: Eerdmans Publishing Co., 2007), 3.
6 Ibid., 1–11.
7 Ibid., 181.
8 Ibid., 185.
9 Ibid., 191–93.
10 White, *Introduction to Christian Worship*, 119.
11 Ibid., 119–126.
12 Brian Castle, *Sing a New Song to the Lord: The Power and Potential of Hymns* (London: Darton, Longman, and Todd, 1994), 49.
13 Ibid., 50–58.
14 Ibid., 59.
15 Ibid., 59–63.
16 William Bradley Roberts, *Music and Vital Congregations: A Practical Guide for Clergy* (New York: Church Publishing, 2009), 16.
17 White, *Introduction to Christian Worship*, 115.
18 Ibid., 115.
19 C. Michael Hawn, *One Bread, One Body: Exploring Cultural Diversity in Worship* (Bethesda, MD: Alban Institute, 2003), 126–127.
20 *Wonder, Love, and Praise: A Supplement to the Hymnal 1982* (New York: Church Publishing, 1997), Hymn 812.
21 White, *Introduction to Christian Worship*, 117.
22 Roberts, *Music and Vital Congregations*, 45.
23 Ibid., 45–59.
24 David J. Montgomery, *Sing a New Song: Choosing and Leading Praise in Today's Church* (Edinburgh, Scotland: Rutherford House, 2000), xiv.
25 Stapert, *A New Song*, 202.
26 Montgomery, *Sing a New Song*, 58.
27 Ibid., 73.
28 Ibid., 76.
29 Ibid., 78.
30 Victoria Sirota, *Preaching to the Choir: Claiming the Role of the Sacred Musician* (New York: Church Publishing, 2006), 91.
31 Ibid., 94.
32 Roberts, *Music and Vital Congregations*, 27–39.
33 Ibid., 40–41.
34 Sirota, *Preaching to the Choir*, 97.
35 Stapert, *A New Song*, 200.
36 White, *Introduction to Christian Worship*, 129.
37 Stephen Darlington and Alan Kreider, *Composing Music for Worship* (Norwich: Canterbury Press, 2003), 10.
38 Castle, *Sing a New Song to the Lord*, 2–4.
39 Roberts, *Music and Vital Congregations*, 57–58.

Annotated Bibliography

Castle, Brian, *Sing a New Song to the Lord: The Power and Potential of Hymns* (London: Darton, Longman, and Todd, 1994).

Viewing song as a universal medium of communication, this book delves into the power of hymns, their relationship to culture, and their ability to teach the faith. Examining the history of hymnody and also the recent wave of new hymns in light of a changing Church, this book also looks to the future implications and possibilities regarding the use of hymns in the worship of the Church.

Costen, Melva Wilson, *In Spirit and in Truth: The Music of African American Worship* (Louisville, MO: Westminster, 2004).
This scholarly yet accessible book traces the development of the music of African American worship back to its origins in Africa, to its emergence in various forms during the North American diaspora, and to its current reality. Arguing against the trend that music in worship has become popular entertainment, the author strongly advocates for the return to the historical, biblical, and theological tradition of African American liturgical music as a means of spiritual empowerment.

Darlington, Stephen and Kreider, Alan, *Composing Music for Worship* (Norwich: Canterbury Press, 2003).
This book is an edited collection of lectures presented by contemporary composers of music for Christian worship at Regents Park College in Oxford in 2000. This text explores both the challenges and the missional opportunities that face those composing music for a postmodern Church.

Fortunato, Frank, Neeley, Paul, and Brinneman, Carol, *All the World is Singing: Glorifying God through the Worship Music of the Nations* (Tyrone, GA: Authentic Publishing, 2006).
This book is a collection of stories based on the idea that in a global mission context, when new believers are encouraged to sing newly translated scriptures in a manner common to the

local culture, the Church can grow dramatically.

Hawn, C. Michael, *One Bread, One Body: Exploring Cultural Diversity in Worship* (Bethesda, MD: Alban Institute, 2003).
A faculty member at the Perkins School of Theology in the areas of music and worship, the author holds in tension the need for theologically informed worship, while at the same time taking seriously the emerging circumstances of an increasingly multicultural society. Using the case studies of four multicultural congregations, he offers ideas and direction to congregations seeking to offer more culturally conscious and inclusive worship.

Kroeker, Charlotte, *Music in Christian Worship* (Collegeville, MN: Liturgical Press, 2005).
Many of the contributors to this volume were presenters at a conference titled "Church Music: Looking Back to the Future" held at Messiah College in 1999. Taking an interdisciplinary and interdenominational approach, this collection of essays seeks to answer the question, how can an understanding of the history of music in liturgy, together with a coherent theological context for the arts, lead to ways of creating more meaningful worship?

Montgomery, David J., *Sing a New Song: Choosing and Leading Praise in Today's Church* (Edinburgh, Scotland: Rutherford House, 2000).
Written from the perspective of the Reformed tradition, this book is an exploration and critique of contemporary praise music. The aim of the book is to set hymn singing in a biblical

and historical context, look at hymns as poetry and music, examine recent developments in hymnody, and finally to offer advice to those who lead music in worship.

Roberts, William Bradley, *Music and Vital Congregations: A Practical Guide for Clergy* (New York: Church Publishing, 2009).

Starting with the premise that "every great congregation has music as a vital component," this aptly named text provides a reasonable and thoughtful path for congregations to achieve that goal. Addressing such important issues as the development of healthy relationships between clergy and musician, the tension between classical Church hymnody and popular religious songs, and their use in worship, and exploring the role of music leader as pastor and congregational leader, this book is an invaluable resource.

Sirota, Victoria, *Preaching to the Choir: Claiming the Role of the Sacred Musician* (New York: Church Publishing, 2006).

Written from the unique perspective of being both a professional Church musician and an Episcopal priest, this book seeks to hold up the ministry of the sacred musician as a calling that integrates not only gifts and skills, but also attentiveness to one's own spirituality and personal wellbeing. The goal of the book is to bring a greater understanding of the forces that work for and against the sacred musician, and it also offers an invitation to deeper commitment.

Spencer, Jon Michael, *Sing a New Song: Liberating Black Hymnody* (Minneapolis, MN: Fortress, 1995).

Professor of African American studies at the University of North Carolina at Chapel Hill, the author coins the term "ethnohymnology" to explore the influence of Eurocentric Christian ideology on Afro-Christian hymnody. It is a discipline that explores hymnody with an overarching concern for the those most alienated from the existing hymnological tradition, namely, women, nonwhites, and the poor.

Stapert, Calvin R., *A New Song for an Old World: Musical Thought in the Early Church* (Grand Rapids, MI: Eerdmans Publishing Co., 2007).

In spite of the fact that the music of the early Church is not available to us, through the writings of the early Church Fathers, the author convincingly makes the case that we have much to learn from the early Church in the area of music. Drawing parallels between the pagan cultures of the early Christian era and the current cultural realities, this book offers an ancient and yet relevant perspective.

White, James F., *Introduction to Christian Worship* (Nashville, TN: Abingdon Press, 2000).

Written by one of the leading liturgical historians of the mainline, with over 40 years of teaching experience in the field of Christian worship, this easily accessible textbook is well organized, succinct, and thorough. This third edition includes a chapter on music and also explores the expansion of Christianity into other cultures and the rich new expressions of worship that have emerged.

Section Three

Leading the People of God

13

Prophetic Leadership and Social Justice

In his landmark book, *The Prophetic Imagination*, Walter Brueggemann has shaped the thinking of an entire generation of biblical scholars, theologians, and congregational leaders. In this important work, he places *prophetic ministry* within the context of the biblical narrative of the Hebrew Scriptures, within the ministry and example of Jesus Christ, and within the life of contemporary congregations. His keen insight and solid grasp of the issues facing mainline Churches provides a perspective that is challenging, without being despairing, and hopeful, without being unrealistic. Borrowing heavily from Brueggemann's influential work, in this chapter we explore the roots of social justice in the Old and New Testaments, and in the early Church. As part of this historical review we also examine different types of justice as well as the inherent tension between the exercise of prophetic leadership and the strong forces of stability that seek to protect the status quo. We also touch briefly on the pursuit of *social justice* in an increasingly multi-faith society, and then lastly, focus on the role of the pastor as prophetic leader.

A basic summary of Brueggemann's argument is that with Moses and the Exodus event, something utterly and completely new happened in the course of human history:

> On the one hand Moses intended the dismantling of the oppressive empire of Pharaoh; on the other hand, he intended the formation of a new community focused on the religion of God's freedom and the politics of justice and compassion. The *dismantling* begins in the groans and complaints of his people; the *energizing* begins in the doxology of the new community.[1]

This theme of breaking down and building up, along with its corresponding theme of lamentation and thanksgiving are constantly recurring throughout the biblical narrative. For instance, the very movement that Moses set out to lead proved too radical for Israel and soon prompted a counter movement. The oppressive history of the Egyptian pharaoh

An Introduction to Ministry: A Primer for Renewed Life and Leadership in Mainline Protestant Congregations, First Edition. Ian S. Markham and Oran E. Warder.

finds new expression in the monarchy of Israel. The monarchy, consumed with self-interest and self-preservation, becomes quite effective in silencing criticism. Yet, the silence does not last. Prophets emerge to challenge royal authority and to reassert the radical tradition inaugurated by Moses.[2] This pattern continues through the narrative of the First Testament and finds its fulfillment in Jesus, and then continues on to the present.

Jesus inherits this prophetic tradition in its entirety. The themes of breaking down and building up, the themes of lamentation and thanksgiving, the themes of challenging oppressive authority and calling for radical freedom and justice, became part of his ministry as well. Jesus stands in a long line of prophets, yet is more than a prophet.

> He practiced in most radical form the main elements of prophetic ministry and imagination. On the one hand he practiced criticism of the deadly world around him. The dismantling was wrought in his crucifixion, in which he himself embodied the thing dismantled. On the other hand, he practiced the energizing of the new future given by God. This future was fully manifested in his resurrection, in which he embodied the new future given by God.[3]

It is within this overarching pattern of dismantling and energizing, the pattern of death and resurrection, that we explore in more detail the scriptural foundation for the pursuit of social justice and the call to prophetic leadership. First we look at the concept of justice found in the Hebrew Scriptures, then as expressed in Jesus and in the early Church.

Walter Brueggemann

UCC minister, theologian, prolific writer, *Walter Brueggemann* (b. 1933) is also one of the most influential Old Testament scholars of the last several decades. Brueggemann places prophetic ministry within the context of the biblical narrative of the Hebrew Scriptures, within the ministry and example of Jesus Christ, and within the life of contemporary congregations. His keen insight and solid grasp of the issues facing mainline Churches provides a perspective that is challenging, without being despairing, and hopeful, without being unrealistic.

Justice in the Old Testament

Justice, as a biblical concept, is first found in the *legal codes* of the Torah, the first five books of the Hebrew Bible. These legal codes contain both prescriptions (what to do) as well as proscriptions (what not to do) in terms of ethical behavior. These three legal codes are found in: the Book of the Covenant (Exodus 20:22–23:33); the Deuteronomic Code (Deuteronomy 12–26); and the Holiness Code (Leviticus 17–26). The Book of the Covenant is the earliest of these legal codes and was written before the time of the prophets, while the other two existed as part of the oral tradition before the prophets but were not written down until later. While all three address issues of justice in a number of ways, it is the Deuteronomic Code that is the most explicit, particularly with regard to the just treatment of the poor.

The main idea expressed over and over again is that providing justice to the poor is key to maintaining a covenant relationship with God. The widow, the orphan, and the sojourner are those most commonly listed among the oppressed and those in need of special care, and are of specific concern. These law codes "set the standard for social justice predicated on the idea that outsiders should not be beyond the reach of compassion and those without advocates have a particular claim on mercy."[4]

It is important to note that one of the largest sections of the code is proscriptive, that is, it concerns, at times in great detail, actions that are prohibited when interacting with the poor. Anything that might further deprive, or take advantage of, the poor is strictly forbidden. Anything seen as a perpetuation of injustice is also banned. There are also many codes that prescribe acts of justice and sometimes provide the rationale for why acting justly is important. Essentially, the people of Israel are to act justly to the poor, the oppressed, and the sojourner, because they too were once poor, oppressed, and strangers themselves. Because the Lord showed compassion to them, they are to show that same compassion to others.[5] This rationale is first, a call to remember, and second, a call to act on that memory.

There are also codes that call for specific gifts to the poor. For instance, a family member who falls into poverty is to be taken in and cared for, and, if needed, provided with a loan, at no interest, until they are restored. Other laws, like those found in Deuteronomy 14:28–29, call for other specific gifts to the poor, such as agricultural provisions, tithes of the harvest, and every seventh year a jubilee, or sabbatical year. This *jubilee year*, based on the agricultural practice of leaving a field fallow every seventh year in order for it to renew itself, also provides a model for the renewal of God's people. Every seventh year debts were to be forgiven, prisoners released, and bond servants given their freedom. This action had the effect of narrowing the gap between the rich and poor, contributing to the leveling of the economic playing field, and providing the poor with the opportunity to extricate themselves from poverty. This practice gave a kind of amnesty along with a chance for a better life.[6] The intended purpose of the jubilee year was to insert social justice as a fundamental aspect of the governing of ancient Israel. This is so important that the guarantee of social justice was written into the legal code of the new nation.[7]

The legal code, as a whole, seems to recognize that without direct and specific intervention, the rich would simply get richer at the expense of the poor. This same ancient code also provided a rather holistic approach to the care of all of God's people by prohibiting unjust acts from happening in the first place, by providing a system to fairly redress the grievances of those who have been wronged, and to stimulate giving as a means of restoration. At its roots, the code strives to model God's vision for humanity that includes the fair and equitable distribution of resources and the caution against the human tendency to accumulate wealth and possessions.[8]

Justice in the New Testament and Early Church

The topic of the jubilee year, and God's vision for humanity, provides a nice introduction to the ministry of Jesus and his strong bent toward carrying on the work of justice that is central to the Old Testament narrative. Quoting Isaiah 61, Jesus begins his ministry by declaring a jubilee year in his inaugural sermon. In Luke's Gospel narrative (Luke 4:14–20) this first sermon comes after Jesus is baptized and after his temptation in the wilderness. Once Jesus is baptized and has rejected the temptations of the world, he is ready to launch his ministry. He returns to his hometown of Nazareth and preaches in the synagogue to a hometown crowd. In this sermon we get the first glimpse of Jesus, in his own words, embracing his messianic ministry. He is the One who has come to reestablish the covenant relationship with God, a relationship and ministry based on the theme of upholding justice. In this passage we learn not only of the centrality of justice, but also of the inherent risk of social witness. Jesus immediately meets opposition, is rejected by his own people, and is run out of town. By refusing temptation, embracing the vision of Isaiah, and offering himself as the fulfillment of that vision, Jesus accepts the way that will ultimately lead to the cross.[9]

Christians continue to look to Jesus as the model for social justice and his witness continues to challenge and inspire. Jesus is the peacemaker who loves his enemies and forgives those who would kill him, even as he is being crucified. He argues for social equality and implores those giving a feast to invite the poor and oppressed and those who cannot repay this generosity (Luke 14:13–14). He endorses the establishment and maintenance of community by summarizing all of God's law by imploring the love of God and the love of neighbor (Matthew 22:39). He rails against corporate greed by cleansing the temple (John 2:14) and warns of the allure of wealth by advising against the accumulation of possessions (Matthew 19:23). For over 2000 years, the Church has looked to the model of Jesus for direction and encouragement, and for many, the standard is set by yet another inaugural sermon. This one, from Matthew's Gospel, is part of the *Sermon on the Mount*, known widely as *the Beatitudes* (Matthew 5:3–12). These words of Jesus again point to God's preferential care for the poor and oppressed, and God's vision for justice and peace. This vision is embodied in the poverty of Jesus, by his own attention to all who suffer, and by his words and his actions. The example of Jesus, as expressed in the Gospel narratives, highlights the fundamental basis for pursuing justice: the belief that every human being is made in the likeness of God and is of intrinsic value. It also reiterates that social justice is not simply optional and something to strive for, but rather, is the commandment of God.[10]

The remainder of the New Testament offers a record of how the early Church struggled to follow the way of Jesus, live into the ideals set forth in his life and ministry, and come to grips with the reality of the new world order brought by his resurrection. One example of this struggle can be found in the apostle Paul's letter to Philemon. This brief letter is an appeal by Paul, on behalf of Onesimus, a runaway slave who has converted to Christianity. Paul appeals to fellow Christian, Philemon, owner of the runaway slave, and pleads for him to accept Onesimus back into his household without reprisal. Paul, who was faithfully served by Onesimus, even agrees to cover any economic loss experienced by Philemon during the absence of Onesimus. Paul's letter to Philemon is not a radical call for the end of the institution of slavery, but it is an appeal for Onesimus to be accepted as a brother in Christ. What is radical in Paul's letter is the idea that their common Christian faith trumped the social conventions of the day. The fact that Onesimus was actually freed by Philemon surely sent a message to the early Church that a new world order had indeed arrived. Yet to be clear, the early Church seemed to accept without question the social order of the day. Their interest appeared to be more in personal reform than social reform.[11] A more expanded view of the role of the Church in pursuit of justice would continue to develop.

Historical Perspective

It would be *Luigi Taparelli D'Azeglio* (1793–1862), an Italian Roman Catholic Jesuit scholar, who would be credited with being the first person to use the term "social justice." His work, drawing heavily on the scholarship and moral teaching of thirteenth-century theologian, Thomas Aquinas, focused on the dehumanizing social problems associated with the rise of the Industrial Revolution. This phrase, social justice, now comes to share a variety of meanings in both the secular and religious domains. The clear inference, however, is that this phrase concerns issues of fairness on a societal level rather than a personal level.[12] By way of definition, most scholars agree that there are five types of social justice:

1. *Distributive justice*. This is an ancient concept of justice having to do with the equitable distribution of both the benefits and the burdens among members of a particular social group. This form of justice is concerned with the adequate availability of necessary resources to meet the needs of community members, while making sure that the burden of acquiring and accessing resources is not excessively or unfairly imposed.
2. *Compensatory justice*. This particular concept of justice has to do with fair restitution because of someone's wrongful act. In other words, this form of justice deals with compensating a person, or whole group of people, in an attempt to restore wholeness. Such restitution can take many forms.
3. *Retributive justice*. This type of justice concerns the way in which blame and punishment are assigned to those committing wrongful acts. Contemporary western theorists consider the conditions under which it is just to blame or punish. They take into account one's ability to act on one's own initiative and fully understand the meaning and consequences of one's actions. Two items are of particular importance in this type of justice, the first is consistency (treating similar cases in a similar way) and proportionality (making certain that the punishment is congruent with the wrongdoing).
4. *Procedural justice*. This term deals almost exclusively with the ongoing debate over the competing models of how to best seek justice within the criminal justice system. The most famous of these debates exists between the "due process" model and the "crime control" model. The crime control or crime suppression model values efficiency and economy, while due process values strict adherence to established rules. The chief virtue of the due process is the premise that one is innocent until proven guilty. The chief complaint is that it is inefficient and overly formal. The chief fear of the crime control model is that speed is a higher priority than accuracy. Critics of both models claim that they are overly connected to the retributive philosophy and overly focused on punishment.
5. *Restorative justice*. One important and significant alternative to the above models has been tried in post-apartheid South Africa. The Truth and Reconciliation Commission was established as part of the Promotion of National Unity and Reconciliation Act of 1995. This commission, a court-like body, was established specifically to bear witness to, record, and in some cases grant amnesty to those who perpetrated human rights violations, as well as providing reparation and rehabilitation. In many cases, perpetrators of violence confessed their crimes directly to victims (or surviving family members). This

process encouraged openness and truth-telling as a strategy for reconciliation. The goal of this type of justice is to restore something that a grave injustice has taken away, and in this case, the restoration of the very fabric of society and the restoration of human relationships.[13]

Prophetic Voice: Desmond Tutu

Archbishop Desmond Tutu (b. 1931) is a South African leader in the Anglican Church, renowned for his perseverance on the behalf of the oppressed and marginalized. Among the many social justice causes that benefited from his influence over a lifetime of ministry and service are his advocacy against the South African apartheid in the 1980s, and his tireless defense of racial and sexual minorities throughout the world. Tutu has won a Nobel Peace Prize and continues to make an impact currently as a public speaker and political advisor.

Contemporary Expressions

With these definitions in mind, and aware of the Church's ongoing development in terms of witness, we turn our attention to the present. It is true that wherever injustice is found, and wherever there are people of faith working for justice, many of them are Christian. It is also true that contemporary expressions of social justice within the Church vary widely in both word and action. In terms of words, many Christian bodies adopt official statements, declarations, legislation, and documents dealing with an array of justice issues. In action, these same bodies are involved in community development, protest movements, advocacy, and policy development in solidarity with the poor and those in need. Again, the particular issues and depth of engagement vary greatly given a particular Church's theology, interpretation of scripture, social location, and political biases. Some contemporary issues of concern to the Church include: peace, poverty, sexism, racism, care for the environment, immigration, sex trafficking, AIDS, abortion, drug and alcohol addiction, domestic abuse, education, human sexuality, incarceration, living wages, socioeconomics, and the list goes on.[14] And, of course, there is the difficult reality of the tension between prophetic leadership and social action, or inaction, and the tension between what the Church says and what the Church actually does. Sometimes the Church is directly aligned with social justice and sometimes the Church is aligned with maintaining the status quo. Sometimes the "words and actions of social justice are directed at the church itself as well as the broader society."[15] Yet how can the Church live within this inherent tension?

Daring to Speak in God's Name

In their book by this same name, Mary Alice Mulligan and Rufus Burrow encourage all Christians to claim a prophetic role and speak the Word of God, especially pastoral leaders.

In the preface of their book they tell the true story of a white supremacist group actively trying to turn a Pennsylvania county into a home base of operation. The leader, an outspoken advocate for the group, claimed to be an ordained Christian pastor who based his racial and ethnic hatred on the words of Scripture. In a nearby town a laywoman confronted her pastor about what their congregation would be doing in response as a rejection of these ideas as Christian. The response that she received was that there would be no response. Knowing that silence would equal tacit approval, this book was written to help individuals and congregations with the resources and encouragement to boldly speak God's Word, and actively refute that which is not God's Word.[16] The authors, both seminary professors, acknowledge that in seminary, students are formed as pastors, priests, and prophets. They also acknowledge that soon after graduation it is typically the pastoral and priestly aspects of their training that predominate. They claim that students get plenty of information about the radical nature of the Gospel of Jesus Christ, but in the congregation a kind of amnesia begins to set in and institutional preservation takes over.[17]

This is not a new phenomenon. To speak God's Word is to be vulnerable and is to face rejection. Reinhold Niebuhr, when reflecting on his early ministry as a pastor, said that he was, at least initially, "too cautious to be a Christian" and he also called the process of pulling back from the prophetic role as the "taming of the preacher."[18] The issue for Niebuhr is that he found that the more he served the congregation, the more he was tempted to remove the prophetic sting from the sharp truth, and the less he wanted to offend.[19] He observed that his problem, a problem shared by countless others, is the "difficulty one finds in telling unpleasant truths to people one has learned to love."[20] He would eventually find a way to preach the prophetic Word of God without alienating the people of God. The correlating fear, of course, is that pastors err too much on the side of saving and preserving the Church without paying enough attention to what it means to actually *be* the Church.[21] Walter Rauschenbusch, the great historian of Christian ethics of the last century, expressed similar ideas, only with blunt force. He declared:

> If a man wants to be a Christian, he must stand over and against things as they are and condemn them in the name of that higher conception of life which Jesus revealed. If a man is satisfied with the way things are, he belongs to the other side.[22]

Undoubtedly, there are times when the prophetic word comes with great cost and alienation cannot be avoided. There are times when the Word of God inspires acts of justice and calls for social action. One classic, inspiring, and soul wrenching example of this form of social action is the life and witness of Dietrich Bonhoeffer. His story is a reminder that the Greek word for witness is *martyr*, in that, his prophetic leadership, like that of Jesus, led to his execution. A theologian in the 1940s during the rise of Nazi Germany, Bonhoeffer struggled to integrate his faith with the oppression and mass killing of Jews. With most of the German Christian churches aligned with the Nazi Government, he stood squarely against the institutional Church, the dominant culture, and the national government. Arrested for his involvement in a plot to assassinate Nazi leader, Adolf Hitler, he died at that hands of the government, but not without writing a theology characterized by prayer and action that would forever change the Church's understanding of social justice and that would soon help bring an end to Nazi rule.[23]

Prophetic Voice: Martin Luther King, Jr

From an Alabama prison on April 16, 1963, the Rev. Martin Luther King, Jr, encapsulated his feelings and interpretation of Scripture in his "Letters from a Birmingham Jail":

> "Love your enemies, bless them that curse you, do good to them that hate you, and pray for them which despitefully use you, and persecute you." Was not Amos an extremist for justice: "Let justice roll down like waters and righteousness like an ever flowing stream." Was not Paul an extremist for the Christian gospel: "I bear in my body the marks of the Lord Jesus." Was not Martin Luther an extremist: "Here I stand; I cannot do otherwise, so help me God."

Source: Letter from a Birmingham Jail, from the African Studies Center at the University of Pennsylvania. Available at: http://www.africa.upenn.edu/Articles_Gen /Letter_Birmingham.html (accessed June 4, 2015).

It was the Confessing Church Movement, of which Bonhoeffer was a leader, which challenged the Church's alliance with Nazi Germany. It was the Civil Rights Movement in the United States, of which *Martin Luther King, Jr* was a leader, which challenged the racial segregation of the American Church. It was the Uniting Reformed Church in South Africa that challenged the Dutch Reformed Church in the 1980s by calling its apartheid theology a heresy. A more recent instance of the failure of the institutional Church and its prophetic witness occurred in 1994 in Rwanda. The racially and ethnically segregated Church of Rwanda collapsed and became a leading player in the genocide that killed over 800 000 of its citizens in a period of 3 months. This occurred in the African nation with the highest percentage of Christians (90%) and with every major denomination and community participating in the violence and with many of the massacres occurring in Church buildings. Today, the Church in Rwanda, using a truth and reconciliation process similar to one utilized in South Africa, continues to struggle as it seeks to create a milieu of social justice.[24]

These examples dramatically reveal how the internal structures of the Church can reflect the injustices and evils found in society. This can happen in ways large and small, even as the Church proclaims itself to be squarely on the side of justice. The Church can make these claims and yet the reality is at times dramatically different.

Many congregations claim to welcome people with disabilities, yet their buildings are inaccessible. Women are told that they are full participants, but few hold leadership positions. Christians preach that all people are created in the image of God and loved by God. Yet when discussions of sexual orientation or gay marriage occur, the rhetoric becomes angry and demeaning, and even hateful. The church declares that reconciliation is central to the Gospel, but most congregations are comprised of one racial, cultural, ethnic, or socio-economic group. Because of these inconsistencies and hypocrisies, the church itself is an arena for social justice action.[25]

In light of all this, and to conclude this section, we now return to Mulligan and Burrow, who claim that the litmus test for all social ministry and the standard for being the Church is found in one short passage from the book of the prophet Micah (6:8):

> He has told you, O mortal, what is good;
> and what does the Lord require of you
> but to do justice, and to love kindness,
> and to walk humbly with your God?

This text is a simple and yet profoundly comprehensive summary of biblical ideals. In this passage God places on believers an unalterable moral obligation. It is the answer to what God requires of us.[26] In the face of injustice, it is not our place to shake our heads in disgust and helplessness, it is not our place to shrink back in fear, but it is our place to speak God's Word boldly in God's name on behalf of God's people. It is our place to be just, merciful, and humble prophets. In the words of New Testament scholar, Luke Timothy Johnson, "Prophets are human beings who speak to other human beings from the perspective of God."[27] This is the ancient calling to which we are the contemporary manifestation.

Prophetic Leadership in a Multi-faith Society

Being prophetic leaders in the modern age, as with any age, is fraught with challenges, not the least of which is the dubious credibility of the Church. The society around us largely forgets our many successes and contributions, tends to recall with great clarity our many failures, and is at best skeptical of what the Church has to offer in terms of addressing the social issues of the day. Contemporary theologian and leader of the emergent Church movement, Brian McLaren, laments the current reality by borrowing the words of William Blake (the English Romantic poet of the late eighteenth and early nineteenth centuries) who once quipped, "A good local pub has much in common with a church, except that the pub is warmer, and there's more conversation."[28]

In addition to the modern, and perhaps not-so-modern, skepticism as to the relevance of the Church, another challenge has to do with our modern context. Germaine to the topic of social justice is McLaren's assertion that twenty-first-century prophetic leadership involves leadership with a multi-faith perspective. He contends that contemporary Christians do two things well in terms of addressing pluralism and interfaith dialogue. The first is that some have a strong Christian identity that responds negatively to those of other faiths. The second is that others have a positive and accepting response to other faiths, yet arrive at this position by weakening their own Christian identity. The latter perspective is one that maximizes commonality, is respectful, strives to achieve coexistence, and would never seek to evangelize or proselytize those of another faith. By doing so, this group makes "matter less that others are of a different religion by making our being Christian matter less.[29]

McLaren argues for a third way of exercising prophetic leadership in the modern world. The third option is to develop a Christian identity that is both strong and kind; strong in the sense of being vital and compelling, kind in the sense of being more than merely tolerant or satisfied with coexistence. This third option seeks understanding, is genuinely interested, and exhibits love and compassion toward those of other faiths. This comes not from a weakened Christian identity but rather is a strong, intentional and explicit way to be a follower of God in the way of Christ.[30] This perspective is of critical importance as we move to the final section of this chapter, which explores the role of the pastor in prophetic leadership and as an advocate of social justice.

The Pastor as Scribe

The genius of Walter Brueggemann's ideas regarding the exercise of the prophetic imagination is not only in his fierce and fearless commitment to the work of social justice, but also his conviction that the Church continues to be the place where the powerful Word of God is spoken and heard. Brueggemann has not given up on the mainline institutional Church as a place of transformation and he has not given up on the role of pastoral leaders as agents of that transformation. The heart of the prophetic imagination is the decision to believe that God, who is beyond human thought and understanding, actively reigns, makes all things new, and is always moving toward hope. To be a prophetic leader is to imagine the world as God imagines and intends it and then to work to bring it about.

Brueggemann also has his feet squarely grounded in reality, and this grounding comes as a welcome relief for those who live in the tension that defines modern life in a complex Church in a complex world. In contrast to what we have come to expect from modern prophetic leaders, he reminds us that the great prophets of Israel rarely spoke directly to special social issues of their day and rarely advocated for specific causes. Rather, they more often spoke to more fundamental issues regarding the reign of God and its implication for those living under God's rule. He adds that even if we were to try to transpose the wisdom of the ancient prophets onto contemporary concerns it would be an arduous and uncertain task.[31] He is also keenly aware that prophetic leadership is practiced within congregations, a place where the leader "must 'speak the truth' and at the same time maintain a budget, membership and a program in a context that is often not prepared for such truthfulness."[32] Yet this is precisely the context for prophetic ministry:

> [I]t is presumed that the practice of ministry is done by those who stand in conventional places of parish life and other forms of ministry derived from that model. We cling to the conviction that prophetic ministry can and must be practiced there, although many things militate against it. The ministry is, first of all, consumed by the daily round of busyness that cannot be ignored. In addition, the ministry most often exists in congregations that are bourgeois, if not downright obdurate, and in which there is no special openness to, or support of, prophetic ministry. Prophetic ministry does not consist of spectacular acts of social crusading or of abrasive measures of indignation. Rather, prophetic ministry consists of offering an alternative perception of reality and in letting people see their own history in light of God's freedom and his will for justice. The issues of God's freedom and his will for justice are not always, and need not be, expressed primarily in the big issues of the day. They can be discerned wherever people try to live together and show concern for their shared future and identity.[33]

The definition of prophetic ministry on the one hand does concern the issues of the day, and on the other hand concerns probing the depths of the biblical narrative with "inescapable side glances at contemporary issues. The latter focusing more on the text than the issue."[34] Brueggemann suggests that this constitutes a valuable approach and is a more realistic way to proceed given the dynamics of congregational life. He suggests that the prophetic leader, in this particular setting, is more in the role of scribe than of prophet. The scribe being the one who carefully and thoughtfully handles the ancient texts and interprets them in a way that sheds light and brings to life their power and authority in a contemporary setting. The scribe is the bearer of the prophetic tradition who brings forth ancient treasure as a resource for the modern world.[35]

For Brueggemann then, the first task of prophetic leadership is to assist people in letting go of the old world and the old ways that are passing away from us. This task echoes the earlier theme of lament, dismantling, and death. The second task is to assist people in receiving and accepting the new world and new ways that are emerging and to see them as a gift of grace, a gift from God. This second task echoes the recurring theme of thanksgiving, building up, and resurrection.[36]

Lest we be too hard on ourselves when acknowledging the enormous gulf that exists between the model of prophetic leadership and social justice that we carry in our minds, and the real-life practice in the life of congregations, we conclude this chapter with Brueggemann's reflections on his own ministry. In these reflections he confesses that the real restraints to his ministry have been neither with his own personal understanding, nor with the receptivity of other people, but with his own uncertainty.

> I discover that I am as bourgeois and obdurate as any to whom I might minister. I, like most of the others, am unsure that the royal road is not the best and the royal community the one which governs the real "goodies." I, like most others, am unsure that the alternative community inclusive of the poor, hungry, and grieving is really the wave of God's future. We are indeed "like people, like priest" (Hosea 4:9). That very likely is the situation among many of us in ministry, and there is no unanguished way out of it. It does make clear to us that ministry will always be practiced through our own conflicted selves. No prophet has ever borne an unconflicted message, even until Jesus. ... It reminds us again that such radical faith is not an achievement, for if it were, we would will it to be done. Rather, it is a gift, and we are left to wait receptively, to watch, and to pray.[37]

Notes

1 Walter Brueggemann, *The Prophetic Imagination* (Minneapolis, MN: Fortress Press, 2001), 115.
2 Ibid.
3 Ibid., 116.
4 Harold T. Lewis, *Christian Social Witness* (Cambridge, Boston, MA: Cowley, 2001), 9–10.
5 Ibid., 11.
6 Ibid., 11–12.
7 Michael D. Palmer and Stanley Burgess, eds, *The Wiley-Blackwell Companion to Religion and Social Justice* (Chichester, West Sussex and Malden, MA: Wiley-Blackwell, 2012), 63.
8 Lewis, *Christian Social Witness*, 11–13.
9 Ibid., 26.
10 Palmer and Burgess, *Wiley-Blackwell Companion*, 46–47.
11 Ibid., 47.
12 Ibid., 4.
13 Ibid., 5–9.
14 Ibid., 61–62.
15 Ibid., 62.

16   Mary Alice Mulligan, and Rufus Burrow, Jr, *Daring to Speak in God's Name: Ethical Prophecy in Ministry* (Cleveland, OH: Pilgrim Press, 2002), vii.

17   Ibid., 20.

18   Ibid., 22.

19   Ibid.

20   Ibid., 213.

21   Ibid., 24.

22   Ibid., 79.

23   Palmer, *Wiley-Blackwell Companion*, 64.

24   Ibid., 71.

25   Ibid.

26   Mulligan, *Daring to Speak*, 65–68.

27   Luke Timothy Johnson, *Prophetic Jesus, Prophetic Church: The Challenge of Luke-Acts to Contemporary Christians* (Grand Rapids, MI: W.B. Eerdmans Publishing Co., 2011), vi.

28   Brian D. McLaren, *Why Did Jesus, Moses the Buddha, and Mohammed Cross the Road? Christian Identity in a Multi-Faith World* (New York: Jericho Books, 2012), 6.

29   Ibid., 10.

30   Ibid., 11.

31   Walter Brueggemann, *The Practice of Prophetic Imagination: Preaching an Emancipating Word*, (Minneapolis, MN: Fortress Press, 2012), 1–2.

32   Ibid., 2.

33   Brueggemann, *The Prophetic Imagination*, 116–117.

34   Brueggemann, *Practice of Prophetic Imagination*, 2.

35   Ibid., 2.

36   Ibid., 136–138.

37   Brueggemann, *Prophetic Imagination*, 118.

Annotated Bibliography

Borschel, Audrey, *Preaching Prophetically: When the News Disturbs: Interpreting the Media* (St. Louis, MO: Chalice Press, 2009).

This book about prophetic preaching is concerned with current events as portrayed in the media, how preachers weigh these issues against or in conjunction with scripture, and how "activist preaching" does not necessarily carry the stigma associated with politicizing religion.

Brueggemann, Walter, *The Prophetic Imagination* (Minneapolis, MN: Fortress Press, 2001).

A landmark book from a landmark author, this revision of the 1978 original anthology of the author's lectures is clearly one of his most important works. Brueggemann contextualizes the prophetic ministry in terms of the life of Jesus, and lays out the facets that comprise an effective prophetic ministry.

Brueggemann, Walter, *The Practice of Prophetic Imagination: Preaching an Emancipating Word* (Minneapolis, MN: Fortress Press, 2012).

A companion piece to Prophetic Imagination, this book focuses on the proclamation of social justice.

Jacobsen, Dennis, *Doing Justice: Congregations and Community Organizing* (Minneapolis, MN: Fortress Press, 2001).

This textbook is focused on congregation-based community organizing, emphasizing ministry to the disenfranchised, primarily in urban settings, for mainline congregations.

Johnson, Luke Timothy, Prophetic Jesus, *Prophetic Church: The Challenge of Luke-Acts to Contemporary Christians* (Grand Rapids, MI: W.B. Eerdmans Publishing Co., 2011).

A preeminent New Testament scholar, Luke Timothy Johnson speaks with his own visionary authority about the mandate from Luke-Acts to be a prophetic Church. This volume addresses the scriptural precedent for social justice and visionary or prophetic calls to service and spreading of good news in the world.

Lewis, Harold T., *Christian Social Witness* (Cambridge, Boston, MA: Cowley, 2001).

This work is part of the New Church's Teaching Series of the Episcopal Church created in an attempt to explore the major traditional themes of the Christian life amid the changes and challenges of the modern world.

McLaren, Brian D., *Why Did Jesus, Moses the Buddha, and Mohammed Cross the Road? Christian Identity in a Multi-Faith World* (New York: Jericho Books, 2012).

In this book, the popular and prolific McLaren spends time addressing pluralism and interfaith relations and dialogue. According to McLaren, prophetic leadership includes being a leader in the Church, while at the same time maintaining a multi-faith perspective.

Mulligan, Mary Alice and Burrow, Jr, Rufus, *Daring to Speak in God's Name: Ethical Prophecy in Ministry* (Cleveland, OH: Pilgrim Press, 2002).

Imploring today's prophets to speak in God's name and to work diligently for the causes of Christ, this work is an examination of justice in the world through the lens of God's expectations for humanity. In some of the sampled pages, the authors glean some "lessons for ministry" from Rabbi Heschel, who is frequently mentioned in works related to prophetic vision and ministry.

Palmer, Michael D. and Burgess, Stanley, eds, *The Wiley-Blackwell Companion to Religion and Social Justice* (Chichester, West Sussex and Malden, MA: Wiley-Blackwell, 2012).

This expansive and comprehensive volume includes the essays of scholars from all the major world religions in the field of ethics as it relates to social justice.

Scholz, Susanne, ed., *God Loves Diversity and Justice: Progressive Scholars Speak about Faith, Politics, and the World* (Lanham, MD: Lexington Books, 2013).

This collection of scholarly essays speaks to social justice in Churches in terms of the need for diversity. This work focuses on the sentiments and spirituality surrounding the need for social justice awareness and activity in the Church.

Wallis, Jim, *The Soul of Politics: A Practical and Prophetic Vision for Change* (Maryknoll, NY: Orbis Books, 1994).

A known figure of political activism from the evangelical Christian left, Jim Wallis, in this book, finds fault with both the conservatives and liberals in the Church on matters of social justice. His thesis is that social change occurs first from within, not from reliance on structures, governments, or institutions.

14

Evangelism and Church Growth

Evangelism and church growth, church growth and evangelism, some in the mainline believe the terms to be interchangeable, others contend they should not even appear in the same sentence. While there is general agreement on the importance and the necessity of both, there is little agreement on the exact implementation of either of these terms. This chapter explores the relationship between evangelism and church growth. First, we will look at the data describing the current state of mainline congregations, which fuels much of the debate about evangelism and the need to grow the Church. Second, we will review the two major responses to the data, one focusing on technique (the doing of evangelism) and the other focusing on church identity (the being rather than the doing of evangelism). No overview of this topic is complete, however, without a conversation about the defining characteristics of the emerging postmodern culture, the mega-church phenomenon, and the challenge of evangelism in an increasingly pluralistic, multicultural, and multi-faith society. In the conclusion we will identify the ways of being and doing evangelism that seem to be working and highlight three areas of emphasis that offer the most hope and encouragement for the Church in this new age.

If *evangelism* is defined as a "set of loving, intentional activities governed by the goal of initiating persons into Christian discipleship in response to the reign of God," then church growth is a byproduct of this effort and not the goal.[1] Walter Brueggemann explains further, "Evangelism is related to church growth, related but in no way synonymous. In speaking of evangelism, one must speak of church growth, but only at the end of the dramatic process, and not any sooner."[2] The distinction here is that the underlying motivation for evangelism is not to grow the church, but rather to summon people to the reign of God. Thus the root of the tension in the relationship between evangelism and church growth lies in the blurring of this distinction, and the welfare of the Church is confused with the extension of the reign of God.[3] For others the two cannot and must not be separated. Any attempt to expand and

An Introduction to Ministry: A Primer for Renewed Life and Leadership in Mainline Protestant Congregations, First Edition. Ian S. Markham and Oran E. Warder.
© 2016 John Wiley & Sons, Ltd. Published 2016 by John Wiley & Sons, Ltd.

enhance the institutional Church is by extension an attempt to expand and enhance the kingdom of God. These actions are seen as one and the same and viewed as necessary and essential. It is within this dialectic framework that our conversation begins.

A Look at the Numbers

There is universal agreement that the mainline Church is in a state of decline if not a state of crisis. The statistics paint a rather bleak picture of the current condition of the Church. One estimation places the figure as high as 80% for the number of congregations in the United States that are either stagnant or in decline.[4] In general terms, most congregations are small, while most worshippers are in large congregations. This dichotomy does not alter the fact that the average congregation has 100 people in attendance each week.[5] Put another way, 10% of US congregations have half of all of worshippers each week, while 90% of US congregations account for the remaining half.[6] These data are based on the assumption that Sunday worship attendance, as opposed to membership, is a more accurate indicator of participation in community life. It also assumes that attendance is a better indicator of the resource base and general health of a congregation. That being said, the data have far-reaching consequences, not the least of which is that it has become increasingly difficult for individual congregations to support a full-time clergy person or a professional staff. In addition, most congregations own their own buildings, struggle with deferred maintenance issues, and have little left in shrinking operating budgets to support basic programs. Add to this an ambivalent attitude toward evangelism and a reticence to reach out beyond the walls of the congregation, and there is certainly ample reason for concern. Yet at the same time, there are ample opportunities for change and reason for hope.

Reclaiming Evangelism

Perhaps a place to start is to examine some of the obstacles that stand in the way of moving forward and envisioning a brighter future. One of the main barriers is the prevailing under-standing, or misunderstanding, of the work of evangelism. In many corners of the mainline, evangelism is a tainted word laden with negative connotations, and in others it is viewed as an unwelcomed necessity for survival. Part of the task of this chapter is to reclaim evangelism as the spreading of good news that is central to active discipleship and a core expression of corporate faith.

In his important book *Evangelism After Christendom*, Bryan Stone begins his discussion by describing a brochure that advertised a gathering of "Women of Faith" on the campus of Boston University where he teaches. The brochure was an invitation for women of all faiths to come together to freely share their views with the promise that there would be no "evangelization." He contends that this small example is indicative of our current environment, where evangelism is increasingly viewed as unnecessary, unwarranted, and something to be avoided if not feared. An embarrassment to Christians and an affront to non-Christians, evangelism has come to be seen as a barrier to respectful conversation, an obstacle to careful listening, and a hindrance to open sharing and cooperation. The very antithesis of the sharing of good news, evangelism is now equated with intolerance, superiority, and judgment.[7]

Given this reality, members of the mainline have reason to be skeptical. The lingering awkward feelings and attitudes about evangelism are deep and difficult to change. They usually stem from three negative associations. The first and most prevalent is the association of evangelism with *proselytizing*, the act of attempting to convert people to a different religion, which is now widely viewed as an intentionally manipulative process that runs counter to a compelling life of faith. The second negative association of evangelism is its historical connection to the *colonial era* and the quest for cultural supremacy, which is now seen as a source of guilt and remorse for which the Church must repent and certainly not something to try to reclaim or revisit. The third negative association of evangelism, closely related to the second, is its connection to the fading dominance of *Christendom*, the idea of Christianity being the dominant religion and the prevailing cultural force in society. This is simply no longer the case and does not accurately reflect the current reality of religious pluralism.[8] For Stone, it is this last item, our close ties to the waning ideals of Christendom, which forms the largest barrier to reclaiming evangelism. Our nostalgia for a bygone era, a golden age of Christendom, makes it difficult to envision a new way of being. Stone contends that most of the recent evangelical movements are merely misguided attempts to "claw our way back to the center of the culture."[9] Rather than a return to the past, he suggests that our greatest hope and greatest witness will come from a Church at the margins of the culture, not from the center. He also believes that our greatest teachers will be those who have themselves been marginalized, colonized, and made minorities by Christendom, and thus have no stake in its survival or restoration.[10]

His sentiments are echoed by others who argue that many of the current evangelical trends assume that people "out there" are eager to be part of the Church and are simply waiting for the doors to be open. The problem in this scenario is simply inertia. If only the Church would make its appeal more loudly and more clearly, people would then respond and come to Church in droves.[11] A critic might say that this kind of magical thinking is akin to accepting the task of being a "fisher of men" and then expecting the fish to simply jump in the boat. In our estimation there are no such silver bullets, trump cards, or easy answers when it comes to reversing the stagnation and decline experienced in our congregations. The work of evangelism is not simply a quick fix for an anxious and alarmed mainline. The circumstances that have led to inertia are as complex as the conditions that will lead to growth. We will say at this point, however, that success for congregations is never a function of just one thing, but growth is always found in a combination of strengths that are unique to every congregation. This combination is not a function of congregational size, nor is it simply a matter of emphasis or focus. It has more to do with a fundamental and comprehensive approach to evangelism and less to do with church growth, and has more to do with spreading the reign of God and less to do with saving the institutional Church as we know it.

Common Threads

While much of this chapter deals with the stark divergence of thinking in the mainline, when it comes to the topic of evangelism, there are also large areas of unanimity. One of the key and fundamental places of agreement has to do with a common understanding of the nature of conversion. Once viewed mainly as a single, sudden, instantaneous, dramatic event, conversion now is viewed more widely as a process rather than an event, a journey rather than a destination, a moment of decision followed by other moments of decision. With this understanding, conversion becomes a never-ending, life-long activity as opposed to a single momentary event. Even the most dramatic conversion stories of the New Testament can be viewed through this lens. They also bear witness to the reality that conversion is not often a linear path. But just to be clear, this view does not at all dismiss the impact of a significant moment of conversion, but merely suggests that such events are the start of a process that is followed by many repetitions, and not an end in and of themselves.[12] This common understanding about conversion points directly to two other areas of mainline agreement. The first is that the process of conversion is highly relational, it involves people connecting to people; and second, and most importantly, the process of conversion is ultimately God's doing. The work of *conversion*, or more expansively, *regeneration* (the ability to bring about rebirth, restoration, and renewal), belongs to God alone.

Another distinct commonality among mainline congregations, which is also indicative of any human institution, is what is known as the *Pareto Principle*. This is the 80/20 theory, the idea that in any organization 20% of the people are committed to providing most of the resources and effort to maintain and promote the mission of the organization, with the other 80% providing only marginal support. While this principle is observed and accepted as a consistent pattern of human behavior, it is also true that this principle does not have to be an immutable law in terms of congregational dynamics. Thus it is a commonly held assumption in the mainline that deeper commitment and greater involvement are directly tied to spiritual growth and formation. It is also a common experience that mainline congregations are better at creating the initial commitment of its members and are less adept at creating the dynamics for sustained commitment. This is connected to the reality that what initially draws people to a congregation is not necessarily what will keep them there for the long term. Therefore, at least part of the work of evangelism is actively engaging the other 80% of our congregations. This work involves listening to those on the edges of the community, working to deepen and broaden their spiritual development, and again, building a relational framework for personal connection.[13]

The Doing of Evangelism

It is important at this juncture to confess that the dialectic framework of this chapter, the tension between the being and the doing of evangelism, is an intentional overstatement. While theoretically these categories are helpful in sorting through the vast amount of literature on this topic, they are less helpful in terms of application. Thinking practically and functionally, no congregation falls entirely into one category or the other, but rather typically leans further in one direction as opposed to the other. For instance, no congregation cares exclusively about numerical growth to the extent that they care little about the formation of disciples, the quality of community life, and the work of mission. Likewise, no congregation is so focused on mission and formation, both individual and corporate, that they care little about welcoming and incorporating new members. Even if they did exist, both extremes would agree that all of these tasks are fundamentally important, deeply interconnected, and differ only as a matter of degree.

With this qualification, we return to our two categories, looking first at the recent trends in evangelism that focus on technique, marketing, and yes, even sales in the doing of evangelism. The underlying theme of these trends is the desire to counter the fact that congregations have become anesthetized, lulled into sleep and inaction. They have come to believe that all that it is necessary for a congregation to do is to strive to live a life of faith in the hope that others may see it and want it for themselves.[14] The antidote to such ineffective passivity is boldness and action. In the book *Selling Swimsuits in the Arctic*, Adam Hamilton, a United Methodist pastor who leads one of the largest congregations in America, makes the case for a proactive, relationship-based evangelism. Acknowledging that in our current culture the Church is now forced to compete with a host of other activities and organizations, he believes that it is imperative that we learn to fully participate in a free-market society. In short, "it is all sales," with every sermon being a sales presentation that conveys spiritual truth, inspires a response, and always includes an invitation to "close the sale."[15] According to Hamilton, the seven keys to growing a congregation are: (i) believing in the product; (ii) believing that people need the product; (iii) understanding the needs of the customer; (iv) offering an excellent product; (v) embodying the product; (vi) effectively marketing the product; and (vii) perseverance.[16] The ideal is for the entire congregation to form a sales force that embodies the product, the Christian faith, through incarnational living.

Other similar perspectives emphasize the importance of the ministries of individual Church members. The first task is to help them overcome the fear of sharing their faith with friends, and then second, to help them to break out of their comfort zones and to enlarge their network of friends. Acknowledging that fear is often the greatest barrier, various authors offer tips as extreme as learning how to share one's faith with the cashier at the grocery store or becoming tattooed with evangelistic body art. The other major component of this category of evangelism is the development of "needs based" or "customer obsessed" evangelism. That is, engaging and listening carefully to those outside the Church community, discerning their needs, and then designing programs based on addressing and fulfilling those needs. And what are the defining characteristics of those outside the Church, the target audience that Church marketers want to reach? Generally speaking, they are diverse, largely indifferent to authority, starved for time, do not hold Sunday as a sacred day, and have little or no prior connection to or experience of Church.[17] So part of the task is learning how to communicate with the wider culture without sacrificing the integrity of the message or losing the message altogether. While Church marketers emphasize that the medium is not the message, they also argue that the medium is, nevertheless, incredibly important. The goal is to reach and engage people. Yet even in this rapidly expanding informational and technological age of new media, direct, relational, "high touch," person-to-person contact remains the best and most effective means of communicating a message of faith.

Before leaving this section, it is worth noting one additional way to think about "doing" evangelism, and that is applying the principles of niche marketing to congregational practice. The basic idea is that the recipe for successful evangelism is the pairing of an unmet need with a niche focus. We highlight this particular idea because of its unique narrow scope. Rather than the usual mass marketing approach, this strategy focuses on the inherent unique strengths of the congregation to develop a "boutique" mentality. Rather than attempting to be all things to all people, this approach emphasizes high quality and high value based on what the congregation does well. This involves studying the "competition," engaging in self-evaluation, and capitalizing on that which is unique or sets a particular congregation apart.[18] This particular approach underscores the effectiveness of a targeted mission to a targeted audience for a targeted purpose.

The Being of Evangelism

Reaction to the market-driven approach to evangelism is widespread and the criticism often quite sharp. Critics argue that too often the focus is superficial, long on style and technique and short on substance. They argue that the consumer mindset, which lures people to church with the promise that they will benefit from what the church has to offer, negates the idea that we are part of a Christian community in order to ask God to use us to make a difference in the world.[19] Critics bristle when they hear the more extreme practitioners of customer-based evangelism make statements like: effective churches are invitational and not confrontational, the Christian Church needs to be friendlier than Disneyland, and the Gospel must be offered but cannot make demands.[20] These statements, described by some as "Christian-lite," are seen as the result of an overemphasis on consumer preferences and market-driven accommodation at the expense of the integrity of the Gospel.[21]

Most critics would argue that the Church's identity is diluted if not lost when embracing a market-focused mentality of evangelism. They reason that if the worship experience becomes focused entirely on meeting peoples' needs, being entertaining and inspiring, and affirming the individual by presenting a relevant and useful God, then this ceases to be Christian worship.[22] To go one step further, they would also reason that when worship becomes a tool for marketing and a means for serving the individual, "the gospel of Jesus Christ becomes just another commodity, just another sign of a self-indulgent culture."[23]

All of this leads Bryan Stone to speak of the failure of evangelism. He contends that the visible signs of the failure of evangelism in our time are "implied as much by the vigorous 'success' of some churches in North America as by the steady decline of others."[24] For him this failure is a theological failure, the result of seeing evangelism as a "bag of tricks" rather than the result of deep reflection and the drawing on the wisdom of Scripture and the tradition of the Church.[25] For him, evangelism is not about providing a more user-friendly product, but about living the contradiction of being both invitational and at the same time subversive proclaimers of the Gospel. Stated directly and simply, his critique can be summed up in a single sentence: "the most evangelical thing the church can do today is be the church … the Body of Christ."[26] As a counterpoint to the doing of evangelism, the perspective of being the Church asserts that the Church's identity is of ultimate importance. Thus "evangelism is not primarily a matter of translating our beliefs about the world into categories that others will find acceptable. It is a matter of being present in the world in a distinctive way such that the alluring and useless beauty of holiness can be touched, tasted, and tried."[27]

Christian evangelism from this perspective is about claiming our true identity. Using the image of Robin Hood, the work of evangelism is the announcement that there is another king, a true king, and one day that kingdom will be fully visible. Evangelism consists of an invitation to become part of that kingdom whose reality can be glimpsed and experienced in the community of a church.[28] This kingdom is for all people, yet it is different from the world and is governed by a different set of values. Recognition of the true king means the rejection of others and the adoption of a lifestyle that is congruent with the values of the kingdom and largely runs counter to the values of the culture around us.[29] Stated again, perhaps the most radical act of evangelism is not necessarily getting people to come to church but rather getting people to *be* that church, claiming its true identity, creating centers of transformation, and being fully present in the foreign field of mission that exists right outside its doors. This presence, this way of being, may actually look quite traditional. With everything, including the mission field, rapidly changing, the same old ways of being might in fact constitute a radical and bold new witness.

An Emerging Church in an Emerging Culture

Attempting to describe definitively the current state of the mission field is an elusive task. Our present age has been called *post-Christian* or *postmodern*. Notice that these terms describe what the current age is not, rather than what it is. These terms simply mark the end of an old era and point to the emergence of a new one that has yet to be born. Beyond a basic rejection of many of the values of modernity, the defining characteristics of the new age are yet to be fully articulated. This is an in-between time, sometimes lamented as a time of chaos and collapse, sometimes celebrated as a time of construction and creativity. At this point however, postmodernity does not represent an organized world view, a distinct culture, or a defined mode of thought. As of yet, there are no postmodern institutions. As the boundaries, structures, and ideals of this new age are still being shaped and formed, postmodernism continues to be a moving target.[30]

In spite of this lack of clarity, there are some things that we do know and these things can be quite helpful, particularly as the Church strives to engage the wider culture during this time of transition labeled by some as a *New Reformation*. This perspective provides a useful reminder that the Church has been through periods of major transition and upheaval before and in every instance has had an uneasy time deciding how closely to relate to the changing culture. The responses have ranged from complete separation to complete absorption, from complete rejection to complete adoption, from complete isolationism to complete incorporation, yet mostly the Church finds itself somewhere between these extremes. It is also useful to remember that this question is never ultimately and finally decided and remains a task for the Church in every generation. The ongoing institutional struggle to find the right and most appropriate way to engage the culture is a recurring theme throughout Church history.

In the current iteration of this question, the Church has a dual problem. On one hand, there are those within the culture who have retained some vestiges of the ideals of Christendom. Unfortunately these ideals usually tend to emphasize religion as being an entirely private endeavor focused solely on the individual. With the lack of a communal dimension, the regrettable consequences of this skewed understanding is that faith can become something that one can assent to but not actively embrace, belief can become something one can ascribe to but does not necessarily follow, and belonging can become something one can claim without offering support or participation.[31] On the other hand, there are ever increasing numbers of those in the culture who have no Christian memory. Given the distortions noted above, this perhaps is more of an opportunity than a liability.

The problem here is that our guiding assumptions about this rapidly growing segment of the population are often misguided and in some instances simply wrong. For instance, it is often assumed that most people in this category possess highly rational, post-Enlightenment, scientific minds, and are actually hostile and openly antagonistic toward the Christian faith. This is simply not true. Generally speaking, postmodern people do not reject the theological positions of the Church because they simply do not know them and are largely unaware of the Christian faith.[32] In fact, some rightly make the case that the largest obstacle that keeps people from faith is not a theological or religious barrier but a cultural and sociological one. "People state the barrier in many ways, but we can state its essence in one sentence: They resist becoming Christians because they don't want to be like church people, which they believe is a prerequisite."[33] It is not the strangeness of the Church that is at issue, but rather it seems that the Church is strange in ways that are unimportant and irrelevant.[34] In other words, postmoderns are aware enough of Christianity to see a disconnect between what the Church professes and what it actually does. Another false assumption about postmoderns is that they are not only anti-religious but also unspiritual and irreligious. On the contrary, postmoderns may have turned away from institutional religion but that does not mean that they are irreligious.[35] In fact many do value and actively seek spiritual resources, but do not seek these resources in or from the Church. Again, this is not necessarily because of antipathy, but because, at least for many postmoderns, there is a failure to see a connection between the two.

So, given this lack of clarity and connection, are there discernible characteristics within the emerging culture that can offer guidance to an emerging and changing Church? It appears as if, again generally speaking, postmoderns "value experience over reason, diversity over conformity, community over individualism, acceptance over tolerance and compassion over idealism."[36] The good news is that all of these characteristics are ones that the mainline Church has the tools to address meaningfully. It is also abundantly clear that while postmoderns may not be interested in maintaining a struggling institution, they are supremely interested in making a positive impact on the world.[37] And herein lies our hope.

All of this points to the expressed need for the *emerging Church* to be in conversation with the emerging culture. Evangelism in this context is more like teaching English as a second language. It means knowing the language and vocabulary of the Church and at the same time knowing the language and vocabulary of the culture and developing fluency in both.[38] Stated similarly, but using a musical image, the emerging Church "must learn to sing the gospel story in a postmodern key."[39]

The Mega-church Phenomenon

One group that has exhibited great promise in the post-Christian religious landscape are the *mega-churches*, loosely defined as Protestant and having over 2000 people in attendance at weekend services. These congregations are not simply a typical congregation grown larger but rather have their own unique dynamics and their own organizational structures.[40] Even though they represent only one half of 1% of American congregations, if combined they would represent the third largest religious body in the US, with 4.5 million people in worship every weekend and an annual income of over $7 billion dollars. Currently there are roughly 1250 mega-churches in existence, with the largest percentage found in California, Texas, and the southeast United States. They are usually found in suburban areas, where land is plentiful and less expensive, and near population growth centers. They are also generally new congregations, which tend to grow faster, and are more nimble and open to change.[41]

There is much that the mainline can learn from the mega-church phenomena in terms of evangelism. Three of the main contributions of the mega-churches are their clear identity and focus, the professional quality of their communications and worship, and especially their intentional, highly organized systems of member interactions. With the mega-church nothing is left to chance in terms of greeting, welcoming, forming, and incorporating new members. The universal assumption for mega-churches is that people do not know one another and left alone they will not make the effort to know one another. Therefore great efforts are made to coordinate fellowship, to create small communities within the larger body, and to instill a sense of belonging. The message is also very clear that involvement in the community is defined by active personal commitment.[42]

In spite of criticism to the contrary, mega-churches are not homogeneous or monolithic, and actually represent a great diversity of theological expression and practice. While most tend toward the more conservative side of the theological spectrum, there are also those that are progressive. The areas of commonality, aside from being large, are their focus on the perspective of those outside the Church and the intentional process of interactions that attract, welcome, and incorporate people and lead them to personal commitment. While there is much to admire and learn from mega-churches, and their impact on the current religious landscape is significant, it is also important to keep this phenomenon in perspective. What has yet to be seen is the stability of mega-churches over time, particularly with regard to the transition of leadership from founding pastors to the next generation of leaders. It is also important to be reminded of their current scope. Even though mega-churches seem pervasive, this is not the case. In reality only 4% of US congregations have attendance of over 1000 worshippers on a weekend and most of those congregations continue to be Roman Catholic.[43]

Globalization and Interfaith Evangelism

One of the major effects of *globalization* is that the world's people, cultures, and religions have been brought closer together. Indeed, the world is getting smaller and ever more deeply interconnected. Our shrinking globe and closer connections have presented exciting opportunities and significant challenges to the mainline. One major opportunity for congregations is the ability to be in close contact with mission partners around the world, many of whom are in parts of the world where Christianity is rapidly expanding if not exploding in terms of numbers and influence. While these relationships can be problematic in terms of divergent geopolitical, cultural, ecclesial, and theological perspectives, they can also be transformative for all involved. Engaging in common mission and shared experience through mutual exchanges, partnership links, and mission trips can provide hope and support to new and often fragile churches abroad, and can at the same time enliven faith and hope at home. An additional challenge that globalization has brought to the home front is the dilemma of how to move from a predominately Christian culture to a multicultural culture, and more specifically, how to appropriately engage those of other faith traditions.

There are generally three responses to the question of appropriate engagement. One is the response of *exclusivism*, the idea that Christianity represents the absolute and only truth and that Jesus is the only way to salvation. The extreme position of this response is the corollary that all other faiths are therefore untrue, misguided, and wrong. A second response is that of *inclusivism*, the idea that a tradition is true but that other traditions are subsumed within that tradition. The third response is the response of *pluralism*, which takes the view that all religions are equally effective vehicles of salvation.[44]

Most of the mainline are either inclusivist or pluralist. At issue is how Christians can affirm the uniqueness and *finality of Christ* as well as affirm that God's grace and truth are active and operative in other expressions of faith. Also at issue is whether or not evangelism has an appropriate place in this pluralistic context. To answer this question, perhaps the place to begin is to acknowledge that God's grace is universal and *prevenient*, that is, it is given to all people, everywhere, all the time. With regard to evangelism, it is also helpful to affirm several tenets summarized from scripture. The first is that God loves non-Christians, that God's grace is at work among non-Christians, and that it is possible, by God's grace, to be saved by Christ without actually knowing it or without taking explicit action. Ultimately, salvation and judgment are left to God. Given this summary, the duty of Christians is to not only love non-Christians, but also to love them enough to evangelize to them.[45]

Perhaps *William Temple* (1881–1944), former Anglican Archbishop of Canterbury in the mid-twentieth century, expressed these sentiments best when he wrote:

> So it may be truly said that the conscience of the heathen man is the voice of Christ within him –
> though muffled by his ignorance. All that is noble in the non-Christian systems of thought, or
> conduct, or worship is the work of Christ upon them and within them. By the word of God,
> that is to say, by Jesus Christ, (others) uttered truths as they declared. There is only one divine
> light; and every man in his measure is enlightened by it.[46]

So it is right to affirm that other religions are at times vehicles of God's grace, yet "the doctrine of Christ's finality means that in several important respects these religions are deficient, but in God's providence they function toward the purposes God has for everyone. From this perspective comes the claim that when persons of other religions are saved, they are saved by Christ."[47] In other words, Christians love and evangelize those of other faiths because we believe that Christianity offers the grace of God in ways that are more true and more complete than the ways that grace is made available in any other faiths. So while salvation is possible without an explicit commitment to Christ, it is certainly more difficult. Just as it is possible to cross the wilderness on one's own, it is much easier when in possession of a map, or better yet, a guide, or even better still, a community of fellow travelers.[48]

Athens Revisited

In the throes of a new Reformation, the mainline Church finds itself journeying through its own kind of a post-Christian wilderness. It is a wilderness marked by breaking down and building up, by obstacles and opportunity, and by pain and promise. There are essentially two mainline narratives for this wilderness journey. One views the past as ideal and longs for a return to former ways of behaving and believing and the reestablishment of a bygone era. The other sees the past as the source of our best ideals and principles, a solid foundation upon which we build a new and brighter future. Both narratives acknowledge problems in the present and both acknowledge that something new is underway.[49] Some have suggested quite convincingly that the circumstances we face in this new age are not unlike those faced by our first-century forebears: a time when Christianity was one faith among many, and a small one at that, and a time when the Church existed at the margins of the culture yet was compelled to speak to that culture in meaningful ways. In the 17th chapter of the book of Acts, set in Athens, the apostle Paul finds the city full of idols. Instead of railing against their heretical ways he commends them for their religious faith and then introduces them to the unknown God whom they are already worshipping unknowingly. This is the God of heaven and earth, who made everything that is, and using the words of Greek poets, he reminds the Athenians that they too are offspring of this same God, the one in whom we "live and move and have our being" (Acts 17:28). A premodernist, Paul understood how to engage the culture constructively, start a conversation right where people were, utilizing insights from other faiths, and then drawing them closer to the one true and only God.[50] Clearly fluent in the language of the culture and the language of faith, confident that God was already present and active among the Athenians, Paul is a model for contemporary evangelism and a perfect wilderness guide.

By way of conclusion, we offer three guideposts, three areas of emphasis, for the being and doing of evangelism. They represent practices that have proven effective for congregations of any size, shape, location, or theological persuasion. We are convinced that every congregation already has the resources it needs, we are convinced that all congregations have innate strengths, and we are convinced that all congregations have something of value from their past that they can draw upon to guide them into a more positive future.[51] As mentioned previously in this chapter, we believe that congregational growth is usually found in building upon a combination of strengths unique to every congregation. We also believe that the revitalization of the mainline will not happen as part of a mass movement, but rather will happen one congregation at a time.

The first guidepost for the journey is meaningful worship. For most congregations worship remains the core task, the primary purpose, and the main event of community life. Much of what people receive when they come to church happens in worship. Compelling, inspirational, transformational, soul nurturing, highly participatory worship is at the very heart of a growing congregation. The second guidepost, not unrelated to the first, is the development of meaningful relationships. A compelling life of faith is all about relationships, a relationship with God and relationships with others. Successful evangelism and church growth finds ways to build and nurture healthy, life-giving relationships, and a way to foster a sense of belonging, a sense of genuine community. Contrary to the mass marketing approach to evangelism, people come to faith through long-term relationships with family, friends, and neighbors. The third guidepost has to do with the development of an intentional process for the welcome, incorporation, and formation of new members. Evangelizing, growing congregations have clearly articulated and broadly understood procedures for the integration of newcomers. Going beyond providing hospitality and welcome, the system must also include some kind of organized formation, spiritual development, or mechanism for making disciples. There are numerous programs and resources on the market that are quite helpful, and congregations should not be shy about adapting them for their personal use. Yet it is important to remember that the most effective programs are home grown and reflective of a particular congregation, in a particular place, with a particular vision and mission. What is also important when considering all of these guideposts is that authenticity and not perfection is the goal. In the end, the work of evangelism and church growth is God's work. While being and doing all that we can, we must also ultimately trust that God's loving purpose for the world will prevail even as a new and largely unknown age is about to be born.

Notes

1   Scott J. Jones, *The Evangelistic Love of God and Neighbor: A Theology of Witness and Discipleship* (Nashville, TN: Abingdon Press, 2003), 114.

2   Ibid., 109.

3   Ibid.

4   George G. Hunter, *Radical Outreach: The Recovery of Apostolic Ministry and Evangelism* (Nashville, TN: Abingdon Press, 2003), 1.

5   Cynthia Woolever and Deborah Bruce, *A Field Guide to U.S. Congregations: Who's Going Where and Why? second edition* (Louisville, MO: Westminster John Knox Press, 2010), 29.

6   Ibid., 32.

7   Bryan Stone, *Evangelism after Christendom: The Theology and Practice of Christian Witness* (Grand Rapids, MI: Brazos Press, 2007), preface/introduction.

8   Richard H. Bliese and Craig Van Gelder, *The Evangelizing Church: A Lutheran Contribution* (Minneapolis, MN: Augsburg Fortress, 2005), preface.

9   Stone, *Evangelism after Christendom*, 11.

10   Ibid., 13.

11   See Graham Tomlin, *The Provocative Church* (London: SPCK, 2002).

12   Mike Booker and Mark Ireland, *Evangelism – Which Way Now: An Evaluation of Alpha, Emmaus, Cell Church and Other Contemporary Strategies for Evangelism* (London: Church House Publishing, 2003), 5.

13   Scott Thumma and Warren Bird, *The Other 80 Percent: Turning Your Church's Spectators into Active Participants* (San Francisco, CA: Jossey-Bass, 2011), 21–26.

14   Bill Hybels and Mark Mittelberg, *Becoming a Contagious Christian* (Grand Rapids, MI: Zondervan, 1994), 47.

15   Adam Hamilton with Cynthia Gadsden, *Selling Swimsuits in the Arctic: Seven Simple Keys to Growing Churches* (Nashville, TN: Abingdon Press, 2005), 1–7.

16   Ibid., 33–35.

17   Yvon Prehn, *Ministry Marketing Made Easy: A Practical Guide to Marketing Your Church Message* (Nashville, TN: Abingdon Press, 2004), 57.

18   Robert L. Perry, *Find a Niche and Scratch It: Marketing Your Congregation* (Bethesda, MD: Alban Institute, 2003), 18–20.

19   Jones, *Evangelistic Love of God and Neighbor*, 188.

20   Stone, *Evangelism after Christendom*, 13.

21   Ibid., 14.

22   Mark A. Olson, *Moving Beyond Church Growth: An Alternative Vision for Congregations* (Minneapolis, MN: Augsburg Fortress Press, 2002), 65.

23   Ibid.

24   Stone, *Evangelism after Christendom*, 14.

25   Ibid., 19.

26   Ibid., 15.

27   Ibid., 120.

28   Tomlin, *Provocative Church*, 28.

29   Ibid., 50.

30   Harry Lee Poe, *Christian Witness in a Postmodern World* (Nashville, TN: Abingdon Press, 2001), 170.

31   Thumma and Bird, *The Other 80 Percent*, 59.

32   Poe, *Christian Witness*, 139.

33   Jones, *Evangelistic Love of God and Neighbor*, 130.

34   Ibid.

35   Bliese and Van Gelder, *The Evangelizing Church*, 109.

36   Kelly A. Freyer, *A Story Worth Sharing: Engaging Evangelism* (Minneapolis, MN: Augsburg Fortress Press, 2004), 179.

37   Ibid., 170.

38   Freyer, *Story Worth Sharing*, 54.

39   Ibid., 13.

40   Scott Thumma and Dave Travis, *Beyond Megachurch Myths: What We Can Learn from America's Largest Churches* (San Francisco, CA: Jossey-Bass, 2007), xvii–xxiv.

41   Ibid., 3.

42   Ibid., 3–17.

43   Woolever and Bruce, *Field Guide to U.S. Congregations*, 117.

44   Jones, *Evangelistic Love of God and Neighbor*, 159.

45   Ibid., 166.

46   Jones, *Evangelistic Love of God and Neighbor*, 168.

47   Ibid.

48   Ibid., 172.

49   Woolever and Bruce, *Field Guide to U.S. Congregations*, 119–120.

50   Steve Hollinghurst, *Mission-Shaped Evangelism: The Gospel in Contemporary Culture* (Norwich: Canterbury Press, 2010), xii.

51   Woolever and Bruce, *Field Guide to U.S. Congregations*, 11.

Annotated Bibliography

Anderson, Douglas T. and Coyner, Michael J., *The Race to Reach Out: Connecting Newcomers to Christ in a New Century* (Nashville, TN: Abingdon Press, 2004).
This book from a United Methodist author focuses on the building of an intentional and systematic process of welcoming and incorporating new members into a congregation. The goal is belonging, and the author suggests that the creation of any process begins working to achieve this goal.

Baucum, Tory K., *Evangelical Hospitality: Catechetical Evangelism in the Early Church and Its Recovery for Today* (Lanham, MD: Scarecrow Press, 2008).
Based on what the author calls "catechetical evangelism," this books provides an outline for effective evangelism in the postmodern world by the recovery of that early Church formula of Christian hospitality, a shared meal, genuine friendship, and sound teaching.

Booker, Mike and Ireland, Mark, *Evangelism – Which Way Now: An Evaluation of Alpha, Emmaus, Cell Church and Other Contemporary Strategies for Evangelism* (London: Church House Publishing, 2003).
This book offers a thoughtful study and evaluation of the key evangelism and church growth resources in use today. Based on the assumption that every community must discern the

best resources to fit their particular context, this work will be a great help in discerning and implementing an effective strategy.

Bliese, Richard H. and Van Gelder, Craig, *The Evangelizing Church: A Lutheran Contribution* (Minneapolis, MN: Augsburg Fortress, 2005).

This book of articles written by Lutheran scholars calls for the death of evangelism and the resurrection of an evangelizing Church. The goal is to reflect on the theology of ministry, to renew the commission to make disciples, and to move from evangelical theory to practice.

Freyer, Kelly A., *A Story Worth Sharing: Engaging Evangelism* (Minneapolis, MN: Augsburg Fortress Press, 2004).

This Lutheran author agrees that some marketing strategies and techniques are quite effective but suggests that this is not the place to begin a conversation about evangelism. Rather the process begins in prayer and in the formation of disciples and evangelical leaders to renew local congregations.

Hamilton, Adam with Gadsden, Cynthia, *Selling Swimsuits in the Arctic: Seven Simple Keys to Growing Churches* (Nashville, TN: Abingdon Press, 2005).

Written by a United Methodist pastor who leads one of the largest and fastest growing congregations in the country, this slim text focuses on seven fundamental concepts of relationship-based evangelism. Designed to be read in one sitting, this is a simple, practical, and easy to use guide.

Hollinghurst, Steve, *Mission-Shaped Evangelism: The Gospel in Contemporary Culture* (Norwich: Canterbury Press, 2010).

Written by a mission practitioner and researcher in the field of evangelism for the Church of England, this book explores the nature of evangelism in our multi-faith and multi-cultural modern world. This book seeks to apply mission thinking to a wide array of contemporary cultural issues with the hope of engaging more effective evangelism.

Hunter, George G., *Leading and Managing a Growing Church* (Nashville, TN: Abingdon Press, 2000).

This Methodist writer contends that the many of the books written to help pastors lead and manage change are based on the false assumption that pastors already know how to lead and manage. This book takes a more fundamental approach to the basics of management leadership in the modern world.

Hunter, George G., *Radical Outreach: The Recovery of Apostolic Ministry and Evangelism* (Nashville, TN: Abingdon Press, 2003).

The author, a professor of church growth and evangelism at Asbury Theological Seminary, presses for the recovery of apostolic mission priorities: to reach out to those with no "Christian memory," those from many tongues, nations, and cultures, and those deemed unreachable and hopeless.

Hybels, Bill and Mittelberg, Mark, *Becoming a Contagious Christian* (Grand Rapids, MI: Zondervan, 1994).

These pastors who serve the Willow Creek congregation, a mega-church known for its successful outreach to the unchurched, offer a personalized approach to relational evangelism that includes the discovery of one's own style of evangelism and the development of a "contagious" Christian character.

Jones, Scott J., *The Evangelistic Love of God and Neighbor: A Theology of Witness and Discipleship* (Nashville, TN: Abingdon Press, 2003).

This exceptional text seeks to ground the practice of evangelism in an understanding of God's love for the world specifically as seen in the incarnation of God in Christ, and contends that the goal of evangelism is to bring people more fully into the reign of God. It is an examination of the relationship between systematic theology and practical theology and a presentation of the thoughtful and coherent theology of evangelism.

Kallenberg, Brad J., *Live to Tell: Evangelism in a Postmodern World* (Grand Rapids, MI: Brazos Press, 2002).

Linking postmodern philosophy to the postmodern evangelism, the author focuses on the task of contextualization; learning to "sing the gospel story in a postmodern key."

McCoy, Linda S., *Planting a Garden: Growing the Church Beyond Traditional Models* (Nashville, TN: Abingdon Press, 2005).

This is the story of the development of an emergent Church that grew out of a large established Methodist Church in Indianapolis. This community embraces innovative thinking and unconventional practices as a way to reach the unchurched and is a successful non-traditional yet progressive Church experience.

McIntosh, Gary L., *Taking Your Church to the Next Level: What Got You Here Won't Get You There* (Grand Rapids, MI: Baker Books, 2009).

Based on the idea of congregational life cycles, this book outlines responses and interventions that can be made at each phase of the life cycle to improve health and creativity and to diminish decline.

Olson, Mark A., *Moving Beyond Church Growth: An Alternative Vision for Congregations* (Minneapolis, MN: Augsburg Fortress Press, 2002).

In a culture where church growth marketing and technique are revered, this author suggests that most of these efforts are counterproductive and argues that hope for the future rests in the Church actually being the Church, with congregational life focused on witness, substance, purpose, and a style anchored in strong leadership, and worship that is passionate and engaged.

Perry, Robert L., *Find a Niche and Scratch It: Marketing Your Congregation*, (Bethesda, MD: Alban Institute, 2003).

The author takes the principles of niche marketing and applies them to congregations.

The basic idea is to identify the gifts and skills of the community and plan a marketing strategy based on those strengths rather than mimicking the perceived success of other congregations.

Poe, Harry Lee, *Christian Witness in a Postmodern World* (Nashville, TN: Abingdon Press, 2001).

Believing that proclaiming the Gospel to a postmodern world is actually more of an opportunity than a challenge, the author contends that the Church has returned to a first-century or New Testament context that can speak directly to the underlying spiritual questions of the emerging postmodern world.

Prehn, Yvon, *Ministry Marketing Made Easy: A Practical Guide to Marketing Your Church Message* (Nashville, TN: Abingdon Press, 2004).

Written by a marketing consultant who is married to a pastor, this text offers ideas and resources for churches marketing to a postmodern world that is indifferent to authority, time-starved, unfamiliar with the Christian vocabulary, and seeking spirituality.

Stone, Bryan, *Evangelism after Christendom: The Theology and Practice of Christian Witness* (Grand Rapids, MI: Brazos Press, 2007).

Addressing the largely negative connotations of the word "evangelism," the author believes that the most radical and evangelical thing the Church can do in this postmodern world is to actually be the Church. He contends that evangelism is not translating our beliefs into categories that others will find acceptable, but rather is more about public witness, being present in the world in a distinctive and alluring way.

Tenney-Brittian, Bill, *Hitchhiker's Guide to Evangelism* (St. Louis, MO: Chalice Press, 2008).

A "how-to" training book related to the idea of relational evangelism, with the emphasis being on breaking out of the "Christian cocoon" and enlarging a network of friends to include the unchurched.

Thumma, Scott and Travis, Dave, *Beyond Megachurch Myths: What We Can Learn from America's Largest Churches* (San Francisco, CA: Jossey-Bass, 2007).

While debunking the seven common myths about the mega-church experience, this extensively researched book offers a clear understanding of mega-churches and also offers insights and ideas that are applicable to congregations of any size.

Thumma, Scott and Bird, Warren, *The Other 80 Percent: Turning Your Church's Spectators into Active Participants* (San Francisco, CA: Jossey-Bass, 2011).

Based on the well-researched premise that spiritual growth and formation are directly related to greater and deeper involvement, this practical guide explores what motivates the inactive to engage in a life of discipleship within a community of faith.

Tomlin, Graham, *The Provocative Church* (London: SPCK, 2002).

More a contemporary theology of evangelism than a "how-to" manual, this helpful text is a blend of theology and practice that focuses on utilizing the gifts of the entire local congregation to create an intriguing, attractive, and provocative community that compels others to come closer and want to know more.

Whitesel, Bob, *Growth by Accident, Death by Planning: How Not to Kill a Growing Congregation* (Nashville, TN: Abingdon Press, 2004).

This work is based on the premise that all growing churches eventually reach a plateau and then begin to decline. It is then that most congregations turn to strategic planning for decision making rather trusting the more responsive and intuitive decision-making process that led to their initial growth.

Woolever, Cynthia and Bruce, Deborah, *A Field Guide to U.S. Congregations: Who's Going Where and Why? second edition* (Louisville, MO: Westminster John Knox Press, 2010).

Based on data from the 2008 US Congregational Life Survey, the largest ever conducted, this volume provides insightful interpretation of the significant changes, current trends, and future possibilities for American congregations. The goal of the book is to provide religious leaders and worshippers with reality-based analysis gleaned from healthy, growing, excellence-oriented organizations. It encourages congregations to move toward data-driven decision making in light of the research facts that are presented.

Woolever, Cynthia and Bruce, Deborah, *Beyond the Ordinary: 10 Strengths of U.S. Congregations* (Louisville, MO: Westminster John Knox Press, 2004).

Utilizing results from the first US Congregational Life Survey (encompassing over 2000 congregations and 300 000 congregants) this books looks at the behaviors of worshippers across the spectrum of denominations and faith groups, and explores the common characteristics of strong congregations.

15

Leading through Change and Conflict

Churches change. Churches fight. There is a certain inevitability to both of these statements. Like any living organism, like any human institution, congregations are constantly pulled between the forces of stability and the forces of change. Whether consciously or unconsciously, the tension between these opposing forces creates conflict at the very heart of the Christian community. Sometimes this conflict is neutralized in a state of equilibrium. Sometimes it is manifest in positive ways and unleashes creativity, growth, and health. Sometimes it negatively erupts into anger, discord, and strife. And as many know from first-hand experience, the latter manifestation of church conflict can be particularly devastating and destructive.

Rather than seeking to actively avoid change and conflict in congregational life, this chapter seeks to embrace its reality and is primarily focused on the role of pastoral leaders in the task of discernment. In brief, the task involves diagnosing the intensity of the conflict or the consequences of the proposed change and prescribing the appropriate level of intervention and leadership. The basic approach is that change and conflict are not problems to be solved but rather are realities to accept and utilize. The overall goal is to help pastoral leaders become more successful agents of change and more effective managers of conflict.

The most common mistakes made by pastoral leaders in the face of change or conflict have to do with properly discerning congregational dynamics and, likewise, discerning an appropriate response. One response to recognizing that a change is approaching or a conflict is brewing is to simply ignore it and hope it goes away. This might be precisely the right and appropriate response in some instances, if pursued in a thoughtful, strategic, and intentional manner, yet the mistake is when pastoral leaders choose blissful ignorance as an automatic default response to any disruption in the status quo. Sometimes issues do not go away and only simmer and intensify and a relatively small problem becomes a larger one, which has grown out of proportion to the initial disturbance.

An Introduction to Ministry: A Primer for Renewed Life and Leadership in Mainline Protestant Congregations, First Edition. Ian S. Markham and Oran E. Warder.
© 2016 John Wiley & Sons, Ltd. Published 2016 by John Wiley & Sons, Ltd.

A second common mistake is to overreact. Pastoral leaders may rightly perceive an imbalance in the congregational system and overcorrect. What otherwise might have been easily addressed and quickly resolved now becomes highly charged. The center of conflict is no longer the presenting issue but rather the heavy-handed or overreaching response of the leadership.

A third common mistake on the part of pastoral leaders is to oversimplify and underreact. In the face of significant disruption and intense conflict a corresponding response is necessary. Oversimplification can cause leaders to offer a response that is often too little and too late. If a tourniquet is required, a Band-Aid is of little use. Even when confronted with the absolute necessity of bold action, pastoral leaders are often timid and reticent to assert the power and authority given them by God, their denomination, and the community they have been called to serve and lead. There is good reason for caution on this front, but caution need not necessarily lead to inaction or inadequate action on the part of congregational leaders. In all three of these scenarios, discernment is key.

Conflict in Scripture

Before we venture too far into this topic it is important to place change and conflict within the context of the larger Christian story. The Book of Acts and the Pauline letters are instructive, inspiring, and encouraging. Acts records the birth of the Church and the history of its early formation. It is a story of the transformation of disciples, from those who followed Jesus, to apostles, those sent forth to continue his redeeming work. This is accomplished by the power of the Holy Spirit and not without a considerable amount of dramatic change and a frightening amount of conflict. The first major Church fight, a conflict between Peter and Paul over the inclusion of gentiles into the covenant community, threatened to kill the Church in its infancy. Eventually, with God's help, a solution emerged and the Church was preserved, only to face the next challenge.

Peter, Paul, and Conflict

But when Peter came to Antioch, I opposed him to his face, because he stood self-condemned.

Galatians 2:11

The early Christian Church in the middle first century did not necessarily begin harmoniously. Peter and Paul, perhaps the two most important apostles with respect to establishing Christianity from its inception following the crucifixion of Jesus, did not always see eye to eye. The heated confrontation in Paul's epistle to the Galatians illustrates this point, based on a vehement disagreement over the conversion of the Gentiles (the non-Jewish peoples) to Christianity. Conversion to this Judeo-Christian religion, from Peter's point of view, meant circumcision for men, as is the Jewish custom; for Paul, this was unnecessary. The conflict between these two was iconic,

> but essential to the fabric of Christianity – and the lesson is that through coping with our tensions and disagreements we may find a pathway to the greater glory of God. In an ironic twist, the Church recognizes a feast day for St. Peter and St. Paul together on the same day (June 29) – united in their disagreements for all time.

In his efforts to plant, grow, and spread the Church throughout the known world, Paul quickly realized that the new congregations needed supervision and guidance. It is a blessing to subsequent generations of Christians that these early communities were embroiled in every manner of conflict and struggled with the forces of rapid change. Were it not for their troubles, we would be deprived of Paul's wisdom and encouragement. These texts provide insight and inspiration as we navigate similar circumstances in our own day. These stories help to normalize the dynamics of change and conflict and place them in their proper perspective. For pastoral leaders, it is reassuring to know that these dynamics have always been part of the reality of congregational life and always will be. The fact that the Church remains is a powerful witness to the continuing presence and activity of the Spirit in the midst of our struggles and confusion, and serves as a reminder that we are not alone in the ongoing work of mission.

Paul also offers another foundational concept in response to the turmoil and division that arose with the churches that he helped to found. In his letters to the churches in Rome and Corinth, he reminds the believers that, like it or not, they are forever bound to one another through baptism, that they are brothers and sisters in Christ, that they are connected to one another in one body (Christ's body) and that each member is an important part of the whole.

In her book, *Living with Contradiction*, Esther de Waal offers a visual image of Paul's profound words. In this excerpt she invites her readers to imagine standing in the nave of Canterbury Cathedral looking up to the vault of the ceiling. Looking at pillar and arch, rib and vault, all are brought together in one great harmonious unity. Each part is separate and individual, yet inextricably linked to its neighbors and to the whole structure. She writes:

> Here is the Pauline analogy of the Body of Christ spelt out in stone … but to discover the secret of this harmonious unity, this peace and concord, one has to climb the hidden stairways and explore the space between the stone vaults and the roof above. Here is thrust and counter-thrust. Here is never-ending conflict. The high vaults strive to push the walls outwards; the flying buttresses strive to push them inwards. Here are columns, arches and walls all locked in unceasing combat. The great cathedral is maintained, and has been maintained for centuries through the interplay and interdependence of contradictory forces, the unremitting pull of opposites. The keystone is firm at the point of equilibrium.[1]

This radical thinking places church conflict and change in a theological framework whereby our unity is found in Christ and not in universal agreement or uniform practice. De Waal argues that the Church needs conflict as part of the equilibrium of the institution to keep it healthy.

In his book, *Faithful Disagreement*, Frances Taylor Gench suggests that Scripture can be a resource and a guide to help foster communication with fellow Christians with whom we disagree. He cautions that the Church's appeal to biblical authority, particularly in times of conflict and change, is often more rhetorical than real and that our arguments about Scripture often expose how very little we know about the Bible itself. More often than not "we appeal to a handful of passages that justify our own positions but lack the ability to order Scripture as a whole."[2] His premise is that we rarely read the Bible in the company of others and more rarely still in the company of those with whom we disagree. He implores Church members to stop shaking the Bible at each other, and instead to actually *open* it, and to *read* it together. When this happens, there is space for God to work, space to listen to the Bible and one another. Reminding us of Karl Barth's famous observation that the "Bible does not always answer our questions but sometimes calls our questions into greater question," he also affirms Raymond Brown's assertion that "a divided Christianity, instead of reading the Bible to assure ourselves we are right, we would do better to read to discover where we have not been listening."[3] In the Church, particularly in unsettled times, we are usually so busy speaking the truth to one another that we fail to listen or to engage in genuine conversation.[4] Scripture has much to teach us about being the Church, particularly in times of conflict and change.

To this point we have discussed change and conflict not only as inevitable but also as inextricably tied. But is this so? Is it possible to have one without the other? And if it is, what is the correlation between the two? While it is our observation that by its very nature, conflict always produces some kind of change, we do not however believe that every change produces conflict.

There is an adage among church planters that it is many times easier to start a new church than it is to change, or redirect, an existing congregation. In the first instance change is expected, anticipated, and welcomed; in the latter, change is often met with at least suspicion, if not outright fear and apprehension. Disrupting the status quo, shifting the balance and equilibrium, even for the health and benefit of the system is risky business and is to be approached with caution, sensitivity, and care. Sometimes it is not the change itself that causes the conflict but the way change is made that creates stress and tension in the system. The reality is that in existing congregations evolutionary change is preferable to revolutionary change.[5] Slow, thoughtful, deliberate, well-articulated, well-communicated change can happen with little or no conflict as a result. It has been said, "congregations are like horses, they don't like to be surprised or startled, it causes deviant behavior."[6]

So even in the absence of conflict, change is an essential part of life. In the prologue of his best-selling novel, *The Lost World*, Michael Crichton offers some profound insights on the subject of change and conflict. In the context of exploring the demise of dinosaurs, he challenges the prevailing theories of extinction and suggests that complex systems of any variety tend to locate themselves on what he calls "the edge of chaos." He continues:

> we imagine the edge of chaos as a place where there is enough innovation to keep a living system vibrant, and enough stability to keep it from collapsing into anarchy. It is a zone of conflict and upheaval where the old and the new are constantly at war. Finding the balance point is a delicate matter. If a living system drifts too close, it risks falling over into incoherence and dissolution; but if the system moves too far away from the edge, it becomes rigid, frozen, totalitarian. Both conditions lead to extinction. Too much change is as destructive as too little. Only at the edge of chaos can complex systems flourish.[7]

To apply this thinking to congregational life, the Church, as a complex living organism, exists in the tension between stability and instability. The Church exists within the tension of two competing realities. In one reality, the Church is seen as a mighty ship whose purpose is to set sail on the adventurous seas of mission. In the other reality, the Church is seen as the anchor whose purpose is to be a place of calm and stability amid the shifting tides and raging winds of change.[8] Put another way, "Christian religiosity seeks to sustain the status quo, Christian faithfulness seeks to challenge the status quo."[9] The truth is that the Church must be both of these realities. Striking the balance and finding equilibrium in the midst of conflict and upheaval, the clash of the new and the old, is the delicate task of discerning leadership.

Assessing Conflict

To be about this task, pastoral leaders need to develop the ability to accurately assess and diagnose the intensity of the change or the level of conflict experienced by the congregation. This requires paying careful attention to congregational dynamics, managing one's own anxiety, acting in communication and concert with parish leaders, and intentionally and strategically leading with a sense of humility and care. It seems that all of the tools and resources for church conflict assessment are based, at least in part, on the seminal work of Speed Leas, a writer and conflict consultant associated with the Alban Institute.[10] Reviewing his work, and that of several others, the task of conflict assessment can essentially be summarized in three basic categories: healthy constructive conflict, transitional conflict, and unhealthy destructive conflict.

Healthy constructive conflict is viewed as normative, if not essential, to a healthy and thriving congregation. At this level, conflict is not seen as a symptom of disease or a sign of pathology. On the contrary, conflict is expected, differences are respected, and there is a genuine sense that all are concerned with the common good of the congregation. At this level the conflict is focused on a specific, well-articulated, and widely understood issue. Generally speaking, people are in problem-solving mode, are not anxious or panicked, and are confident that the issue will be decided one way or another and for the greater good of the community. The appropriate response of the congregational leadership at this level is to work at conflict resolution. That is, successfully dealing with the conflict at this level before it intensifies.

The level of transitional conflict is just that, a conflict that can either be resolved in a positive manner, or remain unresolved, or escalate into a more negative and potentially destructive level of conflict. Rather than being seen as normative and healthy, at this level the people involved can become suspicious of the motives and actions of others and as a result begin to become self-protective. When this happens, a shift occurs. Rather than focusing on a specific well-defined problem, people become focused on preserving and defending their own position. The initial conflict becomes secondary and, rather than addressing the presenting issue, people begin to speak of a general lack of trust and a breakdown of communication. If not successfully addressed, the conflict can intensify to the point where people are not only primarily concerned about maintaining their own position, but now become focused on making sure that their position prevails over and against the positions of others. At this level, if the conflict escalates, there is no longer a perception that differences are honored and there is no longer an overarching sense that all are working toward a common good. Quite the opposite, people are now thought to have malevolent intent and a rift begins to form between groups within the congregation. It is at this point that assigning blame becomes an important focus of time and energy in spite of the fact that "finding fault is the most characteristic dimension and the least helpful dimension of conflict."[11]

Conflict Mediation

The appropriate response by congregational leaders at this level of intensity is conflict mediation. Conflict mediation involves the development of an open and fair process that provides those involved with plenty of opportunities to influence the outcome of the process. To be successful there must be a clear process, a safe environment, and mutually agreed upon ground rules for behavior. The main task is to reduce anxiety, normalize the conflict, seek to return to and specifically define the presenting issue, and develop an agreed upon decision-making process that values and respects difference. If mediation is not initiated, and if initiated and not successful, the conflict could further intensify.

At the level of unhealthy destructive conflict, the conversation has moved far away from the initial source of disagreement, the developing rifts within the congregation have solidified, and it is no longer suitable simply to hold a position, and to prevail against all other positions, it now becomes imperative to seek a divorce. In this scenario, somebody, or some group, is to blame and somebody, or some group, has to go. Taken to the extreme, groups can take on the zeal of religious fanaticism, insist that God and Scripture are squarely on their side, and believe that anyone who opposes this thinking must be eradicated. The appropriate response of congregational leaders at this most intense level of discord is conflict management or conflict negotiation. At this level, the goal is no longer to try to heal and reconcile, rather the goal is to neutralize the conflict, limit the damage, and try to negotiate a settlement that provides at least the possibility of a way forward for all those involved.

Intervention and Resolution

As a general rule it is best to try to resolve and mediate conflicts using the leadership and resources from within the congregation and only turn to denominational resources and the engagement of an outside conflict consultant when local attempts have failed to produce the desired results. Except for instances of intense interpersonal disagreements, most conflicts can be managed without outside intervention. The prevailing wisdom regarding the engagement of outside help is that congregations have to hurt enough to actually believe that they need this kind of assistance before they are open to receiving it. This, of course, does not include outside support and coaching for congregational leaders themselves. Nor does it include congregational education on this subject at a time apart from an ongoing conflict or in anticipation of a major change.

If the engagement of a conflict consultant is deemed necessary, we believe the earliest point of intervention might best occur when efforts to mediate a transitional conflict are found to be unsuccessful. It is also our opinion that outside professional help is an absolute necessity if a conflict reaches the unhealthy and destructive level. Not all conflicts start out small and escalate. Some may erupt quickly and with potentially devastating force. In this case a consultant is also a necessity. The presence of an experienced, neutral third party can make a tremendous difference and can sometimes help to reverse or at least neutralize the conflict and in some cases initiate a lasting process of reconciliation. While conflict at the initial levels can be constructive and life-giving to congregations, conflict at the more intense levels lacks the potential to be either. Conflict in the earlier levels can produce win–win results. Battles waged at higher levels produce no winners.

Power Struggles

It is regrettable that there are some congregations which exhibit a recurring pattern of conflict. In some cases even repeated interventions have not been able to shift or alter the pattern. In fairness it is also true that there are clergy who exhibit similar patterns of leadership. One of the reasons that conflicts within the Church can be so devastating is that most church conflicts, at some level, are struggles for power. As a voluntary institution, a church has structures and processes that not only permit, but even entice, the unaccountable use (and misuse) of power.[12] Lacking the utilitarian control of business and the coercive control of civic institutions, a church cannot force people to behave properly or fight fairly.[13] This reality is an invitation for sinful human behavior and serves as a reminder that "power may not be inherently corrupting, but sinful human beings are inherently fallible in its exercise."[14]

Apart from any conversation about "normal" congregational conflict, it is important to recognize that there are some within a church whose motives are not honorable, but rather are deceiving, disruptive, and intentionally destructive. Part of the task of a prayerfully discerning leader is the ability to differentiate between ordinary conflict and the presence of genuinely antagonistic people and truly evil forces that can exist in congregations. Even still there is a grave danger in equating evil behavior with the evilness of people, which is a judgment that is not ours to make.[15] Yet there may still be a need to act. Using the organic analogy of the congregation as a "living body," Peter Steinke writes that the congregational immune system is either its ruin or its salvation. He adds that congregational leaders make two kinds of mistakes in this regard. They either fail to resist in the presence of real disease, or they overreact and attack that which was not a threat to the health of the system.[16] Again, discernment is crucial.

Pastoral Leadership

Returning now to the discussion of the levels of congregational conflict and the role of the pastoral leader, it is our observation that the ability of the pastoral leader to fully participate and lead in times of difficulty decreases as the level of conflict increases. It goes without saying, yet must be noted, that the pastor is most often the focus of any church conflict at any level. Some believe that even in the absence of conflict, the underlying emotional dynamics of a congregation surface every 7 or 8 years and when they do, they are almost always focused on the pastor.[17] In many mainline denominations this cycle also correlates to the average tenure of a pastoral leader. And in the face of and in the aftermath of actual congregational conflict, clergy are often confronted with the dilemma of whether to leave the congregation or re-engage and stay. Given the highly symbolic nature of the pastoral role, the deep connection of the pastoral bond, and the intricate interconnection of personal, professional, and family considerations, it is difficult to sort out the complexities of the question to leave or stay.

The negative emotions that often accompany a time of intense conflict can sometimes lead clergy to resign too quickly. Resigning prematurely is not only unhelpful, but often unnecessary. The ministry of the pastor and the mission of the congregation may be better served by not acting precipitously, seeing the conflict through to some kind of resolution, and then discerning the call to leave or stay apart from the emotional intensity of the present moment.

Many pastoral leaders consider leaving their congregations because they feel they have mismanaged a change effort or the conflict that resulted. The remainder of this chapter will focus more positively on the role of the pastor as change agent and conflict manager, as well as offer some ideas about how to insulate congregations from destructive forms of conflict.

Any discussion of the management of change and the management of conflict is directly connected to the management of self. It is the pastoral leader who sets the mood, tone, and spirit of congregational life and health, and simply possessing "good cheer is half the battle."[18] Tending to one's own physical, spiritual, and emotional health is paramount. Health begets health. In addition to family and a network of supportive friends and professional colleagues, many clergy find it valuable to establish an intentional relationship with a seasoned mentor who may serve in a variety of roles including pastor, priest, confidant, confessor, coach, and listening friend. The ideal person is a consistent presence to and for the pastor but not directly connected to the congregation.

The Non-anxious Leader

As alluded to earlier in this chapter, one of the primary goals in the management of self as it relates to pastoral ministry is the regulation of one's own anxiety. Any congregation is a highly integrated system of relationships. In such a relational system anxiety is highly contagious, particularly if exhibited by the congregational leadership. If the leader of the congregation is fearful and anxious, these emotions will permeate the entire system. There is much in the literature about the role of the clergy person as the "non-anxious" presence within the congregational system. This term, coined by psychiatrist Murray Bowen (1913–1990) and popularized in the writing and work of Rabbi Ed Friedman (1932–1996), suggests that a non-anxious leader not only has the capacity to be more clear-minded in terms of creative solutions, more adroit in tense and difficult situations, but also and most importantly can help lower the anxiety level of the entire system. This ability alone can do more for conflict resolution than actually coming up with good solutions. The term is often misunderstood and thought to be the equivalent of either being detached and aloof or being cool under pressure. It is neither. Being a non-anxious presence means possessing an inner calm. It also requires a deep connection to people and the system without being caught up in the swirl of emotions. Some have even believed the penultimate goal of the congregational leader is to be completely free of any anxiety, which is not only unrealistic, but also impossible. Bowen himself was once said to have quipped "the idea is not to be completely non-anxious, just less anxious than anyone else in the room."

As a change agent, a non-anxious leader is advised to think strategically and act carefully when initiating change. Throughout the process it is critically important to stay positive and to have a clearly stated, well-articulated, well-communicated, and well-reasoned position. It is important to enlist the support and assistance of congregational leaders and to provide opportunities for open discussion and to move at a slow but deliberate pace. A successful change agent expects, but also resists sabotage, resistance, and reactivity. Lastly it is important to lead in a manner that takes the effort seriously and takes one's self less seriously, to maintain a sense of humor and to not take criticism personally, but rather as a way to gather information about what is happening within the congregational system.[19] The non-anxious leader stays connected, actively listens, and leads with empathy, while at the same time moving forward. A thoughtful, intentional, careful, and deliberate process can minimize conflict and maximize goodwill.

In terms of working to insulate a congregation from destructive conflict, a pastoral leader can begin by acknowledging that conflict is expected and can be an avenue for growth. The leader can work to develop a reputation for being a fair and equitable decision maker, and can also develop an early warning system to deal directly and swiftly with conflicts before they have a chance to escalate.[20] Other ways to be proactive in the work of congregational health include having a clear statement of mission and purpose, one that is regularly reviewed and widely embraced. It is also helpful to educate the congregation in the dynamics of church systems and conflict management; to focus on the good and positive qualities of the community life; to provide forums for open and transparent communication; to deal with conflict in a manner that is consistent with the mission and culture of a church; and to embrace diversity and to model mutual respect.[21] The overarching goal is to help congregations transform potentially malevolent cycles of conflict into benevolent cycles of trust, and to interrupt vicious cycles of fear while encouraging virtuous cycles of faith.

Churches do change, and sometimes that change leads to conflict, and sometimes that conflict can unleash the creative energy of new life and growth. Rather than problems to be solved, change and conflict are realities to be embraced and utilized for the good of the Church and the spread of the Gospel. At issue for the pastoral leader is the prayerful discernment that leads to appropriately assessing congregational dynamics and matching that assessment with appropriate action and leadership. This happens in the context of the larger Christian story and with the full knowledge that the Church's continued existence, through the centuries of conflict and change, is a witness to the ongoing work of the Spirit and to the truth of Paul's analogy of the Church as the living Body of Christ.

Notes

1   Esther de Waal, *Living with Contradiction: An Introduction to Benedictine Spirituality* (Harrisburg, PA: Morehouse Publishing, 1989), 30–31.

2   Frances Taylor Gench, *Faithful Disagreement: Wrestling with Scripture in the midst of Church Conflict*, (Louisville, KY: Westminster John Knox Press, 2009), ix.

3   Ibid., x.

4   Ibid.

5   David R. Brubaker, *Promise and Peril: Understanding and Managing Change and Conflict in Congregations*, (Herndon, VA: Alban Institute, 2009), 117.

6   David W. Kale with Mel McCullough, *Managing Conflict in the Church* (Kansas City, KN: Beacon Hill Press, 2003), 16.

7   Michael Crichton, *The Lost World* (New York: Ballentine, 1995) Introduction.

8   Kenneth A. Halstead, *From Stuck to unstuck: Overcoming Congregational Impasse* (Herndon, VA: Alban Institute, 1998), v.

9   Hugh H. Halverstadt, *Managing Church Conflict* (Louisville, KY: Westminster John Knox, 1991), ix.

10 David B. Lott, *Conflict Management in Congregations* (Herndon, VA: Alban Institute, 2001), 15.

11 Lott, *Conflict Management*, 114.

12 Halverstadt, *Managing Church Conflict*, ix.

13 Ibid., 11.

14 Ibid., 190.

15 Ibid., 190.

16 Peter L. Steinke, *Healthy Congregations: A Systems Approach* (Herndon, VA Alban Institute, 2006), 103–104.

17 Brubaker, *Promise and Peril*, ix.

18 Steinke, *Healthy Congregations*, 85.

19 Lott, *Conflict Management*, 110.

20 Kale and McCullough, *Managing Conflict*, 60.

21 George W. Bullard, Jr, *Every Congregation Needs a Little Conflict* (St. Louis, MO: Chalice Press, 2008), 137.

Annotated Bibliography

Brubaker, David R., *Promise and Peril: Understanding and Managing Change and Conflict in Congregations* (Herndon, VA: Alban Institute, 2009).
Written from the author's experience as a conflict consultant and based on significant research, this book does not focus on causes of conflict but rather on the correlation between conflict and certain kinds of change.

Bullard, George W., Jr, *Every Congregation Needs a Little Conflict* (St. Louis, MO: Chalice Press, 2008).
Building on the foundational work of Speed Leas, and drawing from decades of experience as a conflict consultant in mostly evangelical congregations, this helpful book makes the case for how conflict in congregational life is healthy and constructive and indeed necessary, while at the same time describing levels of congregational conflict that are unhealthy and destructive. Using seven levels of what the author calls "intensities," this volume helps to diagnose, identify, and address church conflict.

Chestnut, Robert A., *Transforming the Mainline Church: Lessons in Change from the Pittsburgh's Cathedral of Hope* (Louisville, KY: Geneva Press, 2000).
Offering guidance, direction, and hope based on his experience of renewing a dying congregation, the author believes that the mainline still has the resources to lead these kind of transformations and turn around strategies for the current age.

Crichton, Michael, *The Lost World* (New York, Ballentine, 1995).

This science fiction novel is a cautionary tale about the unintended consequences of genetic engineering, in this case bringing dinosaurs back from extinction. In the preface to the novel the author makes some insightful and interesting comments about the nature of change and conflict in the created order.

de Waal, Esther, *Living with Contradiction: An Introduction to Benedictine Spirituality* (Harrisburg, PA: Morehouse Publishing, 1989).

Using the Rule of St. Benedict for a framework, this text sees the tension, conflict, and polarization that exists in our personal lives as an opportunity for reconciliation, transformation, as well as new and abundant life. Finding equilibrium, the central position between opposing forces, is at the heart of faith and part of the paradox of Christian life.

Everist, Norma Cook, *Church Conflict: From Contention to Collaboration* (Nashville: Abingdon Press, 2004).

Divided into two sections this book first explores the nature of congregational conflict and then provides an overview of the various ways of dealing with that conflict. The author rightly cautions that each response is potentially helpful and harmful. The overarching goal is to use collaboration in the midst of conflict and to create an environment where such collaboration is normative.

Gench, Frances Taylor, *Faithful Disagreement: Wrestling with Scripture in the midst of Church Conflict* (Louisville, KY: Westminster John Knox Press, 2009).

The book grew out of the author's experience serving on a denominational task force charged with exploring issues that both united and divided the national Presbyterian Church. The premise of the book is that Christians are adept at arguing about the Bible and less adept at actually reading the Bible, in community, and taking time to listen to the text and to one

another. The book consists of seven Bible studies designed to encourage this practice.

Halstead, Kenneth A., *From Stuck to unstuck: Overcoming Congregational Impasse* (Herndon, VA: Alban Institute, 1998).

Utilizing a therapeutic and church systems approach, this text attempts to help church leaders get themselves emotionally "unstuck" in order to help congregational systems become freer, healthier, more creative and adaptive to change, while maintaining necessary stability. The book provides a means of assessing system problems, highlights various approaches to solutions, and most importantly explores the nature of healthy emotional leadership.

Halverstadt, Hugh H., *Managing Church Conflict* (Louisville, KY: Westminster John Knox, 1991).

Drawing on decades of experience coaching church leaders to manage conflict, the author believes that the key to making church conflicts Christian is by offering an ethical, faith-based process designed to evoke goodness, restrain sinfulness, and deal constructively with difference. His process holds up a vision of shalom as the unattainable yet ultimate goal for which to strive in this practical and multidimensional approach to congregational conflict.

Haugk, Kenneth C., *Antagonists in the Church: How to Identify and Deal with Destructive Conflict* (Minneapolis, MN: Augsburg Publishing, 1988).

Written by the pastor and clinical psychologist who is the founder and director of the Stephen Ministries (the interdenominational lay caring ministry), this book acknowledges that although often few in number, antagonists do exist in a church and can disrupt and even destroy congregational life. This books attempts to help congregational leaders discern the difference between healthy constructive conflict and destructive antagonism. It also seeks to offer ways to prevent and lessen the negative effect of congregational antagonism.

Kale, David W. with McCullough, Mel, *Managing Conflict in the Church* (Kansas City, KN: Beacon Hill Press, 2003).

This is a book designed for congregational leaders that seeks to help pastors identify and understand conflict, and also to provide appropriate conflict management practices which include effective communication, mediation, and negotiation skills.

Lott, David B., *Conflict Management in Congregations* (Herndon, VA: Alban Institute, 2001).

This collection of essays from field researchers of the Alban Institute covers a wide range of topics (divided into three sections): the dynamics of conflict, responding to conflict, and situational conflict. The cumulative years of experience and the collective wisdom of the writers make this a valuable resource that includes not only a broad overview of the topic, but also specific, practical, and helpful guidance.

Sawyer, David R., *Hope in Conflict: Discovering Wisdom in Congregational Turmoil* (Cleveland, OH: Pilgrim Press, 2007).

Using the term conflict "utilization" rather than conflict management, the author suggests that conflict offers the opportunity uncover the hidden strengths and wisdom of the congregation. This text explores ways to bring this hidden wisdom to light and use it to bring hope in conflict and lead the congregation to greater health.

Steinke, Peter L., *Healthy Congregations: A Systems Approach* (Herndon, VA: Alban Institute, 2006).

Utilizing systems theory, the author develops 10 Principles of Health that highlight the interconnectedness of congregational life, and focuses on the role of the congregational leader as the chief steward of congregational health.

16

The Business of the Church

Why didn't they teach me this in seminary?

When pastors are asked about their preparation, or lack of preparation, for church administration, this is perhaps the most common refrain. A close second might be a chorus focused on a general disdain for administration and the acknowledgement that most pastors spend most of their time performing administrative tasks. These tend to be the tasks that they enjoy the least and feel least equipped to handle successfully, and for which they feel most vulnerable and most responsible. A third recurring theme could well be the eventual, but nonetheless startling, revelation that rather than shepherding the flock, a vocation they envisioned for themselves, they are instead running a small business, a career they would not have intentionally chosen. This disturbing combination of discordant refrains, choruses, and themes can prove to be a constant source of frustration, disappointment, and disillusionment on the part of those leading congregations. Trained for preaching, teaching, and congregational care, many clergy, especially those newly ordained, are often surprised by the seemingly endless amount of managerial oversight required even in the smallest of congregations. The good news, however, is that even without innate talents or exhaustive study, the necessary administrative skills can be learned and a balance among what seem like competing ministerial challenges can be achieved.

The aim of this chapter is to offer practical advice and to provide a basic overview of the management of ministry. In it we will explore the great divide between the expectations and realities of congregational leadership, the role of the pastor as administrative leader and manager, and then examine the four main areas that constitute the business of the Church: people (human resources); property (land, buildings, and more permanent resources); information technology (communication resources); and money (financial resources). The hope is for a clear, simple, and yet substantive discussion that helps to

An Introduction to Ministry: A Primer for Renewed Life and Leadership in Mainline Protestant Congregations, First Edition. Ian S. Markham and Oran E. Warder.
© 2016 John Wiley & Sons, Ltd. Published 2016 by John Wiley & Sons, Ltd.

solidify the connection between good management principles and good pastoral leadership skills that support and encourage the mission of the Church.

Reluctant Stewards

Why is it that pastors are generally so reticent about assuming the role of administrative leader? And why do lay leaders generally have such low expectations for the ability of clergy to manage the business of the Church? While it is true that seminaries are not noted for their preparation of students in this particular aspect of congregational leadership, this does not completely explain the problem or address the core issues. One major disconnect rests on the false dichotomy that is so deeply rooted in the psyche of congregations that it is often subconscious, yet at the same time can be seen explicitly in the canons, bylaws, and tenets that shape the polity of our various denominations. This is the basic notion that clergy are supposed to deal with spiritual matters and lay leaders are supposed to take care of temporal matters. This delineation between the sacred and the profane is deeply held in spite of the fact that such a clear distinction does not actually exist. Yet, the idea persists.

This seems to be particularly true when it comes to dealing with money. In their book, *Ministry and Money: A Practical Guide For Pastors*, Janet and Philip Jamieson offer the "filthy lucre" rationale for the lingering belief that money is too seemly, too secular, and too profane to be the concern of pastors. Citing the King James Version (KJV) of 1 Timothy 3:8, "Likewise must the deacons be grave, not double-tongued, not given to too much wine, not greedy of filthy lucre," they point to the biblical roots of the issue. Modern translations speak of "not pursuing dishonest gain" (New International Version, NIV) or being "not greedy for money" (New Revised Standard Version, NRSV) and rightly differentiate that the issue is the proper use of money and not the money itself. Thus it is not the money that is condemned, but rather greed and dishonesty in ministry. They conclude, however, that the damage has been done and for many the problem remains that money is seen as unclean, not worthy of seminary study, and we are left with a "tragic inconsistency."[1] This is compounded by the fact that the culture at large has not moved far beyond the KJV understanding of money. Even as churches begin to focus more on money, clergy have little training or experience to aid in this work (unless it comes from a previous vocation, but even then it often lacks any theological basis or understanding). Rather sadly, far too many clergy and far too many people in our pews "depend more upon the adages of Benjamin Franklin for their thinking about money than they do the scriptures."[2]

Aside from this, there are other, more practical reasons that clergy often find themselves unprepared to be administrative leaders. For instance, pastoral ministry continues to be a profession for generalists. Clergy must be able to exercise a working knowledge and possess a basic understanding of many aspects of ministry. In defense of mainline seminaries, there is much to teach, much formation required, and not nearly enough time. For most students, attending seminary represents their first disciplined involvement with Scripture, the history of the church, and engagement with the foundational theology and doctrines of the faith. Given this reality, there is often simply too little space and too little time left in the curriculum dedicated to the issues of church administration.[3]

In addition, reflective of the old false dichotomy, clergy may have picked up the message in seminary, either implicitly or explicitly, that parish administration is not their job. Some arrive in congregations with the expectation the laity run the business of the congregation. The laity, may, in turn, have a different understanding. In this scenario resentments can build quickly. The reality is that even if the details of administration are not the job of the clergy, they are the responsibility of the clergy, and as the "executive director" of this "not-for-profit organization," clergy play a major role. So rather than see this task as an unwelcome burden, it might be better viewed as an opportunity for ministry. Again, the good news is that these administrative skills can be acquired, and the even better news is that pastors do not have to be experts in order to lead effectively.[4]

To be clear, the goal is not to have clergy take over the entire administrative ministry of the parish and displace lay involvement. Instead, the objective is for pastors to claim their appropriate and essential role as managers of ministry who exercise particular authority to coordinate the business of mission.

Why is it Important?

At the macro-level, administration is important because of the shear scope and magnitude of the Church. Even in these lean times, it is important to remember that the Church owns literally millions of acres of real estate, buildings too numerous to count, employs millions of people and holds billions of dollars in assets. The Church is the original multinational corporation and has at least one local branch operation in practically every corner of the earth. It would make sense that a corporation with this kind of reach would make sure to send skilled managers, with ample training and support, into the mission field.[5]

At the micro-level, in spite of the fact that local congregations vary in size, ethnicity, and culture, pastors still have a stewardship responsibility for the resources of a church. It is also true that in spite of these differences, basic administrative principles apply to virtually any congregation and good financial management practices are useful no matter the amount. Regardless of size and make up, almost every congregation will have a program to manage, a church to maintain, and most have some personnel. In brief, the better a congregation can manage its assets, the better God's mission is served. There is a direct line between good and effective management and God's mission.[6]

Business vs. the Church

Skeptics of Management and Business Talk

There are some significant theological movements in the Church that are skeptical about management and business talk. Led by John Milbank and the "Radical Orthodoxy" movement, they insist that the language of the social sciences, which underpins the language of management and business, derives from an anti-Christian foundation. For Milbank, the language of modernity is built on an "ontology of violence" (i.e. it assumes that people are units to be manipulated through control), while the Church witnesses to an alternative foundation which is built on an "ontology of peace." Others have argued that leadership talk is deeply misguided. The concept of a leader is a modern idea, which is shaped by individualist assumptions and isolated heroism. Justin Lewis-Anthony has argued that the concept of leadership is both a myth and "probably a heresy."[7] Instead Christians should use the language of discipleship.

Many bristle at the idea of comparing the Church with a corporation or small business. The government clearly understands the Church as a business, and to that end requires churches to incorporate as not-for-profit organizations. Some within the Church do not share this same understanding. We view the comparison as descriptive and helpful and not pejorative or profane and take the position that although churches and businesses are different in many ways; they also share much in common.[8] We also embrace the idea that good management is good management regardless of the enterprise. Some shortsightedly claim the exceptionalism of the Church allows for less than stellar administrative practices. At the very least we hold that churches must reconcile their bank statements, maintain internal controls, record contributions, utilize standard management principles, and have an annual independent audit.[9] Also, there are some elements of business that work well in the Church, as with any other human organization. Elements such as making sure that roles and relationships are clearly defined and documented, making sure that there are clear management rules and guidelines, making sure that there is a specific mission and that goals are strategically organized, thoughtfully implemented, reviewed, and evaluated.[10] There are also some unique influences in church management that differentiate it and separate it from the business world. First, the proclamation of the Gospel and the formation of Christian community are unchanging in terms of the mission and purpose of the Church. In addition, congregations are organized for service in the world with unique values that are identified with the Church. Second, unlike businesses, churches are perpetual institutions. That is, they may not last forever, but must act as if they will. Lastly, churches are local membership organizations with pastors and lay leaders being held directly accountable to members. In contrast, corporate shareholders have little experience or knowledge of the inner workings of a particular business. This is all the more reason for churches to be as transparent as possible and for church leaders to be as congruent in word and actions as humanly possible. This is true in terms of one's personal and professional life.[11]

Since intentional strategic thinking and planning are critical to the success of any human organization, before leaving this discussion we will review the basic elements of planning. The whole management process, in any enterprise, begins with planning. A *mission statement* provides the general direction and serves as a guide for specifics. Particular *goals* articulate desired outcomes that support and expand the mission, while *action plans* delineate particular objectives. A basic action plan follows a similar form:

1. Identification of the mission statement item for which the action plan is being written (the question is always, how does this action support the mission?).

2. Citing the desired goal or outcome and estimating the financial impact.
3. Assigning responsibility for implementation.
4. Dividing a large task into smaller ones (each with specific actions and measurable objectives).
5. Setting a completion date and periodically following up to evaluate and report on progress.[12]

Management Lessons from the Bible

Churches need not always look to the business world for effective management techniques and principles. Business can also learn from the tradition of the Church. Scripture is filled with resources that are not only consistent with the values and purposes of the Church, but also foster common sense and easily adaptable models for administration.

For instance, from the Hebrew Bible, we highlight Exodus 18:5–27. This story takes place after the Israelites are liberated from slavery in Egypt and are now wandering in the wilderness of Sinai. Moses, the divinely chosen, yet much beleaguered leader of the Hebrew people, receives a visit from his father-in-law, Jethro, the Priest of Midian. Jethro witnesses his son-in-law toil from sun up to sun down dealing with the myriad issues of leading and offers Moses some advice. Although 3000 years old, these ideas are entirely applicable to pastoral leaders today:

1. You cannot do everything all by yourself, so let others help you.
2. Choose capable leaders and give them the responsibility and authority to lead.
3. Teach, train, and support leaders using standard policies and procedures so that actions and decisions are applied consistently.
4. Structure the organization so that each leader is responsible for a smaller segment of the whole and then establish a chain of authority.
5. Push responsibility and decision making to the lowest possible and practical organizational level where there is competence to deal with the matter.
6. Deal personally with only the most difficult cases (not dealt with in #5) or those critical cases that directly impact the survival of the organization.

Lastly, it is important to ask for help when it is needed, and then be open to accepting good advice when it is offered.[13] It is important to note in this example that Moses never relinquishes his responsibility or his leadership of the Hebrew people, yet not even he could manage all the details on his own.

In the Gospels of the New Testament, Jesus consistently and persistently calls his followers to be good stewards and good managers. Over and over again he demonstrates and models an explicit and unapologetic theology of administration and management. One constantly recurring theme is that servants are encouraged to act aggressively in terms of using the gifts with which they are entrusted and are chided when they acted timidly or passively. This is true for stewards who were given talents to invest, for the overseers of large agricultural businesses, and even for the shepherd who makes the risky decision to leave his large flock in search of a single lost sheep. In one story Jesus seems irritated with the disciples for not thinking ahead and bringing enough food for the multitudes to eat. He takes matters into his own hands and transforms the meager available resources into a feast for all.[14] It is important to note in this example that faithful management is not without risk, requires action, and is open to the transformation of ordinary resources for extraordinary and divine purposes.

The Role of the Pastor

As previously mentioned, we readily acknowledge that the work of the Church requires the participation of all of its members, we readily acknowledge that most of the day-to-day details rest in the hands of the laity, and yet we also emphasize the fact that even though many tasks are rightly and appropriately delegated to lay persons, the ultimate responsibility for congregational administration rests with the clergy. To that end, we focus this section on the unique role of the pastor.

While many clergy feel ill-prepared for these administrative and financial responsibilities, this need not be the case always. In terms of professional development and continuing education it might be helpful to think how best to allocate time and resources. For instance, every clergy person is great at something. It would make sense that most personal development time be spent in this area of expertise. It is also true that, generally speaking, every clergy person is competent in two or three other aspects of parish ministry. It would then make sense to invest in ongoing development in these areas as well. Finally, it is certainly true that there are areas of ministry where clergy have little or no interest or expertise, and yet must still exhibit competence in responsibility and oversight. In this case it makes sense to draw on every knowledgeable, skilled, and experienced person and resource available inside and outside a church to make certain that the congregation succeeds in this area as well.[15]

Another helpful way to think about the role of the pastor in administration is to use the image of pastor as the manager of church systems. The task of the systems manager is first of all to see that the congregation is a single system that is composed of many smaller, yet interconnected systems, each interacting to shape the whole. The basic idea is that the pastor is not necessarily involved in the minute details of each system, but rather works to help the systems function effectively and efficiently. The pastor can work to lubricate the system, grease the gears, in order to keep things running smoothly, while at the same time working to maximize the possibilities of each part, making the most of limited resources, and keep the vision and direction clearly stated, in front of the people, while encouraging and enlisting continued support.[16] The very best systems managers learn as they manage and perhaps gain more from mistakes and failures than from successes and victories.

Perhaps to most, effective managing pastors are those driven by a clear purpose, those who have a broad and deep knowledge of the congregational systems, and those who are willing to bring about change patiently without creating destruction. They also possess a genuine care and concern for the people they are called to serve, are willing and able to let the right person lead at the right time, and are also humble enough, when the situation requires it, to be a faithful follower.[17]

Finally, another important characteristic of an effectual pastoral administrator is the ability to discern the difference between management and leadership. Management and leadership are closely related and yet are not synonymous. They sometimes coexist within the same person, but not always. Differentiating between the two is important, particularly when deciding whether a particular situation calls for leadership or management, or some combination of both. Leadership, in this sense, refers to holding up a vision of the future and then marshaling the resources and people to make that vision a reality. Leadership has to do with mobilizing and motivating followers. Management, on the other hand, is the implementation of the vision and works to transform and make it real. Managers get the job done, attend to the details, and deal with the day-to-day issues that either make or break an organization. Managers follow through on the details that others might find boring or distracting. Both leadership and management are essential, and yet both, in the extreme can be disastrous. A strong leader can ignore or disrupt orderly planning and undermine proper management, while a strong manager can discourage necessary risk taking and lack enthusiasm for leadership.[18] Even though the contrast seems sharp and irreconcilable, both are important to the vitality and longevity of an organization. Capable pastors are not only able to discern the difference between the two in specific situations, but are also flexible enough to act accordingly.

The Business of the Church

Four main areas constitute the business of the Church. Each area represents a major subset of administrative responsibility, each requires a different knowledge base, each requires a unique set of skills, and each is present in every church regardless of shape, size, or configuration. Every congregation has to find a way to manage people, property, communication, and money. While each area could easily fill separate chapters if not an entire book, we will deal with each of them as concisely, and yet as comprehensively, as possible in the sections below.

People: Human Resources

First, it must be said at the outset that people are the Church's greatest resource. Nothing else matters in the life of the Church without the involvement of committed and dedicated people. Leadership and management are required for individual people to be transformed into a vibrant community of faith. To fulfill the mission of the Church, the people of the congregation need to be organized and staffed to move in a clear and positive direction with clear and positive results.[19] Churches, however, face a somewhat unique and significant managerial challenge in that they are supported by a mix of paid staff and dedicated volunteers.[20]

Given that the Church is first and foremost about people, one might expect that churches would have a special appreciation and deeper understanding of the importance of the management and care of people. Unfortunately, the track record with regard to the treatment of those in the Church's employ is sometimes less than stellar, at times unjust, and represents an area of our common life where church leaders might learn something from the business community in terms of personnel policies and practices. Most human resource professionals agree that good personnel management involves three things: (i) the ability to bring people together to work efficiently and effectively for a common purpose; (ii) the ability to help and encourage people to maximize their strengths and minimize their weaknesses; and (iii) the ability to foster the ongoing growth and development of the skills needed to succeed. Most businesses are not only aware of employment laws, but also obey them. The best among them have comprehensive personnel policies and follow them faithfully. "The failure of the church to employ some of the best practices used in the business community's personnel management has cost the church dearly."[21] Deeply flawed personnel management is at the heart of the sexual misconduct controversies that have plagued the Roman Catholic Church. In addition to causing irreparable harm, many local dioceses have filed for bankruptcy. Well-managed personnel systems do not allow misconduct to jeopardize the integrity and fiscal solvency of the entire institution.[22]

The key points in church personnel management include being clear about who is managing whom, making sure that ministry descriptions are clear and align with the stated goals and objectives of the congregation, and also making sure that good personnel policies are in place. No system is perfect, and each person brings a unique set of challenges and opportunities, yet most human behavior is remarkably and consistently similar, and standard policies are invaluable.[23]

Extending the right call, making the best hire, can transform a church staff. Getting it wrong can be a nightmare for everyone involved. Do take the time and energy to thoroughly and carefully invite new members to the pastoral team. A good general guide is called the "The three Cs of Hiring": *character* (making sure that candidates genuinely embody values that are consistent with work in a church); *competency* (making sure that candidates have the skill, experience, and abilities to perform the tasks required of them); and *chemistry* (making sure that candidates can get along with, relate to, and feel comfortable with the rest of the pastoral team).[24]

One challenge in the hiring process is the ability to talk with people who really know and are willing to speak honestly about potential candidates. Most candidates will list only those references that will speak positively about them. The goal is to break out beyond the reference list and find someone who will offer a more complete picture of a candidate, and even then do not trust your own opinion exclusively. Make certain to include other trusted colleagues in the process and in the decision.[25]

When it is necessary to fire an employee, unless they have committed a crime, it is essential that a well-documented trail of poor performance be in place. It is incumbent upon the employer to prove that bad behavior and poor performance has been addressed over time with ample opportunity for change. This would include documentation of specific conversations aimed at remedying deficiencies before an actual dismissal.[26] Along these same lines, it is critical to be aware that personnel files are no longer considered to be confidential. The only items that should be included in an employee's file are those that either the employee has provided, or has seen, or has been made aware of, and given a copy.[27] It is also equally important to remember that in spite of the fact that the Church is exempt from many secular personnel laws this does not mean we are exempt from God's laws and the values that undergird our community life. The golden rule applies even when dealing with the most difficult of situations and the most obstreperous people.

In terms of compensation, churches offer an unusual place of employment. While there are immense benefits in performing a job that is, at least ideally, aligned with the will of God, this is no excuse for underpaying those who give themselves to this work. Most denominations and local judicatories provide annual compensation guidelines that are based on actual salaries and often adjusted in terms of geographical regions and varying costs of living. These resources are helpful in calling and retaining good staff members. Given all the time and energy it takes to recruit, orient, and integrate new staff members, it makes sense to compensate staff members in a manner that encourages them to forge a deep commitment, grow in their vocation, and stay in place. The retention of competent staff is one of the main reasons that congregations are stable and grow.[28]

Lastly, in this section, we offer a word about the management of volunteers. The Church's heavy reliance upon volunteers presents an even greater challenge than the overseeing of paid staff. Although practices and policies vary among mainline denominations, it is generally accepted that volunteers cannot be fired (at least not easily) and yet they are absolutely essential in successfully fulfilling the work of the Church. One thing, however, is clear whatever the denomination: when a problem occurs in the congregational system having to do with personnel, paid or unpaid, it is ultimately the responsibility of the pastor. One way to avoid these difficulties, especially with volunteers, is to follow a few basic principles: (i) make sure everyone has a clearly defined ministry description with clearly defined expectations; (ii) make sure that everyone knows where to go with questions or concerns; (iii) make sure that everyone is adequately trained and oriented to their work; (iv) make sure that there is a defined time period in the agreement of engagement, and not an indefinite open-ended arrangement (this allows for re-evaluation); and (v) try to avoid having everyone report directly to the pastor.[29]

People are the Church's primary asset and are key to carrying out the Church's mission. Able pastors find a way to delegate authority without abdicating responsibility. Additionally, to borrow from Peter Drucker on this topic, he says that "management is about human beings. Its task is to make people capable of joint performance to make their strengths effective and their weaknesses irrelevant."[30] This seems not only like sound professional advice, but also like Gospel truth.

Property: Land, buildings, and more permanent resources

It is one thing for the Church to own land, buildings, and other more permanent assets (like clergy housing and cemeteries), and it is quite another for churches to take care of them. When operating budgets are squeezed, among the first places tapped to save money is the line item for facilities maintenance. When this happens consistently, years of deferred maintenance only compounds both the problem and the expense. Then, instead of ongoing maintenance, church leaders are left to deal with one inevitable facilities crisis after another.

One lesson that congregations consistently fail to learn, and do so at their own peril, is that the skills and experience needed to manage and maintain property adequately are usually not found within the church community. While it is more expensive to find qualified "arms-length" assistance, in the long term it will most likely save a church money. Yet congregations choose again and again to either ignore the problem, proceed without proper guidance, put themselves at the mercy of a well-intentioned person who agrees to work for free, or worse yet, get overcharged by someone who has a personal connection to the pastor or congregational leadership. Eventually, after years of constant headaches and unsatisfactory results, church leaders will often conclude that it is better to sell the property, and dispose of the asset simply to be freed from the burden of responsibility.[31] This is usually done in spite of the fact that these assets were created and given to the community as an ongoing resource for ministry.

The long-term care and maintenance of property must be realistically and strategically planned for, including the need for renovation, and the eventual need to address major structural and mechanical systems. Financial support must also be part of the plan. To aid in this endeavor, comprehensive maintenance schedules must be established and updated, with the responsibility for maintenance clear, as well as adequate insurance to protect a church's investment along with a realistic assessment of risk.[32]

A well-selected and well-led facilities committee can accomplish this strategic planning and oversee the maintenance process. The essential tasks of the committee are to: (i) put together a comprehensive list of maintenance issues along with anticipated replacement expenditures; (ii) do the detailed and somewhat tedious work of evaluating insurance policies and reviewing utility options; (iii) collect, organize, and maintain all service contracts, owner's manuals, warranty verifications, as well as all the maintenance records in one location; and (iv) collect and archive all architectural drawings, blueprints, and schematics.[33] With intentional care, insightful leadership, and an engaged congregation, these assets of land, buildings, and other properties can be fully utilized in the present ministry of the Church and also preserved for the generations to come.

Technology Dilemma

We live in an age where expectations for performance and interactive engagement with performance are massive. At home, people have surround sound, high definition, and can tweet, post, and engage in real time with all experiences. These expectations are now part of the Church.

The technology dilemma is acute. On the one hand, our congregations expect a good technologically aware experience, which is expensive to provide. On the other hand, technological progress is so rapid almost anything current will be obsolete in 5 years' time. Faced with this dilemma, many congregations opt to avoid all technology (on the grounds the experience should be counter-cultural) or live with more limited technological experiences. The problem with both of these responses is that for some people, this makes the Church look very "out of touch."

Information technology: Communication resources

This is a relatively new category when considering the scope of the business of the Church, yet in some ways it is the oldest. The primary role of the Church is to communicate the Good News and it has always been so. Over the generations the form and shape of proclamation has changed even as the core content has remained constant. Just as Martin Luther, in the sixteenth century, made it his aim to get Scripture into the hands of God's people in a form they could readily access and understand, so it is in our own day as we utilize the wealth of new information technology for the same purpose. The use of email, web sites, blogs, Twitter, and other forms of social media have opened ways to spread the Gospel in ways never before imagined. For congregations, the challenge is to acquire and maintain the necessary equipment, to keep web sites and other media up to date, to make sure that data are backed up, and to engage reliable technical support. One of the biggest challenges, however, is simply staying on top of the ever-changing technology. There is a problem with buying technology too early (with the bugs not worked out) or buying too late (wasting time and money on obsolete equipment and programs). Church leaders must find the most knowledgeable, the most skilled, and the most experienced people available to lead these efforts and pay close attention to this important area of the Church's common life. Many congregations make the grave error of spending a great deal of money on a new web site and then spend little time and energy to keep it up to date. The two most crucial factors in determining the power and effectiveness of a web site are whether or not information is timely and whether or not information is easy to locate. Of course, all of this takes money. Like deferring maintenance, congregations ignore this portion of a church's business at their own detriment. In the twenty-first century Church, paying attention to information technology is "as important as keeping on the lights."[34]

Money: Finance resources

In the next chapter, we will look at stewardship in detail. Suffice to say here: the essence of Church business is that it is God's business, and money is the common denominator for all of us. Money is not good or bad in and of itself, yet what the Church does with people's money is important. The goal and purpose is to support God's mission in the Church and in the world. That is why clearly communicated, transparent reports of a church's financial health are so important as a statement of how the congregation is living out its mission. Equally important is the accounting for, and recording of, the money that is received by a church. "Almost nothing can undermine the mission the church faster than questions about the credibility of its financial system."[35] Any church financial management system should be mission oriented, full of integrity, informative, systematized, and tailored to the specific needs of the congregation.[36] The overall purpose is to "provide a system to accurately capture and record financial transactions to meaningfully measure progress toward financial goals and to clearly report the results in a way that is transparent, honest, and helpful in making decisions."[37]

Again, as stated before, it is the role of the pastor, not to be involved in the day-to-day details, but to have a working knowledge of the overall financial management system. The basic hope is threefold: the pastor must be able to answer questions with some knowledge and authority; the pastor must be able to ask the right financial questions, of the right people, at the right time; and lastly, the pastor must be able to discern when there is trouble and when additional assistance is required.

In the most basic review of church accounting, there are essentially five types of accounts: (i) *assets* – all the things that a church currently owns; (ii) *liabilities* – all that a church owes in terms of present obligations; (iii) *net assets* – the difference between assets and liabilities (at the end of the year a church's financial position is reflected in what a church owns (assets) minus what the Church owes (liabilities) with the difference in the two being the net assets of a church; this is commonly called the "accounting equation"); (iv) *revenues* – for a church this is mostly income from pledges and offerings; and (v) *expenses* – outflows or the using of assets in support of mission. It is useful to be reminded at this point that, unlike a business, the measure of success for the Church is not the accumulation of wealth but the accomplishment of mission.[38]

In addition to these five types of accounting, accountants also produce three basic financial reports that are essential to the financial overseeing of the congregation. The first is the *income statement*. This document displays the revenue and the expense for a congregation during a specific period of time (month, quarter, year). After totaling all the revenue and expenses, and then subtracting the expense from the revenue, the "bottom line" is produced as either a budget surplus or deficit. The second report is the *balance sheet*. This document shows the assets and liabilities of the congregation at a specific point in time. The liabilities are subtracted from the assets resulting in the net financial worth of the congregation (in terms of tangible assets that can be expressed in dollars on a financial statement). Lastly, the third document is called the *cash flow report*. This report offers a snapshot of the congregation's current cash position (the amount of cash on hand). Given that a church's expenses are usually consistent and regular, and a church's income is rather inconsistent and irregular, this report is of particular importance. The goal is, of course, to manage and match the timing of the inflow and outflow of cash. All three of these reports are tools that can help monitor the financial health of the congregation and monitor how effectively resources are being used to support a church's mission.[39] It is important to keep all of this in perspective and to remember that a "church cannot hurt from too much money but can die from a lack of mission."[40]

Conclusion

Whether taught in seminary, modeled by a mentor, or learned on the job, every pastor leading a congregation requires a basic proficiency in managing the ministry and running the business of the Church. While in truth, it takes all of God's people to fulfill the mission of the Church, it also takes a pastoral leader. Again, to restate the theme of this chapter, able pastors find a way to share leadership and delegate authority without abdicating responsibility.

Notes

1   Janet T. Jamieson and Philip D. Jamieson, *Ministry and Money: A Practical Guide for Pastors* (Louisville, KY: Westminster John Knox, 2009), 5.

2   Ibid.

3   Ibid.

4   Gerald W. Keucher, *Remember the Future: Financial Leadership and Asset Management for Congregations*, (New York: Church Publishing, 2006), 29.

5   John W. Wimberly, Jr, *The Business of the Church: The Uncomfortable Truth that*

Faithful Ministry Requires Effective Management (Herndon, VA: Alban Institute, 2010), 3.

6   Otto F. Crumroy, Jr., Stan Kukawka, and Frank M. Whitman, *Church Administration and Finance Manual: Resources for Leading the Local Church* (Harrisburg, PA: Morehouse, 1998), 4.

7   *You Are the Messiah and I Should Know: Why Leadership is a Myth (and probably a Heresy)*, (London: Bloomsbury Academic, 2013).

8   Wimberly, *Business of the Church*, 3.

9   Keucher, *Remember the Future*, 19.

10 Crumroy, Kukawka, and Whitman, *Church Administration*, 11.

11 Keucher, *Remember the Future*, 19.

12 Crumroy, Kukawka, and Whitman, *Church Administration*, 11.

13 Ibid., 10.

14 Ibid., 2.

15 Bruce L. Peterson, Edward A. Thomas, and Bob Whitesel, *Foundations of Church Administration: Professional Tools for Church Leadership* (Kansas City, KN: Beacon Hill, 2010), 8.

16 Wimberly, *Business of the Church*, 143.

17 Peterson, Thomas, and Whitesel, *Foundations of Church Administration*, 83.

18 Wimberly, *Business of the Church*, 21.

19 Crumroy, Kukawka, and Whitman, *Church Administration*, 2–3.

20 Ibid., 130.

21 Wimberly, *Business of the Church*, 39.

22 Ibid., 39.

23 Ibid., 42.

24 Peterson, Thomas, and Whitesel, *Foundations of Church Administration*, 122.

25 Wimberly, *Business of the Church*, 60.

26 Ibid., 60.

27 Crumroy, Kukawka, and Whitman, *Church Administration*, 131.

28 Wimberly, *Business of the Church*, 66.

29 Ibid., 32.

30 Ibid. 3.

31 Keucher, *Remember the Future*, 28.

32 Crumroy, Kukawka, and Whitman, *Church Administration*, 3.

33 Wimberly, *Business of the Church*, 98.

34 Ibid., 191.

35 Crumroy, Kukawka, and Whitman, *Church Administration*, 2.

36 Ibid., 2.

37 Jamieson, *Ministry and Money*, 53.

38 Ibid., 55–56.

39 Wimberly, *Business of the Church*, 105.

40 Crumroy, Kukawka, and Whitman, *Church Administration*, 59.

Annotated Bibliography

Bacher, Robert N. and Cooper-White, Michael L., *Church Administration: Programs, Process, Purpose* (Minneapolis, MN: Fortress, 2009).
Written by two Lutheran pastors, this overview begins with a historical and biblical perspective on church administration and includes such topics as managing others, working with governing boards, and the importance of communication.

Berkley, James D., *Leadership Handbook of Management and Administration* (Grand Rapids, MI: Baker Books, 1997).
This text includes over 200 articles by experienced pastors in the field of church management covering a wide range of topics (organizational, financial, and legal).

Chaffee, Paul, *Accountable Leadership: Resources for Worshipping Communities* (San Francisco, CA: Churchcare Publishing, 1993).
Although now two decades old, this useful text explores issues of administration through the perspective of the accountability and character of church leaders, both lay and ordained.

Crumroy, Jr, Otto F., Kukawka, Stan, and Whitman, Frank M., *Church Administration and Finance Manual: Resources for Leading the Local Church* (Harrisburg, PA: Morehouse, 1998).

This comprehensive and authoritative guide to church administration for mainline pastors and congregations is an exceptional resource. Written and edited by a team that taught together at the Claremont School of Theology, this work also includes an appendix filled with useful resources.

Engstrom, Ted W., *Your Gift of Administration: How to Discover and Use It* (Nashville, TN: Thomas Nelson Publishers, 1983).

Though dated, this book approaches the topic of administration through the lens of gifts discernment. This carefully organized discussion looks to Scripture for its authority and examines the character traits of a leader gifted in administration.

Hotchkiss, Dan, *Governance and Ministry: Rethinking Board Leadership* (Herndon, VA: Alban Institute, 2009).

Sorting through the myriad ways of organizing, governing, and managing Church life, the author, a senior consultant with the Alban Institute, offers practical, flexible, and sound leadership advice.

Jamieson, Janet T. and Jamieson, Philip D., *Ministry and Money: A Practical Guide for Pastors* (Louisville, KY: Westminster John Knox, 2009).

In addition to using scripture, history, and theology to explore the complex relationship between faith and money, this book is also a primer for the financial management of congregations.

Jarema, William J., *A Survival Guide for Church Ministers* (New York: Paulist Press, 2011).

This work takes a step back and examines leadership in the Church overall with specific chapters that focus on administration.

Keucher, Gerald W., *Remember the Future: Financial Leadership and Asset Management for Congregations* (New York: Church Publishing, 2006).

This very practical, well written, and carefully organized book contains an honest and hopeful view of the economic issues facing many churches of the mainline. Rather than simply managing decline, the author offers useful advice for imagining and securing a better future.

Peterson, Bruce L., Thomas, Edward A., and Whitesel, Bob, *Foundations of Church Administration: Professional Tools for Church Leadership* (Kansas City, KN: Beacon Hill, 2010).

Offering a helpful approach to styles of leadership, strategic planning, budgeting, and building and maintaining a staff, this book is a helpful administrative manual.

Shawchuck, Norman and Heuser, Roger, *Managing the Congregation: Building Effective Systems to Serve People* (Nashville, TN: Abingdon, 1996).

Third in a three-volume set on church leadership, this book focuses on the relationships, structures, and processes that characterize congregational life.

Tyson, John H., *Administration in the Small Membership Church* (Nashville, TN: Abingdon, 1996).

A small yet extremely helpful administrative manual, this work, focusing on small membership congregations, condenses administration and leadership into concise and efficient sections.

Wills, James C., *Handling the People's Trust: A Financial Guide for Churches* (Dubuque, IA: Kendall/Hunt, 1996).

This Certified Public Accountant (CPA) and church treasurer blends his experience in this helpful and entirely practical resource for pastors and congregations. Easily half of the book consists of a thorough appendix of useful resources.

Wimberly, Jr, John W., *The Business of the Church: The Uncomfortable Truth that Faithful Ministry Requires Effective Management* (Herndon, VA: Alban Institute, 2010).

Written by a highly skilled, experienced, and learned pastor, this text analyzes church systems, reminds readers that God is in the midst of administrative details, and offers a plethora of practical and effective strategies for managing the business side of church affairs.

17

Stewardship

Reclaiming Stewardship

A new pastor was called to a large suburban congregation. On an October Sunday morning, early in his tenure, he stood in the pulpit and opened his sermon with this preamble: "I have been told that this is the Sunday for the annual stewardship sermon. I don't like preaching about this, and I know that you don't like hearing about it. But the leaders of the congregation felt that it had to be done; so if you will be patient with me, I will finish as soon as I can."[1]

This single anecdote speaks volumes about the current state of stewardship in the mainline. The issues are essentially fourfold. First, the Church often sends mixed and confusing messages about the nature of stewardship. Second, there is a general lack of biblical and theological grounding to conversations that connect faith and money. Third, when these connections are made, the focus is usually on a church's need to receive funding rather than the giver's need to give. And fourth, more often than not, the pastor is uncomfortable, reticent, or even openly opposed to taking a leadership role. The general reluctance of congregations to talk openly and plainly about money, coupled with the ever increasing competition for charitable dollars, the ever shrinking percentage of those dollars going to support religious institutions, as well as declining membership and rising expenses, make for a seemingly irreversible crisis. This chapter seeks to reclaim stewardship as a biblical and theological concept that is directly connected to discipleship and is therefore central to the life of the congregation, central to the role of the pastoral leader, and central to our hope for the future of the mainline.

Key to this understanding is the idea that congregations, as a whole, model faithful stewardship. Proportional giving, on the part of the community is one way to exercise and model such faithfulness. Congregational giving beyond the walls of the parish in order to address

An Introduction to Ministry: A Primer for Renewed Life and Leadership in Mainline Protestant Congregations, First Edition. Ian S. Markham and Oran E. Warder.
© 2016 John Wiley & Sons, Ltd. Published 2016 by John Wiley & Sons, Ltd.

human need and support the larger mission of the Church can have a positive and lasting effect on the giving of individual members.

A History of Stewardship

Before delving in, and as a way of setting this discussion into a historical context, it is helpful to look at how the Church has funded its mission over the centuries and how we have arrived at our current understandings of stewardship and practices of giving. This broad overview acknowledges the basic truth that the Church does need resources to carry out its work and throughout the ages has found various ways to secure those resources. For most of its long history, beginning with the conversion of Constantine in 313 CE, the Church was supported by taxes, land rents, and benefices (income received in exchange for services rendered or as a retainer for future services). This practice continued throughout the Middle Ages. It is important to note that so-called "free-will offerings," most often equated with alms for the poor, were just that. They were marginal in scope, were received for the specific purpose of offering relief to the poor and needy, and were not used as contributions to support the basic cost of running the institution. It was not until the French Revolution and the subsequent Napoleonic Era that things began to change. Throughout much of Europe Church lands and properties began to be confiscated and, rather than being paid by the Church, clergy began to draw stipends directly from the government.[2]

The American colonies, which were being established during this same time period, began by using the European system. However, increasing discontent with the idea of state-sponsored religion eventually led to the formal disestablishment of any Church. By 1791, with the adoption of the First Amendment to the United States Constitution, which explicitly prohibited the making of any law that either established or impeded the free exercise of religion, most congregations had already separated themselves from state support. This reality forced the creation of a new form of financial support for local congregations, a system known as *pew rentals*. Under this system, congregants who possessed the available means would choose the best pews to "rent" for their own use and in some circumstances would also secure additional, and less desirable, pews for use by those who did not possess adequate means. To supplement these funds churches would also hold special collections, host fairs and offer other forms of subscription. This method of Church financing became the normative practice in America through the time of the Civil War, but came under increasing scrutiny by opponents who saw it as an elitist system that discriminated against the poor. Eventually a "free church" movement took root and gradually pew rents were abandoned altogether for a system of annual pledges to support the mission of the Church. Thus, the current systems of congregational support were largely an invention of the twentieth century.[3] Given this history, it is likely that the funding of ministry will continue to evolve to meet the needs of a changing Church.

Negative Attitudes

The concept of stewardship is distinct and separate from the task of supporting the institutional life of the Church, yet the two are inextricably linked. The relationship between stewardship and fundraising is perplexing and a constant source of bewilderment in mainline congregations. Most churchgoers understand stewardship as simply a euphemism for the annual pledge drive. In most congregations the term has become synonymous with secular fundraising, only covered by a thin ecclesiastical veneer. New Testament scholar Douglas John Hall agrees with this assessment and adds, "stewardship has a very distasteful connotation for the majority of church folk, including clergy. It brings to mind the horror of home visitations, building projects, financial campaigns, and the seemingly incessant harping of churches for more money."[4] So in addition to confused and inconsistent messages, the Church is plagued by negative attitudes about giving. Unfortunately, the only consistent message that seems to be communicated is that the Church needs funds in order to operate and it is up to congregants to provide those necessary funds. While this statement may well be true, it is not an accurate reflection of biblical stewardship.

Terminology

Perhaps the place to begin is with the definition of terms. The word *steward* comes from two Old English words, "*sty-warden*." Just as it seems, the word steward refers to one with the authority to watch over and care for pigs. The sty-warden does not own the pigs, but oversees their welfare for the benefit of the owner and for the benefit of others who depend on the owner for their well-being.[5] A steward, therefore, is someone who watches over something, and that something belongs to someone else. There is no transfer of ownership.

This points directly to a fundamental biblical truth, and the core of any theology of stewardship, that all of creation, 100% of it, belongs to God. There is no transfer of ownership. Embracing this understanding acknowledges that we do not hold title to any of the good things of this world but rather are stewards and are responsible for their proper use. We are caretakers of the creation and even then, only for a limited time. Stewardship involves how we choose to spend that time, how we utilize our God-given skills and talents, and how we deal with all that we have been given to watch over during our lifetime. Stewardship is a way of life that accepts a "total accountability and responsibility before God from whom every aspect of our lives comes as a gift."[6] Note that the biblical emphasis is on the abundant generosity of God and subsequently, the response of all who receive those gifts, and not about the financial support of the Church.

Stewardship, at its core, is about our relationship with God. In biblical terms, money and possessions pose a huge threat to this relationship. At issue is where one places one's ultimate trust and security and the reality that it is impossible to serve both God and wealth. Put another way, often "the one thing standing between God and a person's heart is their wallet."[7] Scripture is filled with stories of the crippling effects of gifts that are hoarded and not shared, and this behavior is consistently viewed as a turning away from God. In contrast, there are countless stories that witness to the idea that one's ability to give is directly related to one's ability to love and serve God. In brief, the portrait of a biblical giver is one who gives with intention, who gives regularly, and one who gives generously of the "first fruits" that they have been given. In addition, a biblical giver gives in proportion to the blessings they have received, gives cheerfully, and with thanksgiving.[8] It is Jesus who put it perhaps most succinctly when he observed, "where your treasure is, there your heart will be also" (Luke 12:34). Indeed there is a close connection between loving and giving.

Faithful stewardship is giving to God and is one of the most tangible expressions of discipleship. Too often congregations approach annual giving as an act of membership. From this perspective giving is treated much like dues that are levied in other organizations with everyone expected to give their fair share in order to be in good standing with the group. From this perspective funds are used to support the institution, and offered so that others can "do" ministry in a mission field that is often far away. In this scenario the goal is to get and keep members with expectations kept relatively low. From the perspective of discipleship, giving is not an annual event or the result of a campaign, but is rather a way of life. For disciples, giving is an outward expression of a growing relationship with God and a deepening connection to the community. Ministry is viewed as a partnership and the mission field is right outside the door of the Church. The goal is for faith to permeate all of life and for new disciples to be welcomed, formed, and sent forth to carry out the work of mission. This is a high expectation scenario with the emphasis on the disciple's need to give rather than the Church's need to receive.[9] "Stewardship is an act of discipleship, not a duty of membership. Faithful giving is part of faithful living."[10]

Stewardship as Worship

Faithful stewardship is also an act of worship. The liturgical act of offering our gifts to God is an outward expression of love. The steward-disciple "receives God's gifts gratefully, tends those gifts responsibly, shares them lovingly, and returns them with increase to the Lord."[11] The offerings of the community are representative tokens of all that we have received, a portion of which we return with thanksgiving. It is important to recognize that although they are token, proportional gifts, they represent the whole of our being. What we offer to God in worship is all of ourselves: heart, soul, mind, and body. Peter Gomes, the famed American preacher, theologian, and professor at Harvard Divinity School, witnessed to this truth when he wrote:

> [W]hite people who visit black churches are often surprised and not a little shocked at the number of offerings given, and with the fine art of encouraging people to generosity. It takes some time to realize that the giving of money is not a necessary condition to the material needs of the people of God, but rather it is the central drama in the act of worship.[12]

We believe that one of the greatest challenges facing the Church in the twenty-first century is effectively reclaiming stewardship as reflective of a faithful relationship with God, an expression of discipleship, and as an act of worship. Indeed the best plan for enhanced stewardship is the "constant immersion in our vocation to a Christian way of life."[13]

Overcoming Silence

To accomplish this, the "conspiracy of silence" around money needs to be broken. It seems that one of the unwritten rules for securing resources for the work of the Church is to do so without ever mentioning money, yet making the connection between faith and money is essential for the health of individual givers and for the life of congregations.[14] One example of breaking the taboo of silence comes from Martin Luther King, Sr., when he

> assumed the leadership of Ebenezer Baptist Church in Montgomery, Alabama, in the 1930s, he ended the long-held tradition of secrecy surrounding what people gave to the church. He opened the pledge records of the church for everyone to see. Anonymous gifts would be accepted but not recorded. "The practice of anonymous giving," he thundered from the pulpit, "leads to the practice of anonymous non-giving."[15]

This may be an extreme example and a practice not likely to be duplicated by mainline congregations, yet the point is well taken. It is generally accepted that the higher the level of secrecy and silence about money in congregations, the lower the level of giving.[16] Giving in most mainline congregations is not a matter of public knowledge and there is much controversy about whether or not the pastor should even have access to this information. This topic will be taken up later in this chapter when we discuss the critical role of the pastoral leader in this area of congregational life. Prior to that we will explore what motivates giving as well as what is not working, and more importantly, what is working, in the Church's efforts to be successful in the work of stewardship.

Tithe

Many Christians talk about the obligation to "tithe to the work of the Lord." In Genesis 14, Abraham gives a tithe back to the Lord. And elsewhere, in the Old Testament, it is mentioned. In actual fact, the ethic of Jesus is much more radical (he seems to want 100% of everything we have). But the language of a tithe remains in many Christian traditions a helpful expectation and standard for giving. The mantra "you should give away 10%, save 10%, and the rest you can live on" has become a piece of advice that gets passed down generations. Most people give away much less than 10%; and members of the mainline are much less likely to tithe than the evangelicals and the historic African American denominations. Naturally any leader of a congregation must always "practice what they preach." And perhaps we would do well to recover the language of the tithe, both for our own giving, and for the purpose of inviting members of the congregation to do likewise.

Reasons for Giving

In examining motivations and attitudes toward giving in mainline traditions it becomes clear that "giving tends to be a matter of choice rather than duty."[17] Understanding this dynamic, and understanding basic attitudes about money are critical to successfully addressing and communicating a theology of stewardship. Generally speaking, it is safe to say that human beings are intrinsically selfish. If we have money we would much rather spend it on ourselves than give it away. For Americans (and perhaps many others) the list of consumer needs continues to expand as the cost of meeting those needs continues to rise. The net result of this insatiable appetite for consumer goods is that Americans have more possessions than ever before, yet at the same time feel poorer than ever before.[18] Helping people to intentionally choose a different approach to life is a difficult yet life-giving, if not life-saving, task. It was Billy Graham, the well-known tele-evangelist, who once aptly noted, "if a person gets his attitude about money right, it will straighten out almost every other area of his life."[19] Getting our attitudes right about money and where we place ultimate value is, of course, at the root of stewardship, and at the heart of discipleship.

It has to be recognized, however, when discussing motivation, that most voluntary giving, when we are completely honest, is not really gift giving at all, but rather a transaction. Money is usually given in order to buy something. This is true even in churches. For many, what is purchased, by giving to the Church, is essentially payment for services rendered. This kind of giving, akin to dues paying and contributing one's fair share, is a motivation that seeks to estimate the direct personal value in order to try to determine an exact amount to be given.[20] Many congregations unwittingly affirm this kind of pay-as-you-go mentality by assigning fees to particular services (usually weddings and sometimes even funerals). For some, what is purchased by giving to the Church is perhaps the strengthening of social ties and connections to important people that might warrant a certain kind of reciprocity. Further still, what is purchased by giving to the Church might also be good feelings and self-affirmation, the hope of continued blessings for self and family that might even warrant a certain reciprocity with God. (There was once a single frame cartoon of a well-dressed businessman on his knees, eyes closed, earnestly praying in Church. As he prays he quietly utters "O.K. God, here's the deal.") This kind of motivation, while incredibly powerful, and unfortunately incredibly widespread, is also incredibly problematic. We enter dangerous territory when God's blessings are directly equated with monetary gifts as some kind of reward.[21] The third-century theologian Tertullian said it simply and clearly: "nothing that is God's is obtainable by money."[22]

These observations may seem harsh and somewhat cynical, yet serve as a reminder that not all who inhabit church pews are inspired or persuaded to give for the same reasons, and those reasons sometimes have little to do with a strong and active faith.[23] They are reflective, however, of a certain reality, but not the only reality, and serve as a starting point for what might inspire deeper discipleship and motivations that spring from love and thankfulness. When motivated by love, giving is a natural extension of the self. If you love what you are giving to, you are in essence giving to yourself. The object of your love and generosity becomes part of you and you become part of it.[24] When motivated by pure thankfulness, one gives freely and joyously, without the expectation of future return. How we move individuals and congregations to embrace this kind of deeper commitment is explored in the next section.

Ineffective Stewardship

Acknowledging that there are no magic formulas, no gimmicks, and no short cuts, one way to begin this part of the conversation is to focus on stewardship practices, that while quite common and generally accepted, are actually counterproductive and ineffective. So before highlighting potentially helpful practices that congregations might consider starting, we begin with those we strongly suggest they consider stopping. In his insightful and hopeful book, *Remember the Future: Financial Leadership and Asset Management for Congregations*, Gerald W. Keucher contends that many mainline congregations are suffering from what he calls a "crisis of confidence" that manifests itself in a survival mentality whereby congregational leaders are more focused on managing decline than visioning for a better future.[25]

When approaching the task of stewardship from this largely institutional perspective, leaders are likely to try one of four strategies, and in more desperate situations might try a blend of all four, when asking people for money. One strategy is to scare people into giving. Keucher calls this the "sky is falling" approach. The basic idea is that if people are fearful of certain consequences if adequate funds are not raised, they might be more generous. This approach does not work at several levels. People cannot stay on high alert for long periods of time, and certainly not for crisis after crisis, and, even more importantly, people are not inspired to give to efforts that are failing. Another strategy Keucher calls the "come help us pay our bills" approach. This is a needs-based approach that invites members to pay their dues, contribute their fair share, and leads to the criticism that all the Church cares about is money. A third strategy he calls the "team spirit" approach, which appeals to the notion that we are all part of this community and all need to do our part. This approach assumes that everyone feels a part of the team and also assumes that everyone believes that the game is worth supporting.

This is not always an accurate assumption. Lastly, there is the "NPR/PBS" (National Public Radio/Public Broadcasting System) strategy, which refers to the periodic public radio fund raising appeals that emphasize the need for participation in order for the institution to continue its work. This approach uses the subtle, and sometimes not so subtle, language of guilt and obligation, especially if you are using the services of the institution and not supporting it financially.[26] Any of these approaches may initially prove effective, but are largely unsustainable and ineffective in the long term. They also tend to reinforce the acceptability of a low level of giving, which only diminishes people's capacity to grow in faith. These approaches also tend to reinforce the idea that instead of stewards, givers are simply donors, and when this happens, there is erosion in the mission of the Church.[27]

In addition to these practices, we would also add a word of caution about the use of numbers and budgets as a catalyst for generosity. While critically important for use by congregational leadership, when communicating about stewardship it is good advice to remember that "numbers are boring to many, misunderstood by others, and uninspiring to just about everyone."[28] While financial information needs to be readily available as a means of accountability and as evidence of prudent management, be advised that this information does not ordinarily inspire a sense of mission and purpose. And as alluded to previously, publishing statistics that represent bad news for the congregation in the hope of spurring increased giving, most often has the opposite effect.[29]

A final word regarding ineffective stewardship practices needs to include a warning against separating the giving of "treasure" apart from the giving of time, and the giving of talent. The three are completely intertwined and are of coequal importance.[30] If biblical stewardship involves the whole person and invites disciples into a new way of life, then giving must encompass the entirety of one's being and the returning of one's life to God. To do otherwise by segmenting our material resources from our unique gifts and skills and the time we choose to offer them in service to God is antithetical to the core message of steward-ship and gives credence to the complaint that the Church is only interested in our money. In fact, experience and research confirms that "time and talent properly precede treasure in the exercise of stewardship."[31]

Effective Stewardship

Keeping all this in mind, we turn our attention now to practices that have proven effec-tive. Relying heavily on the work of J. Clif Christopher and his excellent book, *Not Your Parents' Offering Plate: A New Vision for Financial Stewardship*, we learn that the best way for the Church to raise money is to simply do its job. By this he means focusing on the work of making disciples and developing what he calls a "high expectation" church culture, which, among many other things, includes clear expectations about proportional giving. With a strong bent toward mission, he asserts that the product of our efforts is a changed life, and that is the basis of our witness. He rightly affirms that people do not usually give enthusiastically to institutions or programs yet are eager to give to efforts that really matter, truly make a difference, and result in lives being changed for the better. The redundant and crucial message, communicated in a multitude of ways, is to show people how their gifts are being used to change lives, how their faithful discipleship is making a difference. Consistent with this theme he also advises the use of a narrative, mission budget, which tells of the story of changed lives, rather than an uninspiring numerical line-item budget. Consistent with the biblical understanding of stewardship, he sets the expectation that every disciple will make their "first and largest" charitable gift in support of the mission of the Church, and as disciples, will fully engage, with all their being in the work of changing lives for the sake of the Gospel.[32]

Like others, he also recognizes that not everyone in the pews ascribes to these expecta-tions and must continually be invited into deeper commitment. That being said they remain part of the community and will be motivated to give for a variety of different reasons, there-fore any invitation must be multi-faceted and even generational. Older generations tend to be more loyal to institutions and are more likely to respond to traditional biblical approaches to stewardship. Baby boomers tend to be less trusting of institutions and leaders and often require that a case be made, as well as demanding direct accountability. Younger generations are even less confident in large institutions and are more interested in being connected to efforts that they can see, touch, feel, and experience directly. The challenge for congrega-tions is to be able to not only show them the mission of the Church, but also explain its personal and corporate benefits.[33] In brief, stewardship practices that work are those that are biblically based, are directly related to discipleship, are positive and inviting in approach, are focused on mission, and are timely and consistent with personal thanks to those who give. The only missing ingredient is the critical role of the pastoral leader.

The Leader's Role

As a pious young preacher, John Wesley reportedly earned £30 at his first position. Of this, he kept £28 and gave the other two away. Sometime after, when his salary had doubled, he still kept only £28 and gave the rest away. Eventually, he earned as much as £120 and was still living on £28 and giving away the remainder. His motto regarding faithful stewardship was "gain all you can, save all you can, give all you can."[34]

With this kind of model, there is little wonder that clergy are daunted by the task of leading, teaching, and preaching about stewardship. The awkwardness is only compounded by clergy feeling that perhaps they are not the best role model, feeling a bit hypocritical and they are keenly aware, like everyone else in the congregation, that the money they are soliciting goes directly toward paying their salary.[35] Add to this, according to Douglas John Hall, that many "ministers cringe at the mention of stewardship Sundays" because they feel that they must once again "lower themselves to the role of fund-raisers."[36] This observation points directly to the widely accepted yet false notion that fundraising is the antithesis of religious leadership. The implication is that the subject itself is disconnected from the task of leadership, and therefore separate from the weightier matters of the spiritual life. On the contrary, we take the position that the two are deeply connected and that no one person in a congregational setting is more responsible for fundraising than the pastoral leader.

Many clergy believe that they are not adequately prepared for this important role, with the result being that in many congregations the "clergy and laity collude to create a thunderous silence about money."[37] Alban Institute founder Loren Meade argues that the issue is not a lack of training, but rather the enormous pressure placed upon clergy to avoid the subject altogether due to a general aversion to the topic and because of their own internal anxiety. This is in spite of the fact that money and the use of it is a profoundly spiritual matter that touches our culture and our people more deeply than almost any other. Meade urges clergy to embrace their dual responsibility of "making generous people out of church members and taking care of the financing of the institution itself."[38]

To accomplish this requires open conversation and a recognition that it is incumbent upon clergy to know what people are giving to a church. Remember that asking for money is really evangelism, the main concern being a person's soul and not their money, and "there is nothing more revealing about what is happening in a person's heart than the decisions they are making with their pocketbook."[39] The idea is to preach and teach a *theology* of stewardship that serves as a summons to discipleship, in a manner that is invitational and non-confrontational, and helps folks to move in the direction of a deeper and richer faith.[40]

Planned Giving

Earlier in this chapter we spoke of the evolving nature of giving to provide resources to meet the needs of a changing Church in a changing world. In addition to *annual giving* (funds to support the annual operating budget of the Church), and *capital giving* (funds to support buildings and substantial mission efforts), there is currently an increased emphasis on *planned giving* (funds to support a legacy of faith). Planned giving, while usually associated with wills and estates, is essentially a means to encourage consistent and faithful stewardship in all aspects of life, including the use of accumulated wealth before and after death. In terms of estate planning, planned giving allows people the opportunity to engage in financial planning in order to dispose of their wealth "in a manner consistent with the values and interests that they embraced in life, which will enable the church to meet the challenges of the future."[41] In more recent times the area of planned giving has expanded to include not just bequests, but also planned charitable and legacy giving in one's own lifetime. These gifts include charitable remainder trusts, stocks, annuities, and property that not only help to fund future ministry but can also provide financial benefits to those making the contribution.[42]

Conclusion

All of this talk of money and of faith, the giver's need to give, the Church's need to fund its mission, the reclaiming of stewardship, and the strengthening of discipleship, is unambiguously tied to the generosity of God, who provides all of life as a gift. We know that it is not in our nature to give as we have been given, but we also know that the joyful life that we prize is closely connected to our ability to give generously and with thankful hearts.[43] We know in our heart of hearts that it is in giving that we do, in fact, receive. In light of God's abundant generosity, weighing our affluence against the needs of the world, in the words of John Westerhoff, the question becomes not "what do I need to give?" but rather "What do I have a right to keep?"[44]

Notes

1   Michael Reeves and Jennifer Tyler, *Faith and Money: Understanding Annual Giving in the Church* (Nashville, TN: Discipleship Resources, 2003), 6.

2   Dean Hoge, Patrick McNamara, and Charles Zech, *Plain Talk about Churches and Money* (Herndon, VA: The Alban Institute, 1997), 18–19.

3   Ibid.

4   Michael Durall, *Creating Congregations of Generous People* (Herndon, VA: The Alban Institute, 1999), 23.

5   Charles R. Lane, *Ask, Thank, Tell: Improving Stewardship Ministry in Your Congregation* (Minneapolis, MN: Augsburg Fortress, 2006), 21.

6   Hoge, McNamara, and Zech, *Plain Talk*, 18.

7   J. Clif Christopher, *Not Your Parents' Offering Plate: A New Vision for Financial Stewardship* (Nashville, TN: Abingdon Press, 2008), 27.

8   Lane, *Ask, Thank, Tell*, 45.

9   Ibid., 12–14.

10   Ibid., 6.

11   C. Justin Clements, *The Steward's Way: A Spirituality of Stewardship* (Kansas City, KN: Sheed and Ward, 1997), vii.

12   Durall, *Creating Congregations*, 34.

13   Michael O'Hurley-Pitts, *The Passionate Steward: Recovering Christian Stewardship from Secular Fundraising* (Toronto: St. Brigid Press, 2001), 109.

14   Reeves and Tyler, *Faith and Money*, 5.

15   Durall, *Creating Congregations*, 15.

16   Ibid., 15.

17   Ibid., 5.

18   Ibid., 5.

19   Mark Allan Powell, *Giving to God: The Bible's Good News about Living a Generous Life* (Grand Rapids, MI: Eerdmans Pubishing Co., 2006), Introduction.

20   Hoge, McNamara, and Zech, *Plain Talk*, 47.

21   Ibid., 37–43.

22   Powell, *Giving to God*, Introduction.

23   Hoge, McNamara, and Zech, *Plain Talk*, 51.

24   Ibid., 44.

25 Gerald W. Keucher, *Remember the Future: Financial Leadership and Asset Management for Congregations* (New York: Church Publishing, 2006), 14–17.

26 Ibid., 153.

27 O'Hurley-Pitts, *Passionate Steward*, 23.

28 Durall, *Creating Congregations*, 43.

29 Christopher, *Not Your Parents' Offering Plate*, 29.

30 Patrick H. McNamara, *More than Money: Portraits of Transformative Stewardship* (Alban Institute, 1999), viii.

31 O'Hurley-Pitts, *Passionate Steward*, 101.

32 Christopher, *Not Your Parents' Offering Plate*, 105–110.

33 Christopher, *Not Your Parents' Offering Plate*, 38.

34 Powell, *Giving to God*, 168.

35 Ibid., 67.

36 Ibid., 47.

37 Hoge, McNamara, and Zech, *Plain Talk*, vi.

38 Ibid., vi.

39 Christopher, *Not Your Parents' Offering Plate*, 27.

40 David Mosser and Brian Bauknight, *First Fruits: 14 Sermons on Stewardship* (Nashville, TN: Abingdon Press, 2003), 10–12.

41 O'Hurley-Pitts, *Passionate Steward*, 147.

42 Ibid., 152.

43 Powell, *Giving to God*, 39.

44 Ibid., 168.

Annotated Bibliography

Christopher, J. Clif, *Not Your Parents' Offering Plate: A New Vision for Financial Stewardship* (Nashville, TN: Abingdon Press, 2008).

With the percentage of giving to religious institutions on the decline, the author presents a compelling case for a more sophisticated and arguably more theological approach to congregational giving. This book argues that the best way for the Church to fund its mission is to do its job: witness to changed lives, focus on people and not programs, show how funds are utilized for the sake of the gospel.

Clements, C. Justin, *The Steward's Way: A Spirituality of Stewardship* (Kansas City, KN: Sheed and Ward, 1997).

This easily accessible collection of essays covers a wide variety of stewardship issues and is organized into categories related by topic. It is designed as a creative, challenging, and inspirational resource for those leading stewardship ministries in congregations.

Durall, Michael, *Creating Congregations of Generous People* (Herndon, VA: The Alban Institute, 1999).

With an aim toward creating a congregational climate for generous giving, this book hopes to help leaders understand the motivations of why parishioners give (and don't give) and offers advice for the development of successful and consistent stewardship programming.

Hoge, Dean, McNamara, Patrick, and Zech, Charles, *Plain Talk about Churches and Money* (Herndon, VA: The Alban Institute, 1997).

True to its title, this joint effort (Hoge and McNamara are sociologists and Zech is an economist) provides basic, straightforward, and useful information to clergy and lay leaders about raising money in congregations. Its comparative and comprehensive approach reviews the effectiveness of various strategies, explores the deep ambiguity about money held by many clergy, and seeks to encourage creative and faithful practices for funding ministry.

Holliman, Glenn N. Holliman, and Barbara L., *With Generous Hearts: How to Gather Resources for Your Church, Church School, Church Agency, Chaplaincy, or Diocese*

(Harrisburg, PA: Morehouse Publishing, 2005).

This decidedly "how-to" book covers the landscape of annual, capital, and planned giving for congregations, but also includes information specific to church schools, agencies, judicatories, and chaplaincies. This volume offers sound advice, is biblically and theologically grounded, and comprehensive in scope.

Keucher, Gerald W., *Remember the Future: Financial Leadership and Asset Management for Congregations* (New York: Church Publishing, 2006).

This very practical, well written, and carefully organized book contains an honest and hopeful view of the economic issues facing many churches of the mainline (aging buildings, tight budgets, membership decline, lack of confidence). Rather than simply managing decline, the author, with many years of active experience, not only offers reason to hope, but also offers some useful advice for imagining and securing a better future.

Lane, Charles R., *Ask, Thank, Tell: Improving Stewardship Ministry in Your Congregation* (Minneapolis, MN: Augsburg Fortress, 2006).

With many years of experience at a variety of levels in the Lutheran Church, the author provides a solid foundation and practical guide for leading congregational stewardship. Focusing on the biblical witness, the mission of the congregation, and the role of the pastor as a stewardship leader, this books hopes to help break the taboo of silence that inhibits congregations from talking plainly about money.

McNamara, Patrick H., *More than Money: Portraits of Transformative Stewardship* (Herndon, VA: The Alban Institute, 1999).

Written from his perspective as a sociologist, this book outlines the author's research and interaction with 11 "stewardship" congregations. These congregations, representing a broad range of mostly mainline denominations, each exhibit unique and effective stewardship practices. While not a "how-to" for effective stewardship, some common traits do emerge.

Mosser, David and Bauknight, Brian, *First Fruits: 14 Sermons on Stewardship* (Nashville, TN: Abingdon Press, 2003).

This collection of stewardship sermons, by some of the most noted preachers of the day, is designed to offer encouragement and creative ideas to help pastors articulate a practical theology of giving. The intentional focus and recurring theme is that stewardship is one of the tangible practices of faithful discipleship.

O'Hurley-Pitts, Michael, *The Passionate Steward: Recovering Christian Stewardship from Secular Fundraising* (Toronto: St. Brigid Press, 2001).

Calling into question many commonly held assumptions about Church fundraising, the author seeks to reclaim Christian stewardship as being rooted in a commitment to Christ and the mission of the Church. Not a training manual, this work seeks to connect the theology and faithful practice of Christian stewardship apart from secular fundraising.

Powell, Mark Allan, *Giving to God: The Bible's Good News about Living a Generous Life* (Grand Rapids, MI: Eerdmans Publishing Co., 2006).

Grounded in Scripture, this guide sees faithful stewardship not as a veiled term for fundraising, but as a way of life for Christians. The author focuses in the biblical roots of stewardship as an act of worship, an expression of faith, and as a discipline for spiritual growth.

Reeves, Michael and Tyler, Jennifer, *Faith and Money: Understanding Annual Giving in the Church* (Nashville, TN; Discipleship Resources, 2003).

This excellent resource identifies the many challenges to effective stewardship in congregations, offers biblical, theological, and practical advice about how to connect faith and money. Each chapter concludes with a bibliography of additional resources, and there is an extensive listing of biblical references in the back of the book arranged by a stewardship-related topic.

18

Christian Apologetics

Any person of faith working in the mainline in the west needs to be able to "defend" the faith. This is the territory known as *apologetics*. We need to be able to "defend" the faith because, increasingly, the culture we are working in is less and less sympathetic. We need to give some account of why *theism* (the belief in a personal God) is true.

Some strands of the mainline will be less sympathetic to apologetics. It was Karl Barth, the great Swiss theologian, who complained that apologetics is often linked to natural theology (i.e. it is an attempt to defend faith without making Christ central). Given the only vehicle that God has provided to give us knowledge of God is Christ, the project of natural theology (and with it, apologetics) is doomed to failure. The focus instead needs to be on preaching the Gospel and inviting the response of faith. Our Barthians critic might join the skeptical philosophers (e.g. John Hick) who do not think there are any arguments that are decisive reasons for faith; there are no arguments that should, on the basis of logic, persuade a person of the reality of God. From this perspective, the task of "constructing arguments" that persuade non-Christians is misguided.

Yet in recent years, there has been a widespread and positive resurgence in apologetics. This can be mainly attributed to the so-called *new atheists.* Led by Richard Dawkins, the group includes the late Christopher Hitchens (1949–2011) and Sam Harris among its number. Their aggressive critique has forced the Church to respond. And across the mainline, there have been some good and strong responses.

Atheism

Much of modern Christian apologetics has to do with the response to atheism. The "new atheists," Richard Dawkins, Christopher Hitchens, and Sam Harris (and some might add the American TV host Bill Maher), tend to attack all Christians as one

An Introduction to Ministry: A Primer for Renewed Life and Leadership in Mainline Protestant Congregations, First Edition. Ian S. Markham and Oran E. Warder.
© 2016 John Wiley & Sons, Ltd. Published 2016 by John Wiley & Sons, Ltd.

singular voice. Atheism stands on a self-described non-belief – that there is no God, and that there is no proof that a divine being ordered the universe. As a result, atheists are in constant conflict with the religious world that attests to the existence of God in whatever interpretation that may reveal.

The Critique from the New Atheists

Atheists do have a point. Christians can be their own worst enemy. There are Christians who deny the evidence for some form of natural selection as a key part of the emergence of life on planet Earth; such Christians are forced to postulate a massive conspiracy among biologists at virtually all major universities who are persuaded that the evidence overwhelmingly supports evolution. There are Christians who make little effort to explain what they mean by God, so they do not offer a coherent account of the basic concept of their faith. And there are too many Christians who use the word "faith" as a mechanism to evade questions.

In addition, historically, we have no choice but to concede that the Church was so often a slow and even reluctant supporter of key social causes – for example, the key idea of toleration owes a great deal to secular Enlightenment theorists. And many Christians will concede that the problem of evil and suffering is a deep and strong obstruction to faith.

However, the heart of the objection by atheists is that God is associated with a pre-scientific world view.[1] In other words, science has made God very unlikely. Hitchens made the point like this:

Religion comes from the period of human prehistory where nobody … had the smallest idea what was going on. It comes from the bawling and fearful infancy of our species, and is a babyish attempt to meet our inescapable demand for knowledge (as well as for comfort, reassurance and other infantile needs). Today, the least educated of my children knows much more about the natural order than any of the founders of religion, and one would like to think – though the connection is not a fully demonstrable one – that this is why they seem so uninterested in sending fellow humans to hell.[2]

Pierre-Simon Laplace (1749–1827) and William Ockham (1287–1348) were the heroes for Hitchens. Laplace was the French physicist who had the temerity to explain to Napoleon that his view of the solar system had no need for the God hypothesis. And William Ockham was the one who insisted that the simplest explanation for data is normally the best. For Hitchens, put these two men together and you have the reason why faith is now out of fashion. The aspects of the world that were previously explained by God are now explained differently.

An illustration might help. Once upon a time we were puzzled about why hurricanes and tornadoes occurred. Why is it sometimes sunny? And why does it sometimes rain? The pre-modern picture of the universe postulated a God who was a direct causal agent of the weather. But courtesy of Newtonian physics and modern science, this picture of the universe has been displaced by a meteorological explanation. And of course, everyone accepts the scientific explanation for weather. God has been displaced as an explanation.

For a time, God was moved one stage back. God became the designer of the universe. However, with natural selection, God has been eliminated from this role as well. Hitchens is very critical of those who suggest that evolution is God's mechanism for creating the world. He writes that envisioning God as being behind evolution makes God

> a fumbling fool of their pretended god, and makes him out to be a tinkerer, an approximator, and a blunderer, who took eons of time to fashion a few serviceable figures and heaped up a junkyard of scrap and failure meanwhile.[3]

Given the evolutionary hypothesis makes such compelling sense of the data, it strongly suggests that God does not exist. It is such a long, drawn out process; it is also very cruel. Hitchens writes:

> We must also confront the fact that evolution is, as well as smarter than we are, infinitely more callous and cruel, and also capricious. Investigation of the fossil record and the record of molecular biology shows us that approximately 98 percent of all species that have ever appeared on earth have lapsed into extinction.[4]

For Hitchens, God made some sense in a pre-scientific age and culture. But now, our understanding of the world has moved on. The God hypothesis has been made redundant.

It is important for the leaders of congregations in the mainline to respond to this world view. This is the work of apologetics.

Richard Dawkins on the God of the Old Testament

The God of the Old Testament is arguably the most unpleasant character in all fiction: jealous and proud of it; a petty, unjust, unforgiving control-freak; a vindictive, bloodthirsty ethnic cleanser; a misogynistic, homophobic, racist, infanticidal, genocidal, filicidal, pestilential, megalomaniacal, sadomasochistic, capriciously malevolent bully.[5]

Richard Dawkins is the world's best known atheist (although he tends to describe himself as an agnostic). His attack on the God of the Old Testament is well known. How would you respond?

Our Apologetics Method

The temptation is to reduce the conversation between atheists and theists to a polemic, where the other is crudely and grotesquely caricatured. The Christian tradition at its best does not operate in that way. The remarkable thirteenth-century Dominican friar Thomas Aquinas is the father of apologetics (perhaps the greatest one who has ever lived) and has a deeply generous methodology. Having trained as an Augustinian Platonist, he then spent much of his life exploring the world of Aristotle. He read Muslim and Jewish thinkers with care and sought to synthesize the thought of Aristotle with his Augustinian training. The very structure of his *Summa Theologica* is a testimony to his generosity and care when presenting the arguments of his opponents. In this remarkable text, Aquinas always starts by presenting the strongest arguments he can find against the position that he holds. He then identifies the hinge argument for his position before going on to explain why this position is the correct one. And the position that he takes in the *Summa* was, for his day, controversial and pioneering. In 1270, the views of Aquinas were investigated and condemned by a papal inquiry, which was organized by the bishop of Paris.[6]

Why was Aquinas so willing to read widely and explore a tradition that wasn't his own so carefully? The answer is that Aquinas had a primary obligation to the truth. The quest for the truth is a moral absolute. If God *is*, then God must be the author of all truth. Aquinas saw this clearly. No text was forbidden; no viewpoint inappropriate to explore. And one follows the truth wherever it goes.

A good leader of a congregation should operate with the same set of assumptions. When one enters into a conversation with a skeptic about the faith one should start by making appropriate connections. Atheists have some legitimate insights that Christians can and should accommodate. And the differences should be explored with respect and a deep desire to find the truth.

Working with this methodology, let us look at three areas. The first is the ways in which science is increasingly supporting theism. The second is the whole arena of providence and suffering. And the third is religion and ethics.

Science is a Friend of Faith

For Thomas Aquinas, the quest for explanations in the universe depends on belief in God. This is what lies behind one of his five ways to prove God. To simplify his argument considerably: to assume that the world is explicable is to assume that it is not just a big fluke. If it is a big fluke then a fluke, by definition, isn't an explanation. So if the universe as a whole is explicable, then one needs a creator. Part of the definition of God is that God is the ultimate explanation for the existence of everything.

There is a sense then that God is a necessary assumption of science. However, in recent years, it is another classical argument that is making a comeback. For centuries the strongest argument for faith has been that the universe looks designed. With evolution, this argument looked shaky. For evolution the appearance of design is not due to a creator making sure that everything fits together, but that those things that didn't fit in did not survive. However, it is the work of cosmological physicists who are bringing the concept of design back into contention. This is worth describing in some detail. And it all has to do with the origins of the universe.

The physicist Paul Davies sets out the data with some care. He writes, "The existence of life as we know it depends delicately on many seemingly fortuitous features of the laws of physics and the structure of the universe."[7] So, for example, carbon-based life depends on the production of carbon. The production of carbon in stars requires "a numerical 'coincidence' to produce a nuclear resonance at just the right energy."[8] If this numerical coincidence had not occurred, then life would not occurred.

Along with the size of the universe and the production of carbon, there are a whole range of variables that needed to be just right for life to emerge. So to take another illustration, the forces of expansion and gravity also needed to be just right. Davies explains:

> The large scale structure and motion of the universe is equally remarkable. The accumulated gravity of the universe operates to restrain the expansion, causing it to decelerate with time. In the primeval phase the expansion was much faster than it is today. The universe is thus the product of a competition between the explosive vigor of the big bang, and the force of gravity which tries to pull the pieces back together again. In recent years, astrophysicists have come to realize just how delicately this competition has been balanced. Had the big bang been weaker, the cosmos would have soon fallen back on itself in a big crunch. On the other hand, had it been stronger, the cosmic material would have dispersed so rapidly that galaxies would not have formed. Either way, the observed structure of the universe seems to depend very sensitively on the precise matching of explosive vigor to gravitating power.[9]

It does look fixed. It looks intended. It looks as if there was a decision made that it was important to have life in this universe. And there are so many factors that need to be managed: the order of the universe needed vast quantities of negative entropy; the lack of black holes, which one would expect to dominate a chaotic universe; the uniform structure and behavior of the universe beyond the light horizon; and the fundamental constraints of nature (i.e. those basic entities that have the same numerical value throughout the universe and across all time). As Davies sums up: "There seems to be no obvious reason why the universe did not go berserk, expanding in a chaotic and uncoordinated way, producing enormous black holes. Channeling the explosive violence into such a regular and organized pattern of motion seems like a miracle."[10]

The term Anthropic Principle has been coined to partly explain this remarkable order that makes life possible. Coined originally by the astrophysicist Brandon Carter in 1973, the Principle suggests that all the remarkable variables in the universe have precisely the right values for life to appear. The Anthropic Principle suggests strongly that we were always intended: it looks like we were expected. Since Brandon Carter, a remarkable literature has been generated. It was John Barrow and Frank Tipler who wrote the classic *The Anthropic Cosmological Principle*.[11] Since then, Paul Davies, Martin Rees,[12] and Stephen Hawking[13] have made substantial contributions to the debate. Probably the finest analysis of the philosophy of the debate is Rodney D. Holder's *God, the Multiverse, and Everything*.[14]

It is fun looking at how Richard Dawkins handles all of these data. He is a good enough scientist to know that it is true. He concedes that this universe does look as if life was intended. Dawkins comments on Martin Rees and the way that the six fundamental constraints for life needed to be exactly right, writing: "The bottom line for each of them is the same. The actual number sits in a Goldilocks band of values outside which life would not have been possible."[15] So how does he make sense of it? He starts by excluding *a priori* the concept of a God who intended life to emerge. He rejects this for the rather muddled reason that anything as complex as a God would have to be an end result of a physical process.

He then moves on to suggest that the term "anthropic principle" should be used to describe the skeptic's alternative to theism. So Dawkins writes:

> We have the theist's answer on the one hand, and the anthropic answer on the other. The theist says that God, when setting up the universe, tuned the fundamental constants of the universe so that each one lay in its Goldilocks zone for the production of life. It is as though God had six knobs that he could twiddle and he carefully tuned each knob to its Goldilocks value. As ever, the theist's answer is deeply unsatisfying, because it leaves the existence of God unexplained.[16]

So in what sense is the anthropic answer the alternative? Dawkins uses the term to describe the "magic of large numbers."[17] To explain the remarkable achievement of lifeless matter becoming life on earth, Dawkins reminds us that we live in a vast universe where at least one planet (probably more) will enable the factors to create life to come together. Couple that, he explains, with the remarkable "crane" of Darwinian evolution and the God hypothesis is not needed.

Dawkins opts to explain the improbability of the precision of constants exactly to what are needed to produce life at the cosmological level – across the entire universe – with the multiverse theory. This is the claim that there is a portfolio of universes (all of which exist) and we just happen to be in the one that mathematically enables life to emerge. Naturally we are not in a position to exist in any of the other universes. With physicists postulating multiple universes in one domain, it is attractive to suggest that there are many (perhaps an infinite number of) universes of which only a small number produce life. The multiverse theory attempts to explain the emergence of life as a result of good fortune and chance.[18]

Paul Davies argues that evidence to support the multiverse theory may come from looking at the precise mathematical rules surrounding its probability. As Davies discusses the details of the multiverse hypothesis he suggests that it may extend to "fake universes" (such as the one explored in the movie *The Matrix*). This almost surreal suggestion makes Dawkins' multiverse argument more difficult to explain. With the explanation for how life came to be on earth, we at least know about the millions upon millions of other planets in this universe and the remarkable processes underpinning natural selection, but we do not know about any other universes. Dawkins concedes that the cosmological data are harder for him to explain than the emergence of life on earth:

> We don't yet have an equivalent crane for physics. Some kind of multiverse theory could in principle do for physics the same explanatory work as Darwinism does for biology. This kind of explanation is superficially less satisfying than the biological version of Darwinism, because it makes heavier demands on luck.[19]

The two serious contenders to explain the remarkable math of the universe are either an agency that intended life to emerge (the God hypothesis) or millions upon millions of other universes, most of which don't generate life. It is worth pausing to think about how remarkable the multiverse hypothesis is and that this vast universe is not the only one there is. It provides the skeptic with a view of the world that makes the Christian picture of heaven (the other major universe that Christians postulate) seem rather unimaginative. For the skeptic to evade this remarkable math, he or she needs to postulate millions of other universes (none of which is linked to our space and time). In almost all of these universes, life did not emerge because of an incorrect variable (or combination of variables). So, while some of the proposed universes have planets, most are presumably vast swirling masses of energy, and to provide for the "magic of large numbers" there needs to be an infinity of such universes.

Now on what basis can we argue that theism is a better explanation than the multiverse hypothesis? One important philosophical principle is "prior probability." We do know about the remarkable math of this universe that intended life. When we encounter "intention" in the universe, we normally explain it in terms of agency. We do not postulate unknown and inaccessible universes to provide an explanation for this remarkable math.

It is odd that Dawkins is so enthusiastic about the multiverse theory. It does not look like a scientific explanation and has a certain similarity to forms of the creationism that Dawkins abhors so much. Author Rodney Holder writes:

> Because of its lack of observable consequences, the appeal to a multiverse provides a metaphysical explanation for life rather than a scientific one. But the theory is also unscientific in another sense. This is because it provides a "catch-all" kind of explanation.
>
> Multiverse theories remind me of the argument put forward by Christian fundamentalist *Philip Henry Gosse* in the nineteenth century to reconcile a literal reading of Genesis with geology. Nature is really cyclical and God created it instantaneously in mid-cycle – Adam with a naval, trees in Eden appearing to be 50 years old, fossil birds with half-digested food in their stomachs! Anything can be explained on this basis and no observation can possibly contradict the theory. Multiverse theories are equally sterile. Yes, they explain everything, by the simple formula, "If it can happen, it will happen somewhere sometime, so don't be surprised!" But they cannot be falsified: they are completely insensitive to the empirical facts. This is a far cry from the normal kind of explanation sought in science.[20]

The multiverse theory is deeply unsatisfying. It is implausible that there are so many universes; it is unscientific; and it lacks the simplicity of agency and intention.

Increasingly it looks as if science is supporting faith. The very territory that Dawkins uses to fight faith is now a key reason for faith.

Providence and Suffering

The Anthropic Principle seems to point to God; it is now necessary to look at an area where we are on defense. Why does God allow evil and suffering? If God acts in the world, then how does God act? How does prayer work? Apologetics also requires us to think through these issues.

Keith Ward in *Divine Action* finds the game of dice an interesting way into the issues of suffering and providence. When one plays dice, one needs the game to be random (otherwise there is no game), yet every single time one has a turn one desperately wants to throw a six.[21]

In addition, the game itself is governed by certain basic laws of mechanics, yet the game does not just continue by itself. An external agent in terms of a player is needed to keep the game going. Even though one can reduce the game to the math of mechanics, it is not a complete explanation for what is going on.[22]

So let us unpack this game of dice image. God had certain macro intentions in creating this world (or to use the language of Aquinas – God's antecedent willing), but then has certain micro desires within the world (i.e. the consequent willing). God created a universe in which life with the capacity for freedom emerged. This was God's antecedent willing. However, once these lives are operating in the world, God is constantly calling us to exercise our freedom for love and good (the consequent willing). However, God cannot simply compel us to behave in certain ways because that would override the antecedent willing. In the same way, even though we are desperate for a six to win a certain game of dice, we wouldn't want the game to cease being random. Although God desires a world where humanity lives in peace with each other, God also does not constantly destroy our freedom to bring about that state.

The picture from modern physics seems to support this picture of divine action. Physics has changed dramatically from the mechanism universe advocated by Newton and celebrated by Laplace. Although we should be careful not to overstate the picture emerging from the discoveries in quantum physics, it does open up possibilities for divine action. Ward summarizes:

> [S]ince the development of quantum theory in this century it has become most plausible to see the physical world as a set of emergent, flexible and open systems, and Newtonian mechanics as "no more than an approximation to a more supple reality". In this sense, the material world is open to a purposive shaping of the flexible cosmos of becoming – it is open. ... When the universe is most naturally seen as an open and emergent system, a much more positive space has been cleared for a creative dimension either to emerge within this reality, or, as the theist would believe, to direct its processes as their root.[23]

Thanks to quantum physics, the concepts of human free will (and the related concept of divine agency) are no longer manifestly unscientific. As Immanuel Kant discovered, the Newtonian universe left no room for human free will. For in Newton's universe, the next segment of the world was "caused" by the prior segment: and as Laplace found, the concepts of innovation just didn't seem to make scientific sense. So the presumption emerged, innovation is really an allusion.

Now, however, we are talking about an "open" and "emergent" universe. At the quantum level, we know that this is true. There are in the world of atoms actions that are uncaused. So new models of the universe are emerging: ones in which human agency can make some sense because a decision by a human mind is somehow part of this "uncaused" quantum world.

If human agency is making some sense, then perhaps divine agency can be analogous. It looks as if God can use similar avenues within the universe to bring about certain desired ends. Due to God's antecedent willing, God is – until the eschaton (end of the world) – going to work within the constraints of the creation. So God is not going to suddenly make all missiles into candy floss with a single divine action; but God is going to answer prayers for healing and work to deepen the desire for love inside an individual's human soul.

The picture here is this: the entire universe is part of the life of God. God as spirit is able to embrace everything that is. God has allowed the processes of the big bang and the gradual expansion of the universe to generate a planet with the capacity to shape life. In these processes, God has been constantly at work to ensure certain ends are realized. As creatures emerged with the capacity of decision and freedom, God is now seeking our cooperation in the cosmic project of "love." Sometimes we cooperate; however, sometimes we choose to thwart.

The suffering caused by earthquakes, hurricanes, and other natural disasters is often part of the necessary constraints and structure of the universe. To have a world without these aspects would be a very different world. The suffering we inflict on each other is a necessary part of the project of love. God cannot have creatures with the capacity to love, without also having the capacity for hate and violence.

In this picture, God is constantly seeking to inspire us to cooperate with this love project. And as we exercise decisions and change the world, so God is exercising decisions and changing the world as well. The idea of prayer involves this work of cooperation with God. Keith Ward challenges a popular misconception with prayer. Surely, a person might object, God will do what is best regardless of our prayers? Ward responses to this objection by writing:

> But this neglects the co-operative nature of the Divine action. God cannot heal all suffering, without destroying the structure of this world entirely. But part of that structure is that people can freely help or harm one another. They can increase or decrease suffering by their actions. As they relate to God, they can increase or decrease the possibilities of the Divine governance of things. Sin closes off possibilities of Divine action; whereas obedient love opens up new channels for Divine action. When we show such love by praying for others, we may open up channels of healing that God can use; creatures and creator can cooperate in making the world more transparent to Divine influence.[24]

When we pray, we are creating space for God to act. We are opening up channels – perhaps at the quantum level – for love to act and make a difference.

Now given the interconnected nature of the universe, there is a constant battle between destructive human decisions and loving human decisions. And the matrix of interconnecting patterns is considerable. And in many cases, the factors involved in the patterns are both a mixture of good and bad, tragic and heroic involved. So, for example, if Nelson Mandela had not been imprisoned (bad and tragic) then South Africa would not have had his inspired leadership that managed that nation to move from an oppressive apartheid regime to a democracy (good and heroic). The apartheid regime was upheld by many very determined white people, who were exercising their freedom for evil ends. Now the divine respect for human freedom makes it difficult for God to simply override the apartheid regime. And perhaps – and this is contentious, but it makes sense – God's capacity to predict the future means that God does not simply respond to the prayers of the African National Congress and liberate Nelson Mandela prior to the slow erosion of the apartheid regime. The matrix of factors in this pattern is deeply interwoven with bad and good constantly intersecting.

So let us stop talking about a God who is a remarkable magician and can conjure new situations where everything has changed; let us stop talking about a God who could prevent every evil effortlessly without affecting human freedom and decision. Let us instead see this universe for what it is. This is a universe where God is constantly seeking the cooperation of humans through prayer and through decisions for good to make the world different.

Given the complex intersecting of patterns, it is perfectly proper to talk about the very request from a person who is in a prayerful relationship to God being an important factor. The claim of Scripture is that sometimes God does allow a certain future to materialize precisely because we ask. In the same way as a friend might decide not to play a game of golf but go with another friend to a basketball game instead, so God allows a different feature to emerge because we have asked.

> [I]f the divine plan is to a large extent open, he may consent to realize a certain state just because it is requested. The making of the request is a new fact of the total situation to which God will respond. It is an additional factor of which he will take due account. If he does take account of it, this increases the degree to which a fully personal relationship can exist between creatures and God.[25]

So we have a God who is constantly searching for the way forward, but does so recognizing the complex interlocking matrix of good and bad already in the world. In addition, one of those factors that God must take into account is the prayer of a person with whom God already has a deep relationship. Prayers take different forms: and those prayers already steeped in an understanding and commitment to the reality of God have a real capacity to create both space for God to act and to enable God to respond.

At this point, someone might object in the following way: why doesn't God just take the best possible option in any given situation? Surely an omnipotent being (a being that knows everything that it is logically possible for God to know) would always do this. The problem with this, explains Ward, is that there is no such thing as a "best option." There are many possible futures available to any moment in time. Many of which are good. Granted some are bad (an act of murder for example), but whether one becomes a dean of a seminary or a minister of a church – both can be good. God has created a world where God can take our participation very seriously in the next segment of creation.

So to summarize this section of the chapter: how does God act? God acts by creating a universe that is genuinely open to both human agency and divine agency. Although the universe is predictable in so many ways, there is built in an openness that makes all the difference to the possibility of the exercise of free will and divine agency. Why does God allow suffering? God allows suffering because God could not have a universe of this type without the possibility of human agents being wicked and the structures of the universe inflicting enormous pain within the system.

This brief response to the tragedy of suffering within the world might seem insensitive. So once again we return to the text of Scripture. It is interesting that the Bible never provides an explanation for suffering. The book of Job is a remarkable text, which really struggles over the problem of evil and suffering, and concludes with the declaration that little human creatures can never know the mind of the creator. So although we have suggested that modern physics is providing an insight into why God allows suffering, we do recognize that the response of the Bible is different.

Indeed, it is the Biblical response Dawkins alludes to in passing. He notes how odd it is that a cross is hanging at the front of a church. Dawkins writes:

> It is, when you think about it, remarkable that a religion should adopt an instrument of torture and execution as its sacred symbol, often worn around the neck. Lenny Bruce rightly quipped that "If Jesus had been killed twenty years ago, Catholic school children would be wearing little electric chairs around their necks instead of crosses.[26]

And although Richard Dawkins doesn't get it, this is precisely the point. For Christians, the primary response to the problem of suffering in creation is not an argument, but a person and an event. It is Jesus of Nazareth, who is believed to be the incarnation of God, who hangs and dies on the cross. When we worship God, we worship a suffering God. We worship a God who has identified with the pain of all in creation.

For Christians, this means that when God decided to embark on this creatorial project, God knew that this would extract a significant price for the Creator. It would cost. And as we puzzle from our vantage point as to why God allows so much suffering in the creation, we are constantly reminded through worship of the participation of God in the processes, challenges, and suffering of being human.

Another important response to the reality of evil and suffering within the creation is the constant call to "live differently." A primary goal of the religious life is to live with love. So let us now turn to the problem of religion and ethics. Why are religious people so often unethical?

Religion and Ethics

Let us start by standing back. Why is anyone cruel or unkind? The Christian answer is "sin." Now sin is a complex notion. Sin is often an act of hubris – it is that act of denial of our dependence (on air, food, a world) and interdependence (on each other, on the environment). And ultimately, we are dependent on the Creator, who sustains and enables everything to be. Sin is therefore deeply irrational. It is absurd to imagine that we are not dependent, yet there are countless moments when we imagine we can strike out on our own.

Striking out on our own is almost always an act of selfishness. We assert an egotistical want or need and decide that our "interdependence" does not matter. So to take two illustrations of this – materialism and lust – we find the following. With materialism we focus on an acquisition that we are sure will make all the difference and thereby deny the resource spent on that acquisition that was needed by someone else; and with "lust" (another old fashioned word), the sexual desire so overwhelms us that we forget a promise to another and create havoc and damage as a result.

The Christian claim is that no human life is immune to the illusions of sin. All human lives are sinful. This is not simply true of individuals, but also religious organizations. The fact that a person is religious does not make them sinless. And religion (like all human activities) can be taken over by sin. In fact, good and bad are seen everywhere. In the same way that the game of soccer can become dominated by excessive salaries and crowd violence, so religion can be distorted into a damaging human practice.

Even science is a human activity that can be hijacked. *Fritz Lenz* (1887–1976) was a leading specialist of "racial hygiene" for the Nazis. With a specialization in eugenics, he was an advocate and practitioner of a variety of evil programs. He worked alongside *Otmar Freiherr von Verschuer* (1896–1969), who directed the program that worked on human subjects from Auschwitz. There is nothing that sin cannot touch. So Christians are not surprised to learn that Christian institutions often behave badly. We regret this reality, but we do not deny it. Although we wish it were different, we cannot evade this truth.

Christians should and do repent of a past that includes much ambiguity (to put it kindly) and wickedness (to put it more brutally). So Christians acknowledge that the Crusades were wrong; the imaginative torture techniques involved in the Inquisition were evil; and the cleric from the city of Liverpool in the United Kingdom, who provided a learned justification of the slave trade, was deeply mistaken.

We can also acknowledge and repent of the ways in which religion becomes a part of a wider complex of factors that shape a situation. So in Northern Ireland, there were religious dynamics at work. However, there were also other dynamics – political, social, economic – at work. It is just not true to say that if one eliminated the religious difference then there would never have been a problem in Northern Ireland.

Now granted that there are not very many atheists in history, it is true that religion has played a part in tragic situations more than atheism. However, in the twentieth century, perhaps the century when violence touched more lives than any other, atheists did appear on the scene. Christopher Hitchens spent his time claiming that all tyrants are really religious. In one of the weaker parts of his book, he credits religion with Stalin and Hitler – they show religious characteristics by being tyrants. Hitchens wanted to try and win the argument by definition: religion implies tyranny therefore any tyrant is religious. This is a manifestly fallacious argument. And Stalin, just to take one prominent atheist of the twentieth century, would resent the association with religion. Dawkins is wrong to assert that Stalin's atheism was not a factor in his brutality. He used a variety of tools – persecution, harassment, and murder to minimize the Church. As Borden Painter reminds Dawkins:

> That assertion ignores the historical record as recounted by major historians of modern European history. Stalin's government conducted savage persecutions of believers in the name of scientific atheism as policy, sponsoring the League of the Militant Godless and frequently setting up museums of atheism in churches.[27]

Dawkins suspects that there are fewer atheists in prison. Again given Dawkins has the advantage of atheists being in a distinct minority, this is probably true. Let us also concede that there are plenty of good atheists. Atheists can be found helping their neighbor, advocating for justice issues, and living the life of virtue. However, our worry is the connection between behavior and rationality.

This is a point that Dawkins might find interesting. As Nietzsche demonstrated, moral discourse without God is difficult to justify. So although we are delighted that there are moral atheists, my fear is that they will start thinking and cease using moral categories. There is the very fundamental problem of justification. As we have already noted, one of the oldest question in the history of ideas is – why not be selfish? Or to put it in such a way that acknowledges the Darwinian arguments for altruism – why not encourage others to be altruistic, yet be selfish when one can be undetected? The language of morality implies an external realm that is binding on human behavior. Without this external realm, the temptation of the rational egoist might become overwhelming for the atheist.

In a rational world, where the implications of atheism are faced, there is a real risk of atheism opting for rational egotism. Fortunately, most atheists are not rational. And these atheists continue to use concepts and language, which is formed in a religious culture, as part of their world view. Dawkins is a good example of an irrational atheist. However, we are not sure whether the delightful, yet incoherent, humanism of Dawkins can survive. Ultimately even atheists will end up thinking.

So while empirically, we are willing to concede that there are plenty of examples of religious people behaving very badly, rationally, the moral life does depend on the life of faith. And fortunately, there are plenty of examples of moral people who work hard, serve others, and seek to live their faith with sincerity and love. Robin Gill's excellent study on *Church-going and Christian Ethics* demonstrates that ultimately religious people do behave better than their non-churchgoing counterparts.

Persons of faith are on strong ground in the area of morals. We think the case can be made both with respect to behavior and justification, that religious people are more ethical.

Thomas Aquinas

The thirteenth-century Dominican friar, St. Thomas Aquinas (1224–1274), is the father of apologetics (perhaps the greatest one who has ever lived). His premise that God is the author of all truth, and his own obligation to seek truth, led him into conversations far beyond the Christian tradition. For Aquinas no text was forbidden; no viewpoint inappropriate to explore. And one follows the truth wherever it goes. A good leader of a congregation should operate with the same set of assumptions.

Conclusion

We have examined three case studies in apologetics. We have looked at the relationship between science and faith, the problem of providence and suffering, and the relationship between religion and ethics. These are intended to be case studies. The work of apologetics is a constant task of taking the methodology of Aquinas and constantly being in conversation with traditions around us.

This is strong territory for the mainline. As questions arrive about the relationship of faith and science, the mainline is positioned to do well. We do not require every person who wants to believe to doubt the truth of evolution. We are not afraid of the question. We are confident that appropriate responses can be found. This is deep in the DNA of the mainline.

So the "seeker class" and "theology on tap" are slowly becoming part of the programs within the mainline congregations. A good leader of a congregation needs to have done some hard work in apologetics. In so doing, they are perfectly placed to provide these programs and really help to ensure that thoughtfulness and commitment can go together.

Notes

1   Much of the material that follows is adapted from Ian Markham, *Against Atheism* (Oxford: Wiley-Blackwell, 2010).

2   Christopher Hitchens, *God is Not Great* (New York: Twelve, 2007), 64.

3   Ibid. 85.

4   Ibid. 88.

5   Richard Dawkins, *The God Delusion* (London: Bantam Press, 2006), 51.

6   It did not get as fair as formal censure, although the Archbishop of Canterbury did issue a list of propositions, many of which were linked with Aquinas. This episode is described at the start of Brian Davies' excellent introduction to *The Thought of Thomas Aquinas* (Oxford: Oxford University Press, 1992).

7   Paul Davies, *Cosmic Jackpot: Why Our Universe is Just Right for Life* (New York: Orion Productions, 2007), 150.

8   Ibid., 150.

9   Paul Davies, *God and the New Physics* (London: Penguin, 1983), 179.

10 Ibid., 181.

11 See J.D. Barrow and F.J. Tipler, *The Anthropic Cosmological Principle* (Oxford: Oxford University Press, 1986).

12 See M.J. Rees, *Just Six Numbers: The Deep Forces that Shape the Universe* (London: Weidenfeld and Nicolson, 1999).

13 See Stephen Hawking, *The Universe in a Nutshell* (London: Bantam, 2001).

14 See Rodney D. Holder, *God, the Multiverse, and Everything* (Aldershot: Ashgate, 2004).

15 Dawkins, *God Delusion*, 171.

16 Ibid.

17 Ibid., 165.

18 See Paul Davies, *Cosmic Jackpot* (Boston, MA and New York: Houghton Mifflin Co., 2007), 173.

19 Dawkins, *God Delusion*, 188.

20 Rodney Holder, *God, The Multiverse, and Everything* (Aldershot: Ashgate, 2003), 123–124.

21 Keith Ward, *Divine Action* (London: Collins Flame, 1990), 48.

22 Ibid.

23 Ibid., 126. The quotation inside is from Prigogene and Stengers.

24 Ibid., 166.

25 Ibid., 159.

26 Dawkins, *God Delusion*, 285.

27 Borden Painter, "The New Atheism: Denying God and History," *Conversations in Religion and Theology*, 6(1), May 2008, 93.

Annotated Bibliography

Beattie, Tina, *The New Atheists: The Twilight of Reason and the War on Religion* (London: Darton Longman and Todd, 2007).
A postmodern look at the narratives underpinning science. Beattie argues that the scientific conceit of Dawkins *et al.* is indicative of a crisis within our world.

Clements-Jewery, Philip, *Intercessory Prayer: Modern Theology, Biblical Teaching and*

Philosophical Thought (Aldershot: Ashgate, 2005).

A good survey of the biblical and theological themes around this important topic.

Crean O.P., Thomas, *God is No Delusion: A Refutation of Richard Dawkins* (San Francisco, CA: Ignatius Press, 2007).

With some care, Thomas Crean exposes the philosophical confusions underpinning much of Dawkins' arguments. Less good on the theology and Bible, but outstanding on the arguments.

Davie, Grace, *Europe: The Exceptional Case* (London: Darton Longman and Todd, 2002).

A good accessible summary of her major works (*Religion in Modern Europe: A Memory Mutates*). It provides a global survey of religion throughout the world and explains that Europe is less atheist and less typical than it appears.

Davies, Paul, *God and the New Physics* (London: Penguin, 1983).

Anything by Paul Davies is worth reading. And several of his books are listed in this section. A truly great book, which does not simply describe the anthropic principle, but also explains the mysteries of the physics at the quantum level.

Davies, Paul, *The 5th Miracle: The Search for the Origin and Meaning of Life* (New York, London, Sydney, Singapore: Simon and Schuster, 1999).

In this book, he deals with the factors that generate life and touches on a range of related issues, for example, the possibility of life on other planets.

Davies, Paul, *Cosmic Jackpot: Why Our Universe is Just Right for Life* (Boston, MA and New York: Houghton Mifflin Co., 2007).

A good summary of the growing body of evidence that indicates just how incredible the math is that produced a bio-friendly universe.

Eagleton, Terry, *Reason, Faith, and Revolution: Reflections on the God Debate* (New Haven, CT: Yale University Press, 2009).

A fabulous book, where Eagleton insists that the atheists are treating God as an object in the sky, which is just deeply misguided.

Flew, Anthony with Varghese, Roy Abraham, *There is a God: How the World's Most Notorious Atheist Changed His Mind* (New York: HarperOne, 2007).

It is a pity that the book is not more substantial, but it does tell the story of how Anthony Flew changed his mind on the question of God.

Hart, David Bentley, *Atheist Delusions: the Christian Revolution and its Fashionable Enemies* (New Haven, CT: Yale University Press, 2009).

Probably the best book written on the new atheists. A strong case against the superficial reading of Christian history.

Holder, Rodney D., *God, the Multiverse, and Everything: Modern Cosmology and the Argument from Design* (Aldershot: Ashgate, 2004).

A very competent philosopher looks at the issues and debates around the multiverse hypothesis and shows that the arguments for the alternative are flawed.

Markham, Ian S., *Understanding Christian Doctrine* (Oxford: Blackwell, 2008).

For the person interested in what Christians are trying to say when they use words like "trinity" and "incarnation," then this book is for them.

Markham, Ian S., *Against Atheism* (Oxford: Wiley-Blackwell, 2010).

Much of this chapter is developed in greater depth in this book.

Wallace, Stan W., *Does God Exist? The Craig-Flew Debate* (Aldershot: Ashgate, 2003).

A good summary of the debate between Craig and Flew. Craig is the theist; and Flew is the atheist.

Ward, Keith, *The Battle for the Soul* (London: Hodder and Stoughton, 1985).

A good solid discussion of the challenges facing personhood in modernity. Ward makes the case for the soul and attacks the reductionism pervading so much modern science.

Ward, Keith, *Divine Action* (London: Collins Flame, 1990).

This is an exceptionally good book that makes the case that the world view emerging from the new physics opens up an account of divine providence, which is plausible, powerful, and faithful.

19

Ministerial Integrity

Someone once asked former Methodist bishop, and former dean of Duke University Chapel, William Willimon, "What is the proof of Easter?" He responded by saying:

> The proof of Easter is that this Sunday, in a little crossroads in North Dakota, a preacher I know will stand in the pulpit and proclaim the grace of God in Christ even though in four years at this church none of her fifty parishioners has complimented her work or told her how much her ministry means to them.[1]

This chapter on integrity seeks to highlight the qualities of character that enliven, encourage, and sustain pastoral ministry, particularly in difficult times and challenging circumstances. Focusing on the personal integrity of the pastoral leader we will explore issues of wholeness, balance, the setting of boundaries, and the establishment of holy and life-giving habits. All of which point to the integral connection between *who the pastor is?* (the question of being), and *what the pastor does?* (the question of doing). It is our contention that the opposite is also true, that doing can and does shape being, that action can and does form character, and that practice can and does affect personal identity.

For this exploration we rely primarily on two excellent resources. The first, from which we have already quoted, is William Willimon's work, *Calling and Character: Virtues of the Ordained Life*. Devoted to clergy ethics, this book expands upon the fundamental notion that pastoral leaders are held to higher moral standards, and it stresses that pastors must find appropriate ways to address this reality for themselves and for the sake of those whom they are called to serve. The second resource is titled *Resilient Ministry: What Pastors Told Us about Surviving and Thriving*, compiled and written by Bob Burns, Tasha D. Chapman, and Donald C. Guthrie. Based on a 5-year study funded by the Lilly Foundation, this in-depth and extended conversation with working pastors provides practical advice for building healthy, sustainable, and long-lasting pastoral ministry in the context of the

An Introduction to Ministry: A Primer for Renewed Life and Leadership in Mainline Protestant Congregations, First Edition. Ian S. Markham and Oran E. Warder.
© 2016 John Wiley & Sons, Ltd. Published 2016 by John Wiley & Sons, Ltd.

contemporary mainline Church. Utilizing these resources we will first consider the peculiarities of clergy ethics (as opposed to general Christian ethics), we will then examine what is meant by "ministerial integrity," and, lastly, we will look at the phenomenon of "clergy burnout." The chapter concludes with suggestions about how to build and maintain priestly integrity while at the same time attending to one's own ongoing spiritual formation.

Why Clergy Ethics?

All baptized Christians are called to witness to the death and resurrection of Jesus. All are to represent Christ and the Church in all that they are and in all that they do. All are to use the gifts they have been given to carry on Christ's work of reconciliation in the world. If baptism is the fountainhead from which all ministry flows, and if ordination is a subset within the broader ministry of the baptized, then why is there a separate branch of clergy ethics and not one overarching and comprehensive field of Christian ethics? After all, are not all disciples, lay and ordained, faced with the same ethical challenges and moral quandaries? While this is true in general, there are, in fact, peculiar moral and ethical dilemmas that are specific to clergy. From among the baptized, the Church has found it valuable to call some to lead the Church. More specifically, ordained leaders are called to preach and teach the Word of God, to administer the sacraments faithfully, to pastor to congregations, and to equip and encourage the ministry of all those committed to their care. Ordained pastors have the dual responsibility of serving as role models for those within the community, as well as serving as leaders who visibly represent a way of life that stands in stark contrast to the world outside the Church. It is thus the demands of the pastoral role and the requisite personal integrity that constitute the higher standard by which clergy are judged, and point to the need for a specific ethic of pastoral leadership.[2]

This is not a new idea. Willimon, drawing heavily on the work of the fourth-century Bishop of Constantinople, John Chrysostom:

> believes that the "peculiar nature of the pastorate, caring for the community, makes the priesthood a particularly demanding vocation." It is the politics of it all that makes the pastoral ministry so difficult … "dignified yet modest, awe-inspiring yet kindly, masterful yet accessible, impartial yet courteous, humble yet not servile, vehement yet gentle." … The pastoral overseer must hold all of these conflicting qualities together in his person yet will only one thing, "the edification of the Church." Politically, a good priest must have "a thousand eyes in every direction."[3]

The rite of ordination stands in the shadow of the great sacrament of baptism. However, the peculiar demands of this specific baptismal vocation require a unique embodiment of Christian character and personal integrity.

What is Ministerial Integrity?

To live with ministerial, pastoral, or priestly integrity is to live an undivided life. More specifically, the pastoral leader practices what is preached, holds the same values and behaviors in public as in private, draws no distinction between major and minor moments. Rather, all of life is united in a relationship with God and making that relationship the foundation for everything else. Our current English word for integrity holds within it the sense of two Latin words: *integer* and *integritas*. The first *integer* means whole, or complete; and the second *integritas* means sound, right, or unimpaired. Our modern usage of the term conveys both meanings, and this is particularly true when used in reference to priestly integrity. Rather than pastoral ethics being defined as a set of fixed norms, prescribed moral behaviors, or a list of principles that can be crossed off when achieved, the core of integrity is

> grounded in a relationship to the living God whose wisdom, justice, and love shall forever exceed our own. ... The life of integrity holds God at the very center. It bends the heart, soul, and strength of life itself toward loving God. It grounds all deeds, all thoughts, all comings and goings in the divine-human bond.[4]

While this is true of all Christians, it is especially true for ordained Christian leaders.

This expanded definition serves as a reminder that ordained ministry is also a profession, in the truest sense of the word. In fact the term "profession" was first applied to clergy. A professional is a person who has something to profess: a specific body of knowledge, an allegiance to a higher good, or a vow or commitment to something greater than one's self. Most modern professions see their primary goal as serving customers, while for clergy this is a secondary concern. Clergy profess God, serve God, and are ultimately accountable to God alone, and this is the standard by which ministry is judged.[5] When this is forgotten, trouble is not far behind.

> In a culture of omnivorous need, all-consuming narcissism, clergy who have no more compelling motive for their ministry than "meeting people's needs" are dangerous to themselves and to a church that lacks a clear sense of who it is. ... We must be called, recalled to the joy of being grasped by something greater than ourselves, namely our vocation to speak and to enact the Word of God among God's people ... morality comes as a gracious by-product of being attached to something greater than ourselves, of being owned, claimed, commandeered for larger purposes.[6]

Again, drawing on the life and extraordinary witness of John Chrysostom, Willimon points to the paradoxical nature of priestly integrity. According to Chrysostom, the preacher must toil long and hard in sermon preparation and at the same time be utterly indifferent to the praise or scorn of those who would receive it.[7]

> [A] preacher must "despise praise." At the conclusion of one of his sermons in Constantinople, when the congregation broke into enthusiastic applause, Chrysostom turned on the congregation and mocked them for applauding what they had no intention of taking to heart, derided them as scoundrels unworthy of the gospel, and announced all applause would hereafter be forbidden in the church. ... This announcement brought down the house with applause.[8]

The priestly profession may be accountable to God alone, but it is lived out amid people with differing expectations, amid a Church with rapidly changing demands, and amid a culture with increasing indifference. The next section looks at the toll that differing expectations, changing demands, and increasing indifference can take on those called to this profession.

Clergy Burnout

Willimon believes that the problem that has been termed "clergy burnout" is more a problem of morale than of morals. There is much evidence to support his thesis. A summary of a recent survey of clergy found that:

- 80% of clergy believe the demands of pastoral leadership affect them negatively.
- 33% believe that pastoral ministry is a hazard to their families.
- 75% have had a crisis due to stress at least once in their ministry.
- 50% felt that they are unable to meet all the demands of their ministry.
- 90% felt that they were not adequately trained to meet the demands placed on them.
- 40% reported at least one serious conflict with at least one parishioner at least once a month.
- 70% do not have someone they consider a close friend.
- 37% admitted having been involved in inappropriate sexual behavior with someone in their congregation.[9]

This is only a sampling. In addition, there are disturbing numbers of clergy who are chronically depressed and who are either overweight or obese. All are signs of burnout, which can be defined as the "exhaustion of physical or emotional strength or motivation usually as a result of prolonged stress or frustration."[10] In his book *Clergy Burnout*, Fred Lehr goes so far as to say that these outward signs of burnout are only symptoms of the real disease, which is codependence. He does not equate the terms, nor does he contend that all burnout comes from codependence. However, he does believe that codependence does play a key role. He defines codependence as "a set of maladaptive behaviors that a person learns to survive in an experience of great emotional pain and stress and that are passed from generation to generation. These behaviors and their accompanying attitudes are self-defeating and result in diminished capacity."[11]

The tell-tale sign of codependent behavior in pastoral ministry is the inability to discern and maintain proper professional boundaries. This usually becomes evident in one of three ways: (i) putting an inappropriately high emphasis on caring for others at the expense of caring for self; (ii) lacking a sense of one's own self-worth, which can be inappropriately expressed by being a relationship "junkie or addict," being driven by the desire to please, and losing the ability to know where one's self ends and another begins; (iii) developing "frozen feelings" as a result of losing touch with self and having the inability to know one's own feelings apart from those of others.[12] The sad corollary is that as stress and frustration increase, so does the level of codependent behavior.

In some ways the Church is both the problem and the solution. The apostle Paul wrote to the church in Corinth about his mission strategy of "being all things to all people" (1 Corinthians 9:22). While this idea is ingenious as a way of meeting people where they are, and as a means of interpreting and proclaiming the gospel to the Gentile world, it can also be deadly to well-intentioned church leaders who wear themselves out by striving to meet every demand of every parishioner every minute of every day. While called to sacrifice for the sake of the Church, it is also important to remember that clergy are not the Savior, but serve the Savior. Setting boundaries and limits is crucial.[13]

John Calvin was greatly concerned about the sin of idolatry, the tendency of human beings to worship idols instead of God. He neglected however to see that work itself could be such an idol.

> When a friend asked Calvin if he would slow down and stop working so hard, Calvin responded, "What! Would you have the Lord find me idle when he comes?" Given his concerns about both idolatry and idleness, it is ironic that Calvin married a woman named Idelette. John Calvin and Idelette de Bure Stroder had no surviving children and their home life was marked by Calvin's very long working hours.[14]

The Church is not immune from the life–work imbalance that infects the larger culture. Somewhere between idleness and the idolatry of work there is a balance. Learning to say yes to some things and no to others is a matter of discernment. The medieval theologian *Meister Eckhart* (1260–1328) once wrote "God is found in the soul not by adding anything, but by a process of subtraction."[15] In a more contemporary context, pastor Rick Warren learned about setting limits from his mentor, Peter Drucker, who would always insist, "Don't tell me what new things you are doing; tell me what you have stopped doing."[16] Warren concludes with two leadership lessons: (i) you can't do everything; and (ii) the mark of leadership is often knowing what not to do.[17]

Returning to the idea of character shaping action, and action shaping character, Willimon reiterates that "what pastors do is a function of who pastors are."[18] He warns that the real ethical danger for clergy is not "burning out" but rather "blacking out." The danger is not losing the energy required to fulfill our ministries, but rather losing consciousness and forgetting our vocation (why we are here) and forgetting our identity (who we are called to be for Christ and for the Church).[19] Losing sight of this vision can be deadly for both morale and for morals.

Resilience in Ministry

How then can clergy forge and maintain priestly integrity in a way that builds character, affects action, honors self, strengthens relationships with spouse, family, and community, and leads to health and resilience? While there may be no foolproof recipe for success, there are, however, definite patterns and themes that point in that direction. For help with understanding these patterns and themes, and in an attempt to offer the most useful and practical pastoral survival skills, we turn now to the findings of the *Resilient Ministry* project. While the authors are quick to confess that they do not believe that they have discovered the "holy grail" of clergy wellness, they nevertheless "do strongly believe that an understanding of these themes, and an intentional evaluation of life and ministry through them, will greatly affect the health and resilience of pastor."[20]

These themes follow the premise of this chapter by focusing on who the pastor is and how personal identity and character influence what a pastor does. While seminary training typically concentrates on the mastering of specific content and developing the right skills to accomplish ministry tasks, these are not the reasons that clergy burn out, black out, or leave ministry altogether. As important as these proficiencies are to pastoral work, the "real ministry killers are matters of life skills, behavior patterns, and character."[21] The "Five Themes for Resilient Ministry" that emerged from this extensive study address each of these issues. The five themes are: (i) spiritual formation; (ii) self-care; (iii) emotional and cultural intelligence; (iv) marriage and family; and (v) leadership and management.

Spiritual formation. This theme refers to the ongoing and life-long process of maturing as a Christian. Ideally this follows a daily pattern. It is far too easy for clergy to get so caught up in the busyness of church work that they neglect the actual work of the Church. "Long-term faithfulness in ministry comes from the overflow of one's walk with God."[22] It is important that clergy make the time to cultivate this first love. While pursuing this theme it is crucial to remember that the pressures of ministry do not miraculously evaporate, but ideally are placed in proper perspective. It is Dwight D. Eisenhower who is credited with saying "Important things are seldom urgent, urgent things are seldom important."[23] Spiritual formation is important.

Self-care. This theme begins with the acknowledgment that we are finite human beings with real limits and with the acceptance that we are whole creatures with real needs. "Our responsibility as creatures of God is to nurture and steward our capacities to the glory of God."[24] Part of the acknowledgement of limits and the acceptance of our humanity is helping congregations understand this reality as well. Being part of an active clergy colleague group, developing healthy friendships, and cultivating a trusted mentor and confidant are all part of living into this theme of self-care.[25] This is in addition to tending to one's own physical, emotional, mental, social, and spiritual needs.

Emotional and cultural intelligence. Emotional intelligence is defined as "the ability to manage one's own emotions proactively and to respond appropriately to the emotions of others. Cultural intelligence involves an awareness of regional, ethnic, and general differences and the implications of these differences personally and interpersonally."[26] Most of us assume that our personal perspective and perception is the appropriate, correct, and, sometimes, the only way to look at things. Part of developing emotional and cultural intelligence is acknowledging that our particular understandings of reality, and the corresponding emotions, are limited and are perhaps more narrow in scope than we might imagine. Developing these intelligences allows us to "put ourselves in a position of learning in order to respect the experiences, views and feelings of others."[27]

Marriage and family. This theme underscores the fundamental importance of nurturing and maintaining the primary locus of relationship, that of spouse and children. "We made covenant vows to God regarding our spouse and children that will, at times, conflict with our work responsibilities and vice versa. These promises require great discernment about time and commitments. We need to balance a commitment that honors those we love and serve in our families with a commitment to those we love and serve in our churches. Our congregations need to honor and respect these vows, and we need to expend the physical and emotional energy to fulfill them."[28] The question is whether or not clergy will surrender to the pressure. "Even when consciously and intentionally working to create new healthier habits, there is systemic pressure to conform to old and known patterns of behavior. Will pastors stand firm in their resolve to change?"[29] In order to stand firm, it may well be important to enlist key church leaders so that they can support and encourage this change and see the long-term benefits to clergy, their family, and the entire congregation.

Leadership and management. "Leadership is the 'poetry' of gathering others together to seek adaptive and constructive change, while management is the 'plumbing' that provides order and consistency to organizations. In ministry they blend together."[30] While it is true that a variety of gifts are given to support the mission of the Church, not all of them reside in the pastor. It is important to enlist help, but at the same time not to abdicate responsibility. Again, it is a matter of finding the right balance. Part of the work of leadership is building alliances and partnerships, recruiting others into a united vision.[31]

Understanding these five themes is relatively easy; implementing them is not. Incorporating new practices and the development of holy habits takes intentional and consistent effort, it takes other people, and it takes constancy.

We close this book with this final clerical virtue. Constancy is a "virtue based on the theological conviction that God really is present in the church, in word and sacrament, even though that presence may not always be vivid in the experience of the moment, even though God may not operate on our timetable."[32] This brings us back to the proof of Easter, the North Dakota preacher, and the priestly integrity required to sustain pastoral ministry in difficult times and challenging circumstances. Theologian and ethicist, Stanley Hauerwas, gets the last word:

> I can think of no virtue more necessary to the ministry today than constancy. Without steadfastness to self and to one's task ministry cannot be sustained. Without constancy the minister is tempted to abandon the church to the ever-present temptation to unbelief and unbelief's most powerful ally, sentimentality. A minister must live and act believing that God is present in the church creating, through word and sacrament, a new people capable of witnessing to God's kingdom. The minister must be filled with hope that God will act through word and sacrament to renew the church, but he or she must be patient, knowing that how God works is God's business. From the crucible of patience and hope comes the fidelity to task that makes the ministry not a burden but a joy.[33]

Retreats and Sabbaticals

As many clergy leaders face the daunting challenge of a potential 24-7 ministry expectation, the challenge to seek spiritual, physical, and mental re-energizing is great. Many in mainline ministry find that a structured and ordered space in which to "retreat" is in order. In many churches, clergy have "sabbaticals" written into their contracts – periods of anywhere from weeks to many months, in some cases, in which he or she may spend time on devotion and solitary work for the betterment of his or her long-term ministerial goals. Often sabbaticals are time for quiet reflection, rest, and retreat, that may require travel away from the demands of a church or parish, and generally something more spiritually substantive than a mere vacation. When sabbatical time is not available, many also find that shorter retreats, such as to monasteries or retreat centers specially designed for these recuperative purposes, are a better use of one's limited time. One example of a retreat center is The Society of St. John the Evangelist in Boston, Massachusetts (pictured below), a monastic community of the Episcopal Church.

Source: The Society of St. John the Evangelist in Boston, Massachusetts. Photo: by Daderot (own work) [public domain], via Wikimedia Commons.

Notes

1   William H. Willimon, *Calling and Character: Virtues of the Ordained Life* (Nashville, TN: Abingdon Press, 2000), 119.
2   Ibid., 9–19.
3   Ibid., 20.
4   Steve Doughty, *To Walk in Integrity: Spiritual Leadership in Times of Crisis* (Nashville, TN: Upper Room Books, 2004), 29–30.
5   Willimon, *Calling and Character*, 29–30.
6   Ibid., 24–25.
7   Ibid., 20.
8   Ibid., 14.
9   Fred Lehr, *Clergy Burnout* (Minneapolis, MN: Fortress Press, 2006), 4–5.
10   Ibid., 11.
11   Ibid.
12   John E. Biersdorf, *How Prayer Shapes Ministry* (Herndon, VA: The Alban Institute, 1992), 36.

13   David Edman Gray, *Practicing Balance: How Congregations Can Support Harmony in Work and Life* (Herndon, VA: The Alban Institute, 2012), 41–42.

14   Ibid., 49.

15   Ibid., 52.

16   Ibid., 54.

17   Ibid.

18   Willimon, *Calling and Character*, 21.

19   Ibid.

20   Bob Burns, Tasha D. Chapman and Donald C. Guthrie, *Resilient Ministry: What Pastors Told Us about Surviving and Thriving* (Downers Grove, IL: InterVarsity Press, 2013), 249.

21   Ibid., 252.

22   Ibid., 249.

23   Ibid., 257.

24   Ibid., 250.

25   Ibid., 258.

26   Ibid., 250.

27   Ibid.

28   Ibid., 251.

29   Ibid., 258.

30   Ibid., 251.

31   Ibid., 256.

32   Willimon, *Calling and Character*, 119.

33   Ibid., 118–119.

Annotated Bibliography

Biersdorf, John E., *How Prayer Shapes Ministry* (Herndon, VA: The Alban Institute, 1992).
This publication is a fine resource for the pastor who may need to reexamine prayer as the chief tool in strengthening ministry. Biersdorf touches upon the intimacy of prayer as well as expanding into how to rely on friends and family for support in difficult times without exhausting those resources.

Burns, Bob, Chapman, Tasha D. and Guthrie, Donald C., *Resilient Ministry: What Pastors Told Us about Surviving and Thriving* (Downers Grove, IL: Intervarsity Press, 2013).
A manual for clergy that examines previous works and studies as well as talking to current religious leaders in a "Pastor's Summit." As a result, this book offers sage advice on how to cope with burnout, maintain one's integrity through the work of ministry, and foster one's spiritual formation in the process.

Carroll, Jackson W., *As One with Authority: Reflective Leadership in Ministry*, second edition (Eugene, OR: Cascade Books, 2011).
Considered a newer classic in the field of pastoral leadership, this book emphasizes leadership and integrity, as well as the perceptions and expectations placed upon those in authority.

Doughty, Steve, *To Walk in Integrity: Spiritual Leadership in Times of Crisis* (Nashville, TN: Upper Room Books, 2004).
In this examination of multiple aspects of priestly integrity, including humility, simplicity, honesty, and endurance, Doughty frames his work in the context of crises in a church setting that can cause a leader's true integrity to shine through.

Edman Gray, David, *Practicing Balance: How Congregations Can Support Harmony in Work and Life* (Herndon, VA: The Alban Institute, 2012).
From the Reformed tradition, Gray writes of stewardship, sanctification, self-care, and Sabbath as being essential to maintaining his own balance in ministry.

Epperly, Bruce G. and Gould Epperly, Katherine, *Four Seasons of Ministry: Gathering a Harvest of Righteousness* (Herndon, VA: The Alban Institute, 2008).
Framing the vocation of ministry in terms of the four seasons, the authors invite leaders to be attuned to the rhythm of those seasons. As

with prayer, those who listen and make themselves aware of God's presence will be able to
live fully into the seasons of life and leadership
in the Church.

Kelly, Ewan, *Personhood and Presence* (New
York: T &T Clark, 2012).

Based on the premise that the pastoral care of
a congregation or individual begins with the
self-care and self-understanding of the caregiver, this book examines various aspects of
the introspective work of pastors.

Lathrop, Gordon W., *The Pastor* (Minneapolis,
MN: Fortress Press, 2006).

Emphasizing the scriptural and sacramental
mandates present, the author explores the
character and qualities required for pastoral
leadership.

Lebacqz, Karen and Driskill, Joseph D., *Ethics
and Spiritual Care: A Guide for Pastors,
Chaplains and Spiritual Directors* (Nashville,
TN: Abingdon Press, 2000).

This volume primarily examines personal spirituality as the facet of leaders that is most often
challenged during times of crisis or struggle in ministry. This work methodically traces
historical notions of spirituality in caregivers,
before pivoting to address the ethical challenges and issues raised in "one of the most
demanding and difficult jobs in the world."

Lehr, Fred, *Clergy Burnout* (Minneapolis, MN:
Fortress Press, 2006).

This book, about the pitfalls of clergy burnout
(and the tools to survive it), addresses ways to
reinvigorate one's spirituality and balance.

Standish, N. Graham, *Humble Leadership:
Being Radically Open to God's Guidance
and Grace* (Herndon, VA: Alban Institute,
2007).

Though focused on humility and the fruits of the
leadership that is characterized by this virtue,
the author also focuses on the imperative of
prayer. Humble prayer, and the kind of prayer
life and practices that truly give oneself over
to God, are some of the key points in this
volume.

Steinke, Peter L., *Congregational Leadership
in Anxious Times: Being Calm and Coura-
geous No Matter What* (Herndon, VA: The
Alban Institute, 2006).

Anxiety is often a catalyst for one to examine
their leadership qualities. Employing methods such as the theory developed by Murray
Bowen, Steinke tackles issues of conflict, as
well as the effects of stress on pastoral leaders.

Willimon, William H., *Calling and Character:
Virtues of the Ordained Life* (Nashville, TN:
Abingdon Press, 2000).

This is a work about *clergy* ethics, not general Christian ethics. The implication, which
is expounded upon throughout the book, is
that for better or worse, clergy are held to
higher standards and must address this fact for
themselves.

Glossary

Abrahamic faiths   A term used to describe the three major monotheistic religions (or faiths) that all claim to descend from Abraham: Christianity, Islam, and Judaism.

Adoptionism   The view that at some point in Jesus's life, God "adopted" him as a son.

Agnostics   At a popular level, the term describes people who are not sure whether God exists. More technically, an agnostic is a person who thinks that we can never know the truth about metaphysics.

Ambrose (circa 339–397 CE)   Influential fourth-century Church father, who became Bishop of Milan in 374 CE. He was a defender of the faith and opponent of Arianism.

Anamnesis   A memorial or remembering, and the part in the Eucharist that recalls Jesus' passion, death, and resurrection. The term includes the idea that we participate in that which we remember.

Anglican chant   Developed during the English Reformation and with roots in Latin chant, Anglican Chant puts non-metrical psalms or canticles to short harmonized melodies.

Anglican Communion   The body of Anglicans around the world. The Archbishop of Canterbury acts as convener and leader, however, with no dogmatic or political authority.

Anglicanism   A term used to describe churches around the world that find some origin in the Church of England. The Episcopal Church is a branch of Anglicanism.

Anglo-Catholics   Anglicans who identify more with their Catholic roots. This term originated in the Oxford Movement of 1833 and can be identified by a high view of the sacraments and liturgy (lots of incense and candles), praying to saints, and emphasis on the Catholic tradition.

Anthropology   The study of humankind.

Apocrypha   In Latin meaning "hidden writings." Disputed books of the Bible accepted by Catholics and some, but not all, Protestants. Some of these books include Wisdom, Tobit, Judith and Sirach (also known as Ecclesiasticus).

An Introduction to Ministry: A Primer for Renewed Life and Leadership in Mainline Protestant Congregations, First Edition. Ian S. Markham and Oran E. Warder.
© 2016 John Wiley & Sons, Ltd. Published 2016 by John Wiley & Sons, Ltd.

Apologetics   Defense of the Christian faith. The rational response to objections of the Christian faith.

Aquinas, Thomas (1225–1274)   Born in Italy, a Dominican friar educated at the University of Paris. His great achievement was to weave together the Augustine tradition with the thought of Aristotle. His major work is the *Summa Theologica*, which he never finished.

Archbishop of Canterbury   An office originating with the Catholic Church in England, the Archbishop of Canterbury today acts as the head of the English Province of Canterbury. The Archbishop of Canterbury is also the symbolic leader of the Anglican Communion.

Aristotle (384–322 BCE)   A Greek philosopher who wrote extensively on ethics, cosmology, and logic. For our purposes, he provided the crucial distinction between substance and accidents, two terms that ground transubstantiation and help understand the sacraments.

Arius (ca 256–336 CE)/Arianism   A North African church leader who attracted considerable support for his teaching of subordinationism (i.e. the view that the Son is not equal to the Father). His views are mostly known through works disagreeing with his and it is this view that provoked the council of Nicaea, at which it was condemned.

Asbury, Francis (1745–1816)   The first Methodist bishop in the United States, who was a key figure in planting Methodism in America.

Ascension   Jesus' rising up to the Father after the resurrection. After Jesus is raised the Holy Spirit comes.

Athanasius (296–373 CE)   The significant opponent to Arianism. He became Bishop of Alexandria in 328 and was the primary theological inspiration behind the theology of Nicaea and Constantinople. He was the first theologian to list the 27 books that became the New Testament canon.

Atheists   Those without belief in a divine being. Atheists claim to know God does not exist in contrast to theists, who believe God exists, and agnostics, who don't know if God exists.

Atonement   The saving work of the cross and Jesus Christ. It is the piece of Christian theology that seeks to explain how Christ saves and restores people to God.

Augustine of Hippo (354–430 CE)   One of the seminal patriarchs of the Church who drafted influential works of theology for the western Christian world. His output as a theologian was considerable; there is rarely a question that Augustine did not consider, and everyone since has been forced to take his responses seriously.

Baptism   The Christian initiation rite performed with water and in the name of "the Father, the Son and the Holy Spirit." Though there is some debate about the proper age and preparation needed for one to be baptized, the mainline churches agree on the importance of the sacrament as a gateway into Christian discipleship.

Baptism, Eucharist and Ministry   An important document issued by the World Council of Churches in 1982 that seeks to find common ground and definition among Churches.

Barth, Karl (1886–1968)   The influential Protestant Swiss theologian who saw problems with the liberal theology he was taught in higher education. His major work was *Church Dogmatics*, written over 35 years, in which he expounds on his theology about salvation and the work of Christ.

Basileia   A Greek term for the Kingdom of meaning embracing the values of God's Kingdom.

Beatitudes, the   Sayings of Jesus found in the Sermon on the Mount (Matthew 5:3–12), which are often referenced as ethical guides and encouragement for social justice.

Bishop   A leader of an ecclesial area, such as a diocese or synod. Part of the threefold pattern of ministry, of bishop (episkopos), priest (presbyteros), and deacon (diakonos).

Black theology   Concentrates on the history of oppression of persons of African descent. This reaches into all realms of theology such as the traditional image of God described in terms of a white male.

Bonhoeffer, Dietrich (1906–1945)   Born in Germany and writing at the time of World War II and Nazi occupation, much of Bonhoeffer's theology seeks to address God and suffering. A clear opponent to the Nazis, Bonhoeffer's work also speaks to the action required Christian discipleship. He was killed by the Nazis in 1945.

Book of Common Prayer   A comprehensive collection of liturgical resources, prayers, and psalms, used in the Anglican and Episcopalian traditions for worship.

Book of Discipline   The most current statement of how United Methodists agree to live together and the Book sets forth the theological grounding of the United Methodist Church. It contains the laws, polity, and process by which the United Methodist Church is governed.

Book of Order   The governing document of the Presbyterian Church (USA), made up of three sections: Form of Government, Directory for Worship, and Rules of Discipline.

Boomer era   Named for the "boom" of babies birthed during this time, this generation was alive during the Vietnam War and Woodstock. Tend to be idealists and have a strong work ethic.

Bridgers (a.k.a. Millennials)   Link the twentieth and twenty-first centuries. Multiracial and multicultural, raised in consumerist and fast-paced society, there is a trend to be acclimatized to disturbing extremes resulting in difficulty discerning right from wrong.

Builders (a.k.a. G.I. Generation)   Generation alive for both World Wars and the Great Depression. Strong sense of community spirit and family. They tend to be well organized, structured, friendly, and optimistic.

Busters (a.k.a. Generation X)   Named so because they are not easily categorized. Tend towards individualism, increased suspicion of institutions, and practicality. Raised in technology-rich environments; tend towards short attention span and fast-paced, high-stimulus environments.

Call   A summons from God discerned through deep listening to the heart and, subsequently, the response. Call comes from a central biblical theme of being drawn into relationship to and in response to God. Those discerning a ministerial role will probably be asked about how they were "called" to that role.

Calvin, John (1509–1564)   Calvin is a key figure in the Protestant reformation and known for his reform in Geneva – a "reformed" Protestantism, however, that differed from that of Martin Luther. His most famous work is *The Institutes*, an extensive theological discourse of the reformed tradition. The Presbyterian Church traces its roots to John Calvin.

Canon (music)   A simple round or a single melody sung by multiple voices beginning at different times.

Canon (ecclesiology, scripture)   The approved set of doctrine or rules of the church. Canon also refers to the books of the Bible approved by church to be Holy Scripture.

Canticles   Hymns taken from the Bible (although this is sometimes expanded to ancient non-biblical hymns) that is recited as prayer.

Cantor   A singer in church worship who either leads the congregation or sings a part solo. Cantor is a term referring to a church singer that dates back to medieval times.

Chalcedon, Council of   The fourth ecumenical council of the Church held in 451 CE. At this council Christ was declared to have two natures in one person as opposed to Christ having only one nature. (Christ is human and divine and not one or the other.)

Christendom   Meaning the Christian world, this can refer to a part of the world where Christianity is the dominant religion and prevailing cultural force. It is often heard in reference now to "post-Christendom" or those parts of the world once dominated by Christianity but no longer.

Chrysostom, John (circa 347–407 CE)   Patriarch of the Council of Constantinople in 398 CE. A gifted preacher whose biblical homilies are still widely referenced.

Church fathers   Influential early Church leaders, primarily men, including Ignatius of Loyola, Ambrose, Irenaeus, and Augustine of Hippo.

Church of England   The English Church originating with the Act of Supremacy in 1534. The Episcopal Church grew out of Church of England dissenters (and supporters) who had come to America.

Clement of Alexandria (circa 150–215 CE)   One of the early Church Fathers known for his relating of Christian theology and Greek philosophy.

Collect   From the Latin, "gathering" or "to gather" are prayers for specific occasions (like saints' days or Church seasons) or reasons (like peace and guidance). Collects can be found in prayer books like the Lutheran *Book of Worship* and *Book of Common Prayer*.

Colonial era   Era associated with colonization. In the Church this time is often associated with missionary work that sought to convert natives to the "true" religions (that of the missionaries). Today this era's supremacist attitude is still a source of guilt for some.

Communion   The sacrament of bread and wine also knows as "The Lord's Supper," "Eucharist," and "the Mass."

Conference or annual conference   The annual conference is the main body of the United Methodist Church. It is the annual gathering of both clergy and lay members of the conference. The annual conference votes on constitutional amendments, the ordination of clergy, the election of clergy and lay delegates to General and jurisdictional or central conferences. The term conference is sometimes used in the vernacular to refer to the episcopal area assigned to a bishop.

Constantine (circa 285–337 CE)   Roman Emperor who converted to Christianity and helped facilitate the Edict of Milan of 313 CE, issuing acceptance of Christians throughout the Roman Empire. Constantine was responsible for calling together the 1st Ecumenical Council at Nicaea in 325 CE.

Constantinople, Council of   The second Ecumenical Council held in 381 CE. At this council the Doctrine of God as Trinity was approved. In addition, there the Nicene Creed known by most modern Christians was amended and approved.

Consubstantiation   View of the "real presence" of Christ known in the sacrament of bread and wine, which affirms a significant and objective change but denies the distinction of accidents and substance.

Contextual theology   The branch of theology that seeks to apply theology to everyday living and today's context, understanding that theology looks different depending on the point of view of those doing the theology.

Conversion   The process of finding, changing, restoring, and/or making new faith in God. This is a process facilitated by grace.

Cranmer, Thomas (1489–1556)   Archbishop of Canterbury and compiler of the original Anglican *Book of Common Prayer*. Much of his design, including liturgical rites and prayers, is intact today in even the American prayer book.

Creeds   Statements of belief. The Nicene Creed is the main form of creed that became part of the church in 381 CE. and is recited by many Christians during worship.

D'Azeglio, Luigi Taparelli (1793–1862)   An Italian Jesuit credited with first using the term "social justice." Drawing on the work of Thomas Aquinas, he wrote in response to the Industrial Revolution.

Deacon   A leader in the church designated to serve. Part of the threefold pattern of ministry, of bishop (episkopos), priest (presbyteros), and deacon (diakonos). In the United Methodist Church, for example, deacons are ordained to a lifetime ministry of Word, Service, Compassion, and Justice. Deacons serve in leadership of the Church through teaching and proclaiming the Word of God, assisting in administering the sacraments, forming and nurturing disciples, and serving the Church and the world by embodying love, justice, and compassion.

Diakonia   Greek for "to serve." Serving inside and outside the community.

Diocese   The territory or jurisdiction designated to a bishop.

Discernment   The process of making decisions and how to best judge what may be right or wrong, better or worse, and how God is at work in a situation.

Docetism   The early heretical view that Christ simply appeared to be human but was not actually human.

Doctrine   A set of beliefs held and taught to be true. The Church's doctrine is what is debated by theologians, ministers, lay people, and all who wish to engage with what is taught to be true.

Eckhart, Meister (circa 1260–1328)   A renowned mystic and Dominican preacher, Meister Eckhart is known for his spiritual instruction and teaching that God is in all things and all things are in God.

Elder   A term for a leader of a Church. In the United Methodist Church, an elder is ordained to a lifetime ministry of Word, Sacrament, Order, and Service. Through ordination they receive the authority to preach the Word of God, administer the sacraments, to order the life of the Church for service in mission and ministry. In the Presbyterian Church, Elders are members of the Session, which can include lay people.

Elizabeth I (1533–1603)   She made Protestantism the state religion of England and it was under her rule that the Anglican Church became a distinct Church. During her reign the Puritan movement began in opposition to her strict form of Anglicanism. Though her father Henry VIII was credited with founding the Church of England, it was Elizabeth who united the Protestant theology with Catholic liturgy that became a hallmark of Anglican (and Episcopal) worship.

Emerging Church   A postmodern Christian movement trying to reach out to and speak to the wider culture today. By finding ways to meet culture where it is at there are debates about whether or not this holds to the tradition of Christianity or gives up to much in order to be "relevant."

Enlightenment   An intellectual movement that shaped the eighteenth century. It began in Europe and had a significant impact on religion, with its lifting up of the sciences and reason as supreme. It tended to distrust authority, believing instead in the importance of reason and good argument.

Eschaton   Greek term for the end of the world, end times, or "end of the age."

Eucharist   From the Greek for "thanksgiving," the sacrament of bread and wine also known as "The Lord's Supper," "Holy Communion," and "the Mass."

Evangelism   Telling the Good News, proclaiming the Kingdom of God, and being a witness to God's work in the world today.

Exclusivism   The idea that Christianity represents the absolute and only truth and that Jesus is the only way to salvation.

Exegete   To expound or interpret text, primarily scripture. Exegesis is an important tool for preachers to go deeper into the biblical texts in order to find a transcendent message that speaks to present situations.

Fall, the   Term wrapped up with notions of original sin in the Creation story of Genesis 2. The Fall of humankind can be and has been emphasized heavily making redemption seem impossible.

Family sermon   An intergenerational sermon that attempts to appeal to children and adults.

Finality of Christ   The unique, saving nature of the One Christ. This can be challenging in a pluralist world.

Gay theology   Theology that seeks to move away from the primarily heterosexual discussions around Christian theology and in particular seeks to find a voice in parts of Christianity disapproving of homosexuality.

Globalization   The process of international integration arising from an exchange of ideas; becoming more global results in a greater sensitivity to groups of people throughout the world.

Gloria   Ancient hymn typically used in mainline worship and based on the song of angels in Luke's birth narrative.

Gospel   Translated in Greek, the "good news." Refers to written accounts of Jesus' ministry. There are three synoptic gospels (Matthew, Mark, and Luke) and a fourth independent gospel called John.

Gregorian chant   Plain chant, simple, one-line melody originating in the middle ages. Named after Pope Gregory I (Pope from 590–604 CE). It was under his leadership Gregorian chant was developed for the liturgy and daily office.

Gregory of Nazianzius (329–389 CE)   One of the three Cappadocian Fathers and known for his "Five Theological Orations" and compilation of some of Origen's writings.

Gregory the Great (circa 540–604 CE)   He became Pope in 590 CE, helped establish the political power of this position, and wrote much about pastoral work.

Grosse, Philip Henry (1810–1888)   An English naturalist associated with marine biology, most known for his work attempting to reconcile geology and the Creation account in Genesis 1.

Henry VIII (1491–1547)   The King of England whose controversial desire for divorce prompted the start of the official Church of England. In 1534 his Act of Supremacy made him the "supreme head on Earth under Christ of the Church of England." This opened the English Church to the Protestant influences and beliefs it would later accept.

Hermeneutics   The process of interpretation. How one receives the tradition and applies it to a contemporary situation and setting.

Holy Spirit   Theologically, the third Person of the Trinity. Biblically, the advocate Jesus leaves with his followers after he ascends. Spiritually, the force responsible for moving in humankind and creation today.

Homiletics   The art of preaching and writing sermons.

Hopewell, James (1929–1984)   Professor of Religion at Candler School of Theology, his contributions, in particular his book *Congregation: Stories and Structures*, are important text for congregational studies.

Hume, David (1711–1776)   A Scottish philosopher, whose *Treatise on Human Nature* confronted questions about God as creator, benevolence, miracles, and human nature.

Hymnody   The study of hymns of a time, place, or church.

Incarnation   The term for God in human form. This describes Jesus as both human and God.

Inclusivism   the idea that tradition is true but that other traditions are subsumed within that tradition.

Indulgences   A medieval Roman Catholic practice whereby one could make payments to clergy, and then one could be absolved of sin and leave purgatory (go to heaven). These controversial exchanges contributed to Martin Luther seeking reform.

Infancy Gospel of Thomas   A Gnostic text not included in the canon recounting stories about Jesus' childhood.

Islam   One of the three Abrahamic, monotheistic religions (along with Judaism and Christianity). Members of the Islamic faith are Muslims. The Word of God for Muslims is the Qu'ran.

Jubilee year   Recorded in the Bible, notably Leviticus 25:8–10. If follows the agricultural cycle of leaving a field lay fallow every seventh year in order for the renewal, rest, and restoration of the field. Biblical Jubilee is then applied to God's people calling for, every seventh year, debts to be forgiven, prisoners released, and bond servants given their freedom. This is meant to leave room for more social equality and new opportunities.

Judaism   One of the three Abrahamic, monotheistic religions (along with Islam and Christianity). Members of the Judaic faith are Jews and their inspired word is the Tanakh (what Christians sometime refer to as the Old Testament).

Kant, Immanuel (1724–1804)   A German philosopher who synthesized the insights of Newtonian physics with philosophy, introducing a set of distinctions that continues to dominate contemporary philosophical discussion. Responsible for the term "Enlightenment."

Kerygma   Greek meaning "proclamation," or the sharing of the Good News of Christ.

King, Jr, Martin Luther (1929–1968)   Born in Atlanta, Georgia. Martin Luther King Jr was a Baptist pastor who became the central figure in the American Civil Rights movement. His philosophy of nonviolence found base in Christian teachings on love and he bonded social justice to Protestant theology.

Knox, John (circa 1514–1572)   After persecution in Scotland he went to England in 1549 and defended the Protestant leanings of the English Church. He returned to Scotland preaching and teaching Calvin's ideas. He was a key figure in the Scottish reformation and in the origins of the Presbyterian Church.

Koinonia   Greek meaning "fellowship." Sharing in and building up community.

Last Supper   The term given for the final meal of Jesus and his disciples together on the eve of the crucifixion, which according to the Gospel of John occurred on the night of the Jewish Passover (*pascha* in Greek). At the Last Supper, Jesus instituted the act of breaking bread and drinking wine in symbolic fashion to represent his own body being broken and his own blood being spilt. This is what is memorialized in the 'institution' words in the Eucharist in Catholicism and most mainline Protestant denominations.

Lectionary   A group of scriptural texts set aside to be used on a given day or occasion for Christian or Judaic worship.

Legal code   The legal codes found in the Torah outline the way that the Israelites agreed to live in community with one another and with God. They are found in the Book of the Covenant (Exodus 20:22–23 – 23:33), the Deuteronomic Code (Deuteronomy 12–26), and the Holiness Code (Leviticus 17–26).

Lenz, Fritz (1887–1976)   A leading specialist and scientist who worked on racial hygiene projects for the Nazis with Otmar Freiherr von Verschuer, particularly on human subjects in Auschwitz. This is an example of the cruelty Christians have been capable of in human history, making Christian apologetics' work all the more difficult.

Leitourgia   Greek for "work of the people." Relates to liturgy, offering praise and thanksgiving to God, and how we live and what we do with our lives. Greek word for "charitable gift," applied really to rituals, from which the English word "liturgy" is derived. A liturgy, then, is the people's charitable gift in the form of a ritual of worship to God in some shape or form.

Liberation theology   With roots in Vatican II and South American income inequality, liberation theology interprets theology from the perspective of the poor and oppressed but can also refer to any theology centered around the liberating work of Christ.

Liturgy   From the Greek word *leitourgia*, liturgy is ostensibly public or corporate worship, but is also a field of study and can be understood as an interpretation of theology into a physical ritual act performed in devotion to God. Liturgy can involve music, readings/lessons, preaching, the sacramental performance of acts such as baptisms or communion, and much more.

Luther, Martin (1483–1546)   The major impetus behind the Protestant reformation in Europe. The Cathlolic Church's practice of selling indulgences led him to publish the "95 theses," which eventually led to his excommunication in 1521. He started a new movement called Lutheranism.

Marcion (circa 85–160 CE)   His controversial arrangement of epistles and gospels in an anthology was deemed heretical by the early Church fathers. But Marcion's "New Testament" provided the spark needed for the Church to settle on a definitive New Testament canon.

Mass   The sacrament of bread and wine also knows as "The Lord's Supper," "Holy Communion," and "Eucharist." This is the more Catholic or Anglo-Catholic term.

Mega-churches   Parishes or churches in mainline Protestantism primarily which draw weekly attendances numbering in the thousands, typically due to a number of reasons including worship styles, music, emphases on social justice, or on personal relationships with God.

Merton, Thomas (1915–1968)   A Catholic monk, author, poet, and social justice crusader who is studied and revered for his writings in the fields of Christian mysticism and contemplative prayer.

Messiah   "The Christ," the one who ushers in the Reign of God. In the Abrahamic faiths, the Messiah is derived from the Jewish term for the "anointed one," (*Christos* in Greek), a figure foretold in the

Scriptures who the Hebrews believed would be a divine warrior from the lineage of King David and who would be responsible for their ultimate salvation as a people. For Christians, Jesus of Nazareth was that promised Messiah; for Jews, the wait continues.

Methodology The study of different approaches to theology.

Millennials Often described as "Generation Y" in popular culture, millennials are a taxonomic demographic of the population born in the last 25 years on average, and therefore the subject of much scrutiny and study from current politicians, marketers, sociologists – and religious institutions. See *Bridgers*.

Monotheism The belief in a single god or God, such as that which describes the faith basis of Christianity, Judaism, and Islam.

Natural law An ethical theory holding that truth can be known through reason alone. Thomas Aquinas is an important figure for natural law and believed God gave humans reasonable capacities and that should be enough to determine what is right or wrong.

New age spirituality The term used for spirituality popular among baby boomers that follows no rules. There is no central text or organized structure, creed, or doctrine.

New Reformation A name for the changes happening in Christianity like with the Emerging Church. The changes are labeled as New Reformation referring to a new era of major change in the Church like the sixteenth-century Reformation.

Nicaea, Council of The first ecumenical council called by emperor Constantine. In 325 CE Church leaders met in Nicaea (Asia Minor) to agree upon the nature of God and Christ. Discussions from this council would eventually form the Nicene Creed.

Niebuhr, Reinhold (1892–1971) A pastor and theologian, Niebuhr's writing addressed political and societal issues. He wrote as a "Christian realist" not shying away from sin and evil found in humanity and society.

Ninety-Five Theses Martin Luther's seminal work, which railed against the Catholic Church's general piety, clerical abuses, and indulgences, and which he famously nailed to the door of Wittenburg, Germany's All Saints' Church in 1517. Luther and his writings touched off a sensation that ignited the Protestant Reformation in the sixteenth century.

Ordination A rite for candidates seeking clerical leadership in Catholic and Protestant denominations, ordination is a liturgy where one vested with authority (e.g. a bishop) publicly empowers a member of the laity into formal occupational or vocational ministry (e.g. a deacon or priest).

Pareto Principle The 80/20 theory that 20% of an organization will provide the majority of the resources to maintain and organization. The other 80% provide marginal support.

Parousia Greek meaning "coming." This often refers to the second coming of Christ and the "last things."

Pastor A name for a Christian minister from the Latin pastor meaning "shepherd."

Penance The work you do or are given to do to amend a sin. During the Reformation Luther distinguished between penance given by the Church and penance given by God. On the eve of the Reformation many were afraid they could not be cleared from sin without penance from the Church rather than penance granted by the grace of God.

Pew rentals   A historic system in churches in which parishioners could rent pew space. An early way the Church raised money. This system prioritized money and status as though who could not afford to rent pews sat together in the back of sanctuaries.

Pietism   An approach that stresses the centrality of piety at the heart of Christian interaction with society.

Plainsong   With origins around 100 CE, plainsong is simple, unmeasured, single-voice chant. It would be referred to as Gregorian chant around 600 CE when Pope Gregory I collected and reproduced the plainchants.

Pluralism   Term used to describe the religious landscape comprising multiple religions and beliefs that stresses that each religion is equally effective as a vehicle to salvation.

Polyphony   Multiple voices singing simultaneously.

Popular religious song   Generally considered to be an alternative style of music to classical hymns or anthems in liturgical music, and may consist of any number of more modern to postmodern instrumentations and composition characteristics.

Post-Christian   The name for the age we are now in, where Christianity no longer holds a dominant place in western culture. This era is said to begin as early as the eighteenth century in Europe but reached the United States later. It can also be said that humanism replaced Christianity as the main "spiritual" influence.

Postliberals   A theological movement that moved away from dependence on human experience highlighting the importance of tradition.

Postmodernism/postmodern   A word applying to views on most topics (art, philosophy, literature), of which interpretation is crucial. It denies any absolute truth believed to be held by philosophy, religion, or science.

Predestination   The doctrine that God is in supreme control and already knows the fate of all creation. John Calvin is known for his firm beliefs in predestination and that all are foreordained to eternal life or eternal damnation. The doctrine can be more nuanced and many who believe in predestination will admit that there are mysteries of fate only God knows.

Presbyter   English translation of the Greek word *presbyteros*, meaning a leader in a church setting or faith community (typically referring to a priest or elder in the mainline). Part of the threefold pattern of ministry, along with bishops (episkopos), and deacons (diakonos).

Prevenience   The belief that God's grace is given to all people at all times.

Process theology   Theology that sees God within time and connected to the world. Developed from A.N. Whitehead's philosophy, process theology makes room for a moving, dynamic God.

Prophetic ministry   Ministry that calls out and works against injustice. It recognizes where the world today falls short of the Kingdom of God and seeks to move people towards reconciliation with that Kingdom.

Proselytizing   The attempt to convert others of a different religion to one's own.

Providence   The belief that God intervenes in the world, or God's care for God's creation.

Psalmody   A type of music for worship primarily that sets the Psalter (the book of Psalms in responsory or antiphonal format) to music.

Quakers   Members of the Society of Friends, a Christian denomination outside the mainline that formed in the mid-1600s. Quaker practice is known for silence and peace. Quaker meetings involve sitting in silence until someone is moved by the Spirit to speak. There is no formal saying of creeds or liturgy.

Rabbi   Jewish term for "teacher," and a frequent moniker for Jesus used by the disciples in the four Gospels.

Reformation   A European reaction to the domination of the papacy. It started in Germany in the sixteenth century and spread throughout Europe, leading to the proliferation of Protestant churches.

Regeneration   Spiritual renewal or rebirth. The phrase "Born again" comes from regeneration and can refer to a person becoming spiritually alive due to faith in Jesus Christ.

Resurrection hermeneutic   Reading and interpretation of scripture with a lens that holds the resurrection at its center. An interpretation that cannot separate the resurrection from the rest of the text.

Renaissance   A major European cultural movement from the twelfth to the seventeenth centuries. Classical art and literature went through a major revival during this period that influenced many aspects of culture.

Revelation   How God makes Godself known. Revelation comes from God and is not of human doing.

Revisionism   Theology that revises historically held beliefs to meet present culture and new understandings.

Rite of reconciliation   Also known as "confession," this rite is an opportunity for individuals who want to repent of their sins to do so in front of a priest and receive pardon.

Sacrament   A visible sign considered to be instituted by Jesus Christ and meant to be a means of an inward grace. Baptism and Eucharist are the two sacraments of the Protestant tradition.

Sanctus   Based on two biblical texts, Isaiah 6:3 and Daniel 7:10, the *Sanctus* has traditionally been sung within the Eucharistic Prayer since the fifth century CE.

Scripture   A religious and sacred text. The books of the Bible comprise the sacred and divinely inspired text of Christianity.

Septuagint   The name given to the original Greek translation of the Hebrew Bible from approximately the third century BCE. Commonly abbreviated LXX (referring to the "70" Jewish scholars responsible for translating the first five books, a.k.a. the Torah).

Self-help movement   A modern movement that focuses on the health and well-being of the individual. It seeks healing and wholeness for individuals, this movement has provided endless resources that ensure fixing of problems through various means of helping one's self. Critics point out its self-centered nature and unrealistic promises.

Sermons   The message given following the reading of Scripture. The sermon is a way of interpreting the Word of God and opening it up to listeners.

Service music   Musical settings of fixed sets of words in a particular liturgy or worship service.

Social justice   The view supporting societal equality that covers economic, political, and social rights. Christian social justice acts towards this following the example of Jesus.

Soteriology   The field of study examining salvation, and particularly the Christian notion of how and why Jesus Christ enacts that saving of humanity.

Steward   Someone who watches over something belonging to another; rootward for the Christian practice of stewardship, or giving of ourselves, our gifts and our resources to God.

Supersessionism   Also known as replacement theology, the teaching that the Christian Church has replaced Israel as God's chosen people. It was the dominant assumption of Christianity, though it has been out of favor since the Holocaust in the twentieth century.

Syncretistism   The attempted combining of different forms of values, traditions, or belief. It often takes place when outside beliefs are introduced to indigenous culture.

Taizé   An ecumenical monastic community in France, founded by Brother Roger Schütz. He wrote the inclusive rule the Taizé brothers live by. Many people, particularly young people, from around the world visit Taizé to join the brothers in prayer and song. Taizé songs have simple lyrics and melodies that can be harmonized simply, and often multiple times to allow the singer to listen to other voices, enter the larger experience and pray.

Tanakh   The Jewish Scriptures. TNK in Hebrew, T stands for *torah* (the Law and first five books of the Hebrew Bible), N for *nevi'im* (The Prophets), and K for *ketuvim* (the Writings).

Temple, William (1881–1944)   Born in England, William Temple became Archbishop of Canterbury in 1942. He was an advocate of equality for all and was active in ecumenical and social justice issues. His most well-known works include *Nature, Man and God* and *Christianity and Social Order*.

Teresa of Avila (1515–1582)   Born in Spain and a Carmelite mystic and nun, St. Teresa of Avila is known for her writings about the interior life and spiritual journey. Her book *The Interior Castle* is a spiritual classic.

Tertullian (circa 160–circa 225 CE)   An important North African Church figure and apologist in early Christian theology.

Theism   Belief in a personal God.

Theology   The study of God, or faith seeking understanding.

Tillich, Paul (1886–1965)   One of the great twenty-first-century theologians, Tillich, a Protestant, fled Germany when the Nazis came to power. He taught at Union Theological Seminary and Harvard, and is noted for his ability to synthesize the Christian tradition with modern culture.

Torah   Hebrew for "the Law." The first five books of the Hebrew Bible also called the Five Books of Moses.

Transubstantiation   Belief commonly held by Roman Catholics and some in the mainline that the bread and wine of the Eucharist are changed into the actual body and blood of Jesus during consecration.

Trinity   An often complicated and challenging doctrine of Christianity that ascertains God to be operant in three "Persons" – God as Father or Creator, God as Son or Redeemer, and God as Holy Spirit or Sustainer. The Council of Constantinople in 381 CE solidified this doctrine to proclaim God as both these three persons and yet the one true God regardless. Variants or interpretations of the Trinity have at times led to controversial theologies (such as Process theology, social Trinitarian theology) and heresies (Arianism, modalism, docetism).

Vatican II   A meeting of all Catholic bishops, the Second Vatican Council was held over the course of 1962–1965. Convened by Pope John XXIII and closed under Pope Paul VI, Vatican II was extremely important for change across all Christian denominations. While doctrine was intentionally not changed, major reform was agreed upon to change the face of the Catholic faith. For example, following Vatican II the Mass could be said in vernacular (not just Latin) and lay people had a more recognized role.

Virtue ethics   Rooted in Aristotelian ethics, virtue ethics focuses on the virtuous actions of individuals rather than acting right by duty. Theological virtues include prudence, justice, fortitude, and temperance.

Vocation   From Latin, *vocare*, "to call." The broad calling of an individual, how one responds to and lives out one's relationship with Christ and others.

von Verschuer, Otmar Freiherr (1896–1969)   A leading specialist and scientist who worked on racial hygiene projects for the Nazis with Otmar Freiherr von Verschuer, particularly on human subjects in Auschwitz. This is an example of the cruelty Christians have been capable of in human history, making the defense of the Christian faith all the more difficult and challenging.

Watts, Isaac (1674–1748)   An English hymn writer who pushed against modern standards and included non-biblical texts in hymns. He was a dissenter of the Church of England (those Protestants who did not think the Church of England moved far enough away from the Catholic Church). His hymns were widely used in the eighteenth century and still are sung today.

Wesley, John and Charles (1703–1791, 1707–1788)   The sons of a cleric's daughter, these brothers are founders of the Methodist Church. As members of a group at Oxford called "The Holiness Society" they sought to improve the piety of the Church of England. John Wesley was a gifted preacher who took to open air preaching and Charles Wesley was a gifted and prolific hymn writer. Many of his hymns are foundational to the Methodist and other hymnbooks.

Whitefield, George (1714–1770)   A vibrant preacher heard across England and America he called for conversion and is known for his role in the first American Great Awakening.

Whitehead, A.N. (1861–1947)   A philosopher of science and education who began his career working primarily on mathematics and logic. In 1924 he went to Harvard where he developed his views on religion, eventually propagating the theory of Process theology.

Word of God   Biblical term referring to both the written "words", i.e. Scripture, and the Word Made Flesh, i.e. Jesus Christ – both of which express the notion of how God reveals Godself to creation. In a liturgical context, Protestants believe both Word, what is heard and learned in Scripture, and Sacrament are important.

Yeshua   Hebrew for "The Lord is Salvation." Translated from Hebrew to English the spelling is closest to Joshua, however when translated from Hebrew to Greek to English it is closer to Jesus. Most bibles are translated in the latter way and thus Jesus is the predominant name for Christ for English-speakers.

Zwingli, Ulrich (1484–1531)   A Swiss reformer associated most with Protestant reform in Zurich. He is known for an entirely symbolic understanding of the Eucharist as a memorial to Christ's sacrifice. The Reformed Church from which the United Church of Christ originated grew out of Zwingli's reform.

Index

*An Introduction to Ministry: A Primer for Renewed Life and Leadership in Mainline Protestant
Congregations*, First Edition. Ian S. Markham and Oran E. Warder.
© 2016 John Wiley & Sons, Ltd. Published 2016 by John Wiley & Sons, Ltd.